THE NORTH WILL

John Robb is a leading music journalist and the author of the bestselling biography of the Stone Roses. His other books include *Punk: An Oral History* and *The Charlatans . . . We Are Rock*. He lives in Manchester.

Dancers on the stage at the Hacienda, 1989
(Photo: Ian Tilton www.iantilton.net)

THE NORTH WILL RISE AGAIN

MANCHESTER MUSIC CITY 1976–1996

JOHN ROBB

Quarto is the authority on a wide range of topics.

Quarto educates, entertains and enriches the lives of our readers—enthusiasts and lovers of hands-on living.

www.quartoknows.com

First published in Great Britain
2009 by Aurum Press Ltd
74-77 White Lion Street
London N1 9PF
www.aurumpress.co.uk

This paperback edition first published in 2010 by Aurum Press

A catalogue record for this book is available from the British Library.

ISBN 978 1 84513 534 8

Typeset in Swift by SX Composing DTP, Rayleigh, Essex
Printed and bound by CPI Group (UK) Ltd, Croydon, CR0 4YY

MIX
Paper from responsible sources
FSC
www.fsc.org   FSC® C013604

CONTENTS

ACKNOWLEDGEMENTS

Andy Fyfe for some of the Tony Wilson quotes from Qthemusic.com

Roger Eagle quotes thanks to Phil Welsby at *New Breed* magazine

Selected Ed Banger quotes from http://www.punk77.co.uk

Shake Rattle and Rain, C.P. Lee

Thanks to Manchester District Music Archive,
http://www.mdmarchive.co.uk

Sam Hampson for transcribing some of the interviews. Bob Dickinson and Greg Wilson for some proofreading.

Ann Scanlon.

Respect to Mark Smith.

INTRODUCTION

Of course the Stone Roses come from Manchester; where else could they be from? Where else could the Smiths and Joy Division be from? Where else could Ian Curtis be from? Where else could Factory Records be from? Where else could the Hacienda be? It was so fucking natural. That was an amazing amount of music for such a tiny place in northern England. It was so special: all the bands, all the fashion, all the great writers, all the great people coming out of this city. People say to me round the world, What is it about Manchester? and I say, I don't know!

– Noel Gallagher

Manchester was the right environment for punk rock. It had the perfect conditions. The kind of anger that punk was about was very suited to a post-industrial wasteland like Manchester. The social conditions were exactly right here for punk. It's rather like communism – invented by Karl Marx for 19th century Germany – being adopted in Russia. Punk was invented to get away from the boringness of suburban London and made sense in a derelict post-industrial landscape. Manchester became a punk city.

Manchester has been Britain's immigrant city since 1200, and that openness is essential. And the other reason was something Dave Ambrose, the famous A&R man, said when I asked what he was doing back here. Everything was signed – no one was left – but he said he was back because Manchester kids have the best record collections. And that summed it up. When he said that, I immediately flicked back to a squat in Hulme in the early eighties, ACR's place or somewhere similar, and there on this floor with no carpet and little furniture were 200 albums. And in those albums will be the entire Parliament/Funkadelic catalogue, and 20 Brazilian samba albums, and German metal noise albums. That's the key to all of this.

– Tony Wilson

Manchester is full of gonzoid bullshitters, crazed loons, brilliant musicians, innovative bands, 24-hour freaky party people dancing around the post-industrial cityscape, soundtracking its transformation to post-Hacienda steel and glass. It's a city of poets and outsiders, romantics and lunatics; it's a city of high drama and great songs, bedsit poets and opinionated gobshites shouting from the everchanging rooftops. From punk to post-punk to baggy, the Hacienda, the Smiths, the Roses, the Mondays to Oasis, it's soundtracked generation after generation. And that's just the big bands; there is also an endless collection of mavericks whose musical brilliance has been equally important. This is their story.

John Robb

1

FROM COFFEE BARS TO SUPERSTARS: THE SIXTIES

Sixties Manchester was dancing in the dusk of the Industrial Revolution. With the most vibrant club scene in the country growing out of the coffee bars and a big love for black music that provided the bedrock, Manchester also had a band scene that was as strong as that of any city. Surrounded by the sooty decay, the beat groups stormed the world, while the club scene was a powerhouse of cutting-edge black music, jazz and blues, and psychedelic clubs with a long lost answer to Carnaby Street on the now demolished New Brown Street.

By the end of the decade, the pill-popping mod clubs had been battered by an Act of Parliament specifically aimed at the Manchester clubs, which shut down most of the bars as well as the mass redevelopment of the vibrant city centre area and a chief of police who seemed determined to crush the good times and get things in line with his Protestant work ethic.

Before that, however, there had been a strong music tradition stretching back through the decades. It saw the birth of what would eventually be termed northern soul, which in turn provided a strong foundation for many of the punk and post-punk bands. Arguably Manchester was a black music city, taking full advantage of its multiracial and multicultural mix and its unique history of being the world's first modern city.

Perhaps the key face was the late Roger Eagle, who started DJing and promoting in the sixties and whose expert knowledge and enthusiasm for black music fired the city's prime movers for decades. Roger understood implicitly how all the best music was forged from eclectic tastes and perhaps had the first of the city's famously varied record collections.

ROGER EAGLE (DJ)

I met this black American guy who came over to see me. He's at university in the States and he's doing a thesis on 'Northern British

Appreciation of Black American Music'. He'd been to see everybody on the northern [soul] scene – all the northern DJs and so on – and they all said: 'Go and see Roger Eagle – he started it all.' Eventually he turned up here with a camera and I blew his head off completely. I started playing him tunes . . . he went away with a cassette, with what you would probably think are fairly obvious tunes on it. His mind was completely wrecked. This guy's in his forties, maybe fifties and he's a serious man . . . and he's never heard Ray Charles! I said, if you want to talk about northern soul, there's plenty of people better placed than I am to tell you . . . but if you want the history about white northern English appreciation of Black American music you talk to me! I'll straighten it out for you.

BRUCE MITCHELL (Durutti Column drummer)
Roger Eagle came from Oxford. His mother was Dorothy Eagle who ran the Oxford Press. He came from a very good family. He came to Manchester and got on to the music scene. He was a very tall commanding guy and he was obsessed with R'n'B. He booked people like Sonny Williamson and he ran a magazine called *R'n'B Scene*. He had this amazing record collection that reflected his taste. He was an enthusiast in same way as, let's say, Patrick Moore is!

He was brought in by the Abadi brothers to be their DJ at the first Twisted Wheel club on Brazenose Street.[*]

IVOR ABADI (club owner)
We realised that young people needed somewhere to go and listen to pop music and socialise. We moved into town and opened the Twisted Wheel and got Roger Eagle to DJ because he had a great record collection.

ROGER EAGLE
Before I got the job at the Twisted Wheel, my only DJ experience was taping tracks on one of those reel-to-reel recorders and taking them along to parties to play. One day I received a parcel from the US that contained all of the Chuck Berry and Bo Diddley back catalogue LPs. I took them down to the Left Wing Coffee Bar, just to have a look at them. I was approached by the Abadi brothers, who said 'We're buying this place and turning it into a nightclub – do you know anything about R'n'B?' I said 'Yes' and they offered me the DJ job there and then.

[*] The Abadi brothers had opened one of the first coffee bars in the UK in Macclesfield in 1956 before opening the Twisted Wheel in Manchester, taking over the old Left Wing Coffee Bar in 1963.

To be honest, the Abadis didn't really have an appreciation for the type of music that was popular at the club. They just saw it as a way to get the numbers coming through the door. Only once did they insist that I played a pop record. I argued against it, but to prove a point I played it and emptied the dance floor. After that they never interfered again on the music side.

I wasn't a particularly high-profile DJ. I didn't have the ambition and I certainly didn't have the patter. I was happy playing the music that I loved. I would play six or seven hours solid single-handedly – with just an hour or so's break for the band – for £3 a night. I was happy playing the music that I loved but – with hindsight – I would have appreciated a little more money.

Seven hours of record playing is a long time and there weren't that many soul and R'n'B records available at the time, so I had to mix in rock'n'roll tracks to fill out the time. In fact Carl Perkins was a particular favourite amongst the Wheel crowd. He even played live at the club. In the very early days, when the club first started, we relied very much on word-of-mouth recommendations.

BRUCE MITCHELL

Roger attracted disciples from the way he talked about music. He had a fantastic enthusiasm – he was like the Messiah! He played blues at that time at the Twisted Wheel, which was the original proper blues club. He was so effective that he would have big acts at his club and then he would take the bands back to his horrible flat in Chorlton and they would want to go and listen to him lecture them about music. You would literally get lectured and sometimes he would drop in some criticism of your band: he chose Spencer Davis' first single saying, 'The trouble with you, Winwood, is you're doing this wrong . . .'

When I was a teenager in the fifties, the music I was passionate about was American West Coast jazz. The club where we went to listen to this music was called Club 43 at the Clarendon Hotel on Oxford Road, which was demolished when they built the Mancunian Way.

We would dress like Ivy League [students] with the trousers that finished short of the ankle. It was perfectly tailored – you had mohair suits fitted high with two or three buttons – not that dissimilar to the way mods dressed years later. It was a very sharp, clean image, mainly because all the jazz stars went to a lot of trouble to dress fantastic.

I was astonished by rock'n'roll when it arrived. It was two records at first – Elvis Presley's 'Heartbreak Hotel' and Bill Haley's 'Rock Around the

Clock'. We used to play those tracks over and over again – nothing had sounded like that ever before. Elvis was astonishing – it was very, very alien. When I first heard it, it threw me.

'Rock Around the Clock' was in the soundtrack of a film called *Blackboard Jungle*, about a guy having trouble in a Bronx school. The film started with the rimshot of the drum on the song; the sound was weird and powerful and sent shivers down the spine. I saw *Blackboard Jungle* in a cinema opposite the Free Trade Hall that's not there any more. There was a riot, when everyone left they were jumping on cars – it was a front page story in the *Manchester Evening News*.

I went to see Bill Haley at the Odeon. What I remember most from the gig was that the balcony was actually moving up and down because of the dancing. The band could see it; they just carried on and they pointed at it. After the gig, Bill Haley was mobbed, and this was a chubby guy with a kiss curl – a girl fan even pinched his hat!

I was playing my drums at the time with anyone, mainly jazz – there wasn't any rock'n'roll in England until the early sixties . . .

In Manchester the dominant music of that time was trad jazz. Trad jazz was selling out all the city halls with Kenny Ball, Chris Barber, Acker Bilk.

ROGER EAGLE
I was originally a rock'n'roll kid until I heard Ray Charles. The *In Person* and *Live At Newport* LPs from around 1958/59 really converted me. Rock'n'roll died in 1958. Ray Charles was the first to see the possibilities of mixing different types of music. He mixed R'n'B, rock'n'roll and even country.

BRUCE MITCHELL
In the early sixties I played the Liverpool Cavern in a trad jazz band and the support band was a beat group, which I had never seen before; within nine months beat groups were top of the bill and the trad bands were opening. The beat group had a very strong beat – the drummer played four to the bar on the kit, very solid and very heavy, and played the tom toms.

I did a lot of gigs with various Liverpool groups. They were all great characters. They had multi-band gigs at the Cavern: I remember the Escorts' drummer, who was six foot two. He would get his knob out and piss all over the other band's kits – typical Liverpool (*laughs*). After the gig you would go over in your Transit van and go on to Formby Sands and meet the other groups. Then the groups would get mic stands out and thwack the other bands' vans. You would shake hands and then kick lumps out of their van and they would do same with yours (*laughs*).

ELLIOT RASHMAN (Simply Red manager)

From the age of 12 I became a clothes freak. I'd have arguments with my mum who would say I couldn't have Cuban heel boots, which were the Holy Grail. I got shirts from a shop in Chadderton in the early sixties when I was 13 – they were too big but I still had to have them. The shirts were button down with tab collars, then long collars came in – all different types of collars. I started wearing Cuban heel and zip-up boots. My mum thought they were seditious – she would say, 'You're not going out with those on!'

As soon as I could afford a suit with four or five buttons I had one – even the Norfolk jacket with the belt. I had to have what was in fashion and I never lost that love of clothes.

C.P. LEE (key scenester and mainman in Alberto Y Lost Trios Paranoias)

In the early sixties Manchester had a beat scene and a very strong blues and R'n'B scene. Black music was always big in Manchester. It was a tradition that came from when we supported the North in the American Civil War, fighting against the slave trade. Liverpool depended on the cotton and slaves and supported the South. The John Laird shipyard built Confederate ships in Liverpool whilst in Manchester workers wouldn't side with the Confederate cotton – that's why we got the Lincoln statue in Manchester. From this tradition Liverpool liked rock'n'roll and Manchester liked the blues; there was always a fascination in Manchester with American music, dating back to 1830 when the first minstrel troupe played here. They were huge hits and kept coming back. Because of this, African-Americans would come here and sometimes base themselves in the north in the nineteenth century.

In 1927 people in Manchester were getting jazz 78s from America before they came out. They founded the Manchester Jazz Appreciation Society. They would meet up at the Unicorn Hotel off Oldham Street in the city centre and listen to a wind-up gramophone playing jazz records.

The blues scene was fuelled in the 1950s by John Mayall* with the Bamboo Club, which was a members-only club in Salford where you would listen to records and watch the embryonic Bluesbreakers play in the late fifties. While Manchester was listening to the blues, Liverpool stuck to beat mixed with girl groups, which is where lots of the Beatle harmonies came from; that was what became the so-called Mersey Sound. Mancunian bands had a hardcore R'n'B edge that doesn't come

---

* Born in Macclesfield in 1933, singer, songwriter and multi-instrumentalist John Mayall, with his band the Bluesbreakers, is one of the key players in the British blues scene.

across in the recordings. Herman's Hermits started off as a Chuck Berry-style band before Kennedy Street management picked them and got the Singing Dalek, or Peter Noone as he was better known, to sing with them. The Dreamers played a hard-edged R'n'B set – you get it on their first album, but it's not what they're remembered for.

ROGER EAGLE
There were various coffee bars in Manchester, like the Cona Coffee Bar,[*] where you could take in your own records to play. You would take your own in and also listen to other people's and pick it up from there. There were a few like-minded people around and you would bump into them or meet them in places like the Town Hall pub.

As for getting hold of the records, you could get hold of some but it wasn't long before I was importing records directly from the States. I must thank two guys, Roger Fairhurst and Mike Bocock, who taught me how to import records from the States. I was getting hold of records from the US even before they had been released there!

PETER NOONE (Herman's Hermits vocalist)
The music scene had two main homes, the Twisted Wheel and the Oasis. The Twisted Wheel was a sort of R'n'B soul meets Big Bill Broonzy and Spencer Davis club for people who postured as the folk and blues people. The Oasis was pure pop and the more top 40 types like Wayne Fontana and the Searchers and that sound.

I was comfortable in both places as I was a music enthusiast; I'd been taught to appreciate all music and to keep my gob shut if it wasn't my cup of tea . . .

PHIL SAXE (manager of Happy Mondays)
The first place I went out to was Jungfrau, a little disco-type place near where the Triangle is now. I started going there and graduated to the Oasis.[†] I would see people like Lee Dorsey, the Drifters, Wilson Pickett, that sort of stuff – mainstream mod stuff, soul-orientated. I graduated to the Twisted Wheel when I was older – where it all started happening![‡] It

---

[*] In Tib Lane near Albert Square.
[†] The biggest coffee bar/venue in Manchester, on Lloyd Street; both the Beatles and the Stones played there in the early days, the Beatles playing a sold-out show in February 1963.
[‡] The Twisted Wheel was the key mod club in town and also the birthplace of northern soul. The home of a super-cool club crowd in mohair suits and on pep pills, demanding faster and faster tunes to dance to at the all-nighters, it created a taste for the faster and rawer soul imports that came to be labelled 'northern soul' in 1970 by visiting London-based soul music writer and expert Dave Godin.

was slightly different music from the club soul at other places. It was the first time I realised that there were obscure, rare records, all-nighters and drugs, and I got immersed in that scene and stayed till it shut in 1971.

C.P. LEE

The beat scene had loads of clubs in the centre of town. I counted well over 200. You didn't need a licence in Manchester. You could just open if you didn't sell alcohol. There was the Oasis, the Twisted Wheel, the Heaven and Hell, Beat City and countless others. Then, because kids wanted to dance, every co-op ballroom had a Friday night beat club. There were regular venues in Alderley Edge, Sale Locarno, the Regent Ballroom in Salford. If you were in a band you could play every night – sometimes do double headers, play a short set in one club and then travel to another. It was a great training ground. There was so much work up here that Alexis Korner had a flat in Manchester; he spent half the week up here because he played so many gigs in the north-west.

ROGER EAGLE

The Stones came down to the club and they were standing in the coffee bar having a cup of coffee. The kids were standing round them – just looking at them. Not talking to them – just looking. And I played all of the original tracks off their first album, which had just come out: 'I'm A King Bee' by Slim Harpo, 'Walkin' The Dog' by Rufus Thomas, Arthur Alexander . . . They knew exactly what I was doing. I played them in exactly the same order as the LP. It was just me saying, there's a North/South thing. I'm a southerner by birth but a northerner by emotion. I prefer the north. I'm not saying I don't like southerners, but they tend to be so temporary down there. To me if something's solid then it's worth looking after. Whereas they're into it and out of it. Which is really not the northern style.

GARETH EVANS (Stone Roses manager)

I was a stylist mod. I went to the Twisted Wheel. I was very much into Sonny Boy Williamson, Muddy Waters; I saw Sonny Boy Williamson live at the Twisted Wheel. DJing was the famous Roger Eagle. The thing was, Roger Eagle left the Twisted Wheel because he was into the deep blues, but it was becoming more the Temptations, the Four Tops, Little Anthony and the Imperials down there. My roots are really the Temptations – the original Temptations.

I had the best mohair suits, which I got off the racks with double vents – my trademark was a long yellow suede coat. The first time I tried to ride a scooter I crashed in Albert Square!

ROGER EAGLE

The only other club anywhere that was playing anything like what I was playing at the Wheel was the Scene Club in London. I used to get on well with Guy Stevens* and we used to exchange records. Like I said, I was getting hold of some records before their release even in the States, things like Stax and so on. We weren't consciously trying to create a movement or anything like that. We just liked to have a club that played the right kind of music.

You could say that I tipped my hat towards the things that were happening on the mod scene, style-wise. But it was the music that came first and was paramount above everything else to me. Of course I dressed in the styles of the day. I was smart but I wasn't at the sharp end, style-wise. My money went on vinyl and importing new records. I left the clothes obsession to the kids coming to the club.

I never set out to make it a mod club, it just grew and happened. You knew what was going on though. The punters were generally sharp but some were way ahead. I couldn't keep up with them! I got respect through the records that I was playing. That to me was enough.

GARETH EVANS

The Twisted Wheel on Brazenose Street was the first one, it was small with a lot of different rooms, and next to it was the Clay Door – that was where the footballers went. A lot of Clay Door people came into the Twisted Wheel – the all-nighters with Roger at the Twisted Wheel were great.

The Twisted Wheel became a mod club; that's where I got to know Steve Marriott and the Small Faces. They went back to London in their van with a hundred leather and suede coats which I had got my hands on.

ROGER EAGLE

The Twisted Wheel also had all the live bands. I used to be friendly with Steve Winwood. He would come round to my place and listen to records when the Spencer Davis Group played the club. Georgie Fame did some good things – very King Pleasure influenced. The important thing is to take the influence and then add a twist and take it on further. It's important to remember that there's a big, big difference between club groups and pop groups. Eric Clapton was a good friend at that time. I remember one Sunday morning after he had played at the club, he

* Another legendary music fanatic and a major player in the underground London club scene, Stevens among other things eventually put together and managed Mott the Hoople, and produced the Clash's classic *London Calling* before he died in 1981.

brought a good-looking young mod girl round to my place and she got completely pissed off because all he wanted to do was listen to Freddie King records.

When the club moved from Brazenose Street to Whitworth Street the music policy at the new club was just the same. I moved over with the club; I spent roughly two years at the first Wheel and a year at the second.

PHIL SAXE
Roger Eagle DJed at Brazenose Street at the old Twisted Wheel with Roger Fairhurst. Roger is a legendary figure, playing blues and early R&B which he would import from the States. Maybe one fallacy was that he was to do with northern soul. He would be very upset to be associated with it. He left the Twisted Wheel eventually to set up the Magic Village,* and one of the reasons was that he didn't like the Motown soul that we were playing.

ROGER EAGLE
Well, I left because they wouldn't pay me a decent wage. After three years' hard graft for maybe £3 a night I asked for a fiver and they said they couldn't afford it. I was also getting bored with the music and there were a lot of pills going on. Kids were in trouble with the pills and all they wanted was that kind of fast tempo soul dance. So I was very restricted with what I could play. I thought, 'I'm not getting paid enough money to do this – I ain't going to do it no more.' So I left and immediately got paid a decent wage by Debbie Fogel at the Blue Note Club. I got a fiver a night for four nights, besides doing other things.

I was able to play the kind of music that I liked . . . the range of music. Whereas the pill freaks only wanted the same dance beat – which is what makes it so boring. It's OK, you know, there were some decent sounds, but they made it so boring. You're trying to talk to kids who are off their heads all night on pills and it's really hard.

I set up the Magic Village because I started getting into rock. It was a completely different track. Things like Captain Beefheart, John Mayall, the Nice and so on. But before that I had another night at the Three Coins in Fountain Street. The music policy was similar – it was R'n'B and soul. But you see I was trying to play early funk. In fact, 'Funky Broadway' by Dyke and the Blazers was probably the last record I played at the Wheel.

* The Magic Village on Cromford Court was Manchester's underground rock club, with its own hippie décor and light show. Bands like Pink Floyd and Country Joe and the Fish played there, as did Greasy Bear, the band formed by Bruce Mitchell and C.P. Lee and managed by Roger Eagle.

It was just starting to change and they didn't want it to change. It just split. I was progressing to funk, very early funk, but they didn't want to go with it.

I'm not sure if it was the same crowd. They were just people around town, pill freaks that popped in and out. You can't look at it with hindsight, at the time it wasn't 'Oh, we're going to start a movement!' It was just the place to be. It was the place for the in crowd . . . for a while.

PHIL SAXE

It was at the Twisted Wheel that I witnessed the changes in that scene around 1968, when they came out with the new drugs law that criminalised internal possession of drugs in blood and urine. I perceived that change in the scene as a lot of older era people stopped going to the Wheel and then drifted off.

Me and Brian Phillips started DJing in '68/'69. To compete with other clubs we started playing imports and rarer British label stuff, which is basically where the whole idea of northern soul came from. We were DJing 100 per cent amphetamine dance.

We played faster stuff and the imports. In the north-west we were playing music unlike the rest of the country, though places like Wolverhampton had an influence as well. The music was changing; we weren't going into the ska scene – we'd been through that. We were playing faster and faster music; it was amphetamine-fuelled, we were taking proprietary pharmaceuticals – taking 10 or 20 slimming pills. It was a really buzzing club.

We saw ourselves as distinctive – hipper. We went to all-nighters, we did drugs and we played stuff like Bobby Bland, Freddie Scott, Bobby Sheen, the Valentinos, the Incredibles, the Invitations. Edwin Starr was well known everywhere else through 'SOS', but we played the other tracks. We were chasing obscurities, looking for faster music. We didn't have a name for the scene in adverts we called it discothèque classic. It wasn't called northern soul until Dave Godin the journalist came to the Twisted Wheel in 1970 and coined the term.

MIKE PICKERING (Hacienda DJ and promoter)

The first music I really liked was northern soul and Tamla Motown. I didn't go to the Twisted Wheel – I was too young. I went to Blackpool Mecca where Ian Levine was DJing. I went there three times. It was easier to get in the Highland Room* than the Twisted Wheel, which shut down in 1970. Wigan Casino came afterwards, in the seventies.

* At Blackpool Mecca, where northern soul was played.

What made northern soul so special was that in an era with no instant media, it was like a secret society. I remember getting a train from Stockport to Manchester at the weekend and seeing the kids with blazers and the holdall with the fist badges on it, and I would think: that's one of us going to Wigan or Blackpool. It was so underground.

We wore Oxford bags, tank tops, and your hair would be a bit like Rod Stewart – a feather cut. The area of Manchester where you got these things was where the Arndale is now, on New Brown Street, by the Eighth Day clothes shop; that was the hip area of town. There were great paintings on the wall, like murals. It was crazy when they put the Arndale on top of it, that area had proper boutiques. It was in the area between Market Street and Shude Hill. There was a little square and three roads full of shops a lot of shops. And one great shop that would sell the trousers and the shirts.

JON SAVAGE (journalist and author)
Soul was big in Manchester. I remember when I came here in the late seventies I went to that underground market* and there would still be stalls full of records I'd never heard of – it was a whole new world. Manchester always has been a very big black music town.

GARETH EVANS
I was hanging around helping at the Jigsaw club. I was sent to the owner's house with £1500 in an envelope and said 'There's the money for the week.' I gave him the keys and the money and he said 'I usually have to give them £1000 a week to keep it open!' Obviously they had been ripping him off, so he gave me the keys back and said, 'Run the club.'

I started booking the Yardbirds and Rod Stewart when he played with Long John Baldry, Beryl Marsden and the Rocket Express; I later found I'd booked Elton John.

The Jigsaw was in Cromford Court opposite the Cromford Court casino, where the Krays were thrown out and taken back to Piccadilly station. When I closed the Jigsaw at night I would go to the Cromford Court Casino. I went in there with Martha and the Vandellas; they would only sing two numbers because it was a rat-infested dump! And it was my apparent charm in those days that got Martha to play!

While the club scene was thriving, the band scene was also booming with bands like the Hollies, the Bee Gees, Herman's Hermits, Wayne Fontana and the Mindbenders,

---

* The underground market on Market Street was just that – a market underground with a maze of stalls.

Freddie and the Dreamers. With Top of the Pops being recorded in the city, Manchester was becoming a major pop centre.

Despite being overshadowed by the Beatles, several of the local groups were huge. In 1965 Freddie and the Dreamers, Wayne Fontana and the Mindbenders and Herman's Hermits topped the American Billboard charts consecutively between the middle of April 1965 and the end of May; one week in 1965, the same three bands occupied the top three in the Billboard top 100. And that's not including the Bee Gees, who started in Chorlton before moving to Australia.

ELLIOT RASHMAN

From the age of 11, music ruled everything. I saw the Beatles on *Scene at 6.30* on Granada when they did their first single, 'Love Me Do'. It wasn't a particularly great single or performance but it was one of those things where you walk past the telly and something grabs you.

BRUCE MITCHELL

The beat scene in Manchester operated around St Bernadette's youth club in Withington, where most of the bands would play. Andrew King, who went on to manage Pink Floyd, used to put posters up outside church hall – 'Tonight a beat group, 2/6'.

The Beatles changed everything in their wake when they arrived in 1963. The Beatles changed the way people regarded being a musician; they taught people that anyone can do it.

Manchester groups had great success, like Freddie and the Dreamers. Their singer Freddie Garrity lived in the same flats as me in Merseybank, where I was brought up in the council maisonettes.

PETER NOONE

Mick[ie] Most came to see us at a club called the Beachcomber in Bolton and signed us on the spot. The Beatles paved the way for musicians to have balls and to take the piss instead of the curtsy.

We played any date we could get. We got £4 at Urmston football club and £5 at Shaw Hall youth club, and suddenly we were good enough to travel, and we began playing Liverpool and Wigan and Leeds.

We built up a nice following and paid for the van and the equipment. Most days saw all the local rock sausage at Barratts guitar shop on Oxford Street or the Wimpy Bar, which had a jukebox. This was before bands got pissed all the time; we worked hard and practised and ate Wimpys. All the groups knew each other; I knew them as a fan and a friend or maybe an admirer. Hollies, Freddy and the Dreamers, Mockingbirds, and all the Scousers who dared play. And the Spencer Davis Group who we saw at the Twisted Wheel. We got to play at the

Cavern with the Ravens before they became the Kinks, so we knew about R'n'B in the south.

ELLIOT RASHMAN
Herman's Hermits went to America and were as big as the Beatles in 1965. It's hard to believe now. He was a very pretty boy, very young, and they did novelty songs – so did Freddie and the Dreamers. It was a big time for novelty songs. They played a role in making it a fun-filled time.

PETER NOONE
In '65, Manchester groups had three consecutive number ones: Wayne Fontana, Freddie and the Dreamers and Herman's Hermits. Herman's Hermits sold more records than any other act in the world in 1965.

TONY WILSON
Obviously there was the Beatles and Gerry and the Pacemakers, but then there was Billy J. Kramer and the Dakotas, and then Freddie and the Dreamers. I always thought that Billy J. Kramer and the Dakotas were from Liverpool, but actually the Dakotas were from Manchester. The Beatles' second single came out, Gerry and the Pacemakers put out their second single and Billy Kramer followed, and then came 'We Wear Short Shorts' from Freddie and the Dreamers.

Obviously in '65 the biggest band in the world were the Beatles, but we always forget that in 1965 they were over. Ian Macdonald makes the point in *Revolution in the Head*[*] that they were over, finished, stayed pop for one album too long. *Hard Day's Night* is like *Parallel Lines*, the most wonderful pop album, but instead of moving on they stayed pop while the world moved on and got weirder. We all started to listen to Manfred Mann and the Stones and other things. The Beatles then very cleverly sat down and said, 'We're fucked, what do we do?' and they started writing story-based songs like Bob Dylan, the first of which was 'Norwegian Wood'. For six months the Beatles became irrelevant. In that time Herman's Hermits from Manchester became the biggest pop group in the world.

Then you get the Hollies, and I think we forget how remarkably good a band they were – 'He Ain't Heavy' is a fine, fine song. And then you get 10cc and a pause. Although 10cc begins before that, because [Graham Gouldman] wrote 'For Your Love' for the Yardbirds[†] –

[*] Ian Macdonald's definitive guide to the recording of the Beatles' songs
[†] As well as writing the Yardbirds' 'For Your Love' and 'Heart Full of Soul', Graham Gouldman also wrote the Hollies' 'Look Through Any Window' and 'Bus Stop'. He was also a founding member of 10cc, for whom he co-wrote 'I'm Not In Love', 'The Things We Do For Love' and 'Rubber Bullets'.

and then went on to write 'Bus Stop' for the Hollies before forming 10cc.

ELLIOT RASHMAN
Top of the Pops came out of Manchester. It was fantastic it being here when I was. *Top of the Pops* was hosted by Jimmy Savile, who had built up a name for himself DJing round Manchester.*

C.P. LEE
Jimmy Savile started off in Yorkshire. He did lunchtime sessions playing records for secretaries and clerks who would pay sixpence to dance during their lunch hour. He claims he invented the disco, [although] a disc library, the Peppermint Lounge in New York, was doing the same thing at the same time.

BRUCE MITCHELL
Me and Tosh [Ryan] knew a lot about Jimmy Savile. Tosh's best friend worked for Savile in what might have been the Tropicana – the Mecca Ballroom. Jimmy Savile was the DJ, that was his first gig. He had enormous flair. He had the gig full at dinner time . . . He ran the gig. He had his own security and he got involved in the security sometimes. He ran a very discriminating door and he enjoyed challenging the lads coming in. He had the place rammed all the time and bought a car and put a Rolls Royce grille on it. Then he was sent over to run the Bradford Locarno – it was their equivalent of a musical Siberian salt mine, it was dying a death. Within a month he had that place rammed!

PHIL SUTCLIFFE (journalist)
The uni union was so good on a Saturday night: the hall upstairs and the bar down, standing about three feet in front of G[raham] Bond, G[inger] Baker, J[ack] Bruce, D[ick] H[eckstall]-Smith when they played on the floor of the bar was quite a physical experience.† That's where I saw all those bands, and if there wasn't anything I wanted to see there, then UMIST had some decent stuff, though it was the second student venue really. Seeing all those bands in quite a small place I guess was special. Of course there was the story of how a couple of years earlier the social sec

---

*An ex-coalminer from Leeds, Jimmy Savile started playing records in dance halls in the early 1940s. Savile's claims to have been the first ever DJ are arguably correct and quite fitting in Manchester, which would become synonymous with DJ culture.
† The Graham Bond Organisation launched Jack Bruce and Ginger Baker of Cream, as well as arguably being the first band to employ the classic sound combination created by playing the Hammond organ through Leslie speakers.

had turned down the Beatles for 30 quid, but I'm sure all social secs then did.

In the late sixties pop began to transform from monochrome to full colour. A psychedelic tinge was everywhere and there was magic in the air . . .

ELLIOT RASHMAN

In the sixties everything exploded – feminism, sexuality, drugs, clothes. Movies changed, television exploded. You couldn't miss it in Manchester; you had Swinging London but you also had the North coming out from under the shadows of the Industrial Revolution, producing a lot of creative people – a lot of artists, photographers . . . A lot gets forgotten, because Manchester is fucking awful at honouring those people but it's quite happy to name Mosley Street after a fucking fascist!

TONY WILSON

I was a typical late sixties student. I realised that there are different cycles of life, periods of live culture and dead culture. It was great: LSD, the Dead, demonstrations, revolution, rock'n'roll . . . there was no better time to be a student. Rob Dickens, the great former head of Warner Music, said that to enjoy rock'n'roll you have to have been born in 1950. What he means is that if you were born in 1950 you were eight years old and just beginning to be alive when . . . for example, I heard 'Hound Dog' on television one Saturday night and thought what the hell is going on, how can you call a woman a hound dog? Then you're 13 and in the playground as the Beatles explode around you, then 18 going to university when Jimi Hendrix and the Dead are around and that first Crosby, Stills and Nash album is coming out, and by the time you're 26 and if you've managed to stay alive and not just play old Van Morrison albums to yourself, then you were there when punk happened. If you managed to stay alive a little longer you could even be there when Shaun Ryder came along.

C.P. LEE

I was at the Bob Dylan gig at the Free Trade Hall in 1966 when he was heckled by the audience for 'selling out' with the famous 'Judas' heckle. The gig was a famous bootleg which everyone thought was recorded at the Albert Hall in London.

BRUCE MITCHELL

The psychedelic period was great: you had a couple of art labs and C.P. Lee came out of that scene. There was culture around it – a magazine called *Mole Express*. Acid was legal then! The drugs were always part of the music and I liked taking them (*laughs*). It was fantastic to play on acid!

ELLIOT RASHMAN

At 16 I discovered Roger Eagle's Magic Village. It was the first regular club I went to. I'd been through the mod phase; I then settled into a scene of marijuana and LSD. They did all-nighters where you could stay out all night and trip. I saw everybody play there – John Mayall in all his incarnations of bands, Peter Green, Mick Taylor, Tim Rose. At the same time I saw Pink Floyd on a Sunday at the Palace with Jimi Hendrix. Pink Floyd weren't allowed to use their light show because of the Lord's Day Observance Society rules! Hendrix was sensational. I also saw Hendrix at the CIS building.

The Magic Village was next to New Brown Street, which was a cul de sac. The guy on the door was Rowdy Yates, who started Lifeline. Blackpool act Jethro Tull played there a lot – he was the comedian who played flute on one leg and people would laugh.

New Brown Street* was where all the boutiques were. I got crushed velvet flares, kaftans. The Baked Potatoes caff, where the original Eighth Day† started, was on the corner. It was a fantastic kind of place – food, spices and hippie clothes – stuff you made and took in. There was a real scene. The local junkies would hang out on the street. Junkies were different than now; they held down jobs and led stable lifestyles and were on the National Health.

C.P. LEE

From Shude Hill to Market Street there was a warren of side streets and alleyways. Eighth Day started at New Brown Street, which we used to say was Manchester's Carnaby Street. It's been demolished now and ran from Market Street to the Post Office – a couple of hundred yards long. There were boutiques on each side of the street. You could buy the *International Times* and underground press there. People would hang out and if it was raining you could run across the road to Lewis's, which had a hot air thing, and dry your hair and run out again, which was important if you had an Afro!

Along with Eighth Day there was Stolen From Ivor and Jonathan Silva's Gentlemen's Apparel – purveyor of pointy boots. There was an

---

* New Brown Street was the 'head' street in Manchester. It's now demolished and lies underneath the Arndale shopping centre.
† Manchester's premier health food shop, which is still going strong.

attempt in 1968 to make Brown Street look like Haight-Ashbury; they painted the sides of the buildings.

There was a whole scene going round Manchester. There were love-ins in Platt Fields; it felt like you knew everybody. In 1970 the scene got quite huge; there were underground papers called *Grass Eye* and *Mole Express* – *Grass Eye* was the first one. We were part of the underground press, a shared network of articles that had no copyright. *Grass Eye* had a circulation of 25,000. The scene was divided between the hedonists and the radicals. The Angry Brigade even sent a cell to Manchester to radicalise the Mancunians! There was a bomb in Chorlton. It was a heavy radical period.

I was playing with Jacko Ogg and the Head People, who had Manchester's first light show. We would play art schools and what were left of the clubs after the Manchester Corporations Act of 1966, which closed down a lot of the Manchester bars. The authorities were also worried about what they would call 'men of colour' and white women fraternising. The Chief Constable was John McKay, a Presbyterian Scot who hated people having fun.

The club scene was under siege. A major clampdown followed Chief Superintendent Alan Dingwall's 'Coffee Beat Clubs' report. The report resulted in an Act of Parliament, the Manchester Corporation Act, which when it came into force on 1 January 1966, effectively shut down the city's vibrant network of coffee bars, clubs and venues. Many saw the report and the following act as a deliberate policy to shut down the clubs by the Chief Constable of Manchester, John McKay. McKay's tenure, which lasted from 1958 to 1966, like that of Chief Constable James Anderton in the eighties, was typified by moral high-handedness. The 30 acres of the old town where many of the clubs were located was designated a 'Comprehensive Development Area' by the City Council in the late sixties. In the seventies it was demolished to make way for the Arndale Centre which, when it opened in 1972, was Europe's largest covered town shopping centre.

C.P. LEE

The club scene shrank dramatically. If police believed that they could enter without a warrant they would, and they could close it down immediately. The clubs started to disappear in the next few years: the Wheel, Jigsaw, Mr Smith's.

ELLIOT RASHMAN

The heavyweight drug squad drove things underground and they were something to be afraid of. I spent a lot of my adolescence driving round

Moss Side trying to score pot where possible and acid for Saturday night to go to the Magic Village. It would wear off at six in the morning and we would go to the burger bar at Victoria station and buy breakfast. It was like a ritual.

2

WHAM BAM THANK YOU GLAM:
THE SEVENTIES

If the sixties had been a heady rush of thriving nightclubs and a beat boom, the decade's end seemed to leave a hangover in the early seventies. Clubs were shut down by the police and the beat groups were petering out; the ugly pall of the Moors Murders trial of 1966 seemed to hang over the city for a decade; and the brave new world of concrete that replaced the old town didn't seem to change the post-industrial malaise. Even the glittery glam of the early seventies didn't seem to be helping . . .

GINA SOBERS (punk scene face and member of the Liggers)
Manchester in the mid-seventies was a different world, almost a foreign place [compared] to the experience of the city today. Around the city centre, the warehouses lay empty and rotting, numerous derelict brick-strewn and rubbish-filled sites surrounded them: the Whitworth Street corridor was just a row of boarded-up, ancient-looking shop fronts, a testament to former times of prosperous commerce, the only remaining sign being a ludicrous boat showroom at the far end with massive windows showcasing the latest in yacht design.

MORRISSEY
The T. Rex concert was at Belle Vue in July 1972 and was almost ridiculous. Bolan was messianic, of course, but the screaming controlled the night and the music was incidental. The concert was stopped several times because it all got too dangerous at the front, and thereafter T. Rex suffered the quickest descent I've ever witnessed. If you check their chart span it was alarmingly brief. I also left the concert feeling that they didn't need my support. Sparks I saw at the Free Trade Hall and then the Palace, firstly for *Kimono-Propaganda*, and then for *Indiscreet*. It's forgotten

now, but Sparks attracted a lot of children, so there was a slight gang-show element to what they did, and Russell spoke to the crowd in a very pat-a-cake, pat-a-cake, *Crackerjack* way, and it was very difficult for him to sustain that madcap scattershot vocal pace. I felt out of place because I thought Sparks were Dali-esque, but that wasn't the general consensus. Which is why you'll find their stuff on terrible compilations entitled *Glam Rock* and such.

MARK STANDLEY (V2 guitarist)

This was my first live gig by a real pop star. I didn't even know you could go and see people off the telly in real life! 'What, I'm going to be in a room, and Marc Bolan is actually going to be there at the same time?'

The first rush was getting on the bus at Crown Point in Denton, and the bus being full of T. Rex fans, everyone excited at the prospect of seeing them in 'real life'. When we got to Belle Vue, there were thousands of people there, mostly girls. All in a state of excitement that I hadn't experienced before.

Suddenly, there he was. Marc Bolan in 'real life', smiling and waving to us. Then the band started. It was loud and didn't sound like the records. It was rough and chaotic. I remember Marc broke the neck off his Les Paul after about three songs and seemed really upset. I remember thinking, 'What's up with you? You must have loads of guitars!'

CHRIS SIEVEY (frontman of the Freshies)

I had started in school bands and when I left school my brother and I parked ourselves in Apple Records reception in about 1970 until a Beatle listened to us. After some time someone came to get rid of us. They said the Beatles weren't there and we said, 'Can't we record something?' We were sent up to Tony King's office, who was the head of A&R. We sang a song and they booked us into the studio. George Harrison loved it but was too busy to produce us. Someone else said we were too green and told us to speak to Tony Visconti,* who said, 'It sounds great but I'm working on something at the moment and if that goes big then I can't do it.' What he was working on was 'Ride A White Swan'.† So we were close but not close enough . . .

MORRISSEY

I lived for Thursday when I'd buy *Melody Maker*, *NME*, *Disc*, *Record Mirror*, *Sounds*. I'd read every single word, and [I] had been this way since 1969. It

* Legendary producer of David Bowie and T. Rex.
† A T. Rex classic and the band's first massive crossover pop hit in 1970, marking the beginning of glam rock.

was impossible to hear decent music anywhere – not on the radio, and pop music wasn't used in commercials and films the way it is now. Because it was so commercialised it was considered lowbrow, as opposed to classical music which was highbrow because there had never been a commercialised aspect to it – classical music had never actually *been sold* to people, they just found it.

So, in 1973 you simply did not ever hear music. *Top of the Pops* was the *only* recognition of breakthrough; I'd watch it religiously waiting for something subversive to slip through the net, because there was the belief that if a record sold it would be played by the BBC because the BBC was a public service and had to respond to public taste. The BBC, radio or television, is not like that now – they ignore whatever they wish, irrespective of popularity – but back then they had a duty to respond to what the public nominated. I was astonished when Patti Smith zoomed to No. 5 with 'Because the Night' because although it was a very respectable record she was still considered anarchic, and possibly mad. She refused to appear on *Top of the Pops* because they asked her to mime. The Ramones appeared on *Top of the Pops* too late. The moment had passed.

MARK STANDLEY

At the time, you could either like Slade *or* T. Rex! The trouble was that Slade kept putting records out that I liked too. But that wasn't allowed!

Then it was David Bowie. Not interested – I liked T. Rex.

My friend got me a ticket to see Bowie on the Ziggy tour at Manchester Free Trade Hall. I wasn't that bothered about going, but went along. This time, there were more 'weirdos' than at the T. Rex gig the year before.

I had a smug, 'Go on then, entertain me' attitude. Fuck me, he did! As I stood watching, transfixed by what I was seeing and the quality of the music, a heretical thought kept strolling through my mind: this is better than T. Rex. *Don't be ridiculous!* It is though. That bloke's not human, look at him, listen to what he's saying. I went home very confused, but then realised a pivotal thought: I'm allowed to like more than one thing at once!

Through Bowie, I started listening to Lou Reed, Velvet Underground, Iggy, etc. I never really liked the other side of glam – Sweet, Mud, Gary Glitter, etc. (Even though I ended up in the Glitter Band years later!) At the time, they seemed dim-witted and false. I was already a regular at Pips nightclub.* I walked into the Roxy room and all the women looked like fifties film stars. All the men were like Bowie or Bryan Ferry in an age of cheesecloth shirts and extremely bad hair.

*Perhaps the key Manchester nightclub of the seventies, Pips opened on Fennel Street by the cathedral.

MICK ROSSI (Slaughter and the Dogs guitarist)

I was massively into Bowie, and especially his guitarist Mick Ronson. I was really young, about 14, when I bunked off school and went with a mate over to Sheffield to see him play when he was touring his solo album *Slaughter On Tenth Avenue*. I was down the front shouting at Mick and he gave me the thumbs up; I met him afterwards as he was getting on the tour bus and we got on and I just sat there staring at him. We went back to the hotel where they were having a party. He came over and gave us a set of keys and said, 'There's a room for you and that's where you're staying tonight, I can't have you sleeping on the coach station.' What a top bloke.

HOWARD DEVOTO (Buzzcocks vocalist)

I was working in a record shop in Leeds in my gap year between school and university. This album came out from David Bowie. I remembered having the 'Space Oddity' single, which was a novelty record, and I got to really like *Hunky Dory*, where he still had long hair on the cover. A month after it came out, he had suddenly cut his hair and was in the press. I got in there before the world caught on.

With *Hunky Dory* it was the music and the lyrics, it was very beguiling. There wasn't much image to it at that point, this was before he came out with the bisexuality thing. He was putting about names like Velvet Underground and Iggy Pop and this was fascinating. I had seen an Iggy article in the press a year before and was already interested.

MORRISSEY

The Dolls on *Whistle Test* were the most wild and visionary thing I'd ever seen and heard – 'Jet Boy' sprang at me like a cobra. No one making music had guts or wit or nerve. I had seen Mott the Hoople in 1972 at the Free Trade Hall, and was just slightly terrified. At one point Ian Hunter said: 'Las' Chewsday this song went tuh numbah three in the chaaarts,' and ripped into 'All the Young Dudes' – the Aylesbury Mott hippies stayed in their seats. They didn't see the tide turning. Or, they *did*. I went mad at the front.

I was timid, though, and skulked from gig to gig. I did nothing else and went nowhere else. Luckily, I lived around the corner from the Hardrock in Stretford so in 1972 I also saw Roxy Music, Bowie and Lou Reed. I still have my ticket for the Dolls in 1972, but they didn't turn up because their drummer had died three days earlier in London. The Velvet Underground also came to Stretford, but I didn't go because Lou Reed had left. The Dolls were the have-nots – the kind of people Bowie would think it dangerous to be seen with.

PHIL SAXE
After the [Twisted] Wheel I got into the Velvets and Bowie. I thought northern soul was a cultural cul de sac; it had lost the plot and was nothing to do with soul music.

STEVE DIGGLE (Buzzcocks guitarist/vocalist)
I always wanted to be in a band but it seemed too complicated. I was enjoying running with street gangs and getting into trouble around Rusholme and Bradford and Ardwick. I liked my clothes. I remember walking down the street in a suede jacket and people shouting stuff, that kind of thing toughens you up. If you dressed weirdly in those terraced streets in those days you would get a lot of hassle . . .

KEVIN CUMMINS (photographer)
The first gig I took a picture of was James Taylor and Carole King at the Free Trade Hall. That was the sort of music that people were really into at sixth form. I was always into soul and reggae and that kind of stuff at school and later on I got into Bowie and Roxy Music. We used to organise coach trips to Roxy Music gigs. I went to Ferry's first solo gig at the Albert Hall.*

RICHARD WITTS (The Passage frontman and cultural force)
I'm from Cleethorpes originally and I moved to Manchester to study at the Royal Manchester College of Music. I did what they called the joint course – that's because we smoked joints most the day! It was a five-year course. I was a percussionist. The early seventies was an interesting period in Manchester. The three bands I associated with the conurbation were Van Der Graaf Generator, 10cc and Barclay James Harvest.† Van Der Graaf played at UMIST in the mid-seventies and an argument could be made that that gig was equally important as the two Sex Pistols gigs for a lot of people.

CLINT BOON (Inspiral Carpets keyboard player)
I was always surrounded by music. My mum and dad were always playing music round the house. We had a big radiogram and I can remember Manfred Mann and Herman's Hermits from when I was a kid. My mum

---

* December 1974.
† Formed at Manchester University in 1967, the Peter Hammill-fronted outfit mixed jazz, rock and classical. 10cc dotted the seventies with some intelligent bubblegum pop. They also set up Strawberry Studios in Stockport, named after the Beatles' 'Strawberry Fields Forever'. Formed in Saddleworth near Oldham in 1966, Barclay James Harvest specialised in symphonic/melodic rock with folk, progressive and classical influences and were favourites of John Peel in the seventies with several top 40 albums.

and dad had musicals like *Porgy and Bess* and Burt Bacharach as well as loads of Beatles, though I can't remember any Stones. They also had stuff like Neil Sedaka's *Oh Carol* album and Gary Lewis and the Playboys which, in hindsight, aren't massive albums, but I've still got those albums now, I was always really into the harmonies.

We lived in a corner shop and would sell singles from a box of 45s on the counter as well as vegetables. This box introduced me to a lot of music in 1969–70. I would buy records from Oldham Market. The first single I bought was 'ABC' by the Jackson Five in 1969. I bought Bill Haley's 'Rock Around the Clock' – it was ten bob in Woolworth's. That changed my life, hearing rock'n'roll music like that, and from there I was regularly buying records. I listened to the radio and would watch *Top Of The Pops* religiously every Thursday night.

KEVIN CUMMINS

That was a different era. I had no idea if there was a scene in Manchester in the seventies – it was just another stopping-off point for bands. You didn't think anyone could actually be in a band. We didn't think we could be in a band; it was something that other people did.

LIZ NAYLOR (journalist)

The first gig I went to was with my sister was Lou Reed at the Free Trade Hall.* After that I went to see Mick Ronson, and Fleetwood Mac before they went to America. I saw Captain Beefheart on my own in 1975; my mum came to pick me up after the gig!† I was really young. I would feel slightly edgy at the gigs. It was great; there were all these people in great-coats, hippies – these were the people that you didn't see on the street. If you see footage from the time there are no freaks on the street. At the gigs I had this kind of sense of another world.

RICHARD WITTS

There was a jazz scene going on in Manchester with two modern jazz clubs. Manchester had a vibrant, diverse scene with a lot of activity from the folk movement, with Steeleye Span and Pentangle‡ coming to the Free Trade Hall.

This couple called Silly Wizard were from Manchester. They did really well and ended up supporting Pentangle on tours. There was also the

* 31 May 1974.
† Free Trade Hall, 15 November 1975. At this time the Free Trade Hall was the key venue in Manchester for cutting-edge bands to play.
‡ Led by Scottish guitar player Bert Jansch, whose guitar style was a big influence on Johnny Marr.

emergence in the early seventies of the folk singer/comedian, with Mike Harding and Bob Williamson they were the equivalent of Billy Connolly, coming out of the folk scene and doing a comedy set. There was plenty going on; it wasn't all the rubble of civilisation that Tony Wilson liked to go on about. Barclay James Harvest did their first gig at the Free Trade Hall with backing from the Symphony Orchestra; they were huge in Germany.

There was this great Victorian building by the university and, when the College of Music moved out, nobody knew what to do with it. They couldn't flog it off, it was a Grade Two listed building and it was just there. I thought it was a fantastic place and it was then taken over by productive musicians, squatted and turned into a venue called the Squat, which was an important place.

ANDREW JASPAN (journalist)

The Squat used to be the old Manchester University College of Music. A beautiful building with a concert hall in the centre and rehearsal rooms all around. The acoustics were brilliant.

In 1975 the university decided to pull it down to build a car park. I led an occupation to protect the building and use it to accommodate students who were unable to get lodgings at the start of term. To help pay for the upkeep we put on concerts. After a few months the university reprieved the building, cleaned it out and it continued as a music venue for a few years.

PETER SAVILLE (Factory Records designer)

I grew up on the edge of the city in the countryside. I went to Knutsford Art College and would come in at night to Manchester ever since I was 17 or 18; to me it had the aura of an industrial city, very different to London. I found it all quite exciting. I found the industrial fabric of Manchester quite edgy and exotic, and that was one of the things that would go on to influence the approach and look of Factory Records years later.

PAUL RYDER (Happy Mondays bassist)

Me and our kid had loads of aunties – big Irish Catholic families. One had nine kids and one had six – they were older than us and we would listen to their music. Auntie Winnie's girls were into Motown so when they came to babysit for us we got an earful of Motown all night. My Auntie Mary's kids, Matt and Pat,* their older brothers were into the Eagles. Matt and Pat were the youngest, and the older ones were getting all stuff sent over from America. Their brother Pete worked in a record shop in America and sent stuff not released over here back to them.

* Matt and Pat Carroll, who would become Central Station design and who designed most of the Happy Mondays' sleeves.

My mam and dad's collection was always there: Buddy Holly, Fats Domino and Elvis. So growing up I got a nice big mixture of music.

NOEL GALLAGHER
I came from an Irish background. My dad was a country and western DJ. He used to do Christmas parties – he would play a bit of soul, a bit of Stevie Wonder, a bit of the Beatles, though he wasn't massively into it – and he would play social clubs and that. There's no musicians in my family on either side as far as I know, so I'm not sure where the obsession came from. I guess there's something with being Irish – the Irish are either writers, drinkers, singers or musicians . . .

GINA SOBERS
I remember the three-day week, doing my homework by candlelight, rubbish piling up in the streets, stinking and uncollected, supermarket queues as housewife mums stocked up on sugar, tea and white bread. There was a feeling of grey mediocrity about it all, that Technicolor life was elsewhere, probably down south – that is, in Bramhall, Wilmslow, Hale Barns, the posher parts of the suburbs.

And the music scene wasn't much better. 10cc, a local band, had had chart success; they used the money that to open Strawberry Studios in Stockport – a 24-track recording suite. Sad Café were said to be the next big thing from Manchester. Course we had our own soul group in Sweet Sensation* at number one, but they were all very cabaret, slick and remote like the bands I saw every week on *Top of the Pops*. I thought you needed the attention of a Tony Hatch or a Mickie Most to make it on the pop scene, though me and my schoolfriends loved *Rock Follies*, the story of three women trying to make it in the male-dominated music world.†
Maybe we started dreaming then.

LIZ NAYLOR
My sister was seven years older than me and she was into the glam end of things, so I benefited growing up with Roxy Music and Bowie. When I was ten at primary school, a teacher called Pete Walker gave me a Captain Beefheart album, *Unconditionally Guaranteed*, because I was good at English. He was a hippie teacher and recognised me as a lost ten-year-old. It was utterly weird but I loved it.

---

* Sweet Sensation won TV talent show *New Faces* in 1973 with their homespun Philly soul and scored a few chart hits, including their number one 'Sad Sweet Dreamer'. Their frontman, the late Marcel King, would also later release a single on Factory Records.
† *Rock Follies* was a TV series about a girl group, first shown on TV in February 1976.

NICKY LOCKETT/MC TUNES (rapper)

My dad was a massive rock'n'roll boy. He was in a band. They might have had an album out but my mam was vague on it all. He was into early Van Morrison when Van was a rebel, before he got God. He liked ELO and loved Bob Dylan and Bruce Springsteen the early rebel boys who were a bit naughty. He was also into Jimi Hendrix before anyone knew who Jimi was, but he didn't like the Who or the Beatles. My mam was into George Clinton, Smokey Robinson and the Jacksons. I was listening to that sort of gear while people were into Showaddy-fucking-waddy, fucking Mud. Marc Bolan would sneak in and Bowie fucking brilliant. These were life-changing albums for my parents – fuck all that slack, hippy, 'Ferry 'Cross the Mersey' bollocks! I grew up with lots of black music like Bob Marley, Gregory Isaacs – anything that was black and underground at that time.

TONY WILSON

Manchester did have a couple of venues in the seventies. For example there was the Hardrock, which was a fantastic venue – it was hi tech, beautifully done, very expensive* . . . One of the great gigs at the Hardrock was the Lou Reed concert on the 'Rock'n'Roll Animal' tour.

ALAN ROBINSON (promoter)

I used to work at the Hardrock. I ran the stage when it opened on 2 September 1972, when David Bowie played the first of two nights there.

There were two main halves to the Hardrock: there was a bar, with a gig venue round the back. It was split into two.

When Rank Leisure came in it started to go downhill. There was the Hard Rock café inside but people couldn't afford the burgers, so that shut and turned into a cheap Wimpy burger bar. Soon the concerts were starting to struggle and the promoters pulled out.

BRUCE MITCHELL

The Hardrock saw a lot of the big acts, it was purpose-built. Roger Eagle had the [New York] Dolls booked there at one of his gigs but the drummer, Billy Murcia, died on way to the gig.

DENISE JOHNSON (singer)

As a kid growing up, I was heavily influenced by the radio, therefore pop music, coupled with my mum's collection of ska, American female singers like Gladys [Knight] and Diana [Ross] and really rude filthy reggae

* Located on Greatstone Road in Stretford, the Hardrock was open for a few short years in the early to mid seventies, hosting many big names on the verge of their big breakthrough including Santana, David Bowie, Genesis, Hawkwind and Roxy Music.

with lyrics like 'lie down gal, let me push it up' (*laughs*) – but I wasn't scarred by it!

As I went on I loved Abba, Kate Bush, Karen Carpenter, mid to late eighties American soul, Blondie . . . I could go on and on. But generally, I got into whatever stirred my soul. I was mainly a fan of the song, the artist usually came second.

CLINT BOON

I can't remember when I started listening to John Peel. A lot of kids at school were talking about him. There was a lot of progressive music about so to my mind it wasn't as groundbreaking as when I became a regular listener, when he was playing punk stuff. I was at Rochdale Art School in 1975; at that point my favourite music was fifties rock. I was buying modern British rock'n'roll bands like Showaddywaddy – I was a 16-year-old rock'n'roller into Jerry Lee Lewis, Little Richard, Mud, Rubettes – who were stunning. It was the first music scene I really embraced. I had the brothel creepers, the quiff and the bootlace tie.

I was at Rochdale art college when Showaddywaddy released 'Under the Moon of Love' – I remember the day it got to number one, I was fucking made up that my band was at number one in 1975. Romeo Charger! Fucking brilliant.

GINA SOBERS

We started going out to gigs, one of the first being Roxy Music at the Apollo. There was a queue of trainee hairdressers and apprentice butcher lads stretching round the block. I was a big Eno fan even then, I was wearing a feather boa around my neck as a tribute to his style. I felt miffed that he'd already left the band, but they didn't disappoint.

With a 'Hellooo Manchesterrrrr!' and a roar back from the crowd, Bryan Ferry launched into the opening number. We were committed Roxettes from then on, though the arguments raged over whether David Bowie had more artistic merit and if Bryan Ferry spent as much on hair dye.

MARTIN MOSCROP (A Certain Ratio guitarist)

We all used to go to Pips disco. The Bowie/Roxy room played stuff like *Low* by David Bowie, Kraftwerk, Brian Eno.

KEVIN CUMMINS

I used to go to Pips. They had a generic soul room which played the likes of Barry White – if you wanted to pull a nurse that was where you would go. The Bowie/Roxy room was where we went, where you felt at home. I was never into normal clubs, they were dreadful places.

Bowie/Roxy I think definitely defined Manchester at the time. That's why Manchester bands always had a certain style and edge. Bowie getting so massive in Manchester influenced all sorts of different bands from Ian Curtis to Slaughter and the Dogs . . . You would go to see Marc Bolan and it would be pretty much the same circle as at Bowie and Ronson and Lou Reed. I remember Rossi getting onstage at a Roxy Music gig and playing air guitar next to Bryan Ferry when no one ever dared to get on stage. He did it to Marc Bolan as well . . . He came round to mine when *Diamond Dogs* and *Slaughter on Tenth Avenue* were out. We were trying to think of names for the band and the hybrid of those two albums became their name.

MARTIN MOSCROP
One of the gigs I remember going to was the Fatback Band and Tavares at Belle Vue. At the weekend I worked there at the Pleasure Park – it was a mixture of zoo, funfair, ballroom, ten-pin bowling, greyhound and stock car racing.* I was well in with the general manager of the King's Hall,† so we got in free for the gigs there. It was full of soulboys all pretending we were old enough to drink.

NOEL GALLAGHER
We used to go to Ireland for our six-week summer holiday. There was nothing on the telly in Ireland but I remember one pivotal moment in 1977. The whole family surrounded the radio because we'd heard that Elvis had died. My aunties – who were kind of late twenties, early thirties – all broke down and started crying, 'Elvis is dead!' And I thought, 'Wow, Elvis is dead! That's pretty big.' In those days southern Ireland was a backwater; the fact that the news had penetrated that far and the recital of the Bible passage on the radio or whatever had been interrupted was a big deal.

HOWARD DEVOTO
I was very taken by the improvised theatre performance of Jeff Nuttall's The People Show.‡ Jeff Nuttall was at Leeds and his thing was that performance was a confrontation to try and freak the straights out – like a theatrical version of *Candid Camera*, except The People Show were a bit more artistic and weird about it.

* Belle Vue was the main leisure park in Manchester. It's now demolished.
† Another long-lost venue. Typical of the big Manchester mid-seventies venues, it was not in the city centre, but in Belle Vue. All manner of big bands played here including Rod Stewart, Parliament and Status Quo.
‡ Co-founded in 1966 by Jeff Nuttall, who also wrote one of the seminal books from the hippie era, *Bomb Culture*.

DERMO (Northside vocalist)
My dad used to have a bag full of old seven-inch singles and I'd play them when no one was around. I'd play them in order of what sounded right to me which was the best band name, singer or song title. Little Richard, Abba, Boney M, Duane Eddy, 'Take A Chance On Me', 'I Hear You Knocking But You Can't Come In', etc., all had something interesting in their names. I soon discovered I liked the songs with a faster rhythm, but I still loved a good chorus/melody.

STELLA (Intastella vocalist)
The first music I was into was a collection of jukebox records – records like 'Needles and Pins', a lot of sixties stuff from my dad who got them out of the working men's clubs. There were piles of them with no centres in them. My mum was into modern jazz so I listened to a bit of that, but she was such a snobby mod about it that it made me dislike it. After that I got into T. Rex and David Bowie.

IAN BROWN (Stone Roses vocalist)
My mum had *South Pacific* and was into Perry Como. When I was a kid I was into the Beatles, like everyone in the north; then I heard T. Rex's 'Metal Guru' and that was the first single I bought. I was into Gary Glitter when I was nine – 'Rock'n'Roll Part One' was a great song.

I still think Slade are great. Noddy Holder was one of the best singers to ever come out of Britain he used to sing like John Lennon when you think about it. He sang rough, out there and full-on. I liked Alice Cooper: I had 'School's Out'. I didn't even know what an album was till '76, when I got the *Billion Dollar Babies* album for Christmas. I only thought about singles till then.

MICK ROSSI
Bowie was the first person who really affected me. Before that I listened to my brother Ray's music. We shared bunk beds so I could hardly miss it! He was a mod, so I grew up with Motown, the Who, the Kinks, but when David Bowie came along that was for me. Watching Mick Ronson play guitar was amazing – he was a really talented guy, he put so much into Bowie's sound. He was an angel of a man, very humble, so much talent. He arranged things, he wrote the guitar lines, the piano parts.

There was Bowie and Roxy Music, Mott the Hoople and Lou Reed and T. Rex. And that was it for me.

STEVE DIGGLE

I used to go to the Stoneground* in Gorton and saw bands like Silverhead, who were a bit like the New York Dolls. A mate of mine at the time used to say that grammar school boys listened to Deep Purple and comprehensive boys listened to Led Zep.

HOWARD DEVOTO

For me all of David Bowie's albums in the seventies were fantastic, but live I never really liked his gigs – he was too controlled for me . . . I saw Alice Cooper's first ever UK gig in London at the Rainbow; I got really into him and then the Detroit groups.

MICK ROSSI

The Dolls and Iggy are in there as well, though I got into them later on, to be honest. With me being a Wythenshawe lad we were pretty much isolated. I wasn't really exposed to that stuff. The reason I got into Lou Reed was because Mick Ronson played on the *Transformer* album – he did the classic piano part on 'Perfect Day'.

PETER SAVILLE

In the mid-seventies there was a younger generation who were brought up on Roxy and Bowie and had a strong idea of the things they liked. In the mid-seventies the interesting people at art college weren't doing fine art, they were doing graphics, fashion, advertising – the things that seemed to happen in the world. There were a few of us avant-garde types who wanted things to be different; the rest wanted a job, but we weren't that interested in having a job – we wanted to change things.

ELLIOT RASHMAN

Manchester Polytechnic had the art college with Linder, Peter Saville, Malcolm Garrett and others including Mick Hucknall, who was the last of that art school generation. It produced a generation of people like Ben Kelly, Malcolm Garrett and Barney Bubbles, the guy who did the Blockheads stuff.

CHRIS SIEVEY

I spent the next four years banging my head against record labels' walls. So in 1974 I formed my own label, three years before the Buzzcocks' *Spiral Scratch* was released. I put out three cassette albums.

---

* The Stoneground was Manchester's 'underground' venue in the early to mid seventies. Based in the Corona cinema on Birch Street in Gorton, it later became the Mayflower, one of the key punk venues.

C.P. LEE

Tosh [Ryan] and Bruce [Mitchell] set up Music Force – a musicians' collective which worked for musicians as an agency and several other things.* They bagged the premises from the university on the Oxford Road corridor, which enabled them to set up the agency; the sound side of things was handled by Martin Hannett. Martin had already started producing music he had produced a Nigerian hi-life band and he had worked for Belt and Braces radical theatre company.

BRUCE MITCHELL

We ran Music Force from 100 Oxford Road, putting on gigs in places like Band on the Wall† and Rafters‡ and in pubs. We were involved with lots of musicians and we became agents. We would put on gigs, we would go to the pubs and take them over; we took over Mr Smith's in town, places like that. We would do that to create work at grassroots level. We took our inspiration from Dave Robinson from Stiff Records in London – he invented pub rock because nobody else wanted these bands (*laughs*). We did lots of gigs with Dr Feelgood. They really grafted – we did loads of gigs with them around Europe.

HOWARD DEVOTO

With the hippies, I never believed the ideology; it had all kinds of naivety to it. I never believed the peace and love thing. I was never a relaxed enough person to smoke dope and listen to records. I had some of the paraphernalia associated with it: there are pics of me with Indian embroidered shirts, things like that burning joss sticks in a room. I was a bit too young in a way; you needed to be three or four years older to go off and do hippie things.

I bought the Stooges' first album because I was fascinated by an article I read on Iggy in *Zigzag*, with the classic picture of him standing on people's hands. Even to this day the album doesn't sound that good to

* Music Force was a musicians' co-operative arranging PA hire, booking gigs and setting a fly-posting business. With the money they made, Tosh Ryan and Martin Hannett set up a recording studio. One of Hannett's first commissions was incidental music for an agit-prop theatre group called Belt and Braces Roadshow, as well as the soundtrack for a science-fiction cartoon. Early in 1977 Hannett, Ryan and Lawrence Beadle further expanded, setting up Rabid Records as a vehicle to promote Slaughter and the Dogs.

† The Band on the Wall in the George and Dragon on Swan Street must be Manchester's longest enduring venue, and has a fascinating history.

‡ One of the second wave of post-punk Manchester venues, with gigs initially promoted by Rob Gretton.

me apart from 'I Wanna Be Your Dog'. Then I got *Raw Power* on my way home from college in Bolton just after I moved there. It sounded so different but again it wasn't cementing with me. Lou Reed was the other way round – I liked *Transformer* and then I saw him at the Hardrock and it was disappointing.

I was an Alice Cooper fan by then, so I was a bit interested there. I was tagging him for later investigation. And then of course David Bowie came along and was touting his name around. I was a big Bowie fan. That all added to it. I also liked some of T. Rex's *Electric Warrior*.

TONY WILSON
T. Rex had disappeared. It was short-lived. It was exciting in '72. Unfortunately, for me, Bowie was from London and that put me off Bowie. And I never really liked Roxy Music, not because of Roxy themselves but because of Bryan Ferry – he's all about form over substance. So when Granada asked me to start our own music show in late autumn 1975, we talked about it and decided that music was shite, so we'd be more of a comedy show – which is why Clive James had a spot every week, because music wasn't worth shit except for a few bits of American music which were worthwhile.

It just felt like we were waiting for something to happen.

3

ALL THE YOUNG DUDES: THE PISTOLS AND THE BUZZCOCKS

As the seventies accelerated towards their revolutionary climax, several of the key players in punk were already in place, looking for the magic in the grime of post-industrial Manchester.

RICHARD BOON (Buzzcocks manager)
In the late seventies, Manchester, having been the cradle of capitalism, had become the grave of capitalism.

MORRISSEY
Pre-punk Manchester was a calamitous period of history. The country was done for. Manchester was a maze of dirty streets. Street lighting was still a very dull yellow – none of the sharp white lights that are everywhere now. Violence was everywhere – and accepted. There was a spiritual darkness as well as a literal darkness; still lots of tramps in demob suits, record shops in murky buildings, city squares completely unlit, 70 per cent of city-centre buildings unused, and everything revolving around the last bus home. It was still very visibly post-war, and very industrial-ugly, discoloured with the dirt of 100 years, and rock music was a swarm of misery. Because there was absolutely no money around everyone was in a mode of paralysis. If you think I'm exaggerating, I'm not.

TONY WILSON
I felt let down by the sixties of course. Liz Naylor's famous theory [was] that punk was actually the hippies' revenge:* most of the people at the forefront of punk were people in their mid-twenties who had expected

---

* Not just Liz Naylor's theory!

hippie to change everything and somehow it didn't. Music was dull. British music was dull and we knew something was going to happen.

PETER SAVILLE

The early seventies was a hangover from the sixties, but the waterbed broke. The new generation of pop tutors were Bowie, Roxy, Kraftwerk. They were our favourite professors and linked through to things like the German avant garde of Faust and Neu; they gave us some critical lessons. Bowie gave the lesson in managing pop culture so that you aren't just being a passenger but actually determining your own journey through pop. That was really important.

Roxy Music extended the landscape of pop from music out to fashion, history, style and glamour in a Hollywood kind of way. In a way they were the first modern pop group. Biba was going on then – you could join the dots between different aspects of life. And it wasn't just about music; with Bowie and Roxy Music it was about a romantic attitude towards life. It became the theatre of pop rather than just the sound or the music of pop. And you would learn stuff: David Bowie would mention Lindsay Kemp in an interview in the *NME* and you would go and find out who he was; when Roxy Music mentioned Baby Jane Holzer in 'Virginia Plain', you would think who's she?

You learnt about Warhol. The only art I knew was pop art, because through the sixties I grew up with pop art. And I began to see the connections between things, I started seeing the consecutiveness between things

STEVE DIGGLE

Before punk in Manchester, there was nothing doing. Bowie and Roxy had peaked and we needed something else. You got prog bands who would have one song that would take up the whole side of an album, singing about mushrooms in the sky sort of stuff. Boring.

If you went to Pips nightclub you had to have a suit and tie on to get in. There was a million on the dole . . . the music that was getting made wasn't relevant to our generation. I was going to get a band going, because I was frustrated; it was going to be like the Who smashing their gear up

RICHARD BOON

I knew Howard [Devoto] from Leeds – we were schoolmates. Along with Richard Famous, who went on to join the Poison Girls, we'd messed around with music in the early seventies – sort of folky mumblings! He played piano, and we only managed one gig.

Then I went to university in Reading and did fine art – did some white paintings. It was a bit grim really!

HOWARD DEVOTO

The first band I was in, at Leeds Grammar School in 1972, was a silly Bonzo Dog Doo Dah type of band without the jokes, which I did with Richard Boon. It was a very silly band.

Then I did a little bit with the gentleman who went on to become Richard Famous in the Poison Girls. It was just the pair of us with acoustic guitars; we did a couple of gigs in folk clubs in Leeds and I was the singer. Seeing Bowie with an acoustic guitar made me think there was something left in the instrument.

TONY WILSON

A junkie friend from Cambridge who was a big Dead fan rang me up and said, 'You have to hear this album, *Horses* by Patti Smith.' I trusted him and went and bought it. He was completely right. It was the reason I got John Cale to produce the [Happy] Mondays' first album, which wasn't much use to anybody. What I loved was where Cale placed Patti Smith's voice, sitting right in the middle of your head.

Granada decided to do a *What's On* music spinoff, hoping it would be a network ITV show to rival *Top of the Pops*. We did one pilot and they went, 'Well, it's not a *Top of the Pops* rival but we'll give you a late night series.' That was *So It Goes.**

An envelope arrived with an album sleeve in it – no record – and a note saying, 'Dear Mr Wilson, Your TV show on music was fantastic, could we have more of this please.' The sleeve was the New York Dolls and the note was from Steven Morrissey, in brackets 'aged 14'.

MICK ROSSI

Wayne [Barrett] was in the year above me at school and when we first met we clicked instantly. We were from Wythenshawe, which was a big estate in the south of Manchester.

The first time I went round to his house in October 1975 I remember he had all these garden gnomes in his garden! We started writing straight away and my brother, Ray, got us a gig. We played glam rock but a more aggressive version. In early 1976 we were playing working men's clubs, labour clubs – the reaction wasn't that great (*laughs*) but there was

---

* *So It Goes* was the groundbreaking arts and music TV series fronted by Tony Wilson in 1976/77 that showcased many of the innovative punk acts before anyone else.

Inspirational, intellectual, infuriating, confrontational, energetic, smart, opinionated and loveable, the late Tony Wilson was at the heart of Manchester for decades (Photo: Ian Tilton www.iantilton.net)

nowhere else to play! We did covers and a couple of originals, got paid and told to go home. All this led to Ray promoting the gig at Wythenshawe Forum. We started building our crowd from there. There weren't any other bands around doing our kind of stuff.

Tosh Ryan came to see us with Martin Hannett and talked about putting our single out on his new label, Rabid Records. Pre-Pistols we were carving out a little bit of a following and had our own direction. You can't in my opinion just wake up and be a punk band. I think we were there already anyway. The sound, style and attitude is with you anyway.

Tony Wilson compered our gig at the Wythenshawe Forum. He turned up in clogs and with a handbag (*laughs*), which was unusual to see in Wythenshawe!

'WE'RE NOT INTO MUSIC, WE'RE INTO CHAOS'

In which Devoto and Shelley set off to London to find the Sex Pistols and kickstart the Manchester scene.

On 19 February 1976 the NME ran its famous review of the Sex Pistols gig at the Marquee that concluded with the classic sneer, 'We're not into music, we're into chaos'. It set light to the touch paper of the few people still awake in dreaming England.

Hardly any people around the country noticed the review, but in isolated pockets of the UK it hit home. Two disaffected Stooges and underground music fans at Bolton Institute of Technology (now the University of Bolton) saw the review, which was to set in motion a chain of events that would change Manchester music – and by extension all music – for ever.

HOWARD DEVOTO

In November 1975 I stuck a notice up at college in Bolton to see what would happen. One or two other guys replied to it, including Pete [Shelley], and we started trying to make some music. We were hanging out as much as trying to get that band together, but we had a couple of practices. We attempted to cover the Troggs. We even tried the Rolling Stones' 'Satisfaction' at one point!

We rehearsed a bit at this guy's place on the other side of Bolton. I thought he was a drummer but he assured me that he was a bass player. The three of us were in this room trying to get something together and I was desperately trying to work the Stooges in there. We were trying one or two things from *Fun House*, like 'Loose', and I was trying to work out the lyrics off the record.

PETE SHELLEY

Me and Howard started writing songs in our flat in Salford, but trying to get a drummer wasn't easy. They were like gold dust.

HOWARD DEVOTO

We had no name for the band. We didn't know what we were doing. There was nothing to aim for. We had no drummer so it was hard to get a feel.

PETE SHELLEY

The *NME* used to come out on Thursdays in Bolton and me and Howard were in the college coffee bar flicking through it like we did every week. Howard noticed this review and said, 'Oh look, there's this band that does a version of the Stooges' "No Fun".' He pointed out the review of the Sex Pistols and we were immediately interested.

HOWARD DEVOTO

So we borrowed the car and went to London to find the Sex Pistols.

PETE SHELLEY

There was a committee meeting down in London for the students' union, which I was vice-president of, and it was that weekend. It was the perfect opportunity. Being vice-president sounds grandiose but it wasn't – the rest of the time I was unemployed, so I had still had my punk credentials (*laughs*).

They said that they would pay the train fare to get down there. Instead of getting the train a friend of mine lent us a car and we used the money for petrol. Howard and me went down to London to look for the band, staying with Richard [Boon] who was at Reading University.

RICHARD BOON

This was February 1976; me, Howard and Pete went to see the Sex Pistols after Neil Spencer's celebrated review. We were intensely excited about going to see this band. We didn't know if they were even playing that weekend, so we decided to go to the Sex shop and find out if the Sex Pistols were playing any gigs that weekend.

PETE SHELLEY

When we got to London we bought a copy of *Time Out* magazine, which is where we got the 'Time's Up' song title from. The magazine also had a review of *Rock Follies* that mentioned one of the catchphrases from the series, which was 'that's a buzz, cock'. We thought [it] was a great name for a band and also sounded enough like the Sex Pistols.

We phoned up the *NME* when we were in London to find out if the Sex Pistols were playing anywhere. They said their manager was this guy called Malcolm and he'd got this clothes shop on the Kings Road, [why didn't we] go and ask him. So we got off at Sloane Square and walked all the way down Kings Road and into the shop.

RICHARD BOON
The Sex shop was intimidating, it wasn't like anything else we'd seen before. There was fetish wear on a rail and all these strange clothes everywhere. We must have looked really out of place. My hair was all curly. Howard's looked fairly similar, while Pete was already dyeing his hair – sometimes black, sometimes blond. Malcolm just happened to be behind the counter. He told us that luckily the band were playing two shows that weekend, one that very night and one the next day.*

He was very amiable. He had his rap down about this whole generation of kids' new attitude like a tape loop. It was hard to get him to stop talking!

PETE SHELLEY
So we went to both the gigs that weekend. There was about half a dozen people in the audience who had seen the band before, and no one else – who would have known it would last for years!

HOWARD DEVOTO
Seeing the Pistols did provide a blueprint for what we were trying to do. We had only read a review, we'd never actually heard them. We didn't know what the hell the Sex Pistols would be like. It took a few songs of their set before we found the plot. I wouldn't say they felt quite dangerous, but Johnny was fascinating. I hadn't seen anybody like him in a band before and the fragments of words that came through were really intriguing.

PETE SHELLEY
The Sex Pistols stood out like a sore thumb from all the other bands and that's what made them exciting. It wasn't about how good they could play but how good they were! They were really funny as well. It was the opposite of what you expected from a gig at the time. Johnny Rotten was a charming, erudite man but also the kind of person who doesn't suffer fools gladly.

---

* The Sex Pistols' eleventh and twelfth gigs were on 20 February 1976 at High Wycombe College of Higher Education on 21 February 1976 in Welwyn Garden City.

HOWARD DEVOTO

There was bit of a scene round them as well – the Sex shop and McLaren standing there in his leathers – all that added to it. But John was such a big part of it all. He was, like Morrissey, very British. There was no attempt to Americanise what he was doing. Everything – even his handkerchief constantly getting taken and blowing his nose – was so unusual. He then goes off to be sick in the toilets after a number and returns ten minutes later. There was nothing else like him. Also his lyrics were great, at least the ones I caught – 'I'm on a submarine mission for you baby . . .' Great bits like that were coming through.

There was a lot of aggression, there wasn't anything like a slow song – and no love songs.

RICHARD BOON

After that trip I put the Sex Pistols on in Reading in April 1976 with support from these performance artists called the Kipper Kids.

HOWARD DEVOTO

The audience included the Bromley Contingent – Malcolm, Jordan, Nils Stevenson, Helen Wellington-Lloyd. In their own ways they almost looked more interesting than the band, except that Lydon was so charismatic. We thought they were great: the look, the attitude and the music.

We secretly taped the gig so that we had a tape to take home. It gave us a chance to kind of study them in-depth and suss them out. The style of it was immediate.

Thrilled by their first experience of the Pistols, Devoto and Shelley returned to Manchester and arranged to play a gig as the Buzzcocks at their college in April 1976, attempting a set of cover versions including Eno's 'Baby's On Fire' and songs by the Stooges and early Kinks. Fronted by Howard Devoto with his striking new punk-rock look of freshly taken-in drainpipes and thigh-length leather boots, the band only managed three songs.

HOWARD DEVOTO

We hadn't even managed to rehearse for that first gig. Peter and I had run over the songs. I guess we hoped the rest of the band could play the songs; we had never played with a drummer and a bass player before.[*] I can't imagine what we had in mind or how prepared we were. I hadn't met Garth till he came to the gig.[†] The drummer was someone from

---

[*] Pete Shelley had played before in his own band, Jets of Air, in 1973
[†] Garth played bass at the gig and would rejoin the Buzzcocks a year later. He turned up for the gig wearing a tuxedo.

Bolton called Dennis that we'd never played with before. When we played 'Diamond Dogs' he counted it in at half speed and we played this incredibly slow version! We weren't getting a favourable reaction and they pulled the plug on us after three numbers, but we still got our five pounds! At the end of the gig the drummer actually said, 'I think you guys are on this level, and I'm on this level' (laughs). Despite that, the gig felt like a victory. Even if it wasn't one I was going to present it like that, which I did on a postcard to Richard.

We were working within what we perceived as the punk template. At the beginning of punk rock there was no set lyrical style. There wasn't that much of an idiom. I can't think of anybody else who was on the lyrical side that I was particularly drawn to at that time. The Ramones were kind of funny and all that, I'd hardly heard anything by the Clash, I didn't know much about the Pistols' stuff.

Within the general subject area there was a certain confined space to work in. The words were going to be tough. If you were going to say anything, you had to say it in an angry, thrusting way. The tone of how you say things is tremendously important to the understood message. When we wrote 'Boredom' it felt like a theme – very much of the idiom.

ANARCHY IN THE UK
The Sex Pistols at the Lesser Free Trade Hall, 4 June and 20 July 1976

Can there ever have been two gigs as iconic as the Sex Pistols' appearances in Manchester in 1976?

At a stroke the Buzzcocks, who promoted the shows, realised the punk DIY attitude and took punk out of the London elite and into the rest of the world, while their appearance at the second gig placed them firmly as one of the key trio of UK punk bands.

In several different ways, the Sex Pistols inspired the small audience into action. Peter Hook bought a bass the next day, Morrissey wrote a letter to the NME, Ian Curtis saw his opportunity, Ed Banger got his nickname. Marc Riley went and bought chips, preferring the support band at the second Pistols gig, Slaughter and the Dogs.

Whatever the reaction, there can be no denying that the whole modern Manchester music scene evolved from the Sex Pistols' appearances in the city during that long hot summer. Just before the gigs, there was a whiff of musical cordite in the air.

TONY WILSON
Nothing was going on until spring '76 when suddenly things started to happen.

MORRISSEY

I was torn with the Sex Pistols because they sneered at the so-called New York scene, which was difficult for me because I'd been governed by those first albums by the Dolls, Patti Smith and Ramones. John Lydon mocked Patti Smith at the Roundhouse by mimicking 'horse-shit, horse-shit, horse-shit . . .' and I thought, umm, hang on a minute.

The Ramones' eventual first Manchester gig at the Electric Circus* in 1977 was terrific, and there was something vulnerable about them even then, whereas you could feel charged by the Sex Pistols but you couldn't love them. Manchester gigs always had the same faces. Tony Wilson was never at any of those key gigs. I gave him the Dolls' first album in 1975 and he said, 'Who are they? I thought: well, haven't you at least *heard* of them? I think he knew even less about music than he did about clothes.

TONY WILSON

Then on 15 May that year I got a call from Martin Hannett, who I'd never met but knew of, saying there was a band playing at the Garage in Stockport called Slaughter and the Dogs. I was tremendously excited by this group of Wythenshawe scum all wearing dresses.

MICK ROSSI

Tony came to see us with Martin Hannett before the Pistols gig. We were there first. We were trying to be a street glam band.

RICHARD BOON

Howard had moved to Salford and when I left Reading a room came up in his house so I moved there. A lot of my cohorts were heading to arty spots in London and I didn't fancy that. I had got a place at teacher training college but put it off for a year and moved into Lower Broughton Road. There was a bit of a scene there – Peter lived in a basement flat a few doors down which had no windows. They'd been trying to get Buzzcocks together since the London trip, and Howard was getting the Sex Pistols gig sorted out in Manchester which they were planning to play at as well.

PETE SHELLEY

There was nowhere in Manchester to play, all you could do was do it yourself and hire a hall. No one was interested in having the band, so we

---

* Now demolished, the Electric Circus in Collyhurst was a rock venue that became the key punk venue in the city. It was shut down in autumn 1977; the resulting album, *Short Circuit: Last Night at the Electric Circus*, featured among others the Buzzcocks, Joy Division's first appearance on record and John Cooper Clarke.

hit on the idea of doing the concert ourselves. It was like in those teen movies in the fifties!

HOWARD DEVOTO

I was compiling the listings for a local magazine, just phoning round the venues to see who was playing, so I had an idea of which venues to use. The college at Bolton was the first place we thought of putting the Sex Pistols on. I might have mentioned it to Malcolm and he might have said try to find somewhere else. I can't remember where the idea came for trying the Free Trade Hall.*

The Lesser Free Trade Hall was the smaller room upstairs from the main hall and had a balcony. Everyone knew the main hall but no one had ever heard of the smaller venue.

C.P. LEE

Everything was in place and there was a sense that people were waiting for something. In many ways Howard knocking on the door of Music Force was the catalyst. Because of Tosh Ryan and Bruce Mitchell's knowledge, Music Force had the infrastructure; they knew how to make records and they knew the gigs, they had roadies and PAs. Howard came from Bolton to ask them where to put on the Pistols; Bruce Mitchell told them that the Free Trade Hall was the place and sorted out the PA and the lights for the gig.

PETE SHELLEY

We went to the Lesser Free Trade Hall and found that it cost £32 to hire. We thought we could do that and we printed tickets at a pound each. We did actually make money on the first gig even though there was only about 42 people there!

HOWARD DEVOTO

I was able to get a little picture of them in the *New Manchester Review* and I did a write-up. We also took out a little ad in the *Manchester Evening News*, and then Malcolm McLaren did some A3 posters for the gig and posted them to us. Peter and I went along Oxford Road posting them up. I remember they were very small compared to the other

---

* The Free Trade Hall was already a key venue in the city. Bob Dylan played there on 17 May 1966, shortly after he 'went electric', and was famously branded a Judas by a member of the audience. In 1905 it was where Christabel Pankhurst and Annie Kenney had famously heckled a Liberal Party rally, shouting 'Votes for women' during a speech by Winston Churchill and putting the suffragette movement in the headlines for the first time. Could there have been a more perfect place for the Pistols gig?

posters. Peter and I gave out leaflets as well at two concerts – one of which was a John Miles gig – one at the Free Trade Hall and one at the Palace.

TONY WILSON
I got a cassette in the post with a note saying: 'These are three tracks from a new band from London who I think are wonderful, and I'm bringing them to Manchester on June 4th 1976 to play Lesser Free Trade Hall, yours Howard Trafford'. He was calling himself Howard Trafford at the time, but he later became Howard Devoto.

HOWARD DEVOTO
I got Tony Wilson down for that gig; I had no idea who he was at the time.

TONY WILSON
And then along came 4 June. I went along to the Lesser Free Trade Hall on my own and stood there with my mouth open in shock.

PETE SHELLEY
After all that effort we didn't even play the first gig because we didn't have a drummer! It was very hard to convince people to join the band; this was a vibrant new form of music with no long guitar solos, and most people didn't really understand it.

HOWARD DEVOTO
When we realised we couldn't play it was a disappointment – we didn't have a bass player or a drummer. It was pretty short notice to find another band to play and we were thinking: who do we know? We had to find someone quick. I was working that summer in a mail-order warehouse in Bolton and I'd met this guy who said he had a band, so I phoned him and booked his band, Solstice.* It was the only band I knew. I knew they were very proficient if not quite suited to the event.

HOWARD DEVOTO
Nobody had heard of the Sex Pistols. I don't think we knew of anybody else who knew of them till that first gig. I'm not sure how many came to that first gig. I'm pretty sure about 100 turned up – 30 or 40 comes from somebody who's pretty anxious to present themselves as being really on the ball! I think it was about 100, it had to be that amount for them to

* A Bolton-based progressive rock band who are still going!

feel it was worth coming back a month later. There was enough for John [Lydon] to be very positive about the gig.

PETE SHELLEY
Howard did a lot of the running of the gig. He was very determined that it would happen. Malcolm had sent him acetates of the Chris Spedding demos. People thought that the Sex Pistols were this funny little thing from London till they saw it. Johnny was very unique – abrasive, pissing off the audience, looking like he wasn't having much fun.

They really liked Manchester, that's why they came back a month later.

HOWARD DEVOTO
I don't remember talking to many people. I think I would have been rushing around a lot. I tend to be like that. I'm only half taking it in really. I tend to be a very focused person. Pete's relaxed, while I tend to be very directive. I was concerned with how the gig was going.

One of the few memories of the night was that I'd just got the first Ramones album, which had just been released, and I discovered there was a record player above the stage. We hadn't thought much about interval music. The record player was absolutely ancient so I put the Ramones album on and it wouldn't go very loud. I played the whole album at the beginning of the night and in the interval.

STEVE DIGGLE
The Pistols gig was the first time I met Pete Shelley, and that was by mistake. I was on the way to a meeting about a band I was trying to form, at Cox's bar round the corner from the Free Trade Hall. My mate said, 'I'll meet you outside the Free Trade Hall and we'll go to Cox's because they serve a good pint of Boddingtons.'

PETE SHELLEY
Steve Diggle was waiting outside to meet somebody completely unrelated. I was in the box office taking the money. And Malcolm McLaren, who'd been waiting outside, came down to see how many people were in. He went back outside and said to Steve he should come in and see the band. He then asked him who he was and he said, 'I'm the bass player,' thinking that Malcolm was the person he was waiting for. Next thing I know, Malcolm comes in with this bemused youth behind him and says, 'Here's your new bass player.' And this was Steve Diggle.

KEVIN CUMMINS

I went to the first Pistols gig, not the second one. It was odd really because we didn't even know that the Lesser Free Trade Hall even existed as a room. There was an insane energy about them, an excitement that made you think that going to see the Enid and Ten Years After wasn't that exciting – Sailor and Kiki Dee, that was as exciting as our lives got. It was the energy of the Sex Pistols and the fact that they stood there looking like your mates – rather than people who were getting paid a lot of money to stand there – that was captivating.

On the night you saw odd people you would recognise from Pips, or Bowie people you knew on nodding terms.

After the gig everyone shuffled off and got the bus back and thought: that was pretty good, wouldn't mind seeing them again. Years later everyone was there.

PETER HOOK (Joy Division/New Order bassist)

I was working at the Town Hall and my escape was to read the music press. I devoured it. I knew about everything. In early '76 you started to read about the Sex Pistols and they seemed interesting. I remember being on holiday reading about the Pistols thinking they looked quite appealing – really rebellious, which was very appealing at that age. When I got back to Manchester from my holidays, I noticed the advert in the *Manchester Evening News* for the Sex Pistols playing a gig in Manchester.

PETE SHELLEY

It was the gig that condensed the Manchester scene. People already thinking of doing things saw that there were other people into this kind of music. People were looking at the other members of the audience more than the band and they became nodding acquaintances. So six weeks later, when we put on the second gig, they were there with all their friends.

PETER HOOK

I didn't know anyone else there apart from Bernard's wife, and we met the first Joy Division drummer there.

STEVE DIGGLE

I sat at the back with Pete Shelley and watched the Sex Pistols and it was fantastic. The other gig happened three weeks later and I think that's where everyone gets mixed up about which one they went to.

I agreed to join the Buzzcocks on bass and the next day we had a rehearsal. We were plugged through one little amp and we played a Ramones song and 'Boredom'. Soon we had few other songs on the go, like 'Breakdown' and that sort of stuff.

HOWARD DEVOTO

We met Steve at the first gig, so there was him . . . And then we'd managed to find a drummer.* Steve had now seen the Sex Pistols so he had a bit of an idea of what were trying to do. The songs were starting to come together from Pete and I liked 'Breakdown'. I've got a feeling he didn't have any verses for it but had a chorus, so I built the whole thing round that. I know that 'Orgasm Addict' was like that – he had the chords and the opening two lines and I did the rest of it.

STEVE DIGGLE

We got John Maher, who'd only been playing drums for six weeks. He turned up at rehearsals and he was fantastic. When he said he'd only been playing six weeks, we said 'You must be joking!' We had a great chemistry there. And we had three weeks to get the set together for the second Pistols gig . . .

On 20 July 1976 the Sex Pistols returned for their second gig at the Lesser Free Trade Hall.

PETE SHELLEY

I was more involved with the organising of the second gig.

RICHARD BOON

This time the Sex Pistols brought Caroline Coon and Jon Ingham with them to review the gig, and it got a whole page in *Sounds* and *Melody Maker*. Up till then the Pistols were a curious London gossipy thing. The fact that they came up to Manchester and got a favourable reaction from an admittedly small audience impressed Coon and Ingham, so they wrote it up big and made it look like a national phenomenon.

JOHN LYDON (Sex Pistols vocalist)

Nothing was really going on anywhere and places like the Free Trade Hall in Manchester were basically lying there rotting. It had a good novel combination of different bands that night – the Buzzcocks were always good – but can you call it punk?

* Sixteen-year-old John Maher.

STEVE DIGGLE

At the second Free Trade Hall gig all the press came down vibing on the Pistols; they saw us there and thought: fucking hell, a local band as well. They didn't know what to make of us. *Melody Maker* gave us a really good review but the guy from *Sounds* gave us a bad review, though he took it all back a few weeks later.

It felt like something was happening. Suddenly I felt like I had my place in life.

HOWARD DEVOTO

The reaction to what we were doing was quite good. A few people seemed to understand what punk was about now. The second gig was busier, maybe because Slaughter and the Dogs had brought quite a lot of people with them. It seemed like half the crowd was for them and half for the Pistols.

We wanted to put on a band that fitted better with what we were doing, unlike Solstice at the first show. Even though they were really into Bowie, Slaughter and the Dogs seemed like they could be the right band for the bill even though we weren't particularly close to them. When they put a poster together for the gig themselves with their name in rather large letters, it kind of showed where they were coming from.

MICK ROSSI

We'd heard about the Sex Pistols and we'd heard about the Damned. We didn't know about the Buzzcocks till they played the Sex Pistols gig with us. We felt it was good that there was another band on the scene.

Even though we came from glam we felt part of the punk thing, even if after we saw the Sex Pistols it changed our sound a bit. But they had that effect on everybody I suppose . . .

MARC RILEY (The Fall guitarist and radio presenter)

Me and Steve Hanley used to go and see Slaughter and the Dogs gigs because we knew Mick Rossi. They were a great night out, naïve, very transparent; they did a great version of 'White Light White Heat'. Slaughter's audience were rowdy Wythenshawe bootboys.

STEVE HANLEY (The Fall bassist)

We saw Slaughter at St Bernadette's youth club, which was in a church on Princess Park Way. That was pretty wild actually. They were funny, they were a good bit of glam rock.

MARC RILEY

When we went to the Free Trade Hall gig it was to see Slaughter and the Dogs; we saw the Buzzcocks by mistake because they were the first band on. Mick Rossi had become pally with Bowie's guitar player Mick Ronson and they were the band to go and see.

I'd seen a review of the Sex Pistols in one of the papers, an interview in the *NME*. It was with that famous picture of Steve Jones thumping someone and Lydon bent over in the audience. I was aware of them. I didn't look at them and think, wow, that's for me – it was because Slaughter and the Dogs were on the bill that I went to the gig with Craig Scanlon.*

At that point in time punk didn't exist, so the gig was full of Slaughter fans and people curious about the Pistols. Mark Smith and Martin Bramah† were there, they all had long hair and leathers. It was busy. I don't remember the Buzzcocks having much impact when they played and we went to get chips halfway through the Pistols (*laughs*).

ED BANGER (Ed Banger and the Nosebleeds vocalist)

I was there roadying for Slaughter and the Dogs and it all kicked off. I got hit on the head with a bottle. There was blood everywhere. The Sex Pistols were dead nice about it. They were really concerned. They wanted to get me to a hospital and get me looked at. Someone said, 'There's that headbanger with the nosebleed,' and that's where my name came from.

After spilling our blood for the punk cause, damn right we regarded ourselves as true punks. But we still got labelled bandwagon jumpers.

MARC RILEY

We came back from getting chips just in time for the fight at the end. We were upstairs at this point – the Lesser Free Trade hall had a balcony and we were eating our chips upstairs. Downstairs fists and fur were flying between the Slaughter and the Dogs lot and the Sex Pistols lot. It was handbags really – it was inevitable that it would happen.

MICK ROSSI

I remember those Pistols gigs because everyone who claimed to be there wasn't there at all (*laughs*)‡ At the Free Trade Hall I actually heard the Sex Pistols' soundcheck and they sounded fantastic. Johnny was singing his

---

* Future Fall guitar player.

† Future Fall main man and initial guitar player and future member of the late, great Blue Orchids.

‡ A long-running joke on the Manchester music scene has been the amount of people claiming to have been at the Sex Pistols gigs.

lyrics off bits of paper that he pulled out of his pocket and Steve Jones'
guitar wall of sound sounded great – people forget what a great band
they were.

BILLY DUFFY (guitarist, The Cult)
I saw the Sex Pistols at the second legendary Lesser Free Trade Hall gig in
Manchester on 20 July 1976 and still have the tickets and poster to prove
it. It changed my life forever.

JOHNNY MARR (Smiths guitarist)
I didn't go to the two famous two Pistols gigs but I witnessed the fallout
of it the day after it happened when I bumped into Billy. He went and it
changed him.

PHIL SAXE
I was at the Free Trade Hall the night the Sex Pistols played there because
Soft Machine were on the same night as the Sex Pistols – they played in
the main room upstairs and I went to see Soft Machine.

MORRISSEY
I went to both Lesser Free Trade gigs and I loved them both.

I was jealous though, on behalf of the Dolls, because I wanted it to be
they who saved the world and not anyone else. The distinction between
the first and the second Pistols gig was remarkable. At the first, no one
moved, there was no lighting rig, it was very third-form, and no one had
formed a viewpoint until the second gig which had a mood almost of
increased panic. People edged to the front and began to shout back.
Buzzcocks played their first ever gig on that second night, and at the end
of their set they jumped off the stage into the audience and ran out the
main doors. Linder had introduced them by saying 'Buzzcocks would like
to fuck you.'

LINDER (artist and key player on the Manchester punk scene, singer with
Ludus)
I was living in Whalley Range at the time and I went to the Sex
Pistols/Buzzcocks gig. I didn't know anybody there at that point, so I
went with somebody who designed kitchens! That evening I talked for
the first time to Pete Shelley, who was very friendly, and then to Howard
who was sat next to him. We went for a drink afterwards, somewhere
like the Conti club.

PETE SHELLEY

We met Linder at the second Pistols gig; she and Howard hit it off straight away. She was at the Poly on an art course. She helped Howard, sort of made him over. She was important on the early scene, and, like a lot of women, seems to have been written out of the story.

LINDER

Howard Devoto and Pete Shelley were my knights in shining disarmour.

PETE SHELLEY

Linder moved into Lower Broughton Road and carried on with her artwork. It gave us an imagery to use – all those montages.

LINDER

When I first met Howard that night he looked fantastic. He'd bought some clothes from Sex and Seditionaries and made his own look. Punk was the last DIY movement, it's not really happened since then. It was very exciting, that sense of finding your clothes – you had to make your own clothes. And there was a very literal sense of self-invention – an ideas exchange, like try this with this. It was a two-way thing. Richard Boon was making Pollock shirts. I was starting to make the montages.

Famously the story goes that, after the two Sex Pistols gigs, everyone in Manchester formed a band. Although several people were sparked into action, this is not entirely true.

JOHNNY MARR

In Wythenshawe at the time there were rumblings of these 17-year-old lads in bands like Wild Ram and Slaughter and the Dogs. To be doing that before punk rock broke must have been fairly audacious. One thing I have to give those lads credit for – and one thing that they don't get credit for, because they aren't seen as being as tasteful as Wire, which they weren't, or as clued up or arty as the Pistols – was that they were putting the nuts and bolts together up here, away from art school; away from mentors with an intellectual manifesto, which came later. They did all that on their own as lads, they aspired to put a band together that didn't sound like Deep Purple. That took a bit more doing than they get credit for.

ED BANGER

Me and Toby and Pete were at school together in Wythenshawe and we'd been jamming Slade, T. Rex and Bowie songs in Toby's kitchen. Occasionally I'd nip over to Mike Rossi's house and get chords for Bowie songs – Mike was a big Ronson fan – and we'd talk about forming bands. Mike said he was doing something with Wayne, so me, Toby and Pete formed Wild Ram and Mike and Wayne formed the Dogs. So wherever the Dogs played we'd get a gig a couple of weeks later; we would all go and watch each other's sets and nick bits that would appear in our next shows.

TONY WILSON

I didn't form a band. My job was as a television presenter, and I went back the next day and screamed to my producer that we had to have this band on [So It Goes], it was the most exciting thing I'd ever seen. They said OK, but I had to take Malcolm the researcher to see them to make sure he liked the band too. So we went down to the next show in London that we could get to.* I remember bright blue skies as we drove from Golden Square in Soho to Walthamstow Assembly Hall, and walking into the hall at nine in the evening, still with this bright sky, into this completely dark hall, with 20 people watching in a semi-circle stretching across the whole hall. I soon realised that it was because John was gobbing and they were just out of gobbing distance.

PETER HOOK

The Pistols gig was horrendous. The sound was really terrible. But it was purely the rebellion, the fuck-you attitude that really grabbed you. After that, music went from being this glamorous world to something that you could do as well. It was a total revelation. I went to buy a bass the next day. I borrowed money off my mum. Barney already had a guitar. He could play a little – the odd chord shape.

STEPHEN MORRIS (Joy Division/New Order drummer)

I didn't go to the Free Trade Hall Pistols gig – not even going to pretend I went to that one. I was told they were playing in Didsbury and I went and they weren't on. It was a fucking lie!

BOREDOM

In which the Buzzcocks defy the post-industrial malaise and set about accidentally creating a new music scene

Post Pistols gigs, the Devoto-fronted Buzzcocks played a handful of shows on the nascent punk scene, taking the Pistols template they had already and twisting it with humour and lyrical smarts into something far smarter, far more wired. The Devoto-fronted Buzzcocks were arguably the best punk band of them all.

* Walthamstow Assembly Hall, 17 July 1976.

PETE SHELLEY

The ideas of punk fired people's imagination, I think; we got a big buzz out of that. It was a combination of people waiting for it and people responding to the call of arms of punk. In Manchester the city centre is very small. There were only about two or three clubs you could go to. People would come from a large distance to the Ranch* and the Electric Circus and [there was] nothing else to do when you were there but to talk to people.

HOWARD DEVOTO

The next gig we played after the Free Trade Hall was at the Ranch. At that time it was the only place in town for a punk scene. People into Bowie would go there and they would play Lou Reed. It was a night put on in Foo Foo Lamarr's club and had echoes of the Sex Pistols playing in Soho at El Paradise Strip Club – off the wall, unusual venues.

We thought we should try and do one of those type of gigs and that seemed the only place that was half appropriate. We played there once[†] and not that many people turned up for it. Of course we got stopped, because Foo Foo was doing his act in the next room – there was a sort of hatchway between the two rooms to the main club. We started playing and suddenly after three or four numbers this heavy bloke starts walking towards the stage – which was actually not a stage but just the dance floor – and asked us to end the set. When he came up I said, 'Excuse me, can I help you?' and he said, 'Are you the leader of the band?' and asked us to leave. So we got chucked off because we were interrupting Foo Foo's act in the next room.

RICHARD BOON

The Buzzcocks then did the August bank holiday gig at the Screen on the Green in London.[‡]

HOWARD DEVOTO

There were only three bands playing at the Screen on the Green, so it wasn't quite a festival! I'm not sure if the gig was much bigger than the Free Trade Hall. I remember Malcolm was there listening and encouraging us.

* A small basement room in Foo Foo's Palace, a nightclub owned and run by flamboyant Manchester transvestite performer Foo Foo Lamarr, was converted into the Ranch for a punk/alternative night.
† 12 August 1976.
‡ This event at the Screen on the Green cinema in Islington on 29 August 1976, with the Sex Pistols, Clash and Buzzcocks, was one of the key signpost gigs of the emerging punk movement.

STEVE DIGGLE

We went down to London and did the Screen on the Green gig, which was one of the important early punk shows. For me this was the first time where punk crystallised into a kind of movement, when the Pistols, Clash and us played there. Siouxsie was in the audience, dressed in a very punk way. It suddenly all started to make sense. It started to take off. In London you saw all these people with coloured hair in the Screen on the Green and you knew it was really happening, while in Manchester at the time if you had straight leg [jeans] with a black coat on, that was enough to be a punk.

RICHARD BOON

We needed another bigger gig in Manchester and found the Electric Circus, which was a dying heavy metal venue. We persuaded them to give us a quiet night where we would get the door and they get the bar. Then, when the 'Anarchy' tour came to town, there was an actual place for people to put the gig on.*

KEVIN CUMMINS

The Electric Circus was a khazi! They definitely would not get a licence now. It was in a fairly rough end of town; it was still a wasteland round there. It might have been an old cinema, which became a dance hall and then a gig. Everything was painted black so you didn't see how shitty it was.

STEVE DIGGLE

By the time of the 'Anarchy' tour there were punks everywhere; the scene had got much bigger because of all the press. Because we were from Manchester, it made people aware that things were happening outside London.

CLINT BOON

The Sex Pistols and the Buzzcocks at the Electric Circus was a night. It was inspiring. You thought: I could learn guitar like that in a day – everything I dreamed of was now possible. And at the gig, as art students we felt really at home with what was happening. Everything I've done since has been because of that.

---

* Out of the five gigs that went ahead from the 25-date tour, two were at the Electric Circus – one booked there and another arranged to take place on one of the Pistols' many enforced nights off – further cementing Manchester's position as the 'second city of punk'.

STEVE DIGGLE

The Pistols were always into us. We always got on well with them over the years. There was always that closeness there because we had all started off at the beginning of the scene. They didn't see us as a threat. We were from the north. We weren't in their space. The Pistols and Clash were too close together in London – 'two sides of the town' as they say.

We played the Manchester gig on the 'Anarchy' tour at the Electric Circus. Most of the gigs were cancelled, it was all getting a bit mad.

I remember Malcolm McLaren during the 'Anarchy' tour saying, 'Listen, you've got to sign while the going is good,' but we took our time. It was ages till our next record came out – by that time there was Stiff Records and loads of people making their own records, but we decided to get the right deal.

MORRISSEY

The Electric Circus was the key venue. Briefly the Stoneground edged in, but the Electric Circus managed all the jaw-dropping bookings. It was in the middle of a 1930s council estate on muddy Collyhurst Crofts. I would always go early in the day just to meet the sound crew, which seems laughable to me now. But I *was* a nuisance. The people across the way in this huge council estate would always come out to mock the music kids, and these locals were white working-class mutants of the most deranged cross-eyed variety . . . cross-breed Northerners with club feet and twisted legs and manky hair and humps . . . nine parts Alsatian. It was dog-rough.

RICHARD BOON

We were talking about places to play and I said the Electric Circus. The Sex Pistols' gigs had galvanised Manchester, but it was bereft of any kind of scene or a place where people could meet and talk and say they'd seen the Pistols. I think it was important that early bands like the Buzzcocks were in Manchester.

PETE SHELLEY

Punk affected people really quickly: people were starting their own bands like in skiffle or the Mersey Sound – not since then have so many people wanted to be in bands. It tied into that old Xerox aspect of making your own music

LINDER

I'd done a lot of drawing at soundchecks and gigs. I was in the habit of always drawing. I was at the bus stop at Whalley Range and sketched myself and wrote on [the sketch], 'Going to see the Sex Pistols at Electric

Circus all by myself'. That was where I met Morrissey. The Electric Circus was two bus rides away in a really heavy part of town.

MORRISSEY

I had seen Linder at the Lesser Free Trade Pistols nights, but didn't speak to her until the soundcheck of the third Manchester Pistols gig, which was at the Electric Circus. She was sitting on a table – looking like a sea creature.

I had a quizzy mind and pummelled her. Buzzcocks and Linder were very much a social unit and very courteous, but were older than me and seemed slightly [to belong to a] previous generation – Van Der Graaf Generator and Captain Beefheart. I never understood that kind of music, and I wasn't academic. The only prog-rock LP I had ever bought was *Second album* by Curved Air, which I still love. Howard Devoto loved Iggy, but it seemed as if this punk thing might save him from being a science lecturer. Buzzcocks' clothes were very 1960s schoolteacher, which seemed perverse in young people of the seventies. In Manchester there was nowhere to buy clothes so the most you could aim for was to invent your own quizzical look, which the Fall later did very well with their World War II lice-ridden-evacuee-latchkey-kid look.

I remember around 1979 a lot of young Manchester kids dyed their hair grey, which looked great, and developed into the bleak-and-industrial thing. I much preferred it to the Vivienne Westwood chic, which was only ever adopted by people who'd missed the bus in the first place.

The Clash were also at that Electric Circus soundcheck. Mick Jones approached me and asked me if I was . . . me, and I said, yes, I was . . . He'd placed an ad in *Melody Maker* for a singer for the Clash; I'd telephoned him and he said they'd found someone . . . and London might as well have been Mars, anyway. He was very nice and called me back a week later. At the Electric Circus the Clash were all dressed in what seemed like school uniforms. I also spoke to Johnny Thunders and Jerry Nolan, but they weren't friendly and why should they be? Who was I, anyway? I just kept wondering if all this would happen to me.

TONY JAMES (Generation X, Sigue Sigue Sputnik)

Me and Mick had advertised in *Melody Maker* every other week back in 1975 looking for a singer and a drummer who was into the New York Dolls, Mott the Hoople, the Stooges – that was like asking 'Wanted: a Martian'! Most weeks there were no replies [but] one was a letter from Manchester – from Morrissey. Manchester to us seemed like a million miles away.

LINDER

Lower Broughton Road was very close-knit at the time. Howard and I lived in the same house while Pete Shelley lived in the house next door but one. As years go by it seems important – at the time I took a lot of things for granted . . . Those people in that world were reinventing and re-examining everything. I suppose it was totally intense – me and Howard living together for 18 months or so.

HOWARD DEVOTO

We were also writing songs. I was writing in the punk sense, in that you knew the subject areas that were appropriate. They weren't going to be love songs and I can't remember what else I thought around then – there were certain confirmed areas that would be appropriate. Pete had already written 'No Reply' and we had 'Orgasm Addict' and 'Boredom'.

REINVENTING THE WHEEL
Spiral Scratch *and the DIY revolution*

Spiral Scratch, *released by New Hormones in January 1977, is one of the classic punk singles. With four stripped-down spindly punk rock anthems crammed full of brilliant, totally wired lyrics, it is arguably the quintessential punk rock release. Produced by Martin Zero (Hannett) and paid for by Pete Shelley's father, it was the first proper DIY release of the punk rock generation and the harbinger of the independent scene; the first release from the new Manchester generation, it was an inspiration for a generation of punk rock youth looking to make their own music.*

PETE SHELLEY

It was a madcap thing to do really, in those days no one did it – record companies made records, not bands. But we found out that you could get the factories that made the records to make your record as well. We just wanted to make a record to show our friends. We pressed up a thousand and sold them and then pressed up some more.

JON SAVAGE

My first contact with Manchester was hearing and buying *Spiral Scratch*. When it came out I bought it immediately because there were so few punk rock records. For me it is *the* punk rock record: with its DIY sleeve it was more interesting conceptually than 'New Rose' and it was more modern sounding than 'Anarchy in the UK'. It also had the do-it-yourself conceptuality, the idea of doing first takes and having one-overdub simplicity. Having a Polaroid shot of the band on the cover made it the complete integrated package. It may have seemed simple but it was very sophisticated, the music was very brutal but there's also a psychedelic tinge to it with Pete Shelley's guitar and Martin Hannett's production.

RICHARD BOON

There were hardly any overdubs. Most rock music then was full of overdubs. The whole point of listing the overdubs on the sleeve was to make the point that it was done very simply, without going into all that detail that the Desperate Bicycles and Scritti Politti would later on.

I wasn't strictly the manager now. I just expedited things. What was really important was that there was a phone in the house – that was still quite unusual at that time. So I could hire vans and talk to people and research how you made a record.

STEVE DIGGLE

We went to the studio to see what we sounded like because we'd never heard ourselves properly! We did a session in an afternoon with Andy McPherson, who had a DIY studio in the loft of his house. We just played loads of songs one after another with no overdubs. We had to carry all the gear on the bus to his house, which would be a nightmare now but was quite funny then – in those days you wouldn't dream of hiring a van. The demos eventually got released as the *Time's Up* album years later.

A month later we went in the studio with Martin Hannett producing, to record four songs for a record to give out to people who came to our gigs. Imagine trying to get a record deal then; going to London cap in hand, tongue hanging out, asking some fucker in an office if they would put your record out – it was all Billy Joel, West Coast radio stuff. The idea of music then was to pacify people.

When we did the recording of *Spiral Scratch* we went into another studio near Granada TV with Martin Hannett. Martin knew how to make a good record. He recorded us in the corridor – it was a totally unorthodox approach but it got that unique sound. It just happened there on that day. When it came out people were shocked by the record – the sound of it – but to me it was the sound of punk on record and sounded great.

What was important was that we found out that it was only £500 to make a single, not half a million pounds. We could press 1000 copies – it was an amazing revelation, it seemed so weird at the time. So that really opened things up a bit. Geoff Travis at Rough Trade said he would put it in shops, they said they really liked the record, if we needed any help to distribute it . . . It started selling. We didn't expect it to take off, we were living for the moment . . .

GEOFF TRAVIS (boss of record company Rough Trade)

Spiral Scratch was really the first DIY record that not only captured the spirit of the time but was also a genuinely great record in its own right. We bought copies from Richard Boon, who had to keep coming down to London with more of them.

The fact that it was so good and so popular helped spark our idea of forming a nationwide independent distribution network. We owe the Buzzcocks a debt for their brilliance.

RICHARD BOON

We didn't realise *Spiral Scratch*'s importance at the time. Howard was thinking about resuming his college course and we wanted to make a document of the band. The success of the record took us by surprise and it got us into contact with lots of other people like Rough Trade, who distributed it. In the end we sold 16,000, then we stopped.

MARK STANDLEY

When *Spiral Scratch* came out, it was a shock to realise that 'normal' people from round your way could actually put a record out. The Buzzcocks were on *Granada Reports* around then too. On telly!

'WHAT WAS ONCE UNHEALTHILY FRESH IS NOW A CLEAN OLD HAT'

Howard Devoto leaves the Buzzcocks, January 1977

In perhaps one of the most punk rock gestures of all time, Howard Devoto quit the band just as their debut Spiral Scratch *came out. Just when everyone else was getting into punk, one of its key figures quit the movement, bored with its already narrow confines before most people had even worked out what they were.*

MORRISSEY

Howard played 11 gigs with Buzzcocks. I was distraught when he left. He was neither a pop nor a rock singer – so what was he? There was absolutely no sex in him at all – of any variety which I understood. He sounded a bit like Jake Thackray,* who was also from Leeds as Howard was, and who rattled the words off in a talkative way, just occasionally hitting on melody. Frontmen were still generally all ballsy and Paul Rodgers-macho gestures, so Howard and Pete Shelley seemed a bit potty – which was such a relief, and not unfunny. They were always Buzzcocks and never called *the* Buzzcocks.

* Satirical Yorkshire folk singer who found fame on the BBC's *That's Life* in the seventies

RICHARD BOON

Howard went back to college and Peter took over lead vocals, Garth came in on bass and Steve Diggle moved to guitar. At first they would rehearse in Howard's room in the house and then the basement of Lifeline drug advisory centre.

HOWARD DEVOTO

People still think I temporarily lost my senses but I didn't regret it for a moment. I still sense this thing 30 years on, this element that people can't quite accept what I said. I put out a statement. It was put out as a New Hormones press release.*

LINDER

Howard always had a sense of history being made. It was perfectly choreographed and at the time it was very shocking.

STEVE DIGGLE

It was a bit of a surprise to me and Pete when Howard left. We used to rehearse at Howard's house, and we were sat down in his living room when he opened the door and said he was leaving the band. It was a shock, we'd only done a few gigs really. He was doing his degree, it was his last year and he wanted to finish that off. He said, 'I've done what I wanted to do, I've made a record and now I want to leave.'

When he told us he was leaving, we looked at each other and said, 'Well, let's carry on.' We got Garth in on bass – the standing joke in the band was trying to find him, we would wonder if he would turn up at the gigs in Manchester. He was a schoolmate of Pete Shelley's. When he turned up I thought, fucking hell, what have you got there? He was fucking massive, he towered over us!

RICHARD BOON

We knew that Howard was going to leave. He went back to college – he didn't like it, he didn't want to be a punk any more – and put Magazine together.

GINA SOBERS

On the Manchester front, the Buzzcocks brought punk north and made

---

* Dated 21 February 1977, the statement read: 'I don't like most of this new wave music. I don't like music. I don't like movements. Despite all that – things still have to be said. But I am not confident of Buzzcocks' intention to get out of the dry land of new waveness to a place from which these things could be said. What was once unhealthily fresh is now a clean old hat.'

us aware of our home-grown scene. I loved them from the get-go. And they were tuneful and singing about stuff we could relate to, 'Boredom'.

We saw them at Manchester Poly, Rafters, the Electric Circus, they were all great happenings. There was a real excitement among the young Mancunian crowd. So when they split into Magazine, it was like two great groups for the price of one.

I remember seeing Barry Adamson and John McGeoch lounging round the Poly of a Friday night's disco, looking pretty cool.

STEVE DIGGLE

After we did *Spiral Scratch* we had six major labels phoning every day trying to sign us. CBS offered us as much money as we wanted, but we wanted artistic control and knew what we were getting into. We had *Spiral Scratch* and we enjoyed our crowd – it wasn't about the fame, it was about the music.

Malcolm McLaren died on 8 April 2010, aged 64.

4

'WHAT DO I GET?':
PUNK IN MANCHESTER

When the Sex Pistols played those two shows at the Free Trade Hall, it was like a catalyst: 1977, the year of punk, saw a surge of activity in the city.

JON SAVAGE

Punk was all to do with the compression of time and space and information. It was all about acceleration. It was about a new way of digesting the beginnings of the information overload, which everyone now does on a day-to-day basis. That also has to do with the Debordian idea of the Society of Spectacle,* like the spectacle of celebrity which doesn't mean anything – all it does is take people's attention away from what's really going on.

PETER SAVILLE

Punk came along and created a kind of temporary tear in the order of things, of the incumbent establishment of everything in pop culture. They didn't know what was happening for 18 months and stood still, frozen in time by the blitzkrieg of punk. Some of us walked through the gaps. A lot of it was driven by the fact that youth culture is so entirely commodified and was nothing to do with youth any more. Pop had reached its first period of considered complacency, there were bands playing in front of 3000 people in large auditoriums where you dutifully bought the record. The brilliance of punk – and actually McLaren's vision – was to give youth culture back to the youth.

* Guy Ernest Debord (28 December 1931–30 November 1994) was a French Marxist theorist, writer, filmmaker, and founding member of the groups Lettrist International and Situationist International.

ELLIOT RASHMAN

When punk started I was living in Somerset, which I fucking hated. Then I heard 'New Rose' by the Damned in November 1976. I had to order it from the Hoover shop! I then saw the Bill Grundy show; I left my wife and went back to Manchester and got a job at Granada. When I came back to Manchester I got into the punk scene – it was like a second wind for me. I was reborn!

TONY WILSON

Much the same as many people remember seeing the Sex Pistols on TV for the first time, many north-west kids remember me saying 'And now a young singer who's come up from London, he's actually from Liverpool, Mr Elvis Costello.' We turned round and there's Elvis on a little podium with his electric guitar in his arm. He'd got up there to do 'Less Than Zero', but he'd said that he'd written a new song two days ago and could he do that instead. I said 'Yeah, sure,' and he did 'Alison'. Two days old, amazing.

Anyway, November '76, the 'Anarchy' tour . . . My friend Roger Eagle from Eric's in Liverpool rang to say that he'd had to cancel the Sex Pistols after Merseyside police had been round and told him his licence wouldn't be renewed later that month if he put the band on. I had a graphic made up saying 'What's Off, Sex Pistols at Eric's', but my bosses said I couldn't use it. I argued that this was the most important thing happening, the greatest band in the world being censored, and we had to say something, but I lost the argument. Being what I thought was a professional I did the show without the graphic, then walked upstairs, tore up my cards and walked out the door. They got me back in about five days later and made me sign a piece of paper saying 'I'll do whatever you tell me, because you fucking pay me.'

KEVIN CUMMINS

It was probably February 1977, just after the Pistols at the Circus, that everything kicked off. The Pistols were getting banned everywhere – something definitely was going to happen now. Then we had gigs trickling throughout the year. In May '77, as well as seeing Manchester bands playing that month for less than the price of one ticket today, we saw the Jam, Clash, Ramones, Talking Heads, Blondie and Television! That's when it was exciting, between the end of April and the beginning of October: we were on this ludicrous fairground ride where every stop took us to another gig.

TONY WILSON

That first series of *So It Goes* was a pile of shit except for the last show, when we had the Pistols on. Before that we'd had Eddie and the Hot Rods and Be Bop Deluxe and other safe middle-of-the-road stuff like that, but the second series was brilliant. I would put Buzzcocks and Slaughter and the Dogs on *What's On* through the autumn of '76 and spring '77, but I was told I had a new series of *So It Goes* in autumn '77. I would wake up every night that summer in a sweat, worried that someone else was going to beat us to it.

We launched again and were able to put on Iggy Pop and Elvis Costello, the Jam's first appearance, Magazine, all this great stuff . . . And we had it all to ourselves because the *Old Grey Whistle Test* only put on people who were accomplished musicians or had American accents. They had the Ramones and – to my annoyance – Patti Smith, but hey. Iggy caused all sorts of trouble by swearing during a rambling bit in the middle of 'The Passenger'. My boss wanted to cut it, but I said, 'You can't do that, it's art.' I was told in no uncertain terms that 'If we see the guy with a horse's tail in his arse again you're sacked.'

NATHAN MCGOUGH (Happy Mondays manager)

When I was 14 I came home one day and went downstairs. This bloke off the telly, Tony Wilson, was sitting in a big blue velvet armchair with a white tuxedo jacket, denim shirt and long flowing hair, and he was rolling a joint. He emanated a golden charisma in his white tuxedo – people off the TV, they radiate that charisma. He was a fan of my dad's poetry.*

He was doing the *What's On* programme, so he had to go all over the north-west watching movies and plays. He had a great knowledge of European cinema, an amazing knowledge of all culture. He took a shine to me, so he turned me on and blew my mind with culture; he would take me to gigs and films, that's how I got into Manchester bands more than my hometown ones in Liverpool.

TONY WILSON

So this was my hobby, my passion, my life, and suddenly I realised that I was clutching this thing that had seemed so distant when I went out and bought a Jefferson Airplane album and listened to it on the floor going nuts. You know, Elvis Costello would walk on stage and smile at me in the audience! Malcolm McLaren would give me a T-shirt and ask how things were going. Even Lydon would grunt at me. Suddenly I was

---

* Nathan's stepfather was Liverpool poet Roger McGough.

connected to my heroes and this art form, and I still feel it as an utter, utter privilege.

Then I was told, that's it, no more, but I wanted to stay involved. Then on 24 January 1978 – which is why several of our companies are called something to do with the 24th of January – I got a call from my best mate Alan Erasmus, who'd been managing a band called Fast Breeder for about nine months. There'd been a coup and he was thrown out along with a couple of band members. I said, 'Don't worry, we'll form a band around the remaining guys,' and that was the moment that got me into the music business. Those two, the guitarist was Dave Robotham and the drummer Chris Joyce, who later became Simply Red's backing band, but we put them together with the ex-Albertos bass player and the guitarist from the Nosebleeds, Vini Reilly, and two singers. And that was Durutti Column. We had a group but we needed a place to play; Alan said, 'I know a club in Hulme that we might be able to borrow . . .'

NORMAN COOK (drummer)

I was playing drums with Vini Reilly's band, they were like a progressive Jethro Tull – Norman Gamer used to play flute. Vini played finger style without a plectrum, he was classically trained, [though he was] playing pop rock – this was 1974 to 1977. Vini was in the Nosebleeds at the same time and I also played with them. I stood in for them when the drummer broke his arm. Ed Banger was manic! We played a gig at Jilly's wearing lab coats and brown paper bags over our heads with the eyes cut out. We got fed up with Tony Wilson turning up at gigs with a big long trenchcoat on, browbeating Vini and eventually poaching him and Durutti Column.

JOHNNY MARR

So there were lads were putting these little gigs on; I was amazed the first time I ever encountered punks. It was obviously after the Pistols played up here. Wild Ram not surprisingly changed their name to the Nosebleeds. Even back then I would get narked when people said, 'Are you going to see Ed Banger and the Nosebleeds?' I was one of those people who would say, 'It's the Nosebleeds, right!'

I saw them at that Slaughter gig and maybe a couple of days later there was a smattering of punk rockers around on Market Street. Not too long after that, gigs started to happen at the Apollo as opposed to the Free Trade Hall, which pissed me off because I loved the Free Trade Hall. At the Apollo in spring 1977 the Damned opened for Marc Bolan. We went down; my job was to ask a girl to go into the girls' toilets and then open the window, so we could climb up the drainpipe and squeeze in through the tiny window and run down the stairs and open the back door and get everyone in. At the T. Rex and Damned gig, the guys outside who we got in looked scary and at the same time interesting.

CHRIS SIEVEY
The Freshies were looking for a guitarist and this lad came to my house, but we said he was too young. He was 14 and he was Johnny Marr.

IAN BROWN
I got into punk the day after Bill Grundy. It was on the front of the *Evening News* – I often wonder how the fuck it got on the front page of the local paper when it was only shown in London. My mate went and bought three copies of the 'Anarchy in the UK' single from Woolworth's for 29p each the day after and I got one. The next thing I heard was 'One Chord Wonders' from the Adverts on Piccadilly Radio in early '77, then I heard 'Janie Jones' by the Clash and I had half of each song taped on a cassette.

That spring I started dressing punk. I got a pair of tight cords from Stretford Arndale. They were the only tight pants you could find in the city. At the time everyone wore flares – businessmen wore flares, everyone. In the end we found proper shit-stoppers like Max Wall* pants in Stretford Arndale. You used to have to hunt your gear down. There was a shop by the village barber where downstairs they had a secondhand store where you could get paisley shirts and old sixties jackets. We made punk jackets where you would put pins in – we had the whole look. We used to have to put sugar and water in our hair – there was no gel then – and it would run into your face. That was all part of it – you would get laughed at in the street! I remember guys on our street encouraging their daughters to laugh at us, pointing their finger and laughing!

KEVIN CUMMINS
In Manchester we weren't dressed up like London punks. At the time we were wearing old school shirts, cutting the tie shorter and writing slogans in biro on the shirts. You couldn't buy punk stuff in Manchester. One guy used to go to Seditionaries and buy cheesecloth shirts and everyone would laugh at him.

Same with the bands. We were very parochial. When the Jam were at the Electric Circus people were saying, 'We've got our own bands, we

* A legendary British comedian famed for his daft walk and super-tight tights and big boots.

don't need you.' [Paul] Weller said he was absolutely petrified the first time he played there! He turned up and looked at the place and thought, we'll get battered here.

JON SAVAGE

The difference between London and Manchester punk was that, by the middle of 1977, the London punk scene was very posey, very Generation X. Basically it had gone crap. There were all these terrible groups who were basically 30 year olds, groups like the Police – naff punk groups. I was looking beyond punk – the Pistols were pretty much burned out and had been superseded already. It just shows you how quickly everything was moving. You were starting to get the whole division of labour. If you were a writer you couldn't do montage or DJ and it was also getting very macho – you had the Clash running around with their horrible entourage and it got quite laddish. The only good groups in London were the Subway Sect, Siouxsie & the Banshees and the Adverts – that was kind of it. The Manchester punk scene was very friendly and very inclusive and there seemed like a real community; people weren't dressed in a uniform, they were dressed down. There was still a lot of long hair and T-shirts at the punk gigs. That guy Paul was a fascinating character – a black kid with dyed blond hair – I remember talking to him and being struck by him, he was a real face, he was the face of Manchester punk rock.*

Being gay was a very important strand of punk – [not] least of all because of the name, 'punk'. I could never understand why people got so macho about it because, as everyone knows, punk means a younger guy in a prison who takes it up the arse – so go figure.

LIZ NAYLOR

I was out by then. One of the first pubs on the scene at the time was the Union on Princess Street. I was so clearly underage that there were few places I could go to. I went to Dickens, the Picador.

There was a bizarre unspoken connection [between] being an outsider and a freak and being a punk. Suddenly I wasn't alone; there were other people like me. I was living in Hyde at the time and gangs of kids would shout 'punk' at me for being weird. I was the only punk in Hyde. There was something about being the outsider, creating the space – that's my emotional connection with punk, the fact that it was all right to be weird.

---

* No one knows Paul's second name but he is remembered for being one of the very few black punks.

MARK STANDLEY

The first punk band I saw was the Damned at Middleton Civic Hall in March 1977. I remember being shocked when Captain Sensible and Rat Scabies came into the public bar before the show. That didn't happen at T. Rex or Bowie gigs!

MARTIN MOSCROP

When punk came along I bought Buzzcocks' *Spiral Scratch* EP and the Clash's first album rather than the Sex Pistols, who seemed like a bunch of jumped-up southerners into fashion.

MIKE PICKERING

I didn't go to the Lesser Free Trade Hall Pistols gig. I went to the Electric Circus one in the winter instead. I went to loads of gigs at the Electric Circus – the Ramones with the Talking Heads, who I really liked, the Damned and the Worst who were great. They were brilliant.

I went to gigs with my friend Martin Fry, who was eventually in ABC. I remember a little shop on Peter Street by the Free Trade Hall that would sell lots of secondhand records and magazines. They were the first ones to get the punk singles in and I got *Spiral Scratch*. Only a few people were into the punk scene, especially in Stockport where it was just me and Martin Fry. I remember going to my sister's wedding and playing 'Boredom' and 'Anarchy'. People stood looking at us like we were crazy!

CLINT BOON

Later on in '76, people were bringing records into our class. In the open common room there was a record player which everyone would play their records on. People would bring records in – the first Ramones, early Stranglers – before it was all called punk rock. Looking at the Ramones cover was amazing – it sounded like rock'n'roll, but look at them! I still get goosebumps thinking about that period.

The big music was Genesis and Yes and the tail-end of the British prog era. I went to see the Pistols playing at the Electric Circus with Buzzcocks that December on a weekday night. We went from college straight to Manchester. The line-up was Buzzcocks, Johnny Thunders, the Clash and then the Pistols and it was about a quid to get in! I remember standing there thinking: this is a turning point in my life and it's only cost me a quid . . .

I thought, I've got to get something to remember this night by, so I ripped off a bit of the red vinyl from the seat I was sitting on.

MICK HUCKNALL (Simply Red vocalist)

A friend of mine went to the very early Sex Pistols gigs. He came back raving about it, so I went to see them at the Electric Circus. The excitement, the energy – it was a perfect time for me but I got disillusioned with it very quickly. The whole thing with the early punk gigs I went to was the originality, but by the time it came round to spring 1978 it was all about leather and spiky hair. It was too rock. What I liked about it in the first place was that it was about being original. As that ended I kind of drifted away from it. People always talk about me being a punk and suddenly moving to soul, but it was a very gradual process. I'd been a soulboy before punk.

After the Buzzcocks, Devoto had put together Magazine, who would push the boundaries of punk as far as possible to create a new musical terrain of post-punk. Meanwhile the Buzzcocks, now fronted by Pete Shelley, were about to become one of the great pop bands of the period.

KEVIN CUMMINS

I met Pete and Howard in early '77, just before Howard left, at the Pistols at the Circus. They had a certain educational aloofness about them – whereas the Drones and Slaughter were scallys chancing it, the Buzzcocks were more cerebral. We were a little bit scared of them, we thought they were smart, their lyrics and marketing was smart. The first Buzzcocks gig I shot was at the Band on the Wall in May 1977. They were great with Pete Shelley now singing.

My first piece in the *NME* was a double-page spread on Manchester in July 1977 with Buzzcocks and Magazine, with a big picture of Howard. I was doing pictures of Magazine before they did a record.

HOWARD DEVOTO

After I left I was still helping out the band, I was still really involved with them.

Managing yourself is quite counter to what your image is supposed to be: the 'I'm above all this, above the practical world' attitude, or if you're a punk you're so fucked and anarchic that you can't be bothered with that sort of shit. I ordered the pressings for the record and I continued helping to stick the *Spiral Scratch* sleeves together.

RICHARD BOON

I was becoming manager of Buzzcocks. A&R started turning up at gigs and in 1977 we sorted out a deal in the end with Andrew Lauder – of the people I met he was most sympathetic. The day we signed to UA at the Electric Circus Andrew Lauder came up. I got this phone call from Maurice Oberstein* ranting 'Why don't you sign to us?' but we stayed with Andrew and UA.

HOWARD DEVOTO
I even went down to see the band's first gig after I left at the Harlesden Colosseum with the Clash that March.

JON SAVAGE
I saw Buzzcocks when they played with the Clash and the Slits at Harlesden and I thought they were terrific. I loved all the songs like 'Fast Cars'; they seemed to be about everyday life instead of saying how horrible everyone was.

STEVE DIGGLE
There's a lot of talk about the Pistols and the Clash but the sound of the Buzzcocks is more distinctive and quirky. You can hear it in a lot of other groups or records – I can hear the influence.

HOWARD DEVOTO
I can't remember the point at which we had started talking to record companies about Buzzcocks. Maybe they ran into somebody who said something and they decided to get in touch. I believe we called them up from Manchester thinking, OK, they must have heard of us by now! Do you want to talk about anything?

TONY WILSON
You have to remember that Howard is the one who brought the Sex Pistols to Manchester, Howard is the one who lit the spark. I think we owe everything to Howard.

LINDER
Howard had a very Eno-esque kind of glamour. He was plotting his next step after the Buzzcocks.

HOWARD DEVOTO
I was trying to finish that college course as well. I got my degree. Even after I left I was still writing songs a bit with Pete – 'The Light Pours Out of Me', 'Shot By Both Sides'.

* Oberstein was the boss of CBS Records.

PETE SHELLEY

I had this riff and gave it to Howard. He took it away and changed the verse and made 'Shot By Both Sides'.

HOWARD DEVOTO

Pete showed me 'Shot By Both Sides' at Lower Broughton Road. He showed me the chords and guitar line that gave it the basic feel. 'Lipstick' was Pete's version of it; whether he had all the lyrics at the time I don't know. He had a melody, he didn't just have a guitar phrase. I'm sure he had the vocal melody. I was given the guitar and played the chords whilst he played the lead line. I really liked it and he said, 'You can have that.' It was definitely mine to take away and do something with – all I kept was the guitar phrase. I wrote the rest of the song round that.

The lyrics for 'Shot By Both Sides' are a kaleidoscope. Impressionistic. Take. On. The. Perpetual. Pursuit. Of. The. Point of. Paradox. Which. Will. Illuminate. Finally. The. Dialectical. Binary wotsit. Of existence (*laughs*). I've never managed to articulate it so well before (*laughs*). There are some things you try to reach for, some knowledge or wisdom that is beyond yourself – it means what comes out is not always as understandable as might be. All that political commitment was something I struggled with for many years because I always had the tendency to try and argue the other case with somebody. I guess I was trying to sing about being stuck, it means you can go either way, so you don't have a lot of certainty about anything. It's not always an easy place to be. It can be quite frightening and bewildering.

The first concrete thing I did musically after the Buzzcocks was to meet John McGeoch, who shared a house with Malcolm Garrett. I rehearsed two or three songs with him at Lower Broughton Road. I got together with him in April, then – probably in June or July – he returned to London. He was doing fine art at Manchester Poly.

'Light Pours Out of Me' was one of the earliest songs we came up with. It was the first one to try and do something different from Buzzcocks.

I'm not sure that I had anything very permanent in mind. I actually didn't know what I was going to do. I was feeling out the management thing; there was a point at which I was mulling those two things over – whether to manage the Buzzcocks or continue with making music.

I put Magazine together a few months after leaving Buzzcocks. I put a notice up in Virgin Records in Manchester that said I was looking for people who were into playing fast and slow music. I wasn't into every song going 'rama lama lama lama'. That's how I met Martin Jackson and

Barry Adamson and Robert Dickinson – maybe he was through that notice or he came from another context.

I met them, we rehearsed once, and then I got John involved again. I could tell he was pretty good already. I thought everyone else sounded good as well – Barry told me he'd started playing bass only a few weeks before I met him. Martin Jackson had been in one or two bands before.

BARRY ADAMSON (Magazine bass player)
When punk started, a friend gave me a bass. I'd never played one before. It had a couple of strings on it and when I went to buy the other two strings I saw the ad for Magazine. Even though I couldn't play I went to the audition; I played the root notes and got through it. It was just me and Howard Devoto, it wasn't a band at that point; that came a bit later. I think John McGeoch had already been involved. Howard strummed the chords to 'Shot By Both Sides' and 'Light Pours Out of Me'. Somehow I came up with something and I was in.

HOWARD DEVOTO
When we signed I think I said we'd only sign for one record. I wasn't even sure if we were going to make an album – I'd never done an album properly. That seemed quite a daunting idea. I only wanted to get 'Shot By Both Sides' out. I felt a lot about that song when we recorded it. I know when I recorded the vocals for it, it felt like one of the biggest moments of my life.

BARRY ADAMSON
It was very organic. 'Light Pours Out of Me' was a song in the chord of E; we just played it and it came out in a unique way. We were all adept at musical language, we were lucky to have that line-up; initially it was Howard's vision but the band became a unit. It was never a conscious effort to move away from punk because John McGeoch, despite his style, was still very into that kind of music.

RICHARD BOON
'Orgasm Addict' was the first Buzzcocks single after Howard left.

JON SAVAGE
I loved 'Orgasm Addict' when it came out and I still think that's one of the best punk rock singles ever

PETE SHELLEY
We put a lot of singles out very quickly. In some ways that was what was

good about it – it kept people up to speed with what you were doing. They were like postcards saying 'Hello there, I'm fine'. We managed to put out two albums in one year. I was always toying around, not doing it verse-chorus-middle eight; it fitted in with this idea of being a modern band and not part of the Tin Pan Alley tradition, with a different and more angular edge to it.

RICHARD BOON

We were making a point of taking the Worst or the Fall out with us. It kept that Manchester thing going and gave the impression that there was a lot more actually going on. I think it made a contribution to breaking the Londoncentric hold that the music biz had in those days.

HOWARD DEVOTO

Magazine didn't have that big an advance. I had plumped for artistic freedom over money and it was what they offered us when we accepted.

TONY WILSON

Howard made two mistakes. One was that he refused to go on *Top of the Pops* when 'Shot By Both Sides' stormed into the charts. It was a wonderful song because it was a Pete Shelley guitar riff – it's 'Lipstick', isn't it – and the one thing in this business is that it's always about the song. The other thing is that they went too prog rock, and that was what we were supposed to be against.

It's a shame Magazine didn't reap the reward they should have, and I love them, but they were long over before Factory came along.

STEVE DIGGLE

We were touring and Garth left. Joe Strummer always liked Garth. On the 'White Riot' tour, the Clash had a party in a big concrete hotel. I was stood at the bar with Joe and a few people and the next thing we knew, someone was being carried out. It took six bouncers to do it. Garth was a character! Joe always remembered that.

I remember the spitting. I got one straight in my mouth doing backing vocals. Also when you're running your hand up your guitar with phlegm all over the neck, it would get all over your fingers. I hit someone over the head with a guitar, he had a big scar on his head. I saw him a few weeks later and he said, 'It's better than an autograph.'

The Buzzcocks were not the only punk rock action in town. Slaughter and the Dogs' stomping glam-punk anthems were making an impression . . .

MICK ROSSI

In June we released 'Cranked Up Really High'. Martin Hannett did a great job of producing it. We did Wayne's vocals in the kitchen, it was one of those things where naivety is such a great thing. We recorded it very quickly. We didn't have any idea of what we were doing or how to record. The great thing about naivety is you go off your instincts; that's why a lot of bands lose it in the end.

Wayne wrote the lyrics – I think they're great lyrics. It's obviously a drug reference to cocaine – maybe a fantasy (*laughs*).

JOHNNY MARR

In '75–'76 my best mate at primary school came to grammar school. His best mate played bass in Wild Ram, who Ed Banger sang for. That was my first proper experience of hearing about the machinations of being in a band. They rehearsed instead of practised and they got dressed up for rehearsals – this wasn't someone in school uniform! They went to the rehearsal room in Wythenshawe dressed as you would be on stage. Through the older boys I kept hearing about Wild Ram all the time. Naturally I was always round there.

Wild Ram would play with Slaughter and the Dogs, who to all intents and purposes were a punk band already in 1976. They had slower songs but their attitude was totally punk – they were the real deal. They had Ray Rossi as their manager, everyone locally thought he was a hard lad. Ray Rossi was a formidable character and really completed the picture. I was always a big fan of Howard Bates, Slaughter's bass player. It went some way towards creating my haircut, because it was how Howard had his hair. The band were part of that United/Wythenshawe/Ziggy lot – trendy lads who liked David Bowie. But there was also a soul vibe with people like Rob Gretton being around them as well.

MICK ROSSI

We were playing down in London. We played the Roxy and the Vortex* and we were getting on to the London punk circuit. We played the Marquee – great gig, driving down to London and back in the Transit van, freezing in the back with all the gear. We had a bit of a following down there. Everyone was trying to sign bands on the punk rock scene. We were in Don Letts' *Punk Rock Movie*.

MICK ROSSI

When we did the album we got Mick Ronson in to play on it and help

* The two key London punk venues

produce it. I naively asked him to come and play on the album. I bought this Marshall amp and Mick used the same amp and settings. It sounded amazing! He also left the wah-wah pedal half on and half off; that was his trick to get that really distinctive tone that sounds so Mick.

The album came out and we played the Lyceum. That was great. Then we toured Europe. Wayne met this girl in France and moved out there and left the band.

So we did the obvious thing and got Eddie Garrity [Ed Banger] in to do the vocals. He knew our stuff, he had roadied a bit for us and was an old mate. He's a great guy from Wythenshawe like us – looking back on it, I wish I'd waited and Wayne had come back.

IAN BROWN

Slaughter were a Wythenshawe band – that was sort of our stomping ground . . . Slaughter were important because they were a cool band. I felt like I had a link with them because the guy that lived next door to me worked at Direct Works with Mike Rossi's dad and he had a couple of tapes that he gave to me . . . They made some great records – 'Cranked Up Really High', 'Bootboys' were really great. The reason that the Roses worked with Martin Hannett was because of his production with Slaughter.

We went to see Slaughter and the Dogs at the Wythenshawe Forum with V2. I always remember that when we came out there were all these kids with belts, saying, You're not at home now, you're in Wythenshawe. We had to leg it home.

JOHNNY MARR

Slaughter's gigs were really good as well. They obviously had the Bowie thing going on but they also did a killer version of 'Both Ends Burning' by Roxy. Wayne Barrett, I knew he was hip – even if they were a punk band, he was wearing baggy Bowie trousers.

I liked them when they were proper punks. I didn't like the cartoony talcum-powder vampire thing they did next. I thought they were much hipper when they were real street boys.

The punk scene was signposted by several key venues as it moved around town.

BOB DICKINSON (journalist)

I wasn't living in Manchester until punk was at its height, in mid-1977. But the reason I wanted to live in Manchester was because it was a city I'd known since the early seventies. And I'd seen the Buzzcocks on the 'White Riot' tour at West Runton Pavilion, on the bleak north Norfolk coast, earlier that year. Realising there was more going on in Manchester than East Anglia, I had to go there.

GINA SOBERS

All of a sudden there were new venues opening featuring live punk bands or changing ownership. Rafters* was in an old weekend meat market of a disco where they played the standard chart hits. Previously we'd only gone into the city centre for specific nights at well-established clubs, such as Pips or the Ranch, back of Piccadilly. Manchester Poly had popular Wednesday and Friday night sessions with live music every Saturday and as its bar was subsidised, its prices were more affordable for us too.

ED BANGER

There was the Oaks† who had on Johnny Thunders, the Banshees, Wayne County, the Dogs, and Ed Banger and the Nosebleeds. Then Rafters on Oxford Road and the Electric Circus opened up and Manchester Poly started putting on punk bands. A lot of punks hung out at the Ranch club – a real mix of punks, drag queens and other fetish groups. Pretty cool, eh! There was a tendency for gangs of disco cavemen to hang about outside to give the freaks a good kicking. Unfortunately I got kicked half to death one night and had another bottle smashed on my head. I was beginning to regret being called Ed Banger! I've still got the lump on my head to this day.

MARTIN MOSCROP

I went to gigs at Belle Vue, the Osborne and that sort of thing. I just missed out on the Ranch, being too young. I saw Iggy Pop at the Apollo. By the time I got to the Clash they were already playing to 2000 people . . .

GINA SOBERS

Manchester Poly was where the art students used to hang out; I remember Linder, Malcolm Garrett, John McGeoch, Mick Hucknall from their time at the Poly. It was a cool crowd, posy but still poor. Me and schoolfriends went to some great parties hosted by various students. That's where I first heard Kraftwerk, Iggy and the Stooges, the Velvets and heavy dub tracks.

The general level of aggression and increasing gobbing at gigs made us

---

* After the Ranch and the Electric Circus had closed down, Rafters became the main place to see punk bands in Manchester. It was a subterranean disco on Oxford Road. It's still there now, used as a rock club.
† The Oaks in Chorlton had a short run as one of the key Manchester punk venues.

wary of getting too embroiled in the punk scene. It got so bad at the Electric Circus that one of my friends used to stand at the front under her umbrella, to avoid going home with a slimy wet mohair jumper. On the way there, through Newton Heath, we'd often get yelled at by beer monsters or even accosted by them as they sneered at our clothes and musical taste.

It's hard to believe now that punk was viewed with suspicion and hostility by the general population, because of the dyed, spiked hair, the piercings, and the idiosyncratic approach to clothes, the in-yer-face attitude. Seems so commonplace now that those things are mainstream money-spinners from fashion to graphic design, even via the high street. But back then you risked not being allowed on a bus if the driver felt you looked too offensive.

BOB DICKINSON

I wanted to write about music and I went to a fortnightly listings magazine called *New Manchester Review*. They were based in Waterloo Place, Oxford Road, which happened to also be the post office box address for New Hormones. So some of the first people I got to know were Richard Boon, the Buzzcocks manager, and Andrew Jaspan of *NMR*, who did the magazine's club promotions.

Many of the bands I saw were at the magazine's club nights at Rafters, where the first band I saw were the Fall. They struck me as being very different from anything I'd previously seen, in a seedy and sinister but poetic way.

There were quite a few short-lived punk fanzines, like Paul Morley's *Girl Trouble* and *Out There*, and Steve Shy's *Shy Talk*, and Mick Middles' *Ghast Up*. *Ghast Up* was printed at the Electric Circus on their own printing machine. *Girl Trouble* was probably the best because it was a single photocopied sheet with a collage image on one side, usually by Linder Sterling or Jon Savage, and a page of stream-of-consciousness writing from Paul on the other. Paul had previously written for a prog rock zine called *Penetration* around 1975.

GINA SOBERS

Rob Gretton, later the manager of Joy Division, was the regular Thursday night DJ at Rafters. So he spun up-to-the-minute tracks. It felt like a cosy scene then, made up of familiar Manc faces.

At Rafters, I saw X-Ray Spex, Elvis Costello and the Attractions, Pere Ubu, Big In Japan, Frantic Elevators with Mick Hucknall as the lead singer, Misty In Roots, Selector, Penetration, the Only Ones, Nico – the worst gig I ever saw as she was completely pin-eyed. At the Poly, I caught all the latest Jamaican reggae bands – they had a brilliant social secretary, John Commons, that year. Culture, the Royal Rasses, the Mighty Diamonds, our own Aswad and Steel Pulse, Junior Murvin, U-Roy, Burning Spear, Lee Perry, Linton Kwesi Johnson, Magazine, the Police; all at a subsidised door price. I'm not sure if the Poly actually made any money as John booked his favourite bands regardless. One of my favourite Poly nights was a performance of *Snuff Rock* by C.P. Lee's Alberto Y Lost Trios Paranoias. It was the story of a hapless group desperate for success at any price.

ELLIOT RASHMAN
Tosh Ryan, who ran Rabid Records, was an important part of the Dadaist hard-left politics way of thinking. He was the fly-posterer with an artistic ethos who put up the first generation of hard punk posters in Manchester. He was really important and remained a kind of chronicler with his bits of filming. He was hardest of left politically.

BOB DICKINSON
Another character who'd call into the *New Manchester Review* office during the late seventies was Tosh Ryan, who at that time was releasing records on Rabid by people like Slaughter and the Dogs and later, Jilted John.

He also did fly-posting – you paid him to fly-post your gigs. But, with our little club night, we decided we'd do it ourselves. This got me into big trouble with Tony Wilson, who got me to go and see him at Granada one afternoon and proceeded to yell at me in reception about how I had to 'pay fuckin' Tosh fuckin' Ryan to get yer fuckin' posters put up' instead of doing it ourselves. We kept on putting our own posters up and Tosh's people kept postering them over, in a sort of poster game.

CHRIS SIEVEY
We were on our third EP when Martin Hannett heard me on the radio. I got involved with Rabid, which was great. I got to use the facilities like the printer where they printed the posters. There was a dead small cartel in Manchester. I was doing artwork for John Cooper Clarke and people like that. Suddenly I was working in what I wanted to be working in. Tosh ended up managing me and Martin Hannett produced my single on Rabid. Rabid was great; we did gigs with Slaughter and the Dogs and Jilted John. The Freshies played with everyone – Drones, Buzzcocks . . .

ELLIOT RASHMAN

I lived in Charles Barry Crescent in Hulme in that period, the late seventies, when they started to fill it full of students. It was never well-built and very quickly became a sink estate. The only people who appreciated it were the people who lived there. The best sunsets I've ever seen were from the second floor of a Charles Barry Crescent flat. I went to the shebeens in Moss Side. The Nile club* was a really important scene; you went to score. Hulme was full of lower-middle-class students whose grant had run out. You had the Aaben cinema – an arthouse cinema that was cheap and you would get to see some great movies. There was lots of speed, which was the chosen drug in Manchester – cocaine never touched Manchester, it was speed and Moroccan, they were the drug currency. Speed was not a connoisseur's drug. It wasn't a rock star scene like in London – Manchester had a working-class agenda.

And then there was the glorious Electric Circus in Collyhurst. That was in the middle of nowhere. It was really exotic, it was the first time I saw girls in stockings and suspenders, it was the first time I saw girls push their tits out and not in a sexual way – just to be unique and provocative. The best crowd I've ever seen was at the Electric Circus, they all moved as one – like a football crowd. In the balcony it looked like a raging sea! It was fucking fantastic! The music was part of it. You weren't politely watching the music – it made you jump up and down with the chaos on the stage. The vibrancy was amazing for a couple of years until it all got commercialised. I remember seeing the Prefects – the singer fell into the drums and the drummer was going mad and twatting him.

ROB LLOYD (Prefects and Nightingales vocalist)

We played in Manchester quite a lot and felt some sort of kinship with the bands there, and, for some reason, Manchester seemed to fall in love with us. We played there an awful lot with Manchester bands, and around the country.

In Manchester, I suppose the Fall and the Worst were on the same sort of vibe as us. And there were journalists like Paul Morley and Kevin Cummins the photographer. From the Prefects' point of view we weren't trying to endear ourselves to Manchester or disenfranchise ourselves from London. There was no such plan of action.

---

* The Nile, along with the Reno, the Bengwema, the Barry Fredericks Shebeens, the Capitol and many smaller clubs, were key late-night spaces in sixties and seventies Moss Side. A very mixed clientele of 'Pop stars, actors and actresses, bent cops, pimps, drug dealers, ponces and the rest of the night people' would come down to the Nile club.

There were no Richard Boons or Howard Devotos, no Paul Morleys or spunky Cath Carrolls* in Birmingham where we were from – no semi-intellectual thinkers. We were just making it up as we went along, literally. That's what the Mancs seemed to really like about us. The Buzzcocks were really helpful, as were Magazine and Barry Adamson; people there gave us a guitar or something, they helped us out. We ended up being the only non-Manchester band who played the 'Last Night at the Electric Circus' gig and we got on the album. We just seemed to be adopted. It was weird really.

JON SAVAGE
I travelled up to Manchester for the 'Last Night of the Electric Circus' gigs in October 1977. Manchester was a complete shithole at the time, unrecognisable from what it is now; at the time London had bombsites and derelict buildings but that was nothing like what Manchester had.

Manchester really looked like the end of the world, like a nuclear bomb had hit it. It was endless. It was the detritus of the Industrial Revolution, large areas around the centre of the city had been left to rot. During that trip I interviewed the Buzzcocks – it was one of the first interviews that they had done – and then I went to the Electric Circus gig. I loved the Electric Circus, I thought it was fantastic.

ALAN ROBINSON (promoter)
We shut down the Electric Circus because success was our downfall. We helped make so many of the punk bands famous when they played there. I could put them where other people couldn't, but as soon as they got famous they were asking for five times the money. I couldn't ask the punters for five times the money so they went on to bigger and better venues – to the Apollos – punk was more accepted by then. Financially we started to lose money so we had to close down.

STEVE HANLEY
The Last Night Of the Electric Circus came out as an album – Magazine played, the Fall, Buzzcocks. Warsaw were on the first night, and they were really good.

The early Fall were brilliant. I watched Tony Friel on bass all the time. He was amazing – the bass was the lead instrument in the Fall. And Karl [Burns] . . . Oh man, he was a great drummer. The first time I thought,

* One of the key scenesters of the period, Carroll was to become a pithy and confrontational music journalist.

what the hell is this? It wasn't punk, I don't know what it was. We were into the Velvets and the Stooges – it was kind of more like that.

GINA SOBERS
The Mayflower in Gorton was a punk venue in the middle of east Manchester wastelands. I saw Tapper Zukie there, Crass and the Poison Girls, the Pop Group and much later a young Bjork in Kukl, on an anarchist-sponsored night. Not knowing who she was, just a young girl with an ice-pick voice wearing black.

BOB DICKINSON
I also went to the Squat, the Russell Club* and the Mayflower a lot. But I completely missed the Electric Circus. This was the time punk stopped being such a minority thing and venues like Rafters would be packed way beyond their fire limit for some acts like Elvis Costello. Other times, though, it was great to get up close to the front of the stage at somewhere like Rafters and watch someone like Wayne County or X-Ray Spex. Even though I do remember during the latter event the crowd being so packed that someone pissed down my leg and I couldn't even turn round to tell the perpetrator to desist – using more colourful language.

By now punk had turned a lot of disparate people on to the idea of making music . . .

MARTIN MOSCROP
I bought a guitar in 1975 and 1976 when I started work, and a couple of years later I formed a punk band at school. We didn't know how to tune the bass to the guitar. I could play one barre chord and that was it.

PAUL RYDER
It wasn't just the music with punk. It was the whole attitude. By the time I was in the fourth year I had stopped going to school and got myself a job in the Arndale Centre – first in the clothes shop, Misty Blue, and then the Great Western Jean Company and Stolen From Ivor, just off Market Street just by the underground market.†

I was going to the Portland Bars. I was a bit too young to go to [see] bands. I would go out of the house with my school uniform on, then have to change to go and do my job. One gig I did see was the Ramones and the Talking Heads at the Free Trade Hall. I was watching Talking Heads and thinking, this isn't really punk, but it blew me away – their stuff is

---

* The Russell Club in Hulme hosted many post-punk and new wave bands and would be the venue for the Factory Club.
† One of the places where the clothes shops went after New Brown Street was demolished.

a big influence on me. I went with Shaun. We saw Johnny Ramone outside, we was buzzing to see him in the flesh. I was too shy to speak to him – I just stared at him, drooling at the mouth (*laughs*).

IAN BROWN

Manchester was pretty violent in the seventies. I used to get chased by the Teds in the punk days. On Saturday afternoons I used to see firemen hosing people down in the underground market, Perrys* fighting punks. Kids would be fighting in the bus station at night – battles up and down the bus station! Piccadilly Gardens was pretty violent. I didn't used to get involved in that, although I did hang around with a gang of lads who got into scrapes.

We used to go into town looking at records in record stores and the old Virgin store, where they had old train seats with headphones so you could check the records out. We used to hang out there; we'd hang out in Discount Records in the underground market and the big Teds would come in. They were like men, big men from Belle Vue in drape suits; they seemed ancient even then. There was a big Ted versus punk thing at the time. I remember this big Ted coming into Discount Records and taking the Clash album out and saying, 'Shouldn't this be in the comedy section?' And all the punks looked at the floor!

John [Squire] was into art then. He never used to do games at school, they let him do his art. He would stencil up school shirts Clash style. I used to walk about in shirts that he had stencilled up, with tight pants and braces and baseball boots – that was our look, with a black jacket with pins on.

JOHNNY MARR

It's probably a lot easier to be into punk rock when you're on the Kings Road. When you saw the Kings Road on TV, it might as well have been Venus for us! Some of those kids there were my age and they would be in magazines and on the TV shows – we didn't get on television shows up here!

NOEL GALLAGHER

I remember punk happening and I remember seeing punks but I was just too young to be involved in it – I was ten in 1977. I remember seeing this

---

* Emerging in 1979, the Perry boys were the Manchester equivalent of Liverpool's scallys. A product of the football terraces, they sported Fred Perry polo shirts, Lee cords, Adidas Stan Smith trainers and wedge haircuts. Their look would creep through the musical undergrowth and eventually hit the mainstream in the late eighties care of the Manchester explosion.

guy in Burnage, he had a white skinhead [haircut] with an exclamation mark in the back of his head. It was one of the Stockholm Monsters, who would be the first band to come from Burnage. I remember seeing him on the high street and being like, wow, what the fuck is that! He's got a *what*! I also remember the Sex Pistols being this controversial thing. All my mates' brothers had that album and they couldn't play it to their parents, particularly because of 'Bodies' – the one with all the swearing. When you're a kid you don't particularly understand what it means – you go: wow, he said *fuck* in a song!

JOHNNY MARR

The thing I'm glad that is being put to rights about punk rockers is that they didn't all wear black bondage pants. Up here they looked like the guys you avoided coming out of Deville's on a Friday, Saturday night – probably rent boys. They had side partings, flicks and V-necked jumpers and the fact that their trousers had been taken in was really shocking. And maybe [they had] one or two earrings that were little studs – what was shocking was the minimalism of it all, the lack of adornment. Everything else in the music scene had been flowing scarves. Keith Richards was wearing scarves round his waist and neck. The New York Dolls had taken it to its Nick Kent* nightmare. It was stripped down and brought this austerity and super slick confrontation at the same time. Punk rock was stripped down but still quite dandified in a weird way, maybe because there was an effeminate quality to it.

ANDREW BERRY (Hacienda DJ and hairdresser)

I was still at school so had to rely on going to gigs. We knew this lad who could break open the side doors at the venue and we'd all just leg it in. There was no real security, just an old bloke who worked there during the week when the venue was a cinema. If you wanted a ticket you had to queue at the venue weeks before the gig because there was no Ticketmaster or Visa cards. My school was in town so we could get tickets the day they came out and before anyone else. I saw T. Rex at the Free Trade Hall in '74, Kraftwerk, Iggy and Bowie at the Apollo in '77, Devo, Blondie, Talking Heads, Television, the Clash, the Damned, and Bryan Ferry's 'In Your Mind' tour, all in the seventies. I even saw Fleetwood Mac's 'Rumours' and the first Stiff tour. The first real clubs I went to were the old Polytechnic in Oxford Road with the big Dennis the Menace on the wall and the Russell Club in Hulme.

---

* Rock'n'roll dandy *NME* journalist of the time.

PAUL RYDER

During the third year at school along came punk and it blew me away. I was 13 years old. It was: what the fuck is this, it's scary, man! It must have been like when Elvis or the Stones arrived. Fortunately for me and our kid, our dad liked it; me old fellow is a jack of all trades on musical instruments – he can play a bit of everything. He's not a master, he can play a bit of any instrument. He was a hip guy. We'd bring punk records into the house and he'd say, 'Let's have a look at them.' He'd say 'It all comes from the blues, listen to Fats Domino.'

GRAHAM MASSEY (808 State)

I was at school with Alan Hempsall* and Graeme Clarke, who I still play with. We ended up being into Gong.† We formed a Gong covers band. We were into that early Virgin Records era. When it started Virgin was quite a diverse label, they had a budget series of releases at 49 pence – one was Gong's *Camembert Electrique*, another was *The Faust Tapes*.‡ The one thing our group of people had in common was the 49p records. *Faust Tapes* was an important gluing thing for us and so was *Camembert Electrique*.

Our first gig was on the Queen's Jubilee day in 1977 – that put us smack in the middle of punk – but on that day we did three street parties: we started at ten in the morning at Burnage Congregational Hall before moving on to one in Levenshulme and then one late afternoon in a garage in Didsbury. Our set included rock classics and we would do the Gong cover version in an effort to reach out to the general public with their triangle sandwiches and Union Jack hats. We also did 'All Right Now', 'Rock Around the Clock' and 'God Save the Queen' (*laughs*), which put us at the cusp of old and new culture!

We would sell cassettes in the back of the *NME*. It was very much a DIY culture. Rough Trade were involved – they would let us use their photocopier – and so were Better Badges. My band Aqua played at the Lesser Free Trade Hall for twenty quid. We got the gig because Alan went to the Pistols and got the idea of playing there from that. We did the Phoenix on Oxford Road – that was our social club on Friday and Sunday nights. On Sunday you would bring your own records – that was an interesting night. It was moving away from girls in cheesecloth

---

* Future Crispy Ambulance frontman.
† A seventies/eighties progressive/psychedelic rock band built around Australian musician Daevid Allen, who took Syd Barrett's glissando guitar technique and created a whole new space rock world from it.
‡ Faust were an amazing German underground band in the seventies who are still around.

swirling to Genesis records; we took Magma* records and we'd do these 20-minute Magma dances!

LINDER
I can date the end of punk to my mother's copy of *Woman's Own* from May 1977 when they ran a feature called 'DIY Punk for your Daughter' and I remember thinking, oh, that's the full stop, something brief and exhilarating is over. We have to praise *Woman's Own*, in a way, for signposting that.

* French Krautrock band, if that's not a contradiction in terms!

5

THE MODERN DANCE: IN WHICH MANCHESTER ARGUABLY INVENTS POST-PUNK

By 1978 punk had already started to shift into post-punk as the ideas thrown up by punk were used to create a whole new way of making music in the post trad-rock era. Manchester was the leader of the new scene. The energy of punk had inspired people and opened a door for anyone with an original idea to come through. In Manchester, Magazine were redesigning the zeitgeist and Warsaw were turning into Joy Division, while the Fall were pursuing their own agenda, A Certain Ratio were messing with punk-funk and a whole host of other bands were moving beyond the parameters of rock and, like the city itself, re-emerging blinking from the demolition of familiar landscapes.

PHIL SAXE
I was too old for punk! I thought it was interesting but it didn't excite me tremendously – the first time I got interested again was post-punk and that was early on with Television and Blondie at the Free Trade Hall, where I went with Mike Pickering. In many ways Television were the first band of this scene, taking music somewhere else.

LINDER
The dilution of what was happening was like with the Zandra Rhodes safety pin: it was the high end of fashion moving in. It was an interesting time observing what was happening. The disappointment was that it wasn't what one had hoped it would be. Punk was suddenly very dreary sounding – a disappointment.

LIZ NAYLOR
Manchester in many ways invented post-punk. Magazine were pretty important to this. They may sound almost prog rock now but at the time

they sounded like nothing else. There is a sense that Public Image's *Metal Box* album was the first post-punk album as well. I remember the impact that it had. Post-punk was going on in Edinburgh and Bristol as well at the time, with Fast Records and the Pop Group.* The Buzzcocks albums had some great post-punk ideas on them; their singles compilation, which everyone has, doesn't do them any favours – it's a great pop record but the albums are more interesting. It seemed that just after punk there were quickly loads of interesting bands in Manchester like the Passage and Blue Orchids,† who were both fantastic post-punk bands.

GINA SOBERS

It was a time of many small labels being formed as bands decided to control and distribute their own output. In Manchester we had New Hormones, run by Richard Boon, the manager of the Buzzcocks. London had Rough Trade, a small distribution outlet which grew into a record label. Most of the record sleeves in my punk collection looked like they had been glued together hastily round a kitchen table late of a beery evening. The emphasis of the punk aesthetic was very much a home-baked one before bands were picked up by major labels.

LIZ NAYLOR

The first punk gig I went to, in June 1978 when I was 15, was the Fall at Droylsden Town Hall. It was unbelievable even for someone into Beefheart. I had seen this tiny A4 poster where someone had written 'The Fall live with The Distractions'.‡ I knew I could get there on a bus and I got there bang in doors. I had never seen a band like the Fall, they were quite shambolic but special and they felt like my band. The Fall felt like Captain Beefheart. They had something in them that I recognised, that I thought was amazing.

BOB DICKINSON

There seemed to be dozens of new bands starting up, but they weren't punk-sounding or looking.

The great hope after the Buzzcocks for me was the Distractions. I saw them at Band on the Wall first. I liked Mike Finney's gold lamé jacket and the sexual ambiguity of the band's bassist, Pip Nicholls. They wore T-

---

* A Bristol band who dislocated funk and crossed it with punk to create some fiercely militant and great songs.
† Formed by Martin Bramah when he left the Fall; well worth checking out for paranoiac, seething, keyboard-driven twisted garage rock.
‡ Formed in 1975 by Mike Finney (vocals) and Steve Perrin (guitar), the Distractions stepped up a level when punk arrived in 1977, mixing their sixties pop with punk.

shirts that read 'Distractions Fail the Sex Test'. They were friends of the *City Fun*[*] collective and Pip was featured on the cover of the first issue.

GINA SOBERS
Just after punk, I started growing dreads in my hair as my consciousness of my African-Caribbean heritage grew. I was still one of the few black faces on the Manchester punk scene. Most Rastas couldn't see any connection at first. There was my mate Markus Dread, a skinhead-turned-Rude Boy-turned Twelve Tribes Rasta, and Anthony Bear, with his go-faster blond stripe. None of us hailed from Moss Side[†] so perhaps that made it easier for us to identify with punk. It also made us more visible in the clubs. So I liked Pauline Black, Ranking Roger, Don Letts, Dennis Morris, Poly Styrene as a matter of course.

The Manchester Musicians' Collective had been formed in April 1977. As word spread, more bands became members of the Collective; some for a short while, some for longer. A Certain Ratio, the Fall, the Fast Cars, the Not Sensibles, Slight Seconds, Spherical Objects, Passage, Warsaw/Joy Division, were all Collective members. All the bands were friends and there was a rota of whose turn it was to play a gig and who would headline. Everything was organised by the Collective: members, printing, publicity (fly-posting!).

RICHARD WITTS
We put together a legal framework for the Manchester Musicians' Collective so that it didn't belong to any one person. We hired the North West basement on Kings Street, it was a very posh building. They had a very chic café there and everything was white. We took it over on Monday nights. That's where the Fall first played. I was one of the organisers.

MARTIN MOSCROP
The punk scene for me didn't last very long because all the sort of people into it at the start fell out of love with it quite quickly when it went mainstream. When the *Sun* started writing about the Sex Pistols, everyone was looking for alternatives and that happened quickly. A lot of those alternatives were about in Manchester. The main thing for me was the Manchester Musicians' Collective – this was where the Ratios formed and Warsaw played their first gigs. There was a small scene there.

[*] *City Fun* was the main alternative magazine in the city at the time.
[†] Moss Side is the next area from Hulme going out from the city centre. Originally a densely populated Irish area, it became the centre of the city's black community in the seventies.

GINA SOBERS

The Cyprus Tavern, opposite what became Legends nightclub, was a cheapish venue to hire for gigs, just taking the money from the bar provided you brought in the punters. So quite a few Collective bands played there, myself included with the Liggers. We played one of our best gigs there to a packed house.

The Manchester audience was in thrall to Joy Division, so the venue was awash with pale-faced youths with floppy fringe haircuts and grey gabardine raincoats and army boots.

BOB DICKINSON

The Band on the Wall was where the Musicians' Collective met weekly and many new bands started there – the first time I saw Cath Carroll was when she was playing in Property Of . . . My favourite Collective band was God's Gift – they often played with their backs to the audience, and later released one of the best unknown singles to come out of Manchester, 'Discipline'. God's Gift supported the Dead Kennedys on what I think was their first Manchester gig at the Mayflower, and they publicly complained that the Dead Kennedys were getting paid too much money – various bouncers came on stage and threw the lead singer into the baying crowd. I went and complained to Alan Wise who was promoting this gig, and he of course thought the whole incident was deeply amusing.

STEPHEN MURPHY (God's Gift)

God's Gift were formed initially by school friends. There was a shared love of the Velvet Underground, the Stooges and local music at that time, but everyone had diverse musical tastes, which probably showed. I think GG had a frightening intensity at times and our self-belief and self-commitment were unchallengeable. When playing live, GG were impossible to intimidate and their performance had a very belligerent, aggressive edge. Several gigs ended early due to angry customers or in random violence. The lyrics were always of paramount importance despite the extreme volume we played at. I think the aim was to be disruptive, aggressive, and intimidating whilst keeping up this seamless bombardment of sound. I believe it created a feeling of unease.

MARTINE HILTON (Property Of . . .)

The key was definitely punk rock and its clarion cry that everything had changed. In 1978 I was a student at Manchester Polytechnic and worked nights in a factory to save up for my first bass guitar. Since first going to the Electric Circus I'd wanted to form a girl band and was getting bass lessons from my boyfriend Tony Friel of the Fall. When I met Louise

Alderman she was really into motorbikes and we formed Property Of . . . The name was taken from female Hell's Angels, who wore badges marking them as the 'Property of' their man. The blank after the three dots was the point – we were doing this on our own.

Getting a girl drummer was a problem. We used Tony Tabak, Warsaw's original drummer, and then the late Jeff Bridges, singer with If Only.

Our idea was to hit back against the usual macho rock'n'roll thing. I'd seen how Mark E. Smith totally dominated the Fall so we were keen to be co-operative and democratic. In 1978 Manchester was still wrapped up in that Bernard Manning 'beer and birds' culture. We felt like pioneers because we wanted to be more than ditsy vocalists singing men's lyrics.

LOUISE ALDERMAN (Property Of . . .)
In 1977 I was living in a flat with Dick Witts. I was a member of his NorMedia music group and we had been working with Trevor Wishart, performing some of his pieces at the Ghent Festival. Setting up Manchester Musicians' Collective seemed an obvious step at the time. What we didn't expect was the bands. When it started, it was a mixed bag of musicians but gradually the bands took over. I did a lot of the original organising for the meetings and gigs, as I lived with Dick and also I was one of the few people with transport (a motorbike).

GINA SOBERS
Me and my friends used to go to the Oaks, on the border between Didsbury and Chorlton, which hosted a regular Roxy/Bowie night on Tuesdays with soul tunes filling in the breaks. That was where I first bumped into Paul Morley and an occasional Jon Savage. We knew who they were but to them we were probably just northern teen girls out on the razz. I knew there was a northern soul scene because a girl at school had invited me to go to Wigan Pier with her, but it was too far from my South Manc home. Around that time we met Frank, who was running the Manchester Musicians' Collective from his flat in Burton Road, Didsbury. He invited us to Collective gigs, on Monday nights at the Band on the Wall. We were still underage for pubs but we looked and acted older, so off we went, me and an assortment of friends from my convent school. It was quite an initiatory phase as we'd also started watching European art films at the Aaben in Hulme, having previously grown up on a diet of Hollywood fare. The Aaben was run by Polish John and it was the only independent cinema we knew of in Manchester catering to such eclectic taste – though we felt we were taking our life in our hands walking through the council estates to get there, South Manchester wusses that we were! So the two cultural elements collided in our development

somehow. An awareness of our horizons expanding, of possibilities becoming more concrete. At the Collective we met Warsaw, A Certain Ratio, the Passage, the Fall, God's Gift, Dislocation Dance, Spherical Objects, the Manchester Mekon, Bathroom Renovations, the Spurtz – younger even than us at an average age of 15 to our old 18 – Property Of . . ., the only all-girl group we knew of in Manchester, featuring Cath Carroll on guitar, a Slavic-looking beauty with a sharp taste in charity-shop suits, we thought. It took us a while to get up on stage, but as everyone else seemed to be having a go regardless of whether they could sing or play an instrument properly, we decided to join in the party.

MARTIN MOSCROP

I was in a punk band in Stockport called Alien Tint. I was in the band for a short while. We played a Manchester Musicians' Collective gig at the Band on the Wall with the early three-piece ACR.* I really liked them. When they saw Alien Tint they said, 'What the fuck is he doing in that band!' I had a demob suit on and I already looked like one of A Certain Ratio. I had a decent guitar and amp and looked right and they asked me to join that night. They were very much like their first single 'All Night Party'/'The Thin Boys' with just one guitar – what I added was a lot more rhythm. Pete [Terrell] was quite droney on guitar – initially we didn't have a drummer so me playing with the band made them more rhythmical.

The band's name is taken from the lyrics of Brian Eno's song 'The True Wheel'.† It was a total accident that the name was taken from a Hitler speech on the proportion of 'Jewish blood' that was required to determine whether someone was to be classified as 'Jewish'. It wasn't connected with that at all – we just liked the phrase and it was one of our favourite songs. They were massive Eno fans and that was the catchiest tune on the album. We didn't know where he got his lyrics from.‡

JOHNNY MARR

The spectre of the Buzzcocks was still around. They didn't have that pub rock vibe. They were modern. They looked and sounded modern. Their

---

* Formed in 1977, A Certain Ratio's longest serving members have been Martin Moscrop (guitar, trumpet) and Jeremy Kerr (bass, vocals). Drummer Donald Johnson (drums, vocals), joined early to replace a drum machine. Three original members have left the band, including original vocalist Simon Topping who left in 1983 for Quando Quango and, later, T-Coy, singer Martha Tilson who left in 1982, and guitarist Peter Terrell who left in 1982. Keyboardist Andy Connell, who joined in 1982, left to form Swing Out Sister in 1985.

† From the album *Taking Tiger Mountain (By Strategy)*.

‡ Mildly controversial in the context of the punk and post-punk fascination with the depravity of Nazi regalia, the band's name was, as Martin explains, an unintentional coincidence.

guitar sound was modern. Their melodies weren't blues melodies. I had this 16 year old's attitude that some of the punks needed to move over.

An interesting thing about the punk scene in Manchester – maybe like in London – is that the principal players benefited from the older generations: people like Tosh Ryan and Martin Hannett. Tony [Wilson] was still a fairly young guy then and there were older people round who understood sixties politics, people who had been around the Eighth Day or whatever – they acted like mentors towards the younger bands. In London obviously there was Bernie Rhodes and Malcolm McLaren and the same was true for Manchester as well.

I was 16 and I was at a gig the first time I met Morrissey. It was a Patti Smith gig at the Apollo.* I was at the gig with Slaughter and the Dogs and that's how we met. Him and I were both around Slaughter and the Dogs' orbit; I was in the youngster role – get patted on the head [and] run off to the cig machine, just to bask in the reflected glory of these 17-year-old rock stars!

I was surprised when Slaughter split. Wayne went to France and Mike [Rossi] carried the name Slaughter on. Billy [Duffy] had joined the Nosebleeds who had become the de facto Slaughter and the Dogs support band. Vini Reilly had left and Billy answered an advert in HMV or Virgin and got the job as the Nosebleeds' guitar player, which everybody in Wythenshawe was really impressed by. When Vini was in the band they had released a single, 'Ain't Been To No Music School'.† Some of my mates had been in the cover shoot, which was in a school room. Vini was wearing the blazer from my school – it was a candy-stripe blazer which for years had been the bane of that school's life! Suddenly everybody was trying to find their older brother's blazer, when before we were always getting our arse beaten up for it. Vini left after the single came out and that was when Billy joined, but not for long, because then Eddie Garrity joined Slaughter, thinking he had a better career chance. It was all a bit messy. When Ed Garrity left the Nosebleeds they didn't have a singer; Morrissey was briefly the singer when they supported Magazine at the Ritz‡ for one gig.

MORRISSEY

I met Billy Duffy in, I think, the usual hangout of Virgin on Lever Street. We wrote a few songs – 'Peppermint Heaven' and 'Toytown Massacre' – and he brought in the drummer from the Nosebleeds, who had broken up,

---

* 21 September 1978.

† Apparently written after a somewhat bizarre support slot with Sad Café, when the more musical Mancunian veterans had been sniffy at their more rudimentary support band.

‡ The Ritz on Whitworth Street is one of the last classic dance halls in Manchester. Famous for its sprung dance floor, it still retains some of the great atmosphere of an older venue.

and then the bass player. It was Billy's venture and I virtually did nothing.

One week Billy called it the Politicians, then Providence, and then Studio Sweethearts. We played a gig at Manchester University, about fifth on the bill – I have absolutely no idea who made up the rest of the bill. I wore a dark green nylon shirt. The place was full and applause was great. But it was reviewed as the Nosebleeds, which was irritating, and by the time of the review we didn't exist together anyway. Billy teamed up with Mick Rossi from Slaughter and the Dogs and they immediately made a single as Studio Sweethearts. I wasn't involved, and I don't know who sang on the single or what it was called. This is why local history has me down as an ex member of Slaughter & the Dogs or the Nosebleeds, which is ridiculous, but I find that any details about me from this period are generally believed by whoever wants to believe them. Billy, of course, pointed me towards Johnny Marr, and told me quite graciously that Johnny was a much better guitarist. In essence, Billy walked away from me and didn't want to form a group with me at all, which I completely understand because I was terribly inhibited, so I don't hold any grudge towards him whatsoever.

ED BANGER
Stephen Morrissey and Billy Duffy did one gig before deciding it was a waste of time trying to follow in mine and Vini's footsteps (*laughs*).

JOHNNY MARR
I remember the songs that Billy was playing with the Nosebleeds were things like 'I'd Rather Be In the Electric Chair' – all very punky. 'Living Jukebox' was a big favourite which I remember . . . 'Peppermint Heaven'.

ED BANGER
Slaughter and the Dogs were on the crest of a wave when I joined them. They were about to go top 50 with their single, 'Ready Now', and had a sell-out tour ahead of them. Then Wayne jumped ship for Love in the Afternoon.

JOHNNY MARR
The first proper gig I did I turned up at a soundcheck. I'd been head-hunted by this band Sister Ray – I went to this basement in Whaley and there were these really nasty druggy guys. I thought they were punk rock but they were really nasty bikers. The singer was a complete nutter – looking back, I can understand these guys were really obvious druggies. Anyway, I got to play the Lesser Free Hall with these guys, third on the bill to the Freshies – it was the start of me joining different bands. I was

delighted that the guy doing our sound was the famous Oz;[*] he eventually became the Smiths sound man.

I got to be in a news article in the *Wythenshawe Express*, looking exactly as I do now – same haircut, everything . . .

Devilles was a key place. Funnily enough, the Mayflower and the Banshee were important places to go to but important for me because I was a musician and wanted to be on stage rather than in the audience. I wasn't bothered about going out. I had other things to do, like rehearsing and trying to get in a band. I was now in Sister Ray and did a track on a compilation album called *Identity Parade* which came out on TJM Records.[†] Sister Ray had a song on it called 'Suicide', which as I remember was a kick-ass heavy song along the lines of 'Funtime' by Iggy and the Stooges.

As punk transformed into post-punk, the Russell Club at a West Indian transport workers' club called the PSV in Hulme became the key venue. About a mile from the city centre in the wilds of Hulme, the venue was located in the midst of the stark new architectural cityscapes that would readily be reflected in the new music that was starting to appear.

JON SAVAGE

What everyone forgets was that the Russell Club was pretty important. It was pretty regular and it was like our club – this was all very much a small scene. The Factory crowd were very different from the Music Collective crowd, the Band on the Wall crowd were very different from the Object Music crowd, who were very different from the Fall Prestwich crowd, who were very different from the thousands of kids who went to Rotters disco.[‡] Outside Rotters was always a very edgy corner when we came out of Rafters, which was next to it.

GINA SOBERS

Around that time, Tony Wilson and friends took over the old WISS, a West Indian bus drivers' club in Hulme, in the shadow of a crescent, and renamed it the Factory. We weren't hip enough to link it with Andy Warhol's organisation. It just sounded like an apt name for a club in an

---

[*] Known as the best sound person in Manchester, Oz ran the Oz PA hire.
[†] TJM stood for Tony Joseph Music, Joseph being the middle name of Tony Davidson who ran T.J. Davidson, the now demolished rehearsal studios at 35 Little Peter Street where Joy Division rehearsed and recorded their video for 'Love Will Tear Us Apart'. Many Manchester bands rehearsed there, including bands on the TJM label like Slaughter and the Dogs.
[‡] A club where Manchester's beer monsters went.

industrial wasteland, which was why Alan Erasmus chose the name to begin with. No pretension about it. It showcased numerous punk bands. Some of its patrons still comprised the African-Caribbean bus drivers and their mates, though they usually hung about the door and the bar, staring bemusedly at the young punky clientele. I saw Adam and the Ants, Toyah – I know, all very Derek Jarman. Shame Tilda Swinton didn't make an appearance. Dillinger and other reggae artists played there as well. Sometimes we'd head down there not knowing who was going to appear live, it was such a good atmosphere.

MICK MIDDLES (journalist and author)
It was a noticeable difference between Manchester and Liverpool. They were far more fashion conscious than Manchester. Manchester was heading towards its industrial stage – the Factory was down in Hulme and for some reason we thought that was very industrial! It was grey, anyway.

LIZ NAYLOR
I went to the Factory a lot because the Distractions were managed by Martin X, who lived on nearby Bonsall Street in Hulme round the corner from the club. I had trouble getting into Rafters and there was always a slight edginess to it. If I could get into the Factory I would turn up at sound check and sit there. I could steal beers so it was a cheap night out. I spent most of my time off my face and I just wanted to be there.

The Factory was delightfully seedy, it kind of felt like you were in someone else's space and it was all right for you to be there. It had some kind of edginess, which rock venues don't have now they are owned by Carling. Factory was one for one night a week. Going to Hulme was really frightening. In those days it was full of drug addicts and prostitutes and full of students with long macs on.

One of the great aspects of the DIY liberation promoted by punk was the fanzine scene. An alternative press had already been in place since the counter-culture days of the late sixties; this process was now accelerated, with City Fun *being the main conduit for alternative music and ideas in Manchester at the time.*

BOB DICKINSON
I first met the *City Fun* people in I think 1978 or '79 when I interviewed them for the *Review*. There was a well established alternative press in Manchester in the 1970s – going back to *Grass Eye* and *Mole Express*. The latter was still going in 1977, and the guy who ran it, Mike Don, had a room in the same building as *New Manchester Review*. He was much more of an anarchist than the *Review* editors, who were university graduates

and actually worked on newspapers in the evening. So the *Review*, although it was an alternative fortnightly with left-wing attitudes, aspired to professional journalistic standards and presentation. But it was important in reporting anti-Nazi events, like the time the National Front staged demonstrations in Belle Vue.

Then, after the *Review* went bust in 1980, Andy Zero of *City Fun* rang me to ask if I'd like to join them. We had a meeting at MARC where we all sat in a circle – Andy Zero, Martin X, Liz Naylor, Cath Carroll, Jon Savage, a guy called Neil, and I think Dick Witts as well. Some of us wanted the zine to be better written and better looking. Others like Andy wanted never to lose the punk spontaneity and anger. Anyway, that tension between the two points of view actually spurred us on and gave *City Fun* its edge for the next couple of years.

City Fun also promoted bands to raise much-needed funds. They put on big events at the Polytechnic Student Union and at the Mayflower. We were big mates with Richard Boon still and at this time he was promoting the Beach Club. Liz and Cath had a band, the Glass Animals, who I remember played behind a large white sheet pegged to a sort of washing line. Zero had a band called the Cabbalah. Dick Witts was of course in the Passage. Everyone's favourite band at this time was probably the Spurtz. Their lead singer Corky was a frequent visitor to our shared house.

LIZ NAYLOR

Andy Zero said 'It's got to be punk' and we were against that – ideologically punk meant less to us because we were younger. There were many late nights trying to get *City Fun* done and we were always short of money unless we arranged a benefit gig. After the Fall gig at the Poly, we had loads of money – pound notes being pushed into carrier bags! We had a horrible office with the Fall rehearsal room above us. Cath Carroll declared it to be haunted and it put everyone off! Our office was disgustingly filthy. Despite that, *City Fun* would sell 1500 a month and it did come out once a month. Over a period of time it created a consensus of opinion in Manchester.

Manchester felt very grim, it felt very threatening, the things had that had an impact on me were James Anderton and feeling really frightened because of him.* It felt like *Manchester Slingback*, Nic Blincoe's novel, which captured that period quite well. I used to hang round the Thompson Arms

---

*James Anderton was the controversial, authoritarian Chief Constable of Greater Manchester from 1975 to 1991. A full time Christian, he was nicknamed 'God's Cop'.

a lot. We had no money, we were feeling poor, lots of people were really poor. I didn't know how I could survive at the time. I remember Thatcher getting in for the second time and thinking, we're fucked. It felt like they were coming after us and Anderton felt part of that.

Punk did allow people who were quite isolated and cut off to make a meaningful connection. When *City Fun* initially published something by me it was amazing. I can barely read it now, it was about being 15 and depressed – like early emo!

GINA SOBERS

At a Mekons gig at Band on the Wall, me and some schoolmates were invited onstage to give our rendition of 'Oh Bondage, Up Yours!', an X-Ray Spex song. We loved Poly Styrene but that didn't stop us from murdering the song. Anyhow it was a beginning.

Later we did cover versions of 'The Passenger', 'Gloria', 'I'll Be There'. All classic songs. But as the Mekons were way older than us and a bit hippy, we wanted to get a younger crew to back us. And so we enlisted the help of Andy Zero, then writing for *City Life* fanzine. He became our drummer with a group of his mates on guitars and bass. As we didn't own any instruments ourselves except wooden recorders we'd played at school, it seemed the easiest option. They all could play but their style was too pub rock for our tastes. We decided to tough it out and stay with them for a while, not having any other choice. So we wrote the lyrics and sang as an all-girl threesome while they guitar-thrashed behind us.

MIKE PICKERING

Me and Martin Fry started a fanzine called *Modern Drugs*. There was only ever about three copies – I've still got them, it was a pretty good magazine. Martin had gone to Sheffield University to study English and I had reviewed Joy Division for the fanzine. It was the first review that they had ever had and Rob Gretton came up and said thanks.

I DJed with Rob a little bit. He showed me the ropes. I didn't want to take too many tips off him; people would ask for the Sex Pistols and it wasn't thought cool to play the Pistols by then, post-Grundy, so he would say, 'I told you I'm not fucking playing them!' and the needle would go everywhere. He used to play a mixture of punk and rockabilly tunes like 'This Girl is Red Hot', which was a really big tune. I was playing Dennis Brown, Dennis Bovell and Sugar Minott. In 1977 reggae was big – there was this mixed-race punk, the only one in town, called Paul who was cool as fuck. He would wear amazing gear he made himself, with green satin boxing shorts, a ripped leather jacket and hair different colours in his afro. He looked brilliant. He was a real major face at the time and he was getting a lot of the reggae to us.

THE NORTH WILL RISE AGAIN ... THE FALL

Another key band was operating in the city. The Fall had emerged in early 1977. They started as a band but were gradually becoming the vehicle for the poetic, pointed anger of frontman Mark E. Smith, whose withering commentary made the band as fascinating as their askew, awkward but ultimately and weirdly neo-pop music.

STEVE HANLEY
I saw the Fall play at Rafters with Magazine.* Me, Marc Riley and Craig Scanlon already had a band together. We were still into Genesis and Bowie as well as new bands. The band was called the Sirens – the singer would end up in the Fast Cars. We supported Joy Division at the famous Bowden Vale youth centre and we played Eric's, we played the Russell Club all the time and supported the Fall . . .

We talked to them at the gig and got to know them from rehearsing at TJM's. They got free rehearsals there because the owners had used the Fall's name in an advert. We got to know them and ended up roadying for them. They were really together in them days.

It's really funny – I had never met people like the Fall. They were kind of totally different from us, they had a kind of north Manchester thing going on. They were into everything, they would sit around talking about music for hours.

RICHARD WITTS
I got to know the Fall and they asked me to be their manager. I said, 'I'm not that sort of person but I will help you with your early gigs,' and I did – until a gig at UMIST. I was backstage with Mark [Smith] and he introduced Kay, his girlfriend, to me as his new manager. I said, 'I didn't know I was the old manager!' That was when Tony Friel saw what was going on. Tony had created the Fall and Mark was taking it over. In the early days when they started, it wasn't decided who would play what. I think Tony had a bass already so it would have made sense to make him the bass player, Mark wasn't meant to be the singer at first. Tony Friel was nicknamed Jaco Pastorius† and just from that you get an idea of the diverse influences that came together in the Fall.

* 28 October 1977.
† One of the most respected bassists of all time, the late Jaco Pastorius gave Weather Report a whole new dimension with his distinctive jazz-funk fusion style.

Tony decided he had to leave and he would rather withdraw than confront Mark about it. He asked me if I would be interested in setting up a group and that became the Passage.

STEVE HANLEY

Tony Friel had formed the Fall; at first Mark wasn't going to be the singer, he was going to be the guitarist.

RICHARD WITTS

With the Passage we were interested in taking existing structures of songs – like the verse and chorus – and yet somehow critiquing them. We were also reacting against the punk Luddism that went on, without interest in technology and the progressive side to post-punk.

STEVE HANLEY

I was only 16 when I was kind of drawn into the Fall.

Marc Riley joined them on bass – we were still learning our instruments at this time. I had only picked up the bass the year before I joined. Marc was a bit ahead of me. He joined on bass, me and Craig carried on roadying for them – we travelled all over before we joined. 'Chock Stock' off the second album – that was a song of mine which Mark rewrote the words for.

Martin Bramah left. I think the Fall had started off as an equal band and gradually Mark and Kay took over, and people didn't like it – basically that was the problem. Martin Bramah was great, but now he had gone, which meant that I got to join on bass and Marc Riley moved over to guitar.

MICK MIDDLES

I saw the second Fall gig. Martin Bramah seemed to be leader of the band at that point. The Fall took you away from that central Manchester scene – they would play the Trades Club in Chorley. To some extent the Fall were like hippies in a good way: they would sit around and read Camus and smoke – that's what you did with the Fall.

STEVE HANLEY

One rehearsal and off we go to Scotland and suddenly I'm in the Fall!

There was a kind of unwritten rule about lots of things that were frowned upon, like acting like you're any kind of rock star, acting like other bands.

Joining the Fall was like a natural thing because we travelled round for a year with them, we knew what they were like. We were working all the time. Every ten minutes we were in the studio! We did the 'Rowche Rumble' single and then the *Dragnet* album really quick.

Because of all the shit that's been spoken about the Fall, people forget how good we were in the late seventies and early eighties. We would really push it. God knows how some audiences put up with it: 15-minute-long songs with one riff, the sets were two hours long! There was no pandering to the crowd; people got what they were given.

I always thought the best way to write was that one person has an idea and comes in with it and everybody else works on it. I would have bit of a bass line or Craig would have a finished song, or Marc and Craig would work together on songs. I gradually started writing: the first song I got credited for was 'Fiery Jack', then 'Container Drivers' and then 'Hip Priest', which were all written on bass with other people putting bits in.

Mark Smith sometimes had a tune on guitar, like 'No Xmas for John Quays'. He could do enough to get across the idea; he would rarely turn tunes down. What happened was that you would arrange a songwriting session and most people would turn up with two or three – it was always a battle to get tunes in. There's a magic moment when you know it's working. You don't have to say owt; you look at each other and you know it's working.

Mark's lyrics were absolutely fantastic. He was full of words and really good stories and great ideas – that takes some doing. If there was three or four of us writing music he's got to write the words for everything.

He was a really hard worker in them days. The drinking is an occupational hazard – you turn up at work and there's a fridge full of whatever to drink.

Our relationship with other bands in Manchester wasn't great. We didn't mix with a lot of bands. We knew them, we would run into Joy Division and New Order, [but] we weren't really mates with lots of them, there was a bit of rivalry between the bands in general. Conversely the Fall were a bands' band – that's why we didn't get anywhere! Musicians don't buy records, which is funny because we weren't the best musicians in the world.

I hated all the influx of musicians. I wanted to be in a band like the Clash with people you know and get on with – the perfect line-up was me, Craig, Marc Riley and our kid on drums. It was my brother and my two best mates from school – that was amazing, people you knew and got on with. I hate all that people coming and going shite.

People would leave all the time. Marc Riley wasn't getting on with Mark, there was a lot of friction and he left. I was happy to stand at the back and play the bass. Mark Smith could be difficult to work with, but you could see the point of what he was saying. Later on he'd cause trouble for nothing but at the time he knew what he wanted and he knew how to get it.

Musicians found it hard to deal with Mark. Sometimes I found it hard to deal with him! I got fed up with playing three notes on every song!

When it was in danger of turning into another band he always pulls it back again. He's a control freak but the band is his life. It's absolutely his life – every partner of his has been in the band. The Fall is like Mark's diary; fair enough, but I think I put as much into it as he did. I put everything into it. I did everything apart from sing. I used to do the tour manager bit, sort out the rehearsals and everything else. People think it's all Mark, but there's more to being in a band than doing the interviews.

Having made their name as caustic commentators with a series of uncompromising bass-driven albums, the Fall's innate genius was underlined when the band suddenly became a neo-pop group in the mid-eighties.

STEVE HANLEY

You have to give credit to Brix* for trying to get the Fall a hit. A couple of those songs, though, were already written. We already had 'C.R.E.E.P.' and 'Oh Brother'; she kind of persuaded Mark into that kind of stuff. He had had enough by then and went with it because you can only struggle for so long. We were always big in the midweek charts: we would get a single like 'There's a Ghost In My House' in the midweek charts at number two and then end up at number 40. We gave it our best shot, but I suppose Mark's voice doesn't translate to the mainstream. Although we sold out Hammersmith Odeon, which for me was a life's ambition.

Then when it started unravelling in the late eighties, Brix left. To be fair, Martin Bramah came back and things were good for a while. *Extricate* was a good album.

Eventually I'd had enough. It's well documented that it was going bad. I'm not saying I'm totally blameless. We were all acting like arseholes on

---

* Brix Smith was married to Mark E. Smith from 1983 to 1989, appearing on the band's albums between *Perverted by Language* (1983) and *Seminal Live* (1989), and later rejoining the group for *Cerebral Caustic* (1995) and *The Light User Syndrome* (1996). Her time in the Fall saw the introduction of a more mainstream, pop-orientated element to the group's sound.

that last tour. Somebody said on the internet that it looked and sounded like four guys sick of the sight of each other and there was probably something in that. There was loads of financial problems, financial pressures. I still think it could have been a great band. I'm sure Mark hated my miserable face by then. It ended up with the famous onstage fight in New York in April 1998 and I left.

I can't listen to the Fall now. I saw Tommy, the old Fall guitarist, in Scotland. He had a CD of one of my last gigs at Sankey's Soap in Manchester. I couldn't listen to it. We were full on, there was no subtlety about the gig. It was really poor. There was no space in the music.

'MOVING AWAY FROM THE PULSEBEAT'
The Buzzcocks and Magazine, still living the Real Life

The Buzzcocks were now in their prime. Effortlessly releasing classic singles every couple of months, they were reinventing the love song as a bittersweet vignette with the sharpest and smartest wall-of-sound guitars in punk. Meanwhile Howard Devoto was creating his own vision with Magazine – it was two groups for the price of one. At the same time the third key player in the glorious triumvirate, Richard Boon, manager of the Buzzcocks, was running the New Hormones label that had started with the Spiral Scratch *EP. New Hormones was not just a label, it was a catalyst.*

RICHARD BOON
We had the label New Hormones because we had put the Buzzcocks single out, and we decided to get an office on Newton Street. The office had a beaten-up couch where people – wayward drifters – would hang out with Peter, and his mates and odd people would drop in. It was a mutual space: people would arrive and we made connections. We got to know the Yorkshire lot – Gang of Four, the Mekons and Cabaret Voltaire from Sheffield were constantly around. We wanted to put people and ideas together.

JON SAVAGE
I remember seeing the Buzzcocks at the time playing the Marquee. They had 'Moving Away from the Pulsebeat' in the set, which was fantastic. It was so psychedelic and almost dancey – prefiguring the Stone Roses or trance. In the middle of 'Pulsebeat', Shelley would stop playing while the others would carry on and do what they were doing and he would hand out badges to the fans at the front, which I thought was really sweet and not macho at all. He was very approachable and clever and quite funny, as well as being quite mischievous.

I still think they vie with the Clash for being the second most important British punk group. I had a lot of time for Joe Strummer, but in some ways they were quite traditional. That's why they're so popular now, whereas the Buzzcocks were doing something quite modern.

RICHARD BOON
People started getting in touch. A group from Newcastle called Penetration* called and I said, 'You put us on in concert in Newcastle and we'll put you on in Manchester.' It was grassroots networking.

PAULINE MURRAY (Penetration vocalist)
We always felt a strong affinity with the scene in Manchester. Buzzcocks, Joy Division, the Fall, we would go to Manchester to play a lot at the time.

RICHARD BOON
We wanted to work with people who had sympathetic ideas. There were these pockets of enthusiasts around who you had something in common with.

In Manchester what was desperately important to us was that there was a regular venue. That's where the Russell Club/PSV in Hulme came in. It was a regular gig every weekend which was bringing in people from other places, like the Liverpool bands or Crass. Tony Wilson started putting on the Factory nights there and Alan Wise was starting his nights at Rafters. The Musicians' Collective had started at the Band on the Wall and from suddenly no bands there were a lot of bands of varying quality. Joy Division weren't that good early on but improved tremendously, but we loved the Fall and we still love the Fall – Mark Smith was really compelling, Martin Bramah was a good guitarist and that early garage sound with Una Baines on keyboard was fantastic. The Worst were just that, in the best possible way – they were the real deal, they would get on stage and do it. We took them to the Roundhouse in London as support and they mystified the audience. They were sadly never recorded.

PETE SHELLEY
I thought, well, there's another way you can write love songs. Being bisexual seemed to me the logical description for my sexuality. When David Bowie came out in the seventies, that seemed to say that's who I am. The problem with saying you were gay was that your girlfriend used to get very confused. But the sexuality only happens with the person,

---

* One of the great forward-thinking punk bands. 'Don't Dictate' is a punk rock classic.

rather than the gender. So if you have the right person, something may happen. Or it may not.

LINDER

The Buzzcocks had such a humour and emotional influence; they weren't like the Clash. The Buzzcocks were more sexual, they had that sexual ambiguity and flexibility.

PETE SHELLEY

It was good for us being in Manchester because we weren't tainted by the rush to sign. And once record companies thought, We will buy into this music, they decided to sign up anyone they could. London was more media-orientated. In Manchester no one used to bother us, only journalists – we had Paul Morley writing in the *NME* and Tony Wilson off the telly. That made it less competitive, there was less to fight over.

RICHARD BOON

New Hormones were putting out other records out, like Ludus, who were definitely post-punk – especially early on.* They were wailing over an improvised bass, guitar and drums, then they got a bit melodic. I also loved God's Gift: noise from Prestwich . . .

Factory, when they started their label, were definitely much more an art project. They had an agenda – it was probably more clearly defined. They wouldn't have done it, though, without people stumbling through doors and opening them for them.

LINDER

When I formed Ludus I was interested in 1977 punk rock collage vocal style and lyrics – then we put 20 tempo changes in a twenty-minute song. It was about being unattractive, disappointing and not fulfilling expectations. It's a quite difficult thing to do and I found that people in Europe understood what I was trying to do more when I toured over there; they had a fundamental comprehension of it.

MORRISSEY

Linder and I always remained friends. She had several degrees, but was troubled and constrained and hammered back by, well, the British way of life. When she made that first Ludus EP with Peter Hammill, I loved it so much. They later toured as support to Buzzcocks on, I think, the *Love*

---

* Two years after the release of *Spiral Scratch*, the label returned with 25 releases from the likes of Linder, Eric Random, Dislocation Dance and God's Gift

Bites tour, which was Hammersmith Odeon-type venues, and I thought it was just a matter of time before Ludus broke. They were reviewed ferociously though, at a time when everyone was being let through willy-nilly. As a consequence of the bad reviews they kept losing their rhythm section . . . who would lose heart. Their strongest line-up was right at the end when Dave Formula joined. *But.*

RICHARD BOON

The next New Hormones thing was Jon Savage and Linder's montage, *Secret Public*, which was different. There were lots of fanzines that were the same. An awful lot of them were people typing trivia about bands. *Secret Public* put more noise in the system, it said you can do something else – do a visual thing. The idea of New Hormones was to do something and see where you land.

LINDER

Later on I made the *Secret Public* magazine with Jon Savage and it was published by New Hormones. The printers wouldn't give us any kind of receipt because it was seen to be pornographic; interestingly, left-wing bookshops like Grass Roots wouldn't stock it either. Even trying to get the photomontages photocopied in Manchester was almost impossible.

Montage was a beautifully simple, impersonal method of making art. Very democratic. My work showed quite intimate, claustrophobic domestic worlds, at odds with Jamie Reid's use of monarchical iconography, but still dovetailing neatly with punk's rhetoric of shock and disruption.

I was mainly anti-porn. I suppose it's like that horrible phrase nowadays: raising the debate. If you're working with images and it's normally quite covert or hidden away, then at least people start talking about them

The late seventies were pre-style press, so the images of food, washing machines or record players came from mail-order catalogues and mainstream women's magazines such as *Woman's Own*. In the British pornography I used – *Fiesta, Men Only* – the bodies weren't toned or airbrushed and pubic hair wasn't shaved, so there's a real physicality to them. Now we're fairly at ease with that kind of imagery, but back then women wouldn't have been expected to know about porn, let alone look at it or make work with it.

I was trying to decode pornography. Pornography is sexual shorthand: availability, arousal, gestures – very formulaic. I was really interesting in drawing those bland photographic images.

JON SAVAGE

I had already done a montage for the second issue of my fanzine *London's Outrage*.* I went to Cambridge and I studied classics. I had no art education at all. I always thought the thing about punk was the total expression of 'do it'. If you got an idea in your head then do it. It doesn't matter what it is, do it, whether it's cross-discipline or interdiscipline – just get on and do it!

LINDER

There's a shared kind of philosophy in punk and collage – the images that came to us through cinema and music.

The Buzzcocks were now established as one of the great British singles bands, effortlessly releasing a classic pop rush every couple of months. Each single combined pure melody with an innovative take on the buzzsaw guitar style that they had invented.

STEVE DIGGLE

Joe Strummer said we were a bunch of nerds from Manchester but he liked us soon after. I remember Strummer at the Pistols gig in Manchester. We went to the Grand Hotel with the Pistols and all the papers were after them.

We always went to Tommy Duck's[†] and he really liked it. He would always say, 'I like that pub with all the knickers!'

It was a different scene down there – the London bands were all dressed up and had designer gear on. My brother Phil made some shirts for us. He would rip a corner of them and paint a Co-op stamp on them and draw all over them – things like factory chimneys, stuff like that.

We had no flash stuff; we thought it was cool to buy a shirt from Oxfam and draw on it. Some people say that we weren't really punks, but I would say we were because we would make our own clothes.

When we signed, we got Martin Rushent the producer as part of the package. He was kind of the in-house producer; he had done the Stranglers and was really good and we were happy with that.

The chemistry of the band and Rushent was perfect. It was easy to do because we were tight as a band. A lot of people say our first album is the best produced of all the punk albums. It wasn't polished but it was the

* Jon Savage's punk era fanzine, its title taken from a flyer for a Sex Pistols gig at the Notre Dame Hall.
† Mancunian public house knocked down by redevelopers, famous for the girls' knickers hanging from the ceiling.

right production. We had the HH combo amps we bought from A1.* They said, 'Why don't you have Marshalls?' but we were happy with the HH's. We were in Olympic Studios, where Jean-Luc Godard had filmed the Stones. We were in the middle of this huge room with these two tacky HH amps, but it sounded good.

HOWARD DEVOTO

The next movement along that came along after punk was given a name – power pop. I think the Buzzcocks got that term applied to them; the Rich Kids got called that. Me leaving the Buzzcocks was very liberating for Pete: he could write much more like that – he's got that fantastic facility with melody.

STEVE DIGGLE

After the first album we kept moving on. With the single 'Everybody's Happy Nowadays', Pete was playing chords. I couldn't hear what he was playing but I put that riff to it and it worked, it makes the song. Things were very natural with the way our two styles fitted together, though we were very different people. Pete did the love songs, but I was more interested in writing about social things like Ray Davies did. I wouldn't have hung around with Pete if we'd been at school together but we are similar in some ways. We've sat in a lot of pubs together over the years – one thing Pete Shelley can do is drink!

We released the next album, *Love Bites*. We kept on moving, trying different things which were usually the B-sides of the singles.† And then on the third album, *A Different Kind of Tension*, we decided to really stretch what we were doing. We went into darker areas. We had been touring a lot and we were getting crazy. There had been a lot of partying going on. We were all cracking up at that period! It gets hard to hold it together.‡

EMI had taken over our label and we didn't know who we were meant to deal with any more. No one seemed to be interested in us and we were

---

* A long-established Manchester music shop, now called Academy Of Sound.

† Buzzcocks B-sides were genius as well. Twisting the formula into many shapes without losing the core sound, they celebrated the era when great bands used single B-sides as an opportunity to stretch out. The Buzzcocks never got messy though; the experimentation was always done within a tight, taut framework.

‡ *A Different Kind of Tension*, released in 1979, lived up to its title: a mixture of the classic pop songs that Pete Shelley seems to be able to write at will and Steve Diggle's barking minor-chord punk anthems.

drifting. We recorded six more songs and decided to release them as singles. They were great songs and we released them quickly but they didn't chart. 'Why She's a Girl from the Chainstore'* was about a sociological question of how she got there, it wasn't putting her down. After those singles came out we went back to Pluto Studios.† There were dark clouds hanging over, different tensions. Pete went away with Martin Rushent to sort out his songs and make demos for the album, but when he was there using Rushent's new electronic recording equipment he recorded 'Homosapien' and he sent a letter saying, 'I've finished with the group', leaving me as the only one who has never left this group.

Buzzcocks would reform a decade later and still tour every year.

'THEY WERE THE MILL OWNERS!': FACTORY RECORDS

Factory Records was the key record label in Manchester. Its reputation was built on the major success of Joy Division/New Order and the Happy Mondays, but there were also a whole host of smaller bands making great or bizarre records in its two key phases. Phase one was the Joy Division period, when the label provided the soundtrack to the dying days of post-industrial Manchester; phase two was the Happy Mondays era, when the label was bang in the centre of party-time Manchester, losing money hand over fist through the Hacienda.

Not everyone loved the label – some groups deliberately set out to sign to labels other than Factory and many felt edged out by its suffocating media-powered hipness. But Factory was a brilliant vision; it nearly pulled off the trick of creating a major northern-based music label, until the real world caught up – the bills just got too high.

TONY WILSON

I think Factory in general and myself is a great example of [how] being right and being early doesn't make you rich . . . being late and clever makes you rich.

I didn't stay in Manchester because I'm altruistic; I love my town. I should have gone to London for TV work but my real career is music . . . and I always say: why would a farmer move to worse pastures? So I stay here selfishly.

I'm great at spotting bands but terrible for spotting singles.

---

* In fact, 'Why She's a Girl from the Chainstore' was the only one of the band's last three singles that did chart, although it failed to reach the top 40.
† Long-lost Manchester studio in Granby Row where the Clash famously recorded 'Bank Robber', watched by a very young Ian Brown.

JON SAVAGE

Tony was great in that he was a catalyst in the Factory dynamic; Alan [Erasmus] was the muscle and the bagman whilst Rob [Gretton] was the heart and soul of it. Rob was the one who knew about music and Tony was the intellectual and the PR.

RICHARD WITTS

The Factory story is a story of glorious failure. In many ways New Hormones was the business model – the way it supported bands like Ludus, Dislocation Dance and also ran a club.

LIZ NAYLOR

They seemed to be really capable people and really successful. Tony had been to Cambridge and I was intimidated by that. The Fall were more like people like me – Kay I liked a lot, and Mark – even though he can be a pain in the arse! Factory felt like the mill owners, they owned the city! We were merely the workers.

Manchester was a tiny place, it got bitchy and *City Fun* was very much part of that. We were the constant splinter in Factory's finger, we were there to annoy. Tony Wilson got weird about it all whilst Rob Gretton was mildly amused by it. He was dead funny and he liked the idea that we were there to take the piss out of Factory . . .

TONY WILSON

Everyone thinks that punk was all about some anti-capitalist response to the majors, but it wasn't at all. Malcolm signed the Pistols to anyone, the Clash's first single came out on CBS, and Buzzcocks signed to United Artists the night I saw them at Electric Circus, which was the same night Elvis Presley died. It was all major label stuff until this wonderful distribution network called Rough Trade started, and also Pinnacle, who used to supply Dustbugs. Independent labels at the time were to get your band signed to a major label. I remember interviewing Tosh Ryan from Rabid Records during the *What's On* days and saying to him, 'Why did you sell Jilted John to EMI and John Cooper Clarke to CBS?' He said, 'Don't be such a twat, living in this mythical past, that's what independence is all about, getting your act signed to a major.'

Alan and I were doing what we thought was the right thing and trying to get Durutti Column signed. We managed to get Orchestral Manoeuvres in the Dark signed to Virgin after a bidding war. I did two or three trips to London with Rob Gretton to talk to Andrew Lauder, who was the leading person, to sign Joy Division to Warner Brothers. Then one night at Band on the Wall in Manchester, Rob says to me, 'Er, why don't we do the first Joy Division album and then go to Warners?' I said, 'Are you sure? How much will it cost?' He said Martin Hannett had told him about eight grand, which was a complete lie. I didn't jump on it because it was a complete surprise, but looking back on it that was the dawn of the British independent movement – all from Rob thinking, well the first single Tony spent £5000, we got £5300 back after paying all the costs and we all made £100. If we made an album we would make real money, which would mean, and I quote Rob here, 'I wouldn't have to go to London every week and talk to cunts.'

Also, being Rob, he then said, 'Here's the deal I suggest: 50-50, and you pay publishing out of your per cent.' And that deal, done that day, is the most generous ever for a band, because I didn't want to make money, and it applied to every Factory act ever, most particularly Joy Division and New Order.

JON SAVAGE
Tony was very good at picking up people and giving them an arena to exercise their talent. He was a true impresario. I give endless respect to him for that. In the early days he had a pretty good sense of what was going on; he lost that later when he thought he was a businessman. He took the 'Great rock'n'roll swindle' too seriously and he was becoming the father of Mancunian business. It was the same mistake Malcolm McLaren made – they are just not businessmen, they're arty-farty.

TONY WILSON
It was never conceptualised. It was pure accident the way that Factory worked. There is a wonderful quote from Sam Phillips about allowing musicians the space to expect the freedom to find what they want to do. I was happy to let musicians do what they want.

LARRY CASSIDY (Section 25 bassist/vocalist)
The kudos of Factory was good but it was difficult to get paid.

TONY ASHWORTH (drummer, Tunnelvision)
When Tunnelvision signed to Factory it was a bit surreal, to be honest. A load of young kids being approached by Tony Wilson at Scamps to do a record. It was a Hurrah! moment . . . but we didn't know quite what we were hurrahing!

LINDER

I was asked to do the artwork for Factory. I said, 'I've got another friend who can do it for you,' because I didn't want to make sleeves. I told them about Peter Saville. I was quite good at match-making!

PETER SAVILLE

We had a fresh agenda of just how we wanted it to be. One of the unique things about Factory was that never in any shape or form till the end was it answerable to any establishment organisation – not EMI or NatWest Bank; we didn't answer to anybody. Everybody within it was able to use it to do things the way they would like to be done for themselves. The bands were able to make music in a way they thought it should be and it was the same with the artwork.

Rob Gretton managed Joy Division the way he thought he should manage a band. Martin Hannett produced records the way he thought they should be produced and I stepped into that situation to design covers the way I thought they should be. And Tony Wilson went about being a cultural impresario the way he felt like it should be done – no one told him 'You can't do it that way.'

JONATHAN HURST (sound engineer)

Martin [Hannett] was an industrial chemist and a very clever guy. From working with him at Brit[annia] Row where he was recording Joy Division to Strawberry in Stockport and the Stone Roses he was a brilliant producer. He loved a technical challenge like New Order in quadraphonic at Heaven nightclub.

Martin was a brilliant mentor, but he wasn't clever enough to stay alive.

Factory had started as a business partnership between Tony Wilson and Alan Erasmus, promoting gigs at the Russell Club in Hulme under the name of the Factory Club and putting on bands like the Durutti Column, who the pair of them managed along with Cabaret Voltaire and Joy Division.

Peter Saville was brought in to design the posters and that September, 1978, the three of them decided to release an EP of music by acts who had played at the club – Joy Division, Durutti Column and Cabaret Voltaire, along with comedian John Dowie. Tony wanted to release the EP as Fac 1 but Peter Saville explained that the poster he designed for the club was Fac 1. And so the adventure began.

A few months later Martin Hannett joined as director and in-house producer – a brilliant move, as Hannett was to prove over and over with the distinctive production and singular sonic vision which gave Factory its sound. Months later Rob Gretton joined the label, which now set out on its own course – a mixture of dry northern humour, great records and Situationist pranking.

Other early releases included A Certain Ratio, Orchestral Manoeuvres in the Dark and local reggae act X-O-Dus, but it wasn't until they 'signed' Joy Division that the label started to coalesce. Even the band's contract was 'interesting'.

TONY WILSON

We agreed the deal and a couple of weeks later Rob had his lawyer write it up and sent it to me. It's not like the film where I write the whole thing in blood, but as a joke I think I just signed AHW to this formal contract in blood. You just prick your finger and let it drip on to the page, then take a dry pen nib and write through it.

The central feature of the contract, which caused us disruption later, was the phrase: 'The musicians own everything, the company owns nothing, all our groups have the right to fuck off.' When Polygram and Roger Ames were buying us, it was going along very nicely until a meeting where someone said, 'But you have no contract.' I said that we had a kind of a contract and they looked at it and all the faces on the other side of the table dropped. Roger waved it at me and said, 'Tony, don't you understand, if you have no contract at least you own the catalogue because you paid for it to be recorded. That is, unless you have a piece of fucking paper that specifically says you own nothing.' Far from being the heroic moment portrayed in the movie, I just sort of went, 'Oh well.'

MIKE PICKERING

Rob, because of Joy Division, became a part of it. Hooky said he didn't like what Martin was doing at the time but he was very important – amazing production. I was Rob's boy *(laughs)*. I got the weed and I would drive his car, which he bought with the first cheque, but he couldn't drive. He bought an Audi Quattro – the first one in the country. We were good mates and that's how I came to be part of Factory – I would help mail the records out, everything.

The Factory story is not just about Joy Division. The label's real strength lay in its catalogue, a fascinating collection of maverick outfits. From the excellent brooding bass-driven post-punk soundscapes of Section 25 to the quirky dark neo-pop of Crispy Ambulance, from plaintive singer-songwriter Kevin Hewick to the post-punk funk of A Certain Ratio, every band on the label was breaking new ground.

MARTIN MOSCROP

A Certain Ratio formed as an alternative to being a punk band.

We signed to Factory early on, not long after I joined the band. Rob Gretton saw us play with Joy Division at the Manchester Musicians'

Collective and he told Tony Wilson about us. Tony Wilson put us on at the Factory to come and see us.

That contradiction in our sound between the darker sound and the funk was intentional in one way but quite unintentional in another. We were trying to be rhythmical and we were not trying to be weird – it just came out the other end like that. When we got Donald in on drums we tried to be funky, but we were white boys who couldn't play and Donald loved that. He always went on about how much he liked the guitars in A Certain Ratio.

The way him and Jez [Jeremy Kerr] play as a rhythm section is not like normal musicians but more like two sportsmen, the way they work out drum and bass lines together. The bass and bass drums flow with the same pattern, it gives it that added funkiness and depth at the bottom end. As people they sometimes clashed personality-wise, but if you can shut them up and get them to play the result is just brilliant.

GINA SOBERS

We eventually became good friends with the Ratios, especially Martin, and later he'd bring records around for us to listen to. He was already getting into a Latin vibe even then, which seemed at odds with the rest of Factory output – Doom and Gloom we called it. Though the first Joy Division album produced on the label by Martin Hannett left me breathless – such a different sound from their earlier live stuff, which had been a cacophony.

JOHNNY MARR

One of the people we really admired was a bit of a face round town and that was Jez from ACR – basically he looked like James Woods in a post-punk Factory band. When we were going in clubs in town ACR were starting to be around quite a lot. They played the Ritz a couple of times. They had that new funk aesthetic that was coming into things and strangely you can hear that in the Smiths – it's in the bass playing and that started in the band me and Andy [Rourke] had before the Smiths that was called Freak Party or Freaky Party. It sounded a bit like what the Mondays would sound like. I was playing funky punk guitar, Andy was playing tight basslines and Si [Wolstonecroft] was being funky – everyone knows him as funky Si.

JON SAVAGE

I would go and see ACR rehearse in Stockport with Donald. I went to the Graveyard when they were recording 'Do the Du' and all that stuff with

Martin. The first time I met ACR they were foul and being absolutely rude with me – I just ignored it and then they were fine.

When Donald joined they got funky. The tracks I liked were where they retained the Velvet Underground drone of their early songs like 'Knife Slits Water', rather than the later 'Shack Up', which is good but not as good as the Banbarras' original version. ACR were OK when they were being funky. They then got very much into the slipstream of Joy Division, like Section 25 who were another great band. Joy Division were so big and stamped their sound on Factory that Section 25 and other bands got pulled into the slipstream.

MARTIN MOSCROP

Joy Division were ahead of the game and *Unknown Pleasures* took them beyond. Martin Hannett was stamping too much of his authority on us, making us sound too much like Joy Division – too gothic. Martin imposed the snare sound on us and it sounded like Joy Division. The comparisons continued with Simon Topping's voice, but he already sounded like that before we heard Joy Division. Simon and Ian Curtis were two Manchester lads listening to same sort of stuff and singing in the same sort of tone. It fitted in with Manchester at the time, when it was gloomy, derelict, poor and dirty . . .*

Looking back, I love what Martin did on the album now. When we did *Sextet* in 1982 and got rid of that gothic sound it was too jazz-funk for the press, yet when the album got re-released everyone said it was ahead of its time!

LARRY CASSIDY

I always found Martin really good fun to work with. He brought his wife and new baby to my and Jenny's new house in Poulton one Saturday afternoon. We played with the kids in the garden. It was like Martin was having a real family life for a change, taking a break from the reality of being a leading producer in Manchester. Martin was one of the friendliest people I've ever met in the music industry. He was a top producer with an intuitive passion to bring out the best in you. That he looked like a bit of a hippie didn't matter. He was well good at the desk and you knew he wanted what you wanted – well, I didn't know that, despite what others may say! Of course he was far advanced of me in studio use but he was always open-minded and instructive in the production. I loved his ideas and his input. He was also a good bass

* The resulting album, 1981's *To Each* (Factory), was a perfect synthesis of the dislocated Hannett sound, post-punk darkness and funkiness – creating a template that's still being copied to this day.

player. Martin disabused me of so many dopey ideas I had about music and recording music. Now he's a genius (*laughs*). He got criticised later for doing all the bands the same, particularly by ACR who were jazzy and not rock.

MARTIN MOSCROP

Pete and Jez lived in Epping Walk in Hulme, Simon was nearby and I was in Charles Barry Crescent, a five-minute walk from each other. Hulme was great, a brilliant place then. You didn't have to pay rent and there was a lot of like-minded people about, and it was good having a population of young student females to meet and shag (*laughs*). There was a good vibe there. There were a lot of different people listening to different music, which fed back a lot into A Certain Ratio.

John Lydon was responsible for the way people from the punk era got into reggae and got into soul and jazz and stuff. I also started listening to lot of black music and was being influenced by that sort of music living in Hulme, which was close to Moss Side, which was considered a black area – music started integrating a lot more.

We covered 'Shack Up' after Simon bought the seven-inch single at Tracks Records. They did cutouts and imports, a lot of American stuff. Simon picked it up and because we both played trumpet he played it to us and said 'Listen to how simple this is.' Within five minutes we had shocked ourselves how quickly we could play a funk tune.

We would always try to avoid becoming a cliché. As soon as someone liked something we did we would change it. We were anti-commercial and retained a bit of integrity by trying not to sell out and retain that punk ethic by not doing what you should do to get somewhere. We orchestrated that ourselves.

The famous suntan lotion story? (*laughs*) We asked Tony to get us fake suntan lotion as we were playing the Lyceum in London. We were wearing shorts and we needed it to make our legs browner. We had a sort of military look – it wasn't Germanic as people try to make out. We looked like British army guys in the desert. It was just a fashion thing, we maybe helped to make army fatigues the forefront of fashion! The army fatigue thing comes from reggae. A lot of the reggae guys were wearing army fatigues, which pooh-poohs the idea that people say we looked like German military – we were trying to look like Gregory Isaacs.

JON SAVAGE

I really liked Section 25. Their first album is great. 'Girls Don't Count' is great and I loved 'Key of Dreams' – that long 15-minute track that sounds like an improvisation from San Francisco in 1966; it's that good. Then of course Section 25 went on to do one of the great electro tracks, 'View from a Hilltop'. And there was Crispy Ambulance as well, who had done a great drone track with Martin.

LARRY CASSIDY

The Manchester music scene had always been a bit of a mystery to me, being based in Blackpool, but I saw the Buzzcocks and others at the Factory Club and Throbbing Gristle – that was a particularly good night out. Paul* spent most of the gig in a huge bass bin while Throbbing Gristle did their stuff. After that we decided to do a 'Blackpool night' at the Factory Club with four bands – Section 25, One Way System, Final Solution and Zyklon B. There were seven people there and my girlfriend, but it was good. The lack of audience never bothered us because we were used to it. As Rob Gretton used to say, 'It's the event that counts.' Rob said he thought we should record at Cargo† and put a record out on Factory. So we went to Cargo with Ian Curtis and Rob Gretton. None of us had been in a studio before so we were glad that they were there to help us. The main thing I remember was that it was about five in the afternoon and Ian had to go out and buy some mince meat for his family's tea. I was quite shocked that someone who I'd considered to be a major star was going out to buy mince meat for his tea for his wife and kid. So very ordinary.

We paid the bill ourselves and gave the tapes to Factory and for some reason they took a year to release it! Waiting for Peter [Saville] to do the sleeve, which turned out to be a really good piece of art.

BEN KELLY (designer)

Peter asked me to help with the single sleeve for Section 25's debut Factory release, 'Girls Don't Count'. I hadn't heard of them before. And because I'm a designer and what we do is close to architecture, I produced this abstract drawing with cut-out sections. This was before computers, so at the time we drew on tracing paper. I thought, 'Let's print it and make the sleeve out of tracing paper,' and of course Factory being Factory said, 'No problem.' And as I heard it, they had this elderly

---

* Paul Wiggan, Section 25 guitarist.
† Cargo Studios in Rochdale was arguably the most important studio of the post-punk era. All the main players, from Joy Division to the Gang of Four to the Fall, recorded there at some point.

retired woman sticking the sleeves together and this one won an award as well. I thought: well, this is fantastic! This is easy!

LARRY CASSIDY

We went to Palatine Road* to glue the sleeves and there were hundreds of them. Then it got into Rough Trade Records and they put it on their wall with the Gang of Four. I was proud.

KEVIN HEWICK (singer-songwriter)

With nearly three decades' hindsight, it's amazing how Factory ever got past the starting block of being an idea. Luck, cheek, blissful ignorance and magic all played their part in how Factory became such an influential label.

However, I wasn't to be bracketed as being there at the sharp end, the influential spearhead of Factory. I was part of the miss end of its hit and miss.

Factory saw [there was] something in me – and they were correct, there was. But between my artistic stylistic miscalculations and their brilliant incompetence, Kevin Hewick was a doomed enterprise.

But I should get credit for having the guts to be what I was; I was facing often hostile-from-the-start post-punk audiences with just a voice and an electric guitar, way before Billy Bragg did it with far greater success. Other than me I can only think of Patrik Fitzgerald and Attila the Stockbroker as any kind of solo act at all on that circuit in that era.

What I did was far more fragile. I saw three black bin bags full of hundreds of cassettes in Alan Erasmus's Palatine Road flat, so how mine got picked out I'll never know, though I did get my order in early so to speak, in 1979 – it had been sent to them simply because I'd been turned down elsewhere. Even the champion of alternative music John Peel didn't warm to me, then or ever as it turned out.

Factory's organisation was always informal-meets-irrational – a phone call the day before for a gig halfway across the country, a wonderful idea that *had* to be discussed urgently and then was never heard of again. For every Tony Wilson idea that took off, there were dozens that didn't.

I was dazzled by all sorts of promises and notions and spent much of 1980 convinced I was going to be a major artist of the forthcoming decade.

When Tony loved you he loved you, you were his artist, you were special and the best and the greatest. But you were also a novelty. I soon gave way to Stockholm Monsters and they to whoever [came] next.

* Factory Records' HQ was in Alan Erasmus' flat on Palatine Road, West Didsbury.

JON SAVAGE
Me and Tony were really close for a couple of years but he could be careless with people. We got on because there were very few people who had been to Cambridge who liked pop culture.

LARRY CASSIDY
Vini Reilly was quite well established. The Stockholm Monsters were monsters; the guy out of Blurt was dead good.*

BEN KELLY
It all started with meeting Mr Saville. Peter had moved to London and was working for the record company Dindisc on the Orchestral Manoeuvres in the Dark cover. I met Peter in a bar called the Zanzibar – a private members' drinking club. He explained that he was doing this album cover and he knew I'd done Howie in Covent Garden, which was one of the first fashion shops there after it stopped being a fruit and veg market.

Peter talked to me about the OMD sleeve. He was struggling with it. He wanted a sleeve with the least amount of cardboard possible and as soon as he said that I knew what it should it be. I said 'If you look at the door to the Howie ship, it's got perforated steel panels. I think it would be a perfect sleeve – re-engage with the process of how to make a record.' I showed him the catalogue from a company that did these perforations with several different shapes and sizes, and said it should be this perforation. The OMD sleeve became the perforated sleeve – the outside was turquoise and blue and the inside was bright orange. It was a real zinging combination . . . We put an industrial sticker on and to my amazement it won a big award!

NOEL GALLAGHER
For me, getting from the Beatles to Factory Records was by learning Joy Division bass lines on my guitar because they were so simple. There was this Factory Records thing going on. You've got to remember I'm really young at this point . . . and somehow this guy from *Granada Reports* is involved, he's from Manchester and he had the Sex Pistols on his TV programme, and suddenly it all starts to make sense. This guy was running a record label and he's a TV presenter, bit of an artist and a bit of a Malcolm McLaren, Alan McGee-type thing where he's behind the scenes but he knows everything about Manchester. I started to pick up on that and buying stuff on Factory Records.

* Ted Milton still is Blurt, playing his frenetic jazz punk.

TIM BURGESS (Charlatans vocalist)

Crispy Ambulance's 'Death From Above' is a classic. I remember in hindsight everyone always says the band sounded like New Order/Joy Division, but I don't think they do really.

ALAN HEMPSALL (Crispy Ambulance vocalist)

We were Rob's band really, he signed us. We could tell that Tony never liked us really! Being on Factory meant you got tarred with being Joy Division copyists, which wasn't always fair.

TIM BURGESS

Same with Section 25 – their bass and otherworldliness are similar, but they are really not like New Order. You forget the scenes that crop up all over Britain and everyone is doing the same thing at the same time. I saw A Certain Ratio and I saw Durutti Column and they were great. When I met Vini Reilly years later, I was starstruck.

LARRY CASSIDY

Our sound wasn't 'created' as such. It developed. We got into doing 'disco punk' at the time as Public Image, for which we were pilloried in the NME – unfairly I thought. Fucking reporters!* Our music may have sounded dark, but it wasn't dark at all. I got fed up with the press labelling us as 'doom laden'. I was quite happy at the time, with a wife and a new baby, just singing about stuff that caught my imagination. I'd been to art college and got a first-class degree in sculpture, and turned to music through punk rock. I came back to Blackpool and hooked up with Vin,† and tried guitar players and settled on Paul and started doing it.

I'm not even sure what 'post-punk' is. As far as I'm concerned my attitude was the same as usual – do it yourself and no 'star syndrome'.

TONY WILSON

Factory and Rob and all its members were always obsessed with the black music scene in Manchester – as we all know, black music is the heart of rock'n'roll. But all Manchester black acts fuck up . . . I can remember as a journalist I ended up making a film about this, asking why it's not happening. I can remember interviewing the bass player from X-O-Dus . . . his explanation was that 'we all fall out'. A year later, Factory put out their record 'English Black Boys' and they then broke up – typical!

---

* Section 25 always suffered at the hands of the media, seen as late arrivals when in fact they had been pioneers. Just because they were doing it in Blackpool and not in London shouldn't negate their originality.

† Larry's younger brother Vin was the band's drummer.

We signed 52nd Street and they argued with each other and broke up. Rob was so obsessed with black music that in the mid-eighties he found Marcel King sleeping [in the] back of a car somewhere in Chorlton and signed him, and we got him to record with Bernard Sumner producing. It was one of the best records on Factory – one of the high spots of the entire collection – and he disappears again and then dies.

LARRY CASSIDY

The problem was Factory! It took more energy getting money out of them than doing the gigs and records! I knew that Tony, Martin and Peter were intrinsically good people and we've managed to remain friends. My only regret is not spending more time with Ian, Martin and Rob before they died. How was I going to know they were going to die, any more than when my wife Jenny died in 2004.

6

'LEAVING THE 20TH CENTURY': JOY DIVISION

Out of the ashes of punk came the new sound.

In Manchester, several local bands of various capabilities inspired by punk were moving away quickly from the London punk scene's rock'n'roll roots into something quite different – some called it post-industrial, some called it post-rock.

Rising like the modernist architecture in Manchester's seventies concrete city-scape, these bands were throwing away the rule book with a lot more success than the architects had done in the city.

One of these bands was called Warsaw. They had met at the Sex Pistols gigs and formed as a punk band, but were already moving in their own direction. Their frontman was a charismatic young Bowie/Doors/underground rock fanatic from Macclesfield called Ian Curtis, and his dark worldview and love of Iggy and the Doors and arthouse literature was pushing his band into a different place.

Soon to be renamed Joy Division, they would become perhaps the most influential band of the post-punk era.

KEVIN CUMMINS

Warsaw were terrible. They had a real attitude as well. They were quite aloof and they didn't fit in with other bands in Manchester – they thought they were better than everyone else but they had nothing to back that up when they started.

MICK MIDDLES

I saw them at the Circus first gig supporting John Cooper Clarke. I thought they were the Prefects! Then I thought, I know that guy Ian Curtis from the Electric Circus. They were so nervous; you could tell they just wanted to get off the stage. You wouldn't have known where he would take it from that point. His voice was thin. The band were just learning at this point.

JON SAVAGE

The next big event for me would have been coming up to Manchester to see the first Pere Ubu date in the UK.* I remember seeing members of Joy Division there. When I eventually heard Joy Division, I thought maybe, if they didn't get the idea of the high bass sound from Pere Ubu, then Pere Ubu were [still] very influential for them, because Pere Ubu had a way of dealing with post-industrial space. There were all these link-ups between post-industrial American cities and Manchester, which was then a very post-industrial city – which links up eventually to the Hacienda and all those rust-belt cities like Detroit and Cleveland.

LIZ NAYLOR

I saw Joy Division loads of times and I thought they were fantastic. I appreciated something very special was happening. I saw them at the Leigh Festival. I actually made the effort to see Joy Division.

JON SAVAGE

Their best gig was Leigh Rock Festival in 1979. Most of their gigs were great actually – the Free Trade Hall one supporting John Cooper Clarke with Ian going mental was absolutely unbelievable.

Leigh was great. It was outdoors and a big space, they were getting better and better. The thing about Ian that no one ever talks about is that most great pop performers have stagecraft, which means you're always pacing yourself, holding, giving and stepping back and stepping forward. Watch someone like David Bowie, who's a consummate performer. He knows how to pace his set. It's not calculated – he knows stagecraft and he's brilliant at it. Ian had no stagecraft! He would come on and go 'Waaagh!' and that would be it. [He'd] keep that same level of intensity, which is very hard to do. And he totally opened himself up, which is a very, very hard thing to do in a rock club and is actually very dangerous. I always thought that was part of his problem, ultimately. Ian was too open and he gave too much in his performance.

PETER HOOK

The first time I met Ian Curtis I think was at the Sex Pistols concert at the

---

* Pere Ubu were arguably another of the first post-punk bands, though they formed in Cleveland, USA in 1975, making them a pre-punk-post-punk band, or avant-garage as they termed themselves. Echoes of the band's atmospheric brooding rock could be heard in many post-punk British bands.

Electric Circus. It was the third time that the Sex Pistols had played in Manchester in 1976. You couldn't miss him really; he had 'Hate' written on his back in big white letters. There were so few people around at the time on the scene. You would see them all the time at the same gigs, like the Eater concert or at the gigs at the Squat.

You'd go over and say hello to anyone because you had something in common with them – like having spiked hair and pants all ripped up. It was quite easy to strike up friendships at the time.

When you met someone, the only thing you talked about was your band. Ian told us about his band and me and Barney told him about our band. He had a drummer and a guitarist, Bernard and I had a bass and a guitar. There was talk of joining together but punk bands in those days didn't have two guitarists. It wasn't allowed! It wasn't in the rules (*laughs*).

So we couldn't join together at first, but when his guitar player left he joined Bernard and I as a three piece and then we went looking for a drummer.

Bernard Sumner was fired by the anti-star vibe of the Sex Pistols and felt that the band had 'destroyed the myth of being a pop star, of a musician being some kind of god that you had to worship'. Along with Peter Hook, they had the core of a band, adding fellow traveller Terry Mason on drums.

TERRY MASON

I suppose that the perfect situation would have been that we (me, Hooky, and Barney) actually noticed Ian at the Lesser Free Trade Hall Pistols gig, but that's the bollocks that you'd expect on Joy Division/New Order fan sites. We actually would have seen the 'two Ians'* in the months following the initial outbreak of punk at the gigs round town, including the Electric Circus – and by the time of the two dates on the 'Anarchy' tour that December, certainly we would have been on nodding and grunting terms with Ian Curtis, if not talking. Our earliest conversations would have been about the difficulties in finding drummers, which is where I came in.

RICHARD BOON

In November 1976 at a Buzzcocks/Chelsea gig I was promoting I met Ian Curtis. I got talking to him. He seemed very interested in the emerging punk phenomenon. He said that he had been out to the 1976 Mont de Marsan punk festival in the south of France for his summer holiday, where the Damned had played with a load of pub bands. It wasn't quite

* Ian Curtis and a friend of his named Iain Grey.

what he was expecting, it wasn't where his interests were. He was quite disappointed by it. He was interested in the sources where that music was coming from, more than the music itself. He seemed very, very interested in music.

PETER HOOK

He was just like us. He was bonkers. Mind you, he was a lot nicer than me and Bernard (*laughs*). Me and Bernard were a lot more streetwise than Ian was.

He was much more educated and middle class; me and Bernard were more rough and ready, more working class. Ian was more shy and quiet but he could be as wild as anybody, especially when he'd had a drink, he could be a maniac like everybody else! He was very eager to please, he just wanted to make everybody happy (*laughs*), which is not a bad thing really.

TERRY MASON

As the two Ians had been there from the start of punk in Manchester we saw them as part of the initial wave like ourselves. The Ians both dressed very similar, both wearing donkey jackets to gigs and to the locals of Collyhurst, dressing like normal people – albeit with narrower trousers. Both Ians were quite shy, but once a band got on stage, that's when Ian C. came into his own. He was all over the show.

Ian was very bright and a social chameleon. He could reflect on any situation with anyone. I think it's this ability that means everyone has their own personal Ian. Along with this bright personality was the way that Ian would become very animated, sometimes wildly, over minor issues.

RICHARD BOON

I got chatting to him gradually over the next few months. He and his mates had formed a group by then. He was quite driven to do something. It was a time when people would just form a band and then work out what they were going to do with it. When I used to go and see them rehearse in the early days it was at a pub by Weaste bus depot. I would chat and have a drink and when they seemed ready to play I put them on at another self-promoted gig on 29 May 1977 with the Buzzcocks and Penetration. They were billed as the Stiff Kittens – we tried to foist the name on them and they didn't like it! They went on stage and said 'We are Warsaw.'*

Ian Curtis was smart, intense, and intelligent and had a certain drive

---

* The name was probably derived from 'Warszawa', a track on the recent David Bowie album *Low* and a big favourite with Ian Curtis.

that was a little inarticulate at first. He had a spark about him. He came more from the Iggy and the Stooges side of things. That sort of thing. Simple existentialism.

LINDER
I have a photograph that I've labelled 'Stiff Kittens' which shows Ian Curtis talking to John the Postman at the Electric Circus.

PETER HOOK
Ian finished me and Bernard's musical education. Ian was into the Doors, which we had never heard of somehow. I was into John Cale but not the Velvet Underground, which was pretty weird. Ian was also into Kraftwerk. It's funny, really. We would get compared to the Doors and we would say 'Who are the Doors?'

BERNARD SUMNER (Joy Division guitarist)
Ian introduced me to Chinese dim sum!

MICK ROSSI
We used to rehearse in the room next door to the early Joy Division at T.J. Davidson's in Manchester. Everyone on the scene used to rehearse down there, like the Buzzcocks. The first time I met Ian was down there it was when they were called Warsaw, before they were called Joy Division.

KEVIN CUMMINS
With Joy Division we would go to T.J. Davidson's and sit and watch; Warsaw, as they were then, were terrible. I saw Warsaw supporting Buzzcocks in May '77 and they were awful. They looked like Frankie Goes to Hollywood, refugees from the Bowie/Roxy world. Hooky had gaffer tape round his arms and a leather cap, a moustache and leather trousers – actually he still dresses like that (laughs).

MARK STANDLEY
TJM's is what everyone called it, even though it was also called T.J. Davidson's. There were three directors of the company. Tony Davidson, Michael something and Woody.

Michael was a tramp that Tony Davidson found asleep in his garden one day. He gave him the job of looking after the rehearsal studio. He lived there in the basement. With his Alsatian dog!

The Buzzcocks were downstairs, Joy Division above us. Hucknall across the way and loads of others. There was a place called Brenda's Café on the corner. On any day you could go in and there would be Buzzcocks on one corner taking ages over a cup of tea, us in another in full glam gear sharing some toast. This used to annoy Brenda, as she couldn't fit in the people who bought proper meals and kept her café going.

JOHNNY MARR

The band I was in now was White Dice and we rehearsed underneath Joy Division in T.J. Davidson's – that's where the scene was.

MARK STANDLEY

All the rooms were grimy and cold. You could hardly play because your hands were frozen. After a while, we realised that an old cooker in the corner still worked. So suddenly we had the only room with any heating. I think this might have been the reason that one day in '79, we were asked to let Joy Division use our room to film a video. We were given £10 and asked to go to the pub. We were a bit disgruntled, but didn't mind the free drink! That's the famous 'Love Will Tear Us Apart' video in our room.

There was some rivalry between us and Joy Division. They supported us a couple of times, but we always went to see them live.

GINA SOBERS

I remember playing with the Collective at an early Warsaw gig at an all-day event organised at the Mayflower in Gorton, 'A Wart Hog's Picnic', featuring ourselves, the Fall and Warsaw and several other bands. We all had to share the dressing room so it was a tight fit, with the various bands staking their claim to corner spots. I'd seen Ian Curtis up close quite a few times before, though I never spoke to him; Barney always seemed the most friendly. But I do remember his pale complexion, watery blue eyes, his intense gaze before a gig, an air of wiry concentration about him. Onstage I didn't think much of Warsaw, they sounded as chaotic and raw as the rest of us. However, Ian *was* mesmerising to watch even then, jerking and flailing his arms like a demon possessed, like a man out of place, drowning and waving, in the smoke-filled air. Course, it's easy to see with hindsight that he was both expressive of a generation and cursed with a dystopian introspection. I don't think many people knew he was epileptic at the time. They probably thought it was part of the show, a larger-than-life projection.

LARRY CASSIDY

Me and Paul Wiggin and Vin went to Eric's in Liverpool for a Joy Division matinee gig.* We often did this, we preferred it to going in the evening.

* 15 July 1978.

We thought Joy Division were out of the Salvation Army or something. Then when they came on, just three of them, and started with 'No Love Lost' – after the long intro Ian came out and started to sing. I was completely mesmerised and so was Paul and Vin. At that time we promoted gigs in Blackpool. We hired the Imperial Hotel Ballroom from around lunchtime to 11 pm and we put four bands on – Orchestral Manoeuvres in the Dark, who had just released 'Electricity' on Factory, Glass Torpedoes and Final Solution and ourselves.* All the bands got £30 and we opened early to let the kids come in. In the evening it was more of an adult do. We printed tickets, Joy Division played third on the bill after OMD, then Final Solution with Duncan Disorderly and Fozzie, just the two of them doing weird keyboard stuff. In the dressing room I met Rob Gretton. He seemed to like what we were doing and said he would get us some work supporting Joy Division.

JON SAVAGE
I always found them pretty friendly pretty and down-to-earth. I never got the unapproachable vibe. I was part of the Factory family, but even then I knew that they could be difficult, particularly with journalists. Rob was crucial; he was the fifth JD.

PETÉR HOOK
Everything seemed to move very fast from Warsaw to Joy Division. It was so intense, all that period of time, that it escapes me.

I had a Warsaw live tape that I was listening to and six months later a Joy Division live tape and we were completely different. The songs had changed. It was unbelievable. I was there and I don't know how it happened. I can listen to the two tapes and go: 'Jesus! That's unbelievable!' – from 'Leaders of Men' to having the first Joy Division album done in six months. Unbelievable!

I remember playing the Mayflower. It was the first time we played 'Transmission', which as a piece of music is so simple, but it was so effective. The crowd just stopped dancing – stood there stunned and stopped to watch. The hairs on the back of your neck just go up. I thought, fucking hell, we got something here! It was really a weird moment. We knew we were getting good at that point. It was an amazing moment. One minute there's no one there, then the next the gigs are full and we were playing the same stuff!

* 27 July 1979.

STEPHEN MORRIS

When we started off Joy Division, we didn't feel like we were part of the Manchester scene. There was Buzzcocks, Magazine, the Drones and Slaughter and the Dogs and all that lot – the Manchester music mafia – and then there was them oiks Joy Division.

Eventually me and Ian harangued the Buzzcocks a couple of times. Richard Boon was the manager and we spoke to him and they eventually got us on that tour in 1978. That was one of the big steps up the ladder for us. They were just on the other side of their peak. Before that we thought maybe we should jack it in, but decided to write some songs instead and came up with the album.

BERNARD SUMNER

I had a lot of problems in my youth. I had a lot of very heavy illness in my family. I was brought up by my grandparents, everyone was ill, and people started dying in my family. It was a horrible period for me in my teens because everyone was dying. Basically I was a bit freaked out in my head. My contribution to the band was heavy because of this.

MICK ROSSI

My first impression was that they needed to get cleaner (*laughs*). Their clothes were a bit smelly. Ian always had this coat on, like the sort of coat that bus conductors in Manchester would wear, and they had suits on that were all shiny from years of ironing – really beat-up old-looking clothes! As a person Ian was very nice but a bit introverted. He was always sat there observing from a distance.

But it's always the quiet ones, innit? He said very little but there was always something going on in his head. When people like Ian said something, it was always worth listening to. But when he was onstage, that was when he really came alive, with all that whirling around.

PETER HOOK

He was quiet and he was shy but he would go on stage and go like the bleeding clappers! Which was shocking and inspiring at the same time. When you were playing behind him you thought, this is fucking top!

MICK ROSSI

I saw them play quite a few times. There would be very few people at their gigs at first. Even though their music sounded very grey, in terms of feeling there was always something going on.

PETER HOOK

We all got on quite well. Mind you, it isn't long in a band before all the back-biting starts! It always does! But it never got serious. Steve was very quiet and shy, Ian was quiet, so me and Bernard had a lot of scope really! The best thing Rob Gretton did was to tell us to shut up in interviews because we were a pair of thick bastards (*laughs*)! He reckoned it was better to say nothing than have me and Bernard talk. Most of Joy Division's allure came from Rob Gretton's foresight.

BERNARD SUMNER

We used to rehearse on Sunday in Salford and Steve, because he was the only one who could drive, would drive us into Manchester. On the way we had fun with Steve. When we pulled up at traffic lights if there was any girls there we would shout out of the windows, 'Hey, show us your tits! For me and the driver!' and he would cringe. 'C'mon love, how much? The driver with black hair wants to know!'

We were infantile, fucking idiots. We made this really serious fucking music and then we were quite infantile in behaviour, which made life quite interesting.

BOB DICKINSON

Back at Rafters in 1978 I DJed the night Joy Division played the Stiff/ Chiswick challenge, when they famously went on late after backstage ructions with the Negatives. At first I thought they were some kind of short-haired heavy metal band because they were wearing leather boots and jackets. But it soon became obvious they weren't a metal act, or a pub rock act like the rest of the bands that had previously played. They were really intense, and Rob Gretton, whom I was talking to afterwards, was completely blown away by them. He stood there amid all the broken glass and cigarette ends after the crowd had gone home and just ranted on about how he was going to manage them and they were going to change the world.

TONY WILSON

The first time I ever saw Ian Curtis he came up to me at Rafters and said, 'Fuck you. You're the bastard off the TV, you cunt.' I asked him why he said that and he said it was because I had never put them on the telly. He was really nasty, really confrontational. And this was when they were a completely unknown band. It worked. I put them on pretty soon afterwards. I never saw him like that again in the three or four years that I knew him. He was this thoughtful schoolboy, an emotionally quite deep, thoughtful schoolboy.

MICK MIDDLES

The first feature I wrote was Joy Division and they were hopeless. It was just before they met Hannett and he made them into something amazing; they were sort of half there. They were doing this little tour and they needed publicity. They had one live review by then. I went to the pub with them . . . It was Hooky pretending to be a Nazi and miserable and Ian being really lovely and interesting. They were thrilled by it when they read it. It was a dodgy piece, though!

LINDSAY READE (Factory Records)

I thought Ian Curtis only stood out because he was the singer; singers always stand out, don't they? You don't look at the others. I didn't see him with a superstar quality like Tony did. Tony had a strong first impression of Ian that night! He thought he was weird, especially after their 'conversation'. I don't recall the moment he went up to Tony and shouted at him. Maybe Tony exaggerates that story! Tony is hugely cinematic. Ian was very gutsy though, and he had said something to Tony.

Generally though, Ian was shy. When he met Annik* later on I got to know him a lot better. He was a really nice, honourable and humble person. He would have retained his humility if he had survived and become famous. Ian would have remembered who gave them the leg-up to start with; it was my money as much as Tony's that started them off in the first place and Ian remembered that.

Mick Middles said Ian would never have jumped the queue for a gig even when he was famous. He never had that sort of ego. I'm not sure if he could have gone on with the band even if he hadn't died. He couldn't go on with the epilepsy. He didn't have the character of a superstar, and everyone except Tony said so. He had a lot of conversations with Genesis P. Orridge; they were talking about doing something together, something weird and obscure.

TERRY MASON

There was a major and understandable change in Ian following his major seizure after the first Hope and Anchor gig.[†]

BERNARD SUMNER

Most of the time Ian was all right, there were just odd moments when he would have a bit of a rant and a bit of a rave – everyone loses their temper

---

* Annik Honore was the Belgian journalist with whom Ian Curtis was having an affair at the time of his suicide.
[†] 27 December 1978.

in their own way. He was the most polite person, very, very interesting to talk to – very opinionated but not in a negative way, not judgemental. He didn't go round putting people down; he was pretty positive. I guess the illness took over. Things change. It's very well known that he had epilepsy.

He could be babyish, arsey . . . all day on the way down to London to the Hope and Anchor I had never seen him like that. I remember being very ill and not wanting to play the gig. I didn't want to go down there and play to 15 people and it was shit. Ian was in a very bad mood. The gig was very bad. I had the worst flu ever and was sat under my sleeping bag on the way back. We were driving back in Stephen's car somewhere near Luton and [Ian] grabs my sleeping bag off me. I said, 'Don't be fucking stupid!' and he grabbed it again and just covered himself with it, growling. I yanked it back and he started punching out, he punched Stephen whilst he was driving. We thought, 'Oh, there's something wrong,' and we shouted, 'Pull up, Stephen, pull up!' Stephen was pretty upset because he had hit him.

Me and Hooky and Rob got out of the car on the hard shoulder. We grabbed Ian and realised he was having a fit. I pinned one arm down, Hooky another and Rob his legs. Stephen went inside his pockets and got his cigarettes off him and had one (*laughs*). When he calmed down, we drove really fast to the nearest hospital. They said he was ill and should see a doctor.

TERRY MASON

Ian knew only too well what epilepsy was about. Ian seemed ashamed of his condition, and I got the impression he thought that he was letting the rest of us* down somehow. As Ian's diagnosis and subsequent medication moved forward, Ian moved inwards to himself, and some days it seemed like he was just going through the motions when dealing with the outside world. Poor sod: the drink, drugs and women that most boys from bands get access to were now for others, not him. Ian's concerns were ensuring that he stuck to his prescribed drugs. It wasn't even as if any major money was rolling in to compensate, either!

PETER HOOK

He was ill early on, the dates always escape me. He was ill quite quickly from when we started. He was his own worst enemy. How can you tell the lead singer of a shit-hot band to go to bed early and not to drink? He rebelled against it. As soon as the doctors told him to take it easy he

---

* Having been replaced as the band's drummer, Terry Mason became Joy Division's manager before Rob Gretton took over. He continued to work for the band in various capacities.

rebelled against them, and then he wouldn't let us tell him either. The more we told him, the more he went for it and the more he turned into Iggy Pop on stage. His idol was Iggy Pop, but Iggy wasn't epileptic! If we knew then what we knew now, it would be so different. But unfortunately we didn't.

RICHARD BOON

Well, he did grow more withdrawn; he didn't relish the attention he was getting. Part of him wanted it but part of him wasn't comfortable with the expectations being draped over him. He didn't ask for that.

KEVIN CUMMINS

I had the idea to do some Joy Division pictures around Princess Parkway, the road out of Manchester in Hulme, because that's the road that bands take to get rich and famous and get out of town. We were stood on that bridge over the Parkway. They had gone to the middle of the bridge and I was loading the camera, waiting for people crossing the bridge to go past so that we had the bridge to ourselves. The band were so far away and it looked so bleak that I thought, I can't see who they are, they're just part of the landscape. I took three shots – three frames of that – and I thought, quite nice picture, but the NME won't use them because you can't recognise them! I did a close-up shot of them on the bridge; there were no cars underneath because it was a Saturday afternoon and it had that sort of bleak East European feel. It's probably my best ever session.

JON SAVAGE

I moved to Manchester at about the same time as [Paul] Morley moved down to London, so Morley had been writing about Joy Division and then I was the person writing about Joy Division. And Tony helped me to get a job knowing that I would be writing about Joy Division, so it worked out for everybody.

UNKNOWN PLEASURES AND THE GREAT LEAP FORWARD

Signing to Factory placed Joy Division in the middle of a creative team who were waiting for the catalytic spark the band would provide. In April 1979, the band began recording their debut album, Unknown Pleasures, *at Strawberry Studios in Stockport. From the start, producer Martin Hannett was in control, breaking down the band's sound into its constituent parts – even to the extent of getting Stephen to play each part of his drum kit separately.*

Hannett's methods initially threw the band, who didn't like their proto-Stooges darkness being tampered with and being given a spacier, more atmospheric sound.

Years later, Peter Hook readily admits that the record's sound was down to the brilliant producer.

Unknown Pleasures *was very much an example of teamwork. The Factory family provided all aspects of the band's masterwork, from production to the album's cover design by Peter Saville, who would go on to provide artwork for future Joy Division releases. The band were now seen as the key post-punk act in the UK. The album swiftly sold out its 1000 pressing and has gone on to become one of the great influential rock albums of all time.*

RICHARD BOON

Hannett was their architect. You can't underestimate the big part that Martin Hannett played in the way they recorded – breaking their sound down and building it up again. He gave them articulacy and a sound that they had to learn to replicate live. They didn't like the sound initially but realised later on that something good was going on.

KEVIN CUMMINS

They didn't like the sound Martin gave them but they had to run with it. They wanted it to rock out a bit more.

PETER HOOK

We went in to record the album with Martin Hannett. Which started off all right and then he would go off into the stratosphere. He just went! It was so weird; he was sort of removed from life. Martin got spacier, and he was pretty obtuse when he started! By the time he was off his head he was somewhere else. The best thing he ever did with us was when we were in Strawberry Studios: he used to go in the tape room at the back with these little auritone speakers. He'd connect to these speakers to listen to the mix and he used to say to us, 'If I hear anything I like I will come out.' He never fucking came out! The only time he came out was when he ran out of stuff, and then he went home! That was most surreal.

MIKE PICKERING

Without Hannett they would never have been as good. Hooky said he didn't like what Martin was doing at the time but he was very important, it was amazing production.

PETER HOOK

Tony took the money that his gran had left him and paid for *Unknown Pleasures* – that was a fantastic gamble. Plus it was fair: he gave us a 50-50 deal. It was a hell of a unique thing to be at.

RICHARD WITTS

When I look at Ian's lyrics, at the end of the songs there's always a true turnaround – trying for something better, something very positive that somehow that got missed in the record, and people think the songs are about misery. Martin tended to work by himself anyway; he saw musicians as noise producers who he liked to see fuck off once they had made their noises. Of course he had to have a strong relationship with the singer because the singer added his parts last.

JON SAVAGE

The next thing was I got a letter from Rob Gretton because I was writing for *Melody Maker*, containing a cassette and saying basically, 'My name is Rob Gretton, I'm the manager of Joy Division, I'm sending you a copy of their new album and it's crap. You may have heard their first EP, *Ideal for Living*, and that's crap too, but it's coming out on a twelve-inch.' I really liked the way he wrote the letter. I thought it was really funny.

It was Joy Division's time. They'd just finished recording *Unknown Pleasures*; it wasn't a hit but they were a cult band. Nobody in London was that interested in what was going on in Manchester; despite Morley and myself, there was still a huge media divide. Pete Shelley said it very well, saying Manchester was like the animals in New Zealand – they got on with developing because they were left alone.

I thought Joy Division were terrific because they helped me to make sense of Manchester, which I had just moved to. I had a white label of *Unknown Pleasures* which I had played constantly and that really fixed in my head what Manchester was like. It was very much like the Charles Salem movie, very grey.* Lots of space, yet very claustrophobic.

I definitely thought that Joy Division were psychedelic – 'Autosuggestion' was totally psychedelic. It got that slow drowning vibe of a wet Sunday in Manchester.

Joy Division were so good. Something that people forget about is how uplifting they were, because they really rocked. They made you want to move around; they could swing and be heavy as well – very good musicians. In a way they were a meta-dance band, with the Syndrum and Stephen's beats.

* *No City Fun* was filmed by 20-year-old Charles Salem. Based on an article by Liz Naylor in *City Fun*, it features music from *Unknown Pleasures*.

GENESIS P. ORRIDGE (Throbbing Gristle and Psychic TV frontman)

The first time I came into contact with Joy Division was when Throbbing Gristle played Manchester at the original Factory club. Ian was there. He told me later he wanted to see me but couldn't get backstage. This was his first attempt to make contact. Later on he told me that he was already a big fan of Throbbing Gristle long before we met.

He knew Jon Savage; Jon was living in Manchester at that time.

Ian also knew Crispy Ambulance singer Alan Hempsall* and various people like that, and between them it was probably how he got my phone number. At some point before the Joy Division gig at Hemel Hempstead he began to call me up and talk to me on the phone. We would talk about writers, poetry and how miserable the music business was, all that sort of stuff. I didn't meet Ian in person until Hemel Hempstead. When he called me he said he was playing and to come and watch Joy Division play that night. I did manage to get backstage and hang out.

BERNARD SUMNER

I remember loads of funny stories. Like when he wanted a piss in the car on a really busy road. I said, 'You will just have to piss against the car, Ian, when I stop at the kerbside.' So he's stood there having a piss and no one can see him. I said, 'Steve, put your foot on it now.' Steve drove off and Ian went mad because he had a pair of winklepickers on and the car drove over his feet (*laughs*).

MIKE PICKERING

I knew Joy Division as being really funny, like they always have been. They played this dark and desolate music, but they were also fucking mad, up for a laugh.

GENESIS P. ORRIDGE

The classic image of Ian was wrapped around the mic looking into space. I remember very vividly that as I was watching he seemed to become almost semi-transparent. All the people and everything around began to fade away. There was this very powerful sense of disconnection I experienced when seeing him, not connected fully to this earth.

TERRY MASON

I've got so many memories . . . [one] being after a gig in Preston where we had an incredibly full club, an eventful show, but we got a very poor fee

---

* A big Throbbing Gristle fan, Hempsall had frequently been in touch with Genesis.

and the club owner was unwilling to cough up any more. Our 'dressing room' was the club's kitchen, complete with a solitary comfy chair. We found the club's fridge and deep freezer, and after butter-eating bets we all went home with a bonus frozen chicken. Ian took two because he was so pissed off at our treatment!

GENESIS P. ORRIDGE

I became more profoundly attached to and fascinated by Ian at the same time. I felt that he recognised the feelings I have, that feeling of disconnection from the consensus, from reality, a sense of remaining here in our world by will power.

It's possible that the ethereal quality is something a deeply creative person projects. We made friends and we talked deeply in phone conversations. We were very much best friends; we talked about feelings, and we trusted each other with intimate thoughts. We would share them and try and resolve issues. We would speak for an hour or so on the phone in-between gigs – he was very busy. He would tell me how depressed he was – how much he wanted to escape being in Joy Division.

Ian was truly entrancing. He was in a trance onstage, channelling an energy, an emotion, with as little interference as possible from common sense, something only documented in poetry. That's why he was attracted to Romantic and Symbolist poetry so much – there's this search for a lyrical but modern description of the paradox of existence, the fact that there is this disconnection, of all being completely alone. There was this innate loneliness in the way that Ian Curtis presented himself – not exactly existentialist but a very positive, deep sense of self-loss. You know you are mortal and never completely absorbed into those around you . . .

In March 1980 the band went to London's Britannia Row studio with Martin Hannett and started recording their second album, Closer.

Ian Curtis was becoming more ill. Thanks to the tough life of touring, his epilepsy and seizures were becoming far worse, sometimes occurring during gigs, which further exacerbated his condition. When he was ill at gigs the audience, unaware of his condition, thought it was part of the show, culminating at the infamous gig at Bury Derby Hall on 8 April 1980, which started without the ill Ian Curtis.

ALAN HEMPSALL

My recollections of the Bury gig are still fairly clear. There's been a lot of crap talked about that night. I'm pretty sure 'Decades' was one of the two slow new ones they played after I came off.

The Minny Pops were first on and played a full set, then Section 25 played a short set. They ended with 'Girls Don't Count'. Bernard, Peter,

Steve and myself joined them, with Larry on vocals and me on backing vocals. Section 25 left the stage at the end of song and me, Bernard, Peter and Steve stayed on to play 'Love Will Tear Us Apart' and 'Digital' – or was it 'Passover'? Ian finally came on and did 'Decades' and 'The Eternal', which was all Ian could manage; he then left the stage. I came back on with Larry and Simon Topping from ACR. We did a version of 'Sister Ray' with Larry on lead vocal and me and Simon on backing vocals, before we left the stage with a pissed-off audience.

A pint pot was then thrown and it kicked off. Rob Gretton jumped in the crowd and Hooky had to be restrained backstage from joining in by Section 25's Paul Wiggin. Several gigs were cancelled before the band played what was to be their final gig at the University of Birmingham's High Hall on 2 May.

In May the band were meant to be playing their debut American tour, only adding to the pressure on the frontman, who was trying to deal with his illness, his affair with Annik Honore and his deteriorating marriage. The night before the tour, on 17 May 1980, Ian Curtis went back to his Macclesfield home and asked Debbie to drop the divorce suit she had filed. He then asked to be left alone.

The next morning he was dead.

PETER HOOK

It was odd playing Bournemouth recently; it reminded me of when we played there with the Buzzcocks, when Ian had the longest fit. He was fitting for an hour and half – eventually Rob and me had to take him to hospital. We had to sit on him. It was unbelievable. I was thinking, 'Christ! He's not coming out of this one.' Our roadie went and hid in the cupboard; he said, 'I'm not coming out – he's possessed by the devil, that bastard' (*laughs*). God bless him, he would not come out of the broom cupboard. Ian was really shaking. It was frightening; you'd think, shit, is it worth it? But he wouldn't let you stop. I think he thought what we'd achieved was so huge to us at our time in life that if he stopped or let it go that it might never come back. He didn't want to let everyone else down. Even if you said, 'Stop, don't worry about it – we can stop.' But I don't think he wanted to admit to himself that there might be a chance he might lose it.

GENESIS P. ORRIDGE

Me and Ian had started talking about working together around the time they were in Britannia Row studios recording their second album. He really liked that Throbbing Gristle single 'We Hate You Little Girls'. It had a radical packaging with plastic bag collages, foldout pictures. He asked me to be the intermediary to get the artist Jean-Pierre Turmel to work on the Joy Division sleeve. I said, 'Yeah, more than happy to do something.' I put them in touch and he did the 'Atmosphere' single sleeve.

That was where the French connections started. Jean-Pierre was doing his label Sordide Sentimental and he had been interested for a while in putting Throbbing Gristle on in Paris. He wasn't sure at the time the gig would work, but he thought that combining it with Joy Division made sense as a special event. Ian and I said we could do something at the end of the set in Paris together, a jam session between the bands . . . him and me doing vocals together on 'Sister Ray' because that was an easy one to play . . . From that we talked about working together, trying our voices together . . . As an idea it was a very organic process. Among those conversations, it was apparent to Ian and me that we both felt alienated from our respective bands. We both felt we would like to work on something together. Actually Ian was more mischievous. He wanted to do a gig, a jam session, then announce he was quitting Joy Division and I was quitting TG to do something together. Whatever happened, he was not going to stay in Joy Division anyway.

LINDSAY READE

He became more troubled and more depressed. Like he was labouring under a heavy weight. He stayed with me and Tony for a week after his first suicide attempt. He was with me most of the time because Tony was at work. He was quite deeply depressed just after the first suicide attempt. I think he was kind of annoyed that it had failed.

BERNARD SUMNER

We really didn't have a clue. When he committed suicide he had tried it a couple of months before. The first time we realised that there was something a bit up was when he turned up at rehearsal covered in knife marks where he had slashed himself – he had woken up and didn't know what had happened. He had got it all over and showed us his chest. There were horizontal knife marks, cuts to his chest. We were going, 'What the fucking hell have you done?' He said, 'I just woke up on the floor this morning.' He had slashed the Bible and ripped all the pages out as well. I mean, he used to do pretty mad things like that.

When we played Rafters once he got pretty carried away, pretty kinetic, he started ripping the stage apart, ripping floorboards apart and throwing them at the audience. I did think that was pretty unusual! People threw bottles back, which smashed onstage, and he dived in there rolling around in it, kinda like Iggy. That was pretty unusual actually. He had a bit of a row with the manager of the club. To put his point across he put a bucket on his head and started ranting like Quasimodo!

It's very hard to capture an accurate portrayal of Ian. Everyone has got this picture of him as a depressed person and he was, but only at the end of his career. Most photos you see of him with his head in his hands and unshaven – that's the image the public have. I suppose because of that and his lyrics really he got this image, but he wasn't like that. It didn't capture him. He was quite an odd character really. I think at some point in Macclesfield there was a leak of aluminium oxide in the drinking water. Everyone from there's a little bit strange! It's hard to put a finger on. It's very hard when you're trying to explain what he was like. Very hard, very hard indeed. He was quite intellectual. He read William Burroughs and Nietzsche. Me and Hooky didn't know what the fuck he was going on about half the time, but he had a good sense of humour. He could take a jolly jape.

ALAN HEMPSALL

Ian Curtis was like a regular Joe really. I rather suspect that there were different aspects to his personality. We had a common interest in Ballard and Burroughs – he had some rare Burroughs stuff. Barney and Hooky were just Salford lads – they were the kind of bastards who would give you a wedgie. Ian had a serious side and a troubled side. I knew nothing about that and his private life and it was a total shock to me when he died. And to Bernard, Hooky and Rob, so what would I know?

PETER HOOK

I was reading in Mick Middles' book* about Ian wanting to give up. It was quite odd to hear that he wanted to give up because he was the one that didn't want to give up. Everybody was talking him into taking it easy but he was the one that didn't want to. There's a weird contradiction there – somehow you will never know the truth of it.

GENESIS P. ORRIDGE

He was in a lot of pain, definitely, because there was this gulf and curse of being alone in this very deep mystical way. Normally in a band you would want to embrace it and feel connected to the people around you. He grew and matured very quickly. He was suddenly in this big band and they didn't click . . . There were whole areas that the others would shrug off, say, 'Let's have a beer.' I'm not saying that in a critical way. I really like Bernard and Hooky.

* *Torn Apart* by Mick Middles and Lindsay Reade.

LINDSAY READE

Most of the memories I have are personal memories of what happened that week. I read his palm . . . and told him he wouldn't commit suicide because he didn't have a suicide line. How dumb is that? I dropped palmistry after that.

GENESIS P. ORRIDGE

Maybe that's why Ian was drawn towards me and other people. Annik gave him very much the same mental connection and feeling of belonging; she added other loving aspects as well. He came towards me because he felt I could understand different things, discuss things he was feeling. I was from Manchester originally as well . . .

TONY WILSON

The last conversation I had with him was at the last Joy Division gig in Birmingham. Typically of me I was going on about Ian's use of archaic language in his lyrics. I was interested in modern groups' usage of archaic phrases; it was a very deep conversation.

DAVE HASLAM (journalist, DJ and author)

I was at the last gig at High Hall in Birmingham. It had fallen apart by then – even as a semi-ignorant fan I could tell there was something very wrong. I remember at the gig Ian Curtis left the stage a couple of times, songs started and restarted. I remember coming away from the gig thinking that A Certain Ratio were the future now.

JON SAVAGE

I went to their last show in Birmingham. It shows how little I knew about what was going on with Ian that after I saw ACR, who were supporting, and seeing the band backstage I fucked off before Joy Division came on. We had to get down to London by 11 because Martin was producing the Psychedelic Furs.

TONY WILSON

The last time I actually saw him was when I was getting the train to London. I was driving to Piccadilly station and I saw Ian and Annik wandering around the streets, they had obviously spent the night wandering around. He got on the same train as me but he didn't see me. We didn't sit together. He got off in Macclesfield where he lived and I carried on to London.

GENESIS P. ORRIDGE

We were in the same place; I had tried to commit suicide as well earlier on . . .

I wrote a song called 'Weeping' which explained those feelings, which was one of his favourites – he knew it word for word. I tried to commit suicide because I was trapped. I felt absolutely alone, not understood by those closest to me; he felt so similar to me. When he talked it was uncanny. I did my best to think of ways to direct him away from what happened to me.

I think that Ian was already in motion towards that crisis place, choosing life or death, though maybe he wasn't fully aware of it. It was already in motion. But there were definitely fun times before then at Britannia Row. I went and hung out, I watched them record – there was a cheerfulness, though a lot of it may have been superficial. He was already disconnected and there was a tension, that thing I was trying to explain; it was like being in a family – the band – and it's almost as if it had reached a moment of adolescence where you reject the family and stretch out and create your own identity.

On the last night, when he killed himself, I spoke to Ian. He was singing 'Weeping' over the phone, the song and the tone of his voice was haunting. It was awful: he talked, he sounded anguished, frustrated and very depressed, a feeling that events were slipping out of control. I could just feel it straight away having been there myself. He didn't say, 'I'm going to kill myself.' I tried to get in touch with people but technology was much more primitive then. I spoke to Mick Middles recently when he was doing his book; I told him I'd called everyone in Manchester desperately to go round and try and stop Ian, but it was Mick's wedding night and the people I was calling weren't there. I was always angry that I couldn't get through. I know it wasn't my fault at all; it was a feeling that something was not right.

PETER HOOK

It's like that story of the last phone call he made. I don't know; I'd never heard that story before I read the book. Ian was his own worst enemy – he didn't want to let it go.

He was the one who used to drive us on. When we used to take turns to manage the group, it was always Ian that pushed us on. When we had six months without a gig and we were getting down, Ian was the one who would say, 'We can do it!' He was like a rallying cheerleader. When we felt like we couldn't be bothered, he was always the one pushing it on.

It doesn't surprise me in a way. He was never going to stop till he drove himself to the edge. It still shocks me when I read it in Mick and Lindsay's book, it's something you can never get over when he's been so important in your life for 30 years. I've lived with him every day; I've lived with the thought of him dying or the knowledge of him dying every day. I play the music a lot.

TERRY MASON

I last saw Ian on the Thursday before he committed suicide. He seemed to have got his head around what he was going to do. The divorce was to go through, and Ian was looking forward to the US tour. The tour would sort out the situation regarding his immediate accommodation, plus he was looking forward to the LA gig and staying at the Tropicana Motel, made famous by Jim Morrison. Plus once the tour was completed the band were to take six months off. I was going to get a dog and Ian was going to help me with its training because he missed his dog.

TONY WILSON

I asked Annik some time later how she liked the *Closer* album and I was shocked when she said that she hated it: 'What you have to understand is that he means it.' I said, 'No, it's just an attitude,' but she was right. That's what makes it such a great record. He really meant it.

BERNARD SUMNER

Ian obviously had issues just judging by his lyrics, but, to be honest with you, we never really listened to his lyrics till he died.

STEPHEN MORRIS

That was a bit of an eye-opener when we went through his lyrics!
We wrote them all down and we were going, 'Bloody hell, he was a bit . . . Oh Christ! Why didn't anybody say anything!'

TONY WILSON

I think all of us made the mistake of not thinking his suicide was going to happen . . . We all completely underestimated the danger. We didn't take it seriously. That's how stupid we were.

PETER HOOK

New Order was like driving with a flat tyre for a long time. It took a long time to repair the tyre. Your innocence was lost with Ian's death. When he hung himself, the whole thing became too serious. We weathered his illness with the inexperience of youth. There wasn't the education like there is now. You wouldn't let it happen now, but we didn't know what we were doing. Our innocence died the day Ian died. Everything was completely different after that.

LINDSAY READE
My theory was that his suicide was like a Japanese code of honour type of thing. Like it was the most honourable thing to do. The Iggy Pop record on the turntable isn't that significant. We played that record that week at our house when he was staying over, people read too much into that. But the film he saw the night he died, Herzog's 1977 film *Stroszek* – he related to that character; like him, he couldn't see a way out. He had loads of guilt. He could not see any way of putting it right. He wanted to take care of his daughter. And he loved Annik. Tony [Wilson] had this problem as well at the time. You love someone else that's not the mother of your children but you can't leave your kids. You can't have both.

7

NEW ORDER

The shock death of an iconic lead singer would have spelled the end of most bands, but within days of Ian Curtis's death the three remaining members of Joy Division elected to carry on, quickly becoming one of the key bands of the eighties. They were the link between the punk and post-punk years and the new era of dance and electronic music. All the way to their most recent album, 2005's Waiting for the Siren's Call, *the band has combined cutting-edge music technology with the bass-led melancholy that has become one of the great UK pop sounds.*

PETER HOOK

The thing was, when Ian died we just carried on. We didn't know anything else. We had had a taste of the high life, so to go back to the working world seemed really alien.

We really didn't talk about how we were going to carry on without Ian, but we just carried on – maybe Rob said, 'Fuck it, let's carry on.'

Obviously you couldn't gig, but you could rehearse so we carried on rehearsing. It was the Monday after his funeral that we started rehearsing. His funeral was on the Thursday, we had a drunken weekend and on the Monday we just turned up at the rehearsal room by Pinkies in Broughton. We didn't know what else to do, to be honest; it was like you were completely lost. I don't think even Rob knew what to do, so it was let's carry on. Literally through the shock, we just sat there in the practice room and started playing again. I think it was that weekend that I got the riff for 'Dreams Never End'.* We just went in that day and did what most bands do in the rehearsal room – we fucked about and started playing again, and over the weeks we got quite a lot of music together before we started addressing who's gonna sing.

---

* Sung by Peter Hook, the song was released on New Order's 1981 debut album *Movement*.

Hooky, in low-slung bass viking pose, with Barney at a New Order gig
(Photo: Ian Tilton www.iantilton.net)

Once we started writing again and the songs started to get better, I imagine Tony breathed a huge sigh of relief, thinking: thank fuck for that, they haven't lost it! By the time we got to 'Temptation' and 'Everything's Gone Green' and 'Cries and Whispers', he must have thought: thank fuck, they are good, they're still going to be a great band!

The first gig we played was at the Beach Club,[*] which we did as a three-piece with backing tapes – none of us could play and sing, that's why we used a backing tape. Then we did Scamps in Blackpool[†] and after that we went to America and did the tour, still as a three-piece. When we came back we decided to become a four-piece with Gillian[‡] and played our first gig at the Squat.[§]

I don't know about you but I can't play and sing. You can teach yourself to do it but I've never been interested really; for me it was one or the other. At the same time, Bernard and Steve were finding it difficult as well. It didn't feel that natural to any of us and it's like that thing – if you can't fight, wear a big hat – the more you've got to hide behind the better. So that's why we got the backing tape.

The most obvious thing would have been to get a singer in but – for the life of me I can't remember why – we decided not to. There's been very few occasions when we've talked about getting someone else in. The reason why we brought Gillian in was that she couldn't play. It meant that we kept the power, if you like! But we needed somebody to press the buttons. It was a very selfish reason – not the sort of reason that people bring people into groups. Normally you bring someone into a group because they are really good. Normally you don't bring someone in because they can't play. In all honesty Gillian isn't a very forceful sort of personality, so she was quite happy to take that back role.

The music was fine but the biggest shock for us all was that there was no one sat there saying, 'That sounds good.' That's what Ian used to do. We had to teach ourselves to do that. We had to start recording everything and then listening back to it and picking out bits. It was a much longer-winded way of writing really, but you had to do it because there was nobody there to short-circuit it. The style probably changed because Ian wasn't there spotting the riffs.

[*] 29 July 1980.
[†] 5 September 1980.
[‡] Girlfriend of Stephen Morris.
[§] 25 October 1980.

To me the style changed the most when we decided that Bernard was going to be the singer. That was because he was better at writing vocal lines than I was. Whilst I think that Steve was as good at writing vocal lines as Bernard, I think Steve didn't want the frontman role. So he settled into initially writing the odd vocal line with Bernard singing them. It's quite logical that is how the New Order sound appears, which is Bernard singing and then playing guitar – that way round – and that gave us, I think, our style.

Bernard was always very interested in technology; we'd already started experimenting with it in Joy Division with the Transcendent 2000, which Bernard had got into with Martin Hannett. At the same time, Steve got the Syndrums, the drum machines and the keyboards. We started using the ARP Omnis and Outboard sequencers with Martin Hannett on *Closer*.

I must admit that Rob [Gretton] was very, very good with all this. Rob would give you three grand for a synthesiser in 1981, which was a lot of money then – whereas he wouldn't give you ten quid to pay your tax bill! Whether that was forward-looking or not I'm not too sure!

It was horrible doing gigs at first because of the change. To be honest with you, when we started doing *Movement* we were going through a real period of change. Bernard was changing a lot, if you look back on it now; it was so long ago but there was a lot of change going on.

Because of our age and because of what we were doing, I don't think any of us had had a good breakdown and a good skrike, so it was all pent-up. We started pushing it in different ways . . . Martin Hannett was being so difficult that the whole thing felt dreadfully uncomfortable. People say you can hear that in *Movement* and when I look back to it I can see what they mean.*

Martin was a raddled drug addict, by then he was really bad. He was being very unhelpful, very negative, very sarcastic. It wasn't a pleasant time for any of us, it has to be said. I don't know if that was his way of coping with Ian's death, because nobody ever asked him. Now you would say, 'C'mon, mate, what's the problem?' Now you've got the experience and probably the balls to sort it out, but then you just shut up and stared at the bottom of the pint glass; know what I mean? In a band you never

* A mixed reception greeted the album *Movement* on its release in November 1981. A hangover from Joy Division with two of the tracks dating back to the former band, it would be the last album they recorded with Martin Hannett due to a combination of his spiralling drug and alcohol problems and the band's increased knowledge of working in the studio.

talk about anything constructively. In a way we should have helped Martin out. Now I know alcoholics and I know how difficult it is when people start trying to help you when you're at your worst. Martin to me was at his very worst and he was impossible to work with.

Bernard and I had sat on his shoulder for so long that, after *Movement*, we said to Rob we couldn't work with him again. We said to Rob, 'We'll do this.' I suppose that's what ambition is all about. It was our egos as well. We just thought that we could do it. We were full of it, know what I mean? Purely, though, we got rid of Martin because he was impossible to work with. He was really anti-compromise. He was very divisive in the band. He had been what you would term now a catalyst, but with any catalyst it can go bad as well. I will hold my hand on my heart, though, and say that Martin taught us everything. I saw his new gravestone which they put up recently, and his family put on it: 'He created the Manchester sound'. It's quite interesting in a way – I don't think he created the Manchester sound, but he certainly created the Joy Division sound, which led into the New Order sound. But it's a hell of a claim and it didn't half make me smile when I saw it.

Martin taught Bernard and I right from the word go how to do it. I don't mean he sat there and taught us – he did it and we just copied him. But it made Bernard and I start producing New Order ourselves. Steve and Gillian were really quiet and just sat there, whilst Rob told us to fucking get on with it and make it bigger, faster and louder.

Rob was only involved in the process by shouting at you! He wasn't technical; he would just shout: 'Fucking get on with it, you bastards . . . make it louder, make it go oomph!'

I loved Factory's attitude: we gave Tony our music and he put it out. I remember going with Bernard and Ian and sticking on the sandpaper on that Vini Reilly record, you know, when Vini did the sleeve with sandpaper and it destroyed all your other records.* That was an amazing idea and only Factory would have done that. We got paid 1p a sheet to stick the sandpaper on and we did a thousand in a day, me, Barney and Ian, because we were so skint. Factory was fucking wild and fantastic; everything that we did was interesting and the people when they were together was a great atmosphere. It really felt like you were doing something. And in a way it's been proved because now, thirty years later, how many people look at what Factory and Joy Division did and go: fuck me! No one has ever emulated it. It's scary.

* The 1979 Factory release *The Return of the Durutti Column*. The design was an imitation of Guy Debord and Asger Jorn's book *Mémoires*, which also had a sandpaper cover.

The Factory sampler was Tony's idea, being independent was his idea. That was the whole idea: let's be independent, you sign to us, don't go to a major and we will work together on it.

TONY WILSON
Rob Gretton summed it up best: 'I just put out a record by some mates!' Which is what we did . . .

POWER, CORRUPTION AND LIES

New Order's second album was released in 1983 and was the group's mainstream breakthrough record. It was a perfect combination of their bass-driven minor-key melancholy and their interest in technology and emerging cutting-edge dance sounds, as witnessed on the single 'Confusion', that year's collaboration with Arthur Baker – a groundbreaking producer for Tommy Boy records who worked with Afrika Bambaataa and Rockers' Revenge, and who would regularly pop up to work with New Order over the years – and the iconic 'Blue Monday'.

The seven-and-a-half-minute 'Blue Monday' was the perfect fusion of dance, electronic and New Order themselves. The biggest-selling 12-inch single of all time, it would go on to be a hit on several different occasions with sales over one million, remarkable for a song that breaks all the conventional rules of pop. Although the single itself notoriously lost money thanks to its elaborate packaging, the commercial success of the band's other releases enabled them to make a substantial financial contribution to Factory's latest venture, the Hacienda.

PETER HOOK
Rob was with us all the time. He was literally a hands-on manager. He was there every moment for everything we went through. Managers don't normally do the good bit – managers don't do the partying and the travelling – but Rob did all of it. He wanted to be with us all the time because it was a great crack and he had the freedom to come and do it. We said, 'Yeah! If you wanna come, come!' and Rob would be with us all the time, smoking dope and drinking and saying, 'Make it go oomph.' I suppose that was how he ran the band. It was funny, I've never seen any other manager do that. It was just that he loved the partying and the social aspects of it.

It was odd, because although he loved the social aspects of it he hated talking to record company people. But his reluctance and his stand-offishness gave you an image as well – presumably it scared the fuck out of them. I remember being at a party with Mo Austin when we signed to Warner Brothers in Los Angeles. Mo Austin – the head of Warners – said to me, 'Where's your manager, man? I really need to talk to him.' I said,

'He's over there!' and he said, 'What, there!?' Rob had managed to find the only chair in this party and was sat there with a big joint in his mouth and wouldn't talk to anyone. Every time someone from the record company went over, he would say, 'Fuck off!' It was like the greatest bluff in the world, but it was a great image.

Basically New Order had started earning money at Factory, a lot of money. If they hadn't earned that money they would not have had the freedom to do anything and that's where the Hacienda came about. I think only three bands ever earned any money on Factory, which was us, Happy Mondays and Section 25. Their LP was really popular, it's always been played down about how well they did.

LOW-LIFE, BROTHERHOOD AND SUBSTANCE

Low-Life, *released in 1985, with its singles 'The Perfect Kiss' and 'Sub-culture', saw a further refining of New Order's assimilation of the electric and the electronic, while on 1986's* Brotherhood, *which included the big hit 'Bizarre Love Triangle', each side of the album presented a different face of the band.*

A year later, 1987's Substance, *a compilation of all the band's singles up to that point, accurately depicts their multi-genre merging. It also featured a new recording, 'True Faith', which would go on to be one of the band's biggest hits.*

TONY WILSON

We know that 'Blue Monday' is a great record and we know it sold a lot of records. At the time we would say to the band, 'Go and use a great producer,' and they would say, 'We don't want to use one.' This went on for nine months before they used Stephen Hague and did 'True Faith', which for me is their greatest record.

PETER HOOK

What you have to bear in mind is that you have to write good music to do what you want; you can't write shit music and get that power. Rob wouldn't have been a great manager if he hadn't had a great band; Martin Hannett wouldn't have been a great producer if he hadn't had a great band. I think that sometimes you sort of forget that without the music there would be fucking nothing. I had that argument with Peter Saville all the time. Peter Saville would turn round and say that people would buy our records because of the sleeves; I would say without the sleeves the music would have still been there, but it wouldn't happen the other way round.

TECHNIQUE AND REPUBLIC

1989's Technique *was the band's last album for Factory and was evidence that all those nights spent hanging around their own nightclub was not wasted, with the acid-house soundtrack of the famous venue being soaked up in the album's songs but as ever still managing to sound one step ahead of the pack.*

Meanwhile 1993's Republic *was New Order's last album for eight years. Lead single 'Regret' was a fantastic piece of work, managing to be lilting and celebratory at the same time.*

The album was also their first post-Factory release and saw them having to come to terms with a very different way of working now they were on a major label.

PETER HOOK

We were spoilt really at the start, because as Joy Division and New Order we had a lot of freedom to do what we wanted to do. Nobody told us what to do. We never had an A&R man saying 'You can't do that as your single,' or 'You can't do that.' What happened was that we decided when the song was ready and Rob and Tony said, 'Fine, don't worry about it.' We would write 'Love Will Tear Us Apart' and say it was a single and they would say, 'Fine, let's book the studio, see you in Strawberry on Monday and record it.' Martin would fuck about with it and it would be out in three weeks. Then you get to a major record company, and you have to plan everything three months in advance and have interminable meetings with idiots who don't know fuck all. Being on Factory did mould you; by the time we got to a record company, when we did *Republic*, we were going to them, 'No, you're not doing that.' Because we were used to all that freedom of being allowed to do what we wanted on Factory and we were now working in a completely different way.

GET READY AND WAITING FOR THE SIRENS' CALL

After an eight-year break working on different projects like Bernard's Electronic with Johnny Marr, Peter Hook's Revenge and the other two's, er, The Other Two, the band returned with the guitar-driven Get Ready. *The band's last album to date,* Waiting for the Sirens' Call, *was released in 2005.*

PETER HOOK

To this day Bernard and I and Stephen have never talked about music. We just go into a room and start playing. The only time we ever say anything is 'What kind of song do we want?' We always say the same thing – a fast dancey song – and then you come out with 'We All Stand', a really slow broody number! So it was just one of those funny things when Bernard and I got back together again after he did Electronic and I did Revenge. When he was doing Electronic he used to sit there for hours talking about music with Johnny Marr, and at the time Pottsy* and I would sit there for hours talking about music. But as soon as we got back together again as New Order we stopped. I suppose that's chemistry – we don't need to talk about it, we get on with it. Does that make it a bit clinical? It's rare that you get that chemistry. People always say, 'You're fucking shit apart, why don't you play together?' But if only life was that easy!

I met Bernard when I was 11, I met Steve when I was 21. Bernard was my best friend for a long time till we formed the band. Being in a band is fucking murder! It's like a marriage without the sex! We had a good time though, because Rob ran the band in a different way. We flew around America after the first tour. The first dates we did in America as a three-piece was the only time we drove around America; ever since then we've always flown because Rob insisted we fly everywhere. We never had a tour bus, ever. We came home with no money, but we kept our sanity because you're not cooped up together. You have a hotel room so you're separate from the rest of them. It also meant you got a lot of freedom. It's a much nicer way of travelling than being stuck on a bus. I reckon it gave us an extra ten years as a band, even if it cost us ten years financially!

One of the interesting things about New Order is that every time we were getting somewhere we stopped! As Joy Division we were just getting somewhere when Ian died, so we stopped; as New Order we started again and just when we were getting somewhere we stopped and went off and did all our own things. Then when we got back together, lo and behold, just when we were getting somewhere as New Order we went and stopped again. It's quite interesting. If we did it again we would probably stop, but I can't imagine that – not in a million years.

When I listen back to the music I think: fuck me, we did get something right. And no matter what you say about New Order, we achieved what we did. You know how hard it is to write a song and record it and get it to a point of release – that's a fucking long journey. When you've done that and it's all over, all the pain and anguish you went through to get that song written and recorded and out disappears in a puff of smoke, but the song lasts there for ever.

* David Potts played bass in Revenge and went on to join Peter Hook as lead vocalist in Monaco.

Barney wants to work in his way and I want to work in my way, and Steve will do whatever anyone else wants. Barney likes to work alone but I like to work with people – what I love is everyone kicking around ideas and something coming together in a pot, and Barney doesn't like that. He likes to work on his own. Barney has a way that he likes to write. What he hates most is jamming, but what I love is jamming because you get that magical little kernel of four bars when you all play together and you go, 'Fuck me, there it is!' But you have to listen to six weeks of dross to get the four bars that turn into a top tune, and for him that's six weeks of hell.

New Order eventually petered out. I felt that Bernard was playing down my role in his songwriting. He would say, 'Here's a song. You do the middle eight.' Everything I play has to go through him and he'll say, 'I like that bit, but I don't like that,' and I'm going, 'I don't do that to you, with the bits of yours I don't like.' The thing is, he doesn't feel the bass is the main part of the sound and he's part of the band and if he doesn't feel that, then you got a problem. I mean, it's taste. I'm not saying he's wrong and I'm right.

Currently New Order no longer exist after Peter Hook's 2007 announcement that he had quit the band.

MANCHESTER: A CITY UNITED

Well, sort of! Punk, Joy Division and Factory were still the main story in the city, but after Ian Curtis's suicide Joy Division were brought to a sudden halt, and in the meantime new projects and new bands were emerging. This was an interesting crossover period – the key players in the next big surge of Manchester bands were running around town making connections.

LIZ NAYLOR
Richard Boon started the Beach Club. He wanted to bring people together.

RICHARD BOON
Between the closure of the PSV/Russell Club and building of the Hacienda, the bunch of active misfits around New Hormones thought we – or the city – needed a space for regular counter-culture insurgency or just somewhere we'd like to hang out, with people we'd like to hang out with. It turned out to be Oozits in Shude Hill* – a gay club with a bar on each of two floors. So we started the Beach Club.

LIZ NAYLOR
I knew it as Oozits; it was a horrible firetrap sort of place! I used to go with Pip from the Distractions and it was full of butches and old-school lesbians like in *The Killing of Sister George*. Manchester was such a grim city then. Shude Hill was a dark Victorian maze of streets.

RICHARD BOON
The idea was to have cult films in the first-floor bar area: the likes of *Reefer Madness* and Tod Browning's *Freaks*, for instance; and upstairs, live

* Shude Hill is one of the oldest parts of the city centre and was once Manchester's Fleet Street.

music with the rounding-up of the usual subjects: Eric Random, Ludus, ACR, Swamp Children, Vini Reilly, etc., plus non-Manc bands.

The Beach club was the live debut of New Order, who were unnamed at the time and topping a Factory bill with the Names and Wally Van Middendorp's Dutch outfit, Minny Pops; New Order were sounding like Kraut-traum-rockers Popol Vuh, as it happened.

The name of the club, natch, came from the Situationist Paris '68 slogan: 'Underneath the paving stones, the beach.'

JON SAVAGE
People like Liz Naylor were very much around, with Cath Carroll as the Glass Animals; they were a terrifying pair in their sixties suits. I liked them a lot. Around that time I must have got to know Morrissey as well, because he lived in Stretford on Kings Road. I lived near Stretford and he came round to my house a few times to listen to records.

LIZ NAYLOR
We would walk around Manchester dressed outrageously. Cath wore a cape! When we went back home to Harpurhey gangs of youths would stone us, and we wondered why we were being attacked by these horrible youths (*laughs*).

Then for some reason I got pally with Jon Savage and he got me writing for *Melody Maker*. I was completely useless but he made me go and review a gig. I had no sense of self-motivation or worth. I was a depressed teenager. I didn't have any get-up-and-go but somehow I ended up writing for *Melody Maker*.

PAUL RYDER
In 1979–80 there was a place in Piccadilly called Portland Bars. That's where me and our kid and Matt and our mates would watch bands. It was the Boardwalk* of the day, with all kinds of unknown bands like Clive Gregson's Any Trouble. Four nights a week there was live music on. We went to the Apollo for Adam and the Ants, Teardrop Explodes, Human League.

DAVE HASLAM
Ian McCulloch was the big iconic person in that kind of little moment. In that post-punk era, people were reading and watching films, there

* The Boardwalk on Little Peter Street was a nerve centre of the mid-eighties Manchester music scene. The likes of A Certain Ratio, Happy Mondays, the Membranes and the Inca Babies used the rehearsal rooms downstairs, while upstairs was a 400 capacity venue where all the breakthrough bands of the time played.

was a big period of musical and intellectual exploration. It wasn't done in a pretentious kind of way – more in a hungry-for-information kind of way.

JOHNNY MARR

Joe Moss is an important face in Manchester. He came up with the slogan 'On the eighth day God created Manchester' and he was the first person to get on to flares. Joe told Lloyd to make the trousers wider and wider before Phil Saxe got on them.

I would rush over to Joe's place on Portland Street in my half-hour lunch break and he would play me Little Richard and Phil Spector records. Joe . . . said, 'Why don't you come and work with me?' I was like, 'Can I do that?' and I was given the basement of Portland Street, which Joe had filled full of secondhand clothes.

I would get in at 11. Me and Joe would talk about John Lee Hooker for an hour and I would say, 'I'd better open the shop.' Joe would say, 'Hang on a minute, let's have another cup of tea,' so I would sit there for another half hour talking about Elvis Presley or about the band I was trying to get together. To this day I don't think there's ever been a better boss.

LIZ NAYLOR

At some point we started managing Ludus and we were rubbish at it. I guess Linder liked the idea of two weird lesbians managing her!

Through Linder we were introduced to Richard Boon and I would run around gigs taking lots of speed. I remember Morrissey as some morose figure who was always [hanging] around Linder in an overcoat . . .

In a sense Morrissey and Linder were quite similar; he was very switched on and seemed to be learning from her. Me and Cath spent a lot of time in Newton Street. Nico would always be on the couch; we thought she was some strange woman in a sheepskin coat. She was living in Whalley Range at the time taking smack.

MELANIE SMITH (editor of *Mudkiss*)

My initial experience of Pips nightclub in Manchester was in 1981. It struck me as an adult fantasy playground, exotic creatures decked in wild and wonderful outfits.

The first room I entered was the Bowie and Roxy room with its silver DJ booth on the lower level. It was a small cave-like room with paintings on the wall of Bowie and Ferry, the seating being alcove areas. It could be quite cliquey, though. In here you'd find the Ferry guys, Numan and Bowie clones in various stages of Bowie's career. The dance floor was usually cleared so the Bowie clones could do their thing, dancing in an animated wild-gestured style.

As I recall there seemed to be five rooms in total, all playing different music.

RICHARD WITTS

There is a tendency to think clubs started with the Hacienda, but there were a number of clubs already around, like Pips with its Bowie Room. That was where some of Joy Division went in the seventies. It was another network where people would meet in a room full of narcissists.

BRIAN CANNON (sleeve designer for Oasis and the Verve)

When I found out about New Order and the Fall it made a huge difference that they were from Manchester. It really clicked that you didn't have to be from Mars to be in a band.

JOHNNY MARR

I was the first person to lay a brick down on what has now become Sankeys.* Then it was Decibel Studios and it saved me from being thrown in the nick. I was there on New Year's Eve to get free studio time.

GRAHAM MASSEY

We got connected with Tony Wilson and the Biting Tongues† got signed to Factory, but things didn't really improve for us. When we did a gig we were 100 per cent committed and there was that idiotic, joyful enthusiasm to make music.

I always liked the idea of being the non-musician, the sound manipulator. I liked the idea of that role and I carried it forward from the Biting Tongues. I always liked the idea of being Snakefinger more than Jimi Hendrix. It's about organising sound; it's not about middle eights, verses and choruses.

ANDREW BERRY

In '80–'81 my friend John Kennedy persuaded Bernard Slingsby, who owned Bernard's Bar, to let us use his nightclub Slingsby's on Wood Street. Renaming it the Exit, we set about trying to get a Manchester scene going on. i-D and the Face came down, Spandau and Wham. I was the DJ, pre-Smiths Johnny Marr would play funk and soul tunes . . .

---

* Club located right at the back of the northern quarter.
† A left-field free jazz outfit of which Massey was a member.

Andrew Berry's Exit Top 10

Funky Nassau – The Beginning of the End
Be Thankful for What You've Got – William DeVaughn
Disco Stomp – Bohannon
Sex Machine – James Brown
Family Affair – Sly and the Family Stone
Low Rider – War
Soul Makossa – Manu Dibango
Why Can't We Live Together – Timmy Thomas
Go Bang – Dinosaur L
Funkin' For Jamaica – Tom Brown

JOHNNY MARR

Andrew was someone I knew in Wythenshawe in 1976 and he very publicly decided he was going to be a hairdresser. At that time that meant saying, 'I'm a big poof,' which he was not; the graffiti went round Wythenshawe saying, 'Andrew Berry is a big poof,' but he was super hip. Andrew had four sisters and he knew how girls ticked. He knew they liked a guy who could give them great hair. Andrew was a Roxy kid and a Bowie kid. Later, when the Smiths were forming, he was this very exotic creature who helped me earn dough by DJing with him at the Exit club just off Deansgate. We would play what became known later as rare groove.

ANDREW BERRY

When I started hairdressing in '78, there wasn't that much going on as far as clubs were concerned. The best club at the time was Deville's just off Albert Square. It was hard to get in because it was a gay club and gay and straight clubs were separate then. All the best looking girls would go there. People were slightly older and seemed to have money. They drank cocktails and danced to Giorgio Moroder and Chic in a haze of dry ice and strobe light, whilst sniffing poppers and dressed in Fiorucci. It was the closest thing to Studio 54 we had.

JOHNNY MARR

You can't underestimate the importance of Andrew Berry. He was one of the DJs at the early Hacienda and he knew everybody. He still does. He furnished Bernard Sumner with his haircut, which was very important, and then he would do mine and eventually Morrissey's. He decided that his salon was going to be in the dressing room of the Hacienda . . .

One of the crucial things Andrew brought in was that he played absolutely up-to-the-minute electro at the Hacienda – up-to-date, early electro. That's why in 'How Soon Is Now' the harmonic lick is from Lovebug Starski (Bronx-born electro/hip-hop pioneer): that was me getting one up on the journalists, putting a lick from a hip-hop record into a Smiths song. All the Bobby O releases were amazing stuff. Andrew, from the late seventies, had been very very involved in the Manchester gay disco scene. He brought into my life an awareness of what was going on in the gay scene in Manchester, whether it was Bobby O records or the fashions . . .

Very importantly, Andrew brought me into gay clubs, and very important to me and the Smiths was a club called Manhattan run by this fantastic guy called Dennis. It was a little club, and me and Andrew would go in there at seven when there was no one in there. We would go up to the DJ booth and play the records we wanted. We liked gay clubs – the people who ran them were funny and there was frankly no alternative apart from Corbieres; that was all right, but aside from that it was clubs and pubs, which meant football fans and dickheads.

ANDREW BERRY

Heroes on King Street (entrance at rear) was another gay club but this time more hardcore – a real clone club, San Francisco, almost like Skin Two, slightly fetishy, druggie, a bit seedy with rent boys and old men. The music was amazing: DJ Les Cockell who had come from the northern soul scene and had got into hardcore hi-energy. It was open every night and was always packed. I met Diana Dors there! And Quentin Crisp.

JOHNNY MARR

When the Hacienda opened, Andrew quickly became one of the DJs. He was really into the electro scene coming out of New York. He had everything on the Ze label, like Suicide, James Chance, Was (Not Was), Lydia Lunch, James White and the Blacks, the Contortions, Mars.

ANDREW BERRY

When The Hacienda opened, we were fucked. No one came to the club any more so we had to find a new venue. John Kennedy was amazing; he could talk anyone into anything. We took over a club on King Street and called it Berlin. It was small, a recently refurbished basement where George Best hung out during his seventies champagne years. We would go to the Hac[ienda] midweek to watch the gigs and on Friday and Saturday DJ at Berlin.

The electronic drum-machine driven music that emerged from the Bronx after Kraftwerk influenced a generation of musicians.

GREG WILSON

Piccadilly was the biggest local radio station outside London, broadcasting throughout the Greater Manchester region, so Mike Shaft's weekly soul show, *Takin' Care of Business*, wielded a lot of power. If Mike played a new import, Spin Inn* would invariably order more copies from the States to meet the expected demand. Along with Spin Inn and the all-dayers, it was one of the linchpins of the entire scene up north.

If you didn't buy your records at Spin Inn you couldn't seriously call yourself a black music specialist, simple as. It was the only shop in the region that stocked the very latest imports.

By 1980, Mike Shaft, along with Robbie Vincent and Greg Edwards in London, was regarded as the most influential soul show presenter in the UK, playing a superior selection of soul, funk, disco and jazz-funk, whilst making regular appearances on the all-dayer circuit.

It was around this point that I took over the Wednesday jazz-funk night at Legend,† which had previously enjoyed a purple patch under John Grant's stewardship but was now struggling to survive, given Grant's defection to the Main Event, which was dominating the local scene. I was very much the new kid in town, having announced my arrival via my successful Wigan Pier residency. Nine months later, in May 1982, Legend had hit capacity, turning the entire scene on its head in the process. With its sound and lighting arguably the best in the country, it was the ideal environment for the oncoming electro-funk epoch. Furthermore, I'd placed the emphasis on mixing, which set me apart from all the other black music specialists north of Watford.

What was happening at Legend was a whole new thing. Despite not being the biggest fan of this new electrophonic direction, Mike Shaft, in a similar way to how he reflected the interest in jazz by involving guests like Colin Curtis and Hewan Clarke, invited me to put together a mix for his show – the first of its type in this country, focusing on the imports I was playing at the time.

A GUY CALLED GERALD (Gerald Simpson)

As soon as I heard there was going to be a Greg Wilson mix on the radio

* Manchester's main record shop for dance music in the early eighties.
† Opened in 1980 with a state-of-the-art sound system, Legend was perfect for the funk soundtrack that dominated the club's early days

I would run over to Shadus, the local electronic shop, and buy a brand new chrome C90 TDK cassette tape. I would make sure I was in front of the Amstrad with my finger on the pause button when that mix started. It didn't matter what was happening anywhere else. That mix would get played to death – the tape would be worn out until his next guest appearance on Piccadilly Radio.

GREG WILSON

The end of year 'Best Of '82' mix became something of an underground phenomenon, setting off a sequence of 'Best of the Year' mixes that would run on Piccadilly and later Key 103 for another decade.

From a black perspective, clubbing was a serious business. It wasn't just about going out to party; it was far deeper. These were kids who during their normal day to day were being regularly stopped and searched by the police, many picking up drug convictions for having little more than a spliff's worth of grass on their person. Most were unemployed – it was difficult enough to find a job if you were white working class, let alone black. Then there was the racism, which was a constant in their lives. With all this going on, the need to release the pressure was massive, and, for many, this was done on the dance floor.

The atmosphere in a club like Legend was absolutely intense – this was no hands-in-the-air party vibe, but seriously good dancers losing themselves in the music, which was oozing creativity at the time.

What you must bear in mind was that this all happened in the years that followed the inner-city race riots in England. In my neck of the woods these, of course, included the major uprisings in Toxteth [Liverpool] and Moss Side [Manchester]. Many of the original electro-funk crowd were people who'd been involved in these riots, or were at least caught up in them. They were mainly sons and daughters of West Indian immigrants, and were regarded as British only by place of birth. Black people were third-class citizens at the time, firmly at the bottom of the barrel and outcasts in their own country. Racism still exists in the UK, but back then it was rife, and the black community was the target of constant abuse and often violence from their white counterparts.

Legend was very much a black Manchester thing; most whites felt extremely uncomfortable in the heady reefer-intoxicated atmosphere of the club – it was pretty much a matter of 'spot the white man'. The idea of going to a 'black club' and experiencing what it might be like to now find themselves in the minority, evoked far too threatening a scenario for most white lads (it was slightly different for white girls, who often came along not just for the music, but because they were into the black guys). For blacks, there were precious few places where they could mix with whites on an equal basis; most of the time it was just tokenism, the unwritten rule of door policy in the majority of clubs being to perhaps let a few blacks in, but not too many. For a black kid in those days, one of the few real highs in life was going out to dance, and in the clubs they were always one step ahead, be it the music they were into or the moves that they made . . .

The type of kids who came to Legend were the first generation of black people in this country to really fight back. Their attitude was: 'Fuck you, we're here and you better get used to it.'

In the North and Midlands, the early house releases, before anyone called them house, were played alongside electro in the black clubs and regarded as part of the electro soundscape – just as when Cybotron's 'Clear' was issued on 12-inch in '83, it was considered an electro track that just happened to come from a different city to New York. There was no such category as techno until later down the line. Klein & MBO's 'Dirty Talk' would be another example – this is now seen as an Italo disco classic, but the term Italo disco didn't exist until a German company, ZYX, released an album of Italian tracks towards the end of '83 under the title. For us, 'Dirty Talk' (the instrumental 'USA Connection' version of course) was one of the biggest electro-funk records of '82. It didn't matter that it came from Italy; the country of origin wasn't the criteria, it was the sound and the groove that made it electro-funk to our ears . . .

For London, house was more likely to be heard in the gay clubs post-1988, but in the North/Midlands it was very much part of the overall black music spectrum. The black scene in London was going through the whole rare groove period, where they set the stage for the coming raves via their warehouse parties.

MIKE PICKERING

I was playing really electro stuff – 'Planet Rock', Man Parrish. Greg [Wilson] was only the DJ before I started that played that kind of music.

GREG WILSON

At the time clubbers in London just hadn't considered the possibility that the cutting edge was in Manchester – it was still a time when, for many, north of Watford was regarded as something of a backwater where nothing of importance could possibly be happening.

House was originally another ingredient of the electronic stew, which happened to come from Chicago as opposed to New York. The same goes for the Detroit releases that we'd later refer to as techno. These imports slotted in hand in glove alongside the electro – they were all part of the new direction dance music had taken as far as the people who went to the clubs were concerned, and they'd yet to be compartmentalised into separate genres, and later sub-genres.

JOHNNY JAY (DJ and producer)
I would pick up on music from the radio when I was young. I was influenced by the pop music at the time in the seventies – which was pretty dodgy (*laughs*) – until I saw the Jackson Five, and it was probably how they looked to be truthful. It didn't move me to make music. Even at school I was a football nut and that was it, not music at all. I'm Cheetham Hill born and bred and I used to hang out at Abraham Moss college in the evenings where they did art and music stuff.

I got into music with body-popping.* I was a body-popper; the first thing to hit me was Kurtis Blow whose first single, 'Christmas Rapping' had just come out.† I knew something was happening in America and I didn't have anything solid to reference – there were only three TV channels in England and they were pretty bad, so we picked up bits and pieces as we found them. The first thing I saw long enough to copy the dance moves was Jeffrey Daniel on *Top of the Pops*.‡ It wasn't the music; it was him and his performance. He had the white gloves and he did the moonwalk, the robot, and those Marcel Marceau mime things. Then we saw the documentary *Style Wars*, the film *Wild Style*, and that brought everything into focus.§

---

* Jerky dance style from seventies California that in the early eighties became a street craze in the UK, where it was used to dance along to funk, disco and electro.
† Born in Harlem, New York, Kurtis Blow was one of the first stars of hip-hop, coming out of the original block party scene with his crossover classic 1980 hit 'The Breaks' at a time when the music business had no understanding of hip-hop.
‡ Daniel performed the 'moonwalk' on television in 1982 during a performance of Shalamar's 'A Night to Remember', almost a year before Michael Jackson moonwalked for the first time.
§ *Style Wars* was a key 1983 New York documentary on the new hip-hop culture; *Wild Style* was the first hip-hop feature film, released in 1982. Many of the UK hip-hop scene talk about how the film introduced a generation to the hip-hop culture of dancing, graffiti art and clothes as well as the music.

BREAKDANCERS

One of the key subcultures in eighties Manchester was breakdancing. Dancers would lay down pieces of lino in the street and, in a blur of Sergio Tacchini and Fila tracksuits, Puma trainers, sovereign rings and gold rope chains, throw a complex series of dance shapes. Broken Glass were the pioneers, Street Machine the upstarts; between them they imported New York's street culture to the greyness of Manchester. The roots of breakdancing go back to the mid-seventies, when DJ Kool Herc, a Jamaican-born New Yorker, started mixing funk records to create a seamless flow of dance beats, which he called 'cutting breaks'. The kids who danced to those breaks he called B-boys, meaning either 'boogie boys' or 'break boys'. At block parties, Herc would shout out, 'B-boys go down!' and the dancers would hit the floor with an upgraded version of what they did on the streets – a mixture of dance styles and martial arts moves they adapted from kung fu films.

Hip-hop culture first made a serious impression in the UK in 1982, when Grandmaster Flash and the Furious Five released 'The Message', a piece of social commentary that made an impact on young black Britons in the aftermath of the 1981 riots. But the record that brought breakdancing to the UK mainstream was Malcolm McLaren's 'Buffalo Girls'.

GREG WILSON

Malcolm McLaren's 'Buffalo Girls' was the first video where you could see a DJ scratching. The World Famous Supreme Team were scratching a seven-inch single. The video also introduced three of the four elements of hip-hop – scratching, graffiti and breakdancing – into this country.

BENJI READ (playwright and former dancer)

When I first saw people doing those moves, spinning on their heads, I couldn't believe it. It was the first time you had seen a physical depiction of the culture. You got to see the dancers doing headspins, backspins. It showed us the moves.

GREG WILSON

Smac 19 were a breakdance crew from Sheffield, who travelled around to places like Wigan Pier and the all-dayers for battles against other crews like the Wolverhampton B Boys,* Nottingham's Rock City Crew, who were named after the Rock City club and, of course Manchester's Broken Glass, who by 1984 were picking up national TV exposure, taking things

---

* One of whom was Goldie.

to a whole new level with appearances on shows like *The Tube*, *CBTV* and *Some You Win*.*

The first time I saw Broken Glass was one night when the people from Huddersfield came on to the floor first, but the Manchester kids responded immediately with their moves. I soon found out that the Broken Glass Street Crew, as they were known then, had been practising, getting ready to unleash in a club.

Broken Glass would go on to play a big part in helping acclimatise the Hacienda clientele to the electro sounds I was playing in 1983, especially during my hour-long Saturday night spots, when they took to the Hacienda stage. At this point breakdancing was regarded as extremely cutting edge and people would stand back and admire their energy and athleticism.

At first, the indie kids in the club were bemused, but the dancing helped turn them on to electro, paving the way for the house revolution a few years later, and providing an often-overlooked link in the city's musical heritage. Perhaps they taught Manchester how to dance. They certainly gave a curiously Mancunian bent to an American street culture.

JASON ORANGE (Take That)
You can't describe the atmosphere in the clubs when Broken Glass were there. All those different crews at the time – the competition was fierce. It was like the film *The Warriors*, without the violence.† They were the most important days of my life.

BENJI READ
We'd be out there battling, seeing who had the best moves. It kept us out of trouble. When I joined Broken Glass, I had to work hard. You had to rehearse and go out on tour.

SEFTON (breakdancer with Broken Glass)
It gave us a life. I was a latchkey kid, I was 12 or 13 at the time, and I would go round the country doing the human beatbox, playing to 5000 people in London. That was something.

KERMIT (rapper with Ruthless Rap Assassins and Black Grape)
I remember meeting Greg Wilson for the first time at Legends and

* *CBTV* was a children's TV programme; *Some You Win* was a Saturday-night peak-time variety show, hosted by Lulu.
† Walter Hill's entertaining and influential cult gang-warfare film *The Warriors* (1979) featured suitably outrageous, sci-fi style gangs battling it out on the streets of Brooklyn

discovering the club nights down there in the mid-eighties. I also remember when we were doing Broken Glass and we were putting out our mats in the centre of town, getting ready, you know, stretching and things and these coppers come and arrest me!

JOHNNY JAY

You saw the lifestyle and you would aspire to that lifestyle, everything you got in bits and pieces – the Sugarhill Gang, Kurtis Blow, Dr Heckle and Mr Jive, Funky Four Plus One. You got Africa Bambaataa as well. Early on *Wild Style* gave you the lifestyle. Grandmaster Flash was in *Style Wars* and I was totally blown away! We then had a little crew in Cheetham Hill, which we called Soul Sonic Rockers or something really dodgy! But it sounded enough like Africa Bambaataa's Soul Sonic Force.

We used to go to my mate's house who had a video and watch and practise the moves. It was an interesting time. It hadn't exploded then. I went to the High School of Art on Cheetham Hill Road. Kermit was there from Broken Glass. Kermit was a bodypopper at the time. He was good and original and creative. There was a good little scene. When we were about 15 to 19, 60 of the guys would go to Legends.

We got to see more of the breakdancing when we saw *Style Wars*. We saw the Rock Steady Crew and Crazy Legs.* These performances would come on the telly and, the week after, everyone would be practising the moves, but it was very underground. It was the black youth, it was our way of expressing ourselves. The ska and Two Tone thing was more about the Jamaicans. My parents were Nigerian. I didn't have rice and peas till I was 18 at a Jamaican girlfriend's house when I went round for tea (*laughs*).

EVO (Street Machine)

In New York they would dance to original funk breaks, James Brown, stuff like that. Over here it was electro, and that changed the way we danced.

JOHNNY JAY

We were Thatcher's generation. We were the 'How can she fuck the miners and all that' generation. We were on the dole, we were the '1 in 10', and it means we couldn't identify with the soul music coming out of America – guys with makeup on and roses in their mouths singing about love. I remember Grandmaster Flash's lyrics: 'Rats in the front room, roaches in the back. Junkies in the alley with a baseball bat . . .'† These

---

* One of the original members of the Rock Steady Crew.
† From Grandmaster Flash's seminal and brilliant 'The Message'

were the first lyrics that I thought were exactly my life. I fell into the imagery of New York and that particular black experience. 'The Message' for us was life-changing, although we didn't get the outfits (*laughs*). There was no other music – the only other music was Duran Duran. It was a good grounding for music; it sounded so different and it sounded right and exciting. For me the Stooges are cut from the same cloth; for me it feels the same – 'I Wanna Be Your Dog' (*laughs*). Brilliant! It's someone else's truth and it got me into music. I didn't ever think of this as a career. I started with the dancing, then moved to DJing and then promoting my own gigs.

GREG WILSON

I first started playing electro before Afrika Bambaataa and the Soul Sonic Force's seminal electro classic, 'Planet Rock' on Tommy Boy exploded on the scene in May '82. There had already been a handful of releases in the previous months that would help define this new genre. D Train's 'You're the One for Me' (Prelude), which was massive during late '81, would set the tone, paving the way for 'Time' by Stone (West End), 'Feels Good' by Electra (Emergency) and two significant Eric Matthew/Darryl Payne productions, Sinnamon's 'Thanks To You' (Becket) and, once again courtesy of Prelude, 'On a Journey (I Sing the Funk Electric)' by Electrik Funk (the term electro-funk originally deriving from this track, 'electric-funk' being amended to electro-funk following the arrival of Shock's 'Electrophonic Phunk' on the Californian Fantasy label in June). However, the most significant of all the early releases was 'Don't Make Me Wait' by the Peech Boys (West End), for this was no longer hinting at a new direction, it was unmistakably the real deal.

JOHNNY JAY

I bought records to dance to like Kurtis Blow's 'Christmas Rappin' and then some records on Tommy Boy Records. The Africa Bambaataa records were expensive when you'd got no money – especially the imports. I would buy one a month. I DJed at a youth club so I could get more records because I got paid. I fell into that lifestyle of getting records and DJing. The records were sold in plastic bags from Spin Inn and I got a reputation for carrying records in plastic bags before I elevated to my mum's shopping bag.

I turned up at Abraham Moss and they found the old decks in a cupboard, a pair of Jimmy Savile double decks with a microphone on it. I thought, wow! And I went there every night and practised when I should have been doing college work. They would pay me £2 a night and the UK imports were £1.50, so I worked out very quickly that I had to look for youth clubs that could pay me so I could buy more records. Quickly I was working everywhere. Eventually I built up a collection of electro and early rap imports.

Mike Shaft, who was the big local radio DJ, did Saturday afternoons at the Music Box/Rafters. I went down with my shopping bag full of records and said, 'I'll help you promote your club if you let me DJ.' I took the flyers to all the places I was DJing at the time – Abraham Moss, Moss Side, Chorlton, West Didsbury and Wythenshawe, Baguley and Longsight, and handed them out everywhere I went. The next week, instead of 20 people being at the Music Box he had 200 kids paying about three quid. I didn't get to DJ much but at the end of the night I was paid four quid. I didn't care. I said, 'Give me more flyers,' and I put Mike Shaft's and my name on the same flyer! The third week the kids came down and robbed the cigarette machine and Shaftie closed it down. I was devastated.

But I now knew how to promote my own club, so I got Satellite in Cheetham Hill and promoted my own night. The first night I made £31; we had about 50 kids. Broken Glass and Street Machine were there at the club. I was playing only electro and the second week we had 400 people and I pocketed 800 quid – I had never seen so much money in my life! I remember putting the money on my bed going, 'Oh my God!' From there I got into promoting various things – all-dayers and all-nighters, hiring the Gallery.*

GREG WILSON

After this the controversy started, with what the purists called the 'blatant' electro-funk – 'Planet Rock' of course, stuff like 'ET Boogie' by the Extra T's, 'Dirty Talk' by Klein & MBO, which broke out of Legend as an Italian import, 'Nunk' by Warp 9, etc. These were despised by the old guard, and dismissed as mindless machine muzak that had no place on the 'soul scene'. The crowd definitely began to split as a result; we lost a fair chunk of the white kids who'd been regulars at Wigan Pier whilst jazz-funk held sway, but filled the gap with black kids, who instantly went for this new electro sound. Legend, being a black club, didn't have the same dynamic – it just went through the roof and became the most cutting-edge night in the country. It was way ahead of the game – everything was lined up for it, with the club building momentum in the months leading up to 'Planet Rock's release. It was perfectly positioned for this new musical direction, and was the ideal venue, given its state-of-the-art sound and lighting system.

---

* A long-gone and demolished venue, the scene of early Stone Roses shows and one of REM's first ever UK gigs.

Legend opened in 1980. It was so impressive that even now, over a quarter of a century on, it would blow people away if they walked into such a venue – they just don't make clubs like Legend any more (must say at this point that the black crowd always, for some reason, called it Legends). It was the first club I'd worked in with a sub bass system, it was the first British club I'd worked in with SL1200s (three of them), its light show was described in *Black Echoes* as like something out of *Close Encounters of the Third Kind* – suffice to say that this was a truly amazing club

What should be remembered is that before Wigan Pier and Legend, black music nights had generally been held in run-down venues that were struggling for trade (hence allowing the black crowd there in the first place). Wigan Pier and Legend bucked the trend somewhat, welcoming the black audience into an environment that they'd never experienced before, with arguably the best sound and lighting in the UK at the time.

Before rave, most white guys would only take to the dance floor if they wanted to make a move on a girl, and would certainly not have dreamed of getting up and starting to dance on their own, with the exception of those who were involved in specialist scenes like northern soul and jazz-funk.

It was the total opposite with black kids, as dancing was an integral part of their culture; it was completely natural for them to go out to dance. They were fluid on the dance floor and the best dancers were held in high regard – deservingly so, because their moves were something to behold! There was a lot of footwork involved, so floor space was necessary – when challenges developed, even before the whole breakdancing period, circles would form around the dancers, with those at the front pushing back to create more space for the dancers to utilise.

Before electro-funk there was northern soul, disco and jazz-funk, after electro-funk there was hip-hop, house and techno. The electro-funk era was the catalyst that enabled the old to become the new – it was right at the crossroads as far as British dance culture is concerned. Without it things could never have worked out in the way that they did.

THE HACIENDA MUST BE BUILT

The Hacienda wasn't just another nightclub. Transplanting a piece of New York-style club architecture into the collapsing old warehouses of the back end of the city centre arguably fast-forwarded Manchester's renovation. In the 21st century the whole of Manchester looks like the Hacienda.

The Hacienda was conceived as an arts centre/club/gig venue/cinema in a way that was radical then and would be radical now. It was Factory's Situationism in 3D and it became a nerve centre for a lot of the city's culture in the next few years.

JON SAVAGE

The Hacienda came about because the Russell Club, which was our club, wasn't there any more. It was that critical post-JD moment when everybody was pretty depressed. Ian's death had caused a real pall to fall over Manchester. I have a very good memory but I can't remember anything I did in May 1980 . . . I have a hole in my memory, which was obviously to deal with the shock.

It was pretty dreary in Manchester after that – Buzzcocks were breaking up after those three last great singles with Martin Hannett.* People were getting into Dislocation Dance and for me that was really dreary territory – I remember getting the record thinking it was just nothing. At this point Manchester needed something.

RICHARD BOON

I was down at some gig at the Music Machine in London. I went with Cath Carroll and Tony Wilson and we were saying, 'This environment is awful to go and see a band in.' Tony Wilson said, 'We got to make a decent venue in Manchester.' Add to that their early adventures to New York, which were so influential – there was an idea that there should be something like a New York loft place, incongruously in the middle of Manchester.

HOWARD JONES (manager of the Hacienda and Stone Roses)

Rob Gretton was looking to do shows for New Order just after Ian had died. He was very delicately figuring out how to put the band back into gigs. Rob rang me and asked what I was doing. I was putting on a gig and Rob said New Order might be up for doing that. I rang Phil Jones, who was the social sec at the Poly, and he said, 'Yeah, let's do it.'

PHIL JONES (promoter)

Rob wanted to put New Order on and we did it. We had 1200 in on a cold Tuesday night. After that gig there was some sort of meeting in the dressing room and the idea of a club came up.†

HOWARD JONES

It was a brilliant gig, one of their first gigs. After the gig we were sitting

---

* 'Are Everything', Strange Thing' and 'Running Free', the last three Buzzcocks singles, were released in quick succession before the band split up in 1980.
† In fact it was New Order's seventeenth gig, on 6 February 1981

in the dressing room. We shut the doors and Rob Gretton said, 'Instead of promoting from one place to another, why don't we do it in one club?' He said to me that he and Tony were thinking of doing that. They didn't own the Factory club in Hulme, where they were already promoting gigs, and the club kept upping its price. The more successful they got, the more it cost them. So he said, 'Are you interested in running a club?' I said 'Of course,' and that was it sorted out.

HOWARD JONES
In March Rob rang me and said, 'The Marine Centre on Whitworth Street is closing down. Why don't we go and have a look at that as the location for the club?' I went down there on 19 March 1981. As soon as I walked in, we knew that it had to be there. We also looked at a couple of other clubs. [We looked at] the Tropicana on Oxford Road but it was too sleazy. And ironically we also looked at the site of what would become the Dry Bar, and somewhere by the church at the bottom of Deansgate.

BEN KELLY
Peter said to me that Factory were talking about doing a club. Peter did everything graphics-wise for Factory and they assumed that he would be designing the club, but when he realised the enormity of the task and the discipline involved he said he had no idea about it. And he told Tony Wilson he knew someone who could get the job done.

PETER SAVILLE
When the Hacienda design came up, Ben Kelly enjoyed the same sort of autonomy of design that we had. No one told Ben Kelly what a nightclub should be like. No one said what he could or couldn't do. He had the autonomy to do what he wanted to do.

BEN KELLY
I got off at Piccadilly Station and was met by Howard 'Ginger' Jones in a red sports car and whizzed off to the building. We did a tour of the building; Tony was there and Alan [Erasmus] as usual turned up halfway through with Rob. We went round this filthy, dirty, shambolic space, but I could see amazing potential. They said, 'Did you want the job?' and I said, 'Of course I want the fucking job!'

I think Factory probably thought, A coat of paint, tart it up and put in some toilets and a bar and you're away. But I could see it was a bigger job than that! There was an existing mezzanine balcony in there which was a rickety thing – they thought that could stay. They had no sense of building design or the local authorities and all the hoops you have to jump through. It became clear to them early on that this was a bigger project than they thought. New elements were going in, new thinking – like what was the club going to be? A full-on nightclub? A bar? Or a club? What attracted me was it had the potential to be a hybrid environment. Consequently the biggest decision that had to be made was where to put the stage. That argument went on for a long time. Rob had strong feelings about it, and because he was managing a band his logic said put it at the far end of the space where the bar was going to go. My view was that its primary function was to be a venue which they were calling a club, whereas Rob wanted a club to 'ogle the birds in', which was his famous quote.

PETER SAVILLE

Ben's work is about the industrial urban environment. He grew up working class in Yorkshire; he had his own fantasy of the industrial aesthetic and he was playful with it. He saw it as something you could articulate in a positive way; you didn't have to see it as oppression. Ben's use of the diagonal stripe is quite up, whereas very often we encounter it in an oppressive way – i.e. 'Be careful, hazard warning, don't go here'. Ben turned that round and said, 'Hey, this is fun, it's quite exciting!'

BEN KELLY

The black and yellow stripes I came up with because there were a number of columns on the dance floor that could be perceived as quite hazardous. People could hurt themselves if they weren't careful. In industrial premises there is a way of coding hazardous elements, so I thought that was the explicit language that the clients, who were called Factory, would be perfect for.

HOWARD JONES

Whitworth Street was the perfect location. It was worked out was that most of the potential clientele at that point would walk from Hulme, where they were living, and that was just down the road.* It made sense. You'd think there would be a more scientific approach, but we looked at the way our friends went out and what we wanted from a club, and hoped everyone else would agree!

---

* The Hacienda was also round the corner from the recently vacated Joy Division rehearsal room TJM's. Had someone spotted the building on the numerous journeys to rehearsal?

BEN KELLY

Once it was agreed where all the main compartments went, it was a blank canvas. Clearly it was the biggest project I had ever delivered. I was obsessed with popular culture and interested in what Factory were doing. Perhaps without realising at the time, what I wanted to produce was a three-dimensional version of what Peter was doing.

PETER SAVILLE

The Hacienda was a kind of a three-dimensional manifestation of it all. Space and buildings get to people more than pictures, music gets to people – you can close your eyes and music can take you anywhere. It's a remarkably emotive force – the visual arts are a little bit more limited, but architecture and spatial design can take you somewhere because it envelops you. The Hacienda was a brilliant realisation of a kind of end-of-twentieth-century romance of who we were. It was a certain sort of romance of the culture that many people had experienced in the twentieth century.

BEN KELLY

It was like an abstract piece of sculpture, but it had to do its job. It had to be practical. It had to have a dance floor, toilets, a bar and a stage. I'm really interested in the use of geometry within a 3D space. And the use of geometry to set up the idea of a journey. You can introduce a narrative, so if you go through the front entrance you go into this small lobby where you pay or show your membership card, then there is a second set of doors which, because all Factory's projects have a catalogue number, had FAC 51 set into the door. It was using the language that had been developed and it's the first clue that there may be more to this place than just getting pissed.

Then you go through those doors into a bigger space and start to get a view of the massive cathedral space inside, which was a raised level. To get there I had these monolithic slabs like in the film *2001: A Space Odyssey* where the apes congregate around these slabs that have all knowledge in them. I thought: I'll have a bit of that! The slabs also gave a notion of entering Rome, like it was a heroic feeling entering the [cathedral] space . . . I set up the path round the dance floor to the main bar so that you had to go through the space and you would have to read other clues as part of this narrative. I was always interested in the use of strong and bold colours and the balcony, which had steel structural supports, gave me another element that could have this treatment on it. You build this great big picture up as you go along.

Tony said the name of the bar was the Kim Philby bar, which was his obsession with the Cold War and spies. I made the sign difficult to see, almost elusive, to fit into that Cold War idea. The whole club was like that – if you don't see everything immediately, you will discover things the more times you go back. That was part of getting a sense of ownership.

There was the practical issue of the dance floor, which was raised one step above the main space. I was worried about people falling off the dance floor, so the bollards were there to mark the edge, with hazard markers to create a filter system. The cat's eyes were part of that language; the reflections were picked up from the lighting rigs. I liked the taking of things out of context.

JOHNNY MARR

Peter Saville comes into the shop – which is quite incredible now when you think about it – the day they got the plans from Ben Kelly about the Hacienda, and he was so excited. He came in the shop and spread them out on the counter to show me. I was just a 17-year-old kid. That's how excited they were about it.

When the Hacienda opened on Friday 21 May 1982 with a typically off-the-wall party starring Bernard Manning winding up the punters and a cast of Factory all-star bands, it hit the headlines. After all, how many cult bands and underground labels build clubs a decade ahead of their time in pop history? The name itself came from a 1950s political text, The Situationist International Handbook, *which Rob Gretton had been leafing through. The piece, written by Ivan Chtcheglov in 1953, contains the phrase, 'The Hacienda must be built', and there in front of Gretton's eyes was the name, the 'hacienda' in the text being an idealised co-operative community. The club began its curious relationship with its naturally sceptical city as though it was trying to find a role for itself.*

MIKE PICKERING

When the Hacienda opened, it was amazing. It frightened people a bit – a real shiny, bright place, no one had ever seen anything like it before. It was Hulme that took it to its heart.

It's a myth that it was always empty before house [music]; that's bollocks. The Friday night I started in 1985 was always packed and the Saturday night for the *Face* readers was always packed as well. There was a load of gigs that we sold out. We got the bands cheap before anyone else, because everyone wanted to play the Hacienda.

ANDREW BERRY

Mike Pickering and Rob Gretton came to the club, Berlin, one night to check out the scene. They were looking for local DJs to play at the Hacienda. They were stuck outside; the bouncer hadn't heard of Factory Records. I went to the door, got them in, bought them a drink and played 'Blue Monday' very loud. The next day I met Tony Wilson and Howard Jones at the Hacienda and they offered me the job. I said I would do it if they let me cut hair in the dressing room during the day. They gave me a FAC number: FAC 98 – Factory Hairdresser and Hacienda DJ. I was there from '82 until '88.

During the day I would be downstairs cutting hair for friends, bands and the Hacienda staff. There were fashion shows, hair shows, performance art, installations, film. I DJed all the gigs upstairs, Friday Nude Night and Saturday nights. I even did the goth night for a while because no one wanted to do it. I saw the Cramps, Jesus and Mary Chain, the Birthday Party – all the Smiths gigs, local band nights.

Andrew Berry's Hacienda Dance Top 10

Boogie Down Bronx – Man Parrish
Stone Fox Chase – Area Code 615
Set It Off – Strafe
The Dominatrix Sleeps Tonight – Dominatrix
Dirty Talk – Klein and MBO
Padlock – Gwen Guthrie
Just Be Good To Me – SOS Band
Thinking of You – Sister Sledge
Genius of Love – Tom Tom Club
Atomic Dog – George Clinton

Andrew Berry's Hacienda Indie Top 10

Everything's Gone Green – New Order
What Difference Does It Make – Smiths
Cruisers Creek – Fall
Hymn From a Village – James
Cool As Ice – 52nd Street
Shack Up – A Certain Ratio
Delightful – Happy Mondays
Looking From a Hilltop – Section 25
Rip It Up – Orange Juice
Way Out – The La's

DAVE HASLAM

Before the Hacienda there was nowhere to go in Manchester in terms of a night out. It was places like Jillys, with lager-lout wankers fighting. The clubs had dress codes and you had to put on a suit to go. The Hacienda was somewhere without a dress code and where people didn't go fighting.

I remember going there on Tuesday nights to watch underground gay films and weird biker movies. They showed films on big video screens and there would be 40 of us shivering, watching these films.

RICHARD WITTS

The Hacienda looked great. I remember going in there thinking I would meet some people, but I didn't meet anybody because you would be the only people in there! I would go to the Gay Traitor; the rest of the Hacienda was like a dark cavern, like a cathedral.

RICHARD BOON

When the Hacienda started it was almost always empty, but it was the place to go.

IAN BROWN

The Hacienda used to be freezing cold and empty with four of you sat in the balcony watching *Tron* on those screens, which at the time seemed super-modern.

LIZ NAYLOR

The Hacienda seemed pompous; it felt corporate and it felt like Factory being decadent again. A New York disco?! We had never been to New York. I never knew anyone who had been to New York and the idea of it being a New York disco was like: great, I can go to a New York disco full of posey fucking twats! I was really affronted by it, but I went to it all the time of course (*laughs*). I still have my membership. I'm number 52.

It was an odd relationship: we would take the piss but we'd still be there. We'd get in free and blag free drinks and take the piss out of it!

DAVE HASLAM

I remember the Hacienda taking out a full-page advert in *City Fun*. Inside the magazine was ranting on about some night when they went there and how it was a white elephant and how long would it last. Then they would phone up and get on the guest list and take advertising from them (*laughs*).

MIKE PICKERING

I had been living in Holland . . . I was DJing, playing Chic and American disco records. I was also into the early electro scene, New York electro, [as well as] Arto Lindsay, DNA, Tuxedomoon, and European bands like Liaisons Dangereuses and DAF. I was playing [bands like] that with disco, and I was booking English bands to play there, like A Certain Ratio and Durutti Column. I got one of New Order's early gigs.* After the gig Rob said, 'I want you to come home. I'm thinking of opening this club in Manchester.' Once the idea was in his mind, he would do it; Rob was the only one who really wanted to do it.

I met Tony. He said I should be the A&R for Factory because I was the only one who was hearing new stuff – he was too busy

At the time they had ACR, Section 25, Royal Family and the Poor; the Wake, who were a bit like New Order. We then had a few new things like Quando Quango, 52nd Street. I loved ACR, they were amazing, the whole way they looked. They weren't approachable – Simon [Topping], their singer, ended up in a band I was in for years. He's still a miserable get (*laughs*).

JON SAVAGE

Of course Factory wasn't the only noise in town. There was also black music. When the Hacienda opened, I DJed there with Mike Pickering and Claude Bessey and Hewan Clarke. I really got on with Hewan; we really bonded over this track 'How We Going To Make the Black Nation Rise' by Brother D, which was an early rap track.† Mike played the Peach Boys and a real mixture at the early Hacienda, which was great. It was very avant-garde and very early electro mixed with Cabaret Voltaire being crossed over with rap and early electro. You would play 'The Message' or 'Planet Rock' alongside 'Hydraulic Pump' by P-Funk All Stars, alongside Gang of Four and then some electro track. It was all mixed in together.

MIKE PICKERING

It's a myth that no one took drugs before acid house. We were totally into drugs. I remember Teardrop Explodes playing the Hacienda really early on. It was a mad night, about 200 people turned up and it was a great gig; at the end of the night we shut the doors and partied. There was so much acid and everyone was having cocktails. Everyone was still there when the cleaners came at midday the next day!

---

* 13 December 1980.
† Arguably one of the first socially conscious hip-hop tracks. It was originally released in 1980.

GREG WILSON

Although the Hacienda reacted to, rather than instigated, the Manchester dance era, it was much to the club's credit that they'd noted what was happening at Legend and decided that this was a direction they wished to pursue.

MIKE PICKERING

I remember Alan McGee brought down the Jesus and Mary Chain for a gig in the mid-eighties* and it was like he wanted a riot. Me and Alan still laugh about it now. Rob was saying, 'Whatever he wants give it him, because he's trying to get you to pull the gig.' This went on for hours – all night. In the end Alan and Rob were both sat in the office downstairs and they couldn't find an argument, so the gig goes ahead and it was great.

PETER SAVILLE

It was an intellectual conceit that the Hacienda was just for middle-class intellectuals, as were my covers. Without the music in them that the kids adored, they wouldn't have looked twice at the covers. The music got to people; it got to people's hearts and eventually the aesthetic came through to their heads. It's interesting that pop music is the agent of culture.

GRAEME PARK (DJ)

There used to be a train that went to Manchester. I would get off at Deansgate and walk two minutes up Whitworth Street and go to the Hacienda and see bands like Orange Juice, Aztec Camera, Josef K.

PHIL THORNTON (pop culture author)

The first time I went to the Hacienda, when I was 17, was a bit of a letdown . . . It was almost empty, it was freezing, the sound was shite, the ale was dead expensive, I didn't smoke weed, the music was shite, the people were nobs – divs dressed like Haysi Fantayzee, straw hats, dungarees. Real kind of *i-D* and *Face* magazine types, no lads, scallys or whatever at all. I felt totally out of place.

TIM LAWRENCE (author)

The *Observer* ran a piece on Broken Glass's impact at the Hacienda in November 1983, but just in case any of the Hacienda's regular clientele were thinking about spinning on their heads or, more realistically,

* 26 June 1985.

giving themselves up to the rhythms of black music, Tracey, the Saturday night resident, would break the spell with an end-of-night flourish that revolved around records such as the theme song from *Thunderbirds*, Lulu's 'Shout' and Frank Sinatra's ode to New York.

The electro music coming out of New York and the related early hip-hop scene were making connections on the Manchester streets that were soon to have a profound influence on the music produced in the city.

JOHNNY JAY

I did a club called Strawberries, playing electro and rap. It was very much with the B-boys scene. I remember putting on 'Ain't Nothing Going On But the Rent' by Gwen Guthrie and dancers didn't dance to it, but then I put on an electro track by Chaka Khan, 'I Feel For You'. Everyone would [usually] go in a respectful circle and the guys would dance and then cop off with the girls. But for the first time the circle disintegrated and the girls started dancing, and they were kicking the guys out of the way. From then on I was playing for a different audience: girls had always turned up at breakdance things and one or two would breakdance, but in truth they wanted songs and lyrics; the music they were listening to had gone from Anita Baker to Lisa Lisa and Mantronix. It was interesting to see how the music metamorphosed to a tougher sound and the girls were into that as well.

We had the explosion of electro. It had gone from 50 black kids in Moss Side and Cheetham Hill, everyone bodypopping on lino in the streets, to everywhere. It was absolutely crazy. I did a gig at the Ritz and it was packed. I was just there to play electro. The whole thing had really exploded and then six months later it had gone back to the diehards – everyone had stopped because of getting bumps on their heads (*laughs*).

We heard the beats that had been used on these records and that got me thinking, maybe we can do our own records. I formed my own crew through people I had met from promoting. [A Guy Called] Gerald was in it, and believe it or not MC Tunes and a guy called Prince Cool. It was a bit like the Zulu Nation. I thought we were going to do some music. Gerald had his first bit of gear – he was always at home in his bedroom doing his bits and pieces. I was doing shows at the Gallery where people in the crew would come and perform. I didn't know how to organise, but we started a crew and called it the Rock the House crew.

I had a four-track recorder and Carl had a Mirage keyboard. We would record people in Carl's front room and send it to record companies. We soon realised that they would all send the same letter back: 'Thanks but no thanks – but keep us informed. It's not what we are looking for at the moment.'

I tried to be in Broken Glass but I didn't go to the audition. I used to bodypop with Benji Read. Benji was fearless; we'd practise our moves in Cheetham Hill a couple of hours before and then Benji just went and he got in. He was a brilliant dancer.

MC TUNES
Johnny Jay was one of the first guys my age who got off his arse, putting nights on at the Gallery for breakdancers, bodypoppers and rappers. He started at Strawberries and then moved to the Gallery, but, like everything else, it got shut down.

MC TUNES
Broken Glass and Street Machine were the street wave. A lot of guys went on to do naughty things! They were two big rivals. It was brilliant. It was fucking really good. It got a lot of people off their arses, saying, 'If they can do it so can I.'

I remember Chad Jackson was doing the music.* He was the DJ.

We were called Heatwave. That was my crew. We should have had a stupid name like Propeller From Hell or something like that. We lost every breakdancing challenge we had because we were all stoned. A lot of the time we would travel miles on the bus to a challenge somewhere and by the time we got there we were hammered – all the Thunderbird had gone and we had smoked all the resin.

GREG WILSON
The Playpen was once the infamous Slack Alice's, the sixties nightclub owned by Georgie Best. The owners of the Pier and Legend bought it in '84 and it became a really influential underground dance venue throughout the mid-eighties, with people like Colin [Curtis], Hewan [Clarke] and Stu Allan having regular nights there. Along with the Gallery, Berlin and Legend it completes a quartet of city-centre venues that would lay the groundwork for the coming house era.

MC TUNES
When I was a kid, till [the age of] 14 I would go out to the Sunday night disco at the youth club. We would all go there and take our seven-inches and bully the DJ to play them and get on the floor; that was until they started closing all the youth centres down.

* Chad Jackson was the 1987 Technics World Mixing Champion and creator of the track 'Hear the Drummer Get Wicked'

When I was 14 I was always at parties in Moss Side. It was killer, man – the Taurus sound system, Selector sound system. We all did a fair bit of rapping – especially when I met Johnny [Jay]. He was always passing me the mic, bigging me up. I was then in his crew – Rock the House – for years, with Sefton, Martin Green, Prince Cool.

We wanted to get rich, meet pussy and get laid. I [had] made my first record by the time I was 15. I had got into rapping from the first time I had heard the first Sugarhill Gang.* I saw them on *Top of the Pops* and I thought it was fucking brilliant: it was the same sort of music I already liked, but no love songs on top of it! I liked listening to Motown but it was Grandmaster Flash's 'The Message' that set me off. I remember seeing the video on *Top of the Pops*. Stood in front of the camera, Melle Mel was smashing it – I thought, 'Ohmigod, that's brilliant!' and that got me into bodypopping. I was already rapping – dissing people with a few lines while my boys were still dancing.

BRIAN CANNON
My first sleeve designs were for the Ruthless Rap Assassins.† I met Greg Wilson in 1984 when I did a New York-style piece of graffiti on a warehouse in Wigan; it was 25 feet long and 10 feet high and Greg saw it and said I got to meet this guy. Greg was a happening, trendy DJ and I was into punk and hip-hop. He had a really impressive record collection – enough to sink a battleship. He was 24 and I was 18. I was in awe of him.

ANDREW BARKER (808 State)
The first music I liked was Kraftwerk and then early hip-hop. I started DJing playing LL Cool J and some old electro stuff. I was playing in a youth club in Ancoats – an old Salvation Army building set up for kids to do something. I blagged the guy who ran it into getting a set of decks, so we ran a disco in there. We were playing electro, had a following of kids who were breakdancing and bringing in their linos doing headspins. I was never fit enough to do that (*laughs*).

A few crews would come round to do challenges. That was that was the beginning of all that scene in Manchester with Broken Glass and Street Machine.

PHIL THORNTON
The thing I first noticed about Manchester was that it was far more

---

* 'Rappers' Delight', released in 1979.
† The Ruthless Rap Assassins' two albums with EMI, 1990's *The Killer Album* and 1991's *Think, It Ain't Illegal Yet*, were two of the best British rap albums of the time.

culturally diverse than Liverpool and that the black kids were really into the clothes, the same as the white kids; there hadn't been that split between what would become hip-hop fashion yet, and places like Hurleys up by Piccadilly Station were rammed with black and white kids after the latest sportswear imports. I'd got into funk and electro, hip-hop by this time, so we'd go down to the old Spin Inn, opposite the Royal Exchange. It was tiny and had this three-bar heater in there. You'd listen to the latest 12s, they had all these Kangols behind the counter, the red felt ones that LL Cool J wore, and I remember buying one but never having the bottle to wear it. I did see a few in the United Road actually and there was this bit of a crossover thing going on, but musically there still is this massive rift between black music or dance music and the indie scene.

MARTIN MOSCROP

We used to go to Legends on Wednesday night. Colin Curtis was the DJ and then Greg Wilson; it was mainly a black club but you would get white females in there. We were the only white guys there. Another club was Hewan Clarke's night, where we met people like the Jazz Defektors. The first night we met the Jazz Defektors they had Perry Boy gear on and we had demob gear on. The week after it was the other way round! We copied each other! Hewan's was on a Sunday night and you couldn't dance in Manchester on a Sunday [at the time] because it was illegal. James Anderton, or God's Cop, was running the police force. He was a religious nut, which was ironic as the Jazz Defektors would dance in this club on Sunday . . .

PHIL THORNTON

I was only buying black American music by this time – really got into P-funk, became pretty rigid with it too, wouldn't entertain anybody with a guitar unless it was Eddie Hazel. The indie scene then was a mix of New Order types and goths and even a few more clued-up scallys. I secretly liked bands like Echo but couldn't get into 'em because McCulloch looked such a twat; that whole eighties pop star look put me off most bands to be honest. Even New Order – I just couldn't understand why they were so popular. 'Blue Monday' was OK but it had fuck-all to do with New Order really; the production was pure New York electro. I think they milked that, even though underneath it all they were pretty ropey, just another tired rock'n'roll band. And Barney's horrible tuneless voice, I used to be embarrassed for him.

The only thing was that anyone who wasn't into that desperate chart music of the times was classed as 'alternative', so you'd go to these shite 'alternative nights' at various clubs and discos and wait all night to hear a few ancient James Brown tunes, and then it'd be like Lloyd fucking Cole or Bauhaus for the rest of the night and that'd be it. It was terrible! There was literally nowhere to go in small towns, or even in the big cities at that time. You couldn't really go to the black clubs, because we were too scared to go to them if I'm being honest. Whether that's fair or not, you just felt out of place and a bit nervous. Plus if you were white and into hip-hop, you felt as if you were encroaching on their scene. I could understand that from a black kid's perspective.

You felt pretty isolated, white kids into black music and not really into the whole hip-hop fashion thing, just dressing like a normal footy lad because at that time, the footy mobs weren't really big music heads.

ANDREW BARKER

Because I was playing all this music I wanted to know how to make this kind of music. So I started researching it. I bought a keyboard. I had a little set-up with a drum machine, a keyboard and a four-track Portastudio. At that time in the mid-eighties there were a lot of different little acts hanging round Eastern Bloc listening to all the new tunes coming in.* We had our own group which was called the Spinmasters, which was me and Darren† and a rapper called MC Shine. There was four or five of these little groups. We did a couple of Boardwalk gigs where we put our own show together with Gerald. Martin Price‡ was involved. We would get all our mates and family to come down and watch it.

HEWAN CLARKE (DJ)

The Reno§ for me was like some kind of rebirth. The Reno was something totally different. The Reno opened at eleven and it shut at six in the morning. It used to get totally packed. It was a dive basically. The toilets were like – oh – we won't even talk about that. The Reno had been going since, I believe, the fifties. In the fifties and the sixties it was a respectable jazz club.

GRAHAM MASSEY

We used to go to the Gallery on Friday night. Manhattan Sound on Saturday night had a reputation for having a really good sound system. They chose records that sounded good on the sound system. Sound

---

* Eastern Bloc on Oldham Street became the main dance record shop during the acid house period.
† Darren Partington, future member of 808 State.
‡ Price, who worked at Eastern Bloc, was later a member of 808 State.
§ Now demolished club in Moss Side.

system culture at the time was at the Moss Side carnival. That was around until the On U Sound System did their take on sound systems at places like the Berlin and the Ritz.*

ADRIAN SHERWOOD (producer)

On-U was me doing my own thing, interpreting the music I was really into. I didn't try and copy Jamaican music; I also used elements of noise and distortion. I was working with people as diverse as Tackhead and Mark Stewart and the Mafia to Bim Sherman. The idea was to use the space of dub and reggae but build my own sound up. I worked consciously to develop my own sound. We used to take out a package tour of all the acts on the label because I wanted to try and make it interesting.

CLINT BOON

I went to the Boardwalk on the first night it opened and I went there for years [afterwards], from when it was a venue to [when it became] a dance club. It was a great place; I saw some amazing gigs down there. It's like the Hacienda. It's a tragedy that it's shut down. It will end up like the Cavern in Liverpool. They shut that down and really regretted it. When it reopened it wasn't even in the same building! They had to rebuild the place and that's what will happen with the Hacienda or the Boardwalk.

DAVE ROFE (DJ and manager of the Doves)

House started in '86 – Colin Curtis used to play a little house set every week. One by one the records came out, another song came out, but there were so few records to play a set.

I used to go to the Playpen and Colin Curtis and DJ Patrick, who I think was the first person to do a house set in Manchester, although Colin Curtis claims he was first.

The eighties saw the development of a very diverse musical scene, as the era after punk saw a fracturing of pop into several different strands which in turn would influence a disparate collection of young fans.

STELLA (Intastella vocalist and actress)

My best education was Moston youth club. [That was] where I first heard the Who's *Quadrophenia*, which came out round then, and then there was the mod revival with Secret Affair and all that. Mod was the first

---

* Now demolished club in Moss Side.
† Adrian Sherwood's On U Sound System played a couple of seminal gigs at the Ritz in the late eighties. Although rarely mentioned, their twisted take on the sound system culture and heavy dub vibe was one of the many important influences on the scene.

music I got really into, but I really liked Adam and the Ants as well. I remember going to see Adam and the Ants at Rafters when I was very young and still at school, when their first album, *Dirk Wears White Sox*, was just out.

NOEL GALLAGHER

I would read Weller interviews in *Melody Maker* and *Sounds*. He would go on about the Beatles and I thought, 'I've heard of the Beatles, I like the Beatles,' 'cos I'd heard 'She Loves You' on the radio when I was holiday in Ireland. Weller would go on about 'Strawberry Fields', the Small Faces, the Kinks and the Who. Down the road from our house in Burnage was Sifters record shop, which was a secondhand record shop. I started to buy secondhand cassettes from there at 50p. I would buy all these bands' greatest hits. That's when guitar music took over for me, I fucking loved it. I would just buy greatest hits because I wasn't really aware of the bands' albums; because I didn't have much money I would buy the record with all the hits on it. That's where I started getting into sixties stuff.

STELLA

Around that time I went to see Nico at the Library Theatre. It was the first time I had clapped eyes on her. I knew the Fall because my band used to live below Mark E. Smith. I used to go round there at a very young age with my school uniform on and he used to terrify me. I didn't realise how young I was and how old these blokes were!

DAVE ROFE

A Certain Ratio did a warehouse party. There was no licensing but we got around that by saying that we were shooting a video and would give beer away for a ticket that cost a pound. Steve Adge put that one on.

JOHNNY MARR

In the north there was a big rockabilly culture. I learnt a lot from those guys who used to come into the shop and were getting the rockabilly look down places like Fleetwood. Then Robert Elms did that article and killed it.

My best mate Billy Duffy had joined Theatre of Hate* and they were the hippest thing in town for a few of us. Me and Andy Rourke would go to Theatre of Hate gigs with an enclave of people from outside Manchester

---

* Kirk Brandon's super-stylised, bequiffed post-punk outfit

. . . They are why when I first came out with the Smiths I played a Gretsch, because that was what Kirk Brandon played. He had a green Gretsch Tennessean.

SCOTT CAREY (Paris Angels bassist)

We used to go to get our brothel creepers from X Clothes just off Cross Street. I was still at school then. I remember I wagged school and we went to see King Kurt one night. I got covered in flour and shit. I woke up and couldn't open one eye and I didn't go to school next day.

JOHNNY MARR

The other thing that was going on big time in town was secondhand clothes shops. There were four or five of them. Just behind the antique market there was a place called Rocket that was run by my mate Rick; there was some secondhand stuff sold at Joe Moss's other place on Portland Street in the Crazy Face basement which I went on to work in eventually, which was where the Smiths HQ would be. There was Carl Twigs as well . . .

There was a place on Cross Street where you could buy old seven-inch singles, and Rare Records on John Dalton Street where Ian Curtis bought records; he worked there as well, I think. There was this place near the Gallery called Savoy* where you could buy bootlegs; it was a hangover directly from the post-punk days where you could buy books. And there was Paperchase as well† – Pete Garner did for Paperchase what I did for X Clothes, he updated the stock for his own age group.

ELLIOT RASHMAN

I discovered Mick Hucknall by booking the Frantic Elevators at the Poly. I booked them because my friend Tony Bowers from the Albertos said 'You've got to book them, they are funny.' They used do a number called 'Hunchback of Notre Dame' which went: 'I'm an ugly sod, it's not my fault' – and it was Mick talking about himself! They were managed by Roger Eagle, so they were doing a bit of rockabilly; they were also trying to do black music, but they couldn't play it. It was a really weird mix at the time. They were on in Liverpool a lot. Roger always had them on in Eric's.‡

In some ways Hucknall came out of no scene in Manchester. He knocked about with bands in Liverpool like Lawnmower and he would

---

* A fantastic counterculture shop that was imbued with the spirit of the Merry Pranksters.
† Paperchase was an alternative book and record shop in the mid-eighties.
‡ Roger Eagle was now booking at Eric's and was still on the cutting edge of music.

play with slightly different influences, with the stuff Roger Eagle gave him.

JON SAVAGE

I liked Morrissey at the time. He came round two or three times to my house to listen to records and talk about books. He was listening to sixties girl pop. I don't remember talking about the Dolls but I remember him giving me a single by Rita Pavone.* He was very enthusiastic and I liked him. He wanted to be a writer. I wonder whether or not he had this vague idea that he would do the script for the mythical ACR film that never happened, called *Too Fast Too Live, Too Young to Die*. He was hugely involved with that scene.

JOHNNY MARR

Me and Andy and Si were cooking up post-punk funk (In their ad hoc band Freak or Freaky Party.) and considering getting singers . . . I went home from rehearsals one night and walked into my friend's house where I was staying. One of my mates was shooting up another mate with heroin, so I went upstairs and got my bag and said to [my girlfriend] Angie, 'Come on darling, we're out of here!' I didn't go back there for a year-and-half. All my friends were doing heroin and as much of a badass as I was, I had to draw the line somewhere. I found myself for the first time in my life a one-man band, just me and Angie; it coincided with when I nearly went to prison. And I still needed a singer.

I knew this guy Morrissey was good, but he had dropped out of sight for some time. He was almost definitely in my mind. He may have been part of a different era but he was really good. The age difference makes a difference – he was five years older and I regarded him as part of the punk scene. But I knew he was first division.

My idea was to go and see him.

* Italian sixties singer and actress.

9

'DESTINATION – ANYWHERE': MARR, MORRISSEY AND THE SMITHS

When Johnny Marr knocked on Morrissey's door in late May, 1982, it was one of the pivotal moments in Manchester music history. Surrounded by mythology, it equals the Pistols gig or Ian Curtis's death as one of those catalytic moments when Mancunian – and, by extension, all-pop culture shifts.

MORRISSEY

I had scant resources and I was getting older. This was the worst time of my life. I couldn't bear to go to gigs any more because I couldn't bear to be a member of the audience any more. I had always wanted to sing, but suddenly it was an illness. I didn't take drugs or drink, but I was suffocated by the need to sing. My life was right on top of me all the time. A close friend called Simon Topping started his own group (A Certain Ratio), and I collected the money at their first gig at the Band on the Wall in Manchester. I had no idea why I was doing this. They needed a drummer and I placed an ad for a *Nimble Applicant*, and Donald Johnson replied. Again, I had no idea why I was placing the ad. We went to Eric's in Liverpool in someone's van. The band looked great, very sourly Germanic. Tony Wilson burst in and said, 'I'm taking this band to Bel Air!' and a few months later Simon was on the cover of *NME*. I couldn't bear it. He was off. I was face-down in the weeds. We never saw each other again.

RICHARD BOON

I had known Morrissey for quite a while. I met him at the bar of the Piccadilly Hotel shortly after the second Sex Pistols gig. Our John Maher had a mate who had put an ad in *Melody Maker* to find likeminded people in Manchester. Morrissey was around trying to make music in the middle of town.

LINDER

I had met Morrissey in 1976. He came to speak to me when he was writing for *New York Rocker*.* He wrote a couple of fantastic pieces for them and he was very interested in talking to Howard and Peter about Buzzcocks. They were soundchecking and he spoke to me instead. If he wants to know something he will speak – he's not shy, he's very economic. We hit it off pretty quick. He's very funny. It's hard to say if we had a good creative relationship but it was a really dynamic relationship. We were both really into the America/Warhol Factory scene. That was really important. At that point we both had a fascination with Warhol's Factory, British cinema and that notion of the past. Even though punk was rebelling against the present, we had a fascination with the recent past of our childhood and our formative years . . .

JOHNNY MARR

I was talking to Joe Moss about pop history, like we did all the time. We were talking about how Mike Stoller had got Leiber's address and went round and knocked on his door and gave him this pitch about how he would write the music and how he would write the words, or maybe the other way round.† Joe said, 'You should do that with that Morrissey bloke,' and suddenly a lightbulb came on in my head.

NOEL GALLAGHER

Johnny [Marr] was always the ambitious one in the Smiths. He wanted to play Wembley Stadium and have the biggest guitar collection in the world, whereas Morrissey was going to take on the vivisectionists and all that carry-on.

JOHNNY MARR

I rang up Stephen Pomfret‡ and got Morrissey's address and asked if he knew where the house was. He obliged really beautifully – we both got on the bus and went there and he took me to the door and knocked. Pommy is quite a shy guy but he actually introduced me and said, 'Hiya Steven,' [though] they didn't know each other well enough for Morrissey to say barely more than hello, and certainly not to say, 'Come in.' Stephen Pomfret just said, 'This is Johnny,' and he literally took about five steps back. I told Morrissey that I was a guitar player and I was forming a band and had a manager, which was Joe. He'd never managed

---

* A long-defunct but excellent New York-based music paper.
† Jerry Leiber and Mike Stoller are one of the key songwriting partnerships of the twentieth century, writing several of Elvis's better-known tunes as well as other standards.
‡ Ex-member of the Nosebleeds and a mutual friend of Morrissey and Johnny Marr.

Handsome Devils: The Smiths defining 1980s cool at 'G-Mex at the 1986 Festival of the 10th Summer'
(Photo: Ian Tilton www.iantilton.net)

a band in his life and didn't know what they did, but he just made it up as he went along, which was brilliant . . .

I said I was going to write some songs, and [told him] I knew Billy [Duffy] and Mike Rossi – that was all probably going against me! But, quite importantly, I had a pair of fifties Levis on with proper American bike boots and a Johnson's sleeveless jacket and a Johnson's shirt, and a real proper old American flying men's cap and a superquiff which was faultless. And then, amazingly, he let me in – amazing not because I was a stranger, but because he is so private to this day.

He let me in his bedroom, sat down and asked me did I want to put a record on, which I knew was a brilliant test. So I went over to this box with only a few singles – which was quite impressive in itself, that he was so very selective. I flicked through them, and the Monochrome Set was in there and a lot of old girl group records. There was a Marvelettes record in there, I think it was 'Paper Boy', which to an aficionado is really obvious, so I played the other side as some sort of cute gesture.* When I pulled the Marvelettes out I sensed this kind of stroking of the chin and this intrigue. So I put that on and sang along with it. And he sensed my exuberance, with my talking nonstop at several hundred miles an hour.

MORRISSEY

There seemed to be so much language of despair in those songs by the Marvelettes or Crystals or Supremes . . . penalised for being in love, laughed at for being poor or unloved, danger and death everywhere in Shangri-Las' songs . . . and you can't get more despairing than Timi Yuro's singles of the sixties: 'Make the World Go Away', 'Insult to Injury', 'Hurt' or 'I Apologise'. The Supremes are overlooked because they were so establishment-successful, but their output was apocalyptic – 'Remove this Doubt', 'I Hear a Symphony', 'I'm Livin' in Shame' are terrific bursts of emotion.

I had first met Johnny Marr at a Patti Smith concert at the Apollo . . . but I can't remember if it was *Easter* or *Wave*. I had seen her in Birmingham in either '75 or '76, and the slope was in full evidence a few years later. Johnny and I got on very well. He looked a bit rockabilly, a bit wired and very witty, but also hard and indifferent, but it was the exact opposite of the few rehearsals I'd had with Billy [Duffy] because with Johnny it was instantly right and we were instantly ready.

I had no doubt that Johnny was *the moment*, and I was grateful that nothing had ever happened for me earlier on.

We moved very, very quickly. I thought of the name the Smiths, but it was Johnny's venture. We both had an astonishingly solid sense of direction, and we very rarely disagreed, which was unusual because we were opposites – he was full of excitement for everything, and I was . . . *not*.

We were formidable and a lot of people tried to squeeze in between us. The first song we wrote was called 'Blow Your Own Horn', and the singles we listened to early on were 'Shoes' by Reparata† – which became the blueprint for 'A Rush and a Push and the Land Is Ours' – and 'Are You Sure Hank Done It This Way?' by Waylon Jennings, which showed the way for the travelling beat of 'The Hand that Rocks the Cradle'.

---

* American girl group who had twenty Top 20 US hits, including the classic 'Please Mr Postman'. 'Paper Boy' was the B-side of 'You're the One', released on Motown in April 1966.
† Reparata had been the lead singer of the late sixties girl group Reparata and the Delrons, who had a great run of emotion-drenched bubblegum-pop singles.

JOHNNY MARR

He had a life-sized cardboard cutout of James Dean doing the crucifix thing from *Rebel Without A Cause* in his room. Curiously there was also the poster from *Beyond Belief: The Moors Murderers: The Story of Ian Brady and Myra Hindley*,* which was pretty intriguing. He obviously knew that I knew what I was on about and I talked about how I wanted to form a band a bit like the Dolls and hit all the right spots. His look was like an impoverished version of how we first came out with the Smiths – cardigan and faded baggy Levis, which were probably the only pair he owned, and kind of studenty flat shoes.

We clicked on this superhuman kind of level. I thought to myself, OK, we made this arrangement that he's going to call me tomorrow afternoon and there's probably a 60/40 chance against it. I sensed that he was into it, but against that was the fact that I was so used to trying to get bands together and having people not be up to the mark in terms of their commitment.

But right on the money, at one o'clock the next day he called me and I knew we were on. Two days later he came over to mine. He got off the train in Altrincham; Angie picked him up in this old VW and took him to my house, to this attic place I was living in.†

I lived in this really tiny room that was stacked full of records . . . Morrissey brought the lyrics to 'The Hand that Rocks the Cradle' and 'Suffer Little Children'. He'd posted me this cassette of him singing 'The Hand that Rocks the Cradle' with no music against it, which I'd got the day before. I couldn't really quite fathom it because he was singing so quietly and in such a low key.

It wasn't the first time he had done this. There's that famous story of him sending a recording of him singing a song called 'Wake Up Johnny' into the tape machine to Richard Boon about a year before.

When he actually came to my place we talked about music and the fact that we both loved Patti Smith, so that was a good place to start. So we started playing 'Kimberley' by Patti Smith to get us off the ground. I had this riff that I had been carting around that wasn't quite right for what I had been doing with Andy and Si in Freaky Party. The riff worked with 'Suffer Little Children' and that kind of set the template for the next lot of songs we wrote. And then we were off – my life and his just became unstoppable. I had more than I hoped for and so did he, and our hopes were fucking high, really high! Our standards were really high, but I still got more than I bargained for, and so did he.

* Emlyn Williams's 1968 book about the Moors Murderers.
† The attic room was rented from Granada presenter the late Shelley Rohde.

'MY BABY MUST BE A MAGICIAN'

In which Morrissey and Marr get busy. Very busy . . .

JOHNNY MARR

That first day we mapped out a lot of what we wanted the band to be. Almost all of it came true. I threw concepts at him, like how we would be in photographs. It was as detailed as this: the idea was that we should be really close together all the time and hanging off each other like the Dolls did. You never saw that at the time. In band photos you would have one guy behind the synthesiser and another guy 500 yards away behind the drum machine. I grew up with Patti Smith and bands like that were all draped round each other – especially the Dolls. We talked about that, and we talked about how we should sign to Rough Trade and not Factory.

TONY WILSON

I don't think we missed out on anybody, but the bands I didn't sign that were successful were obviously the Smiths and the Stone Roses. I always thought Steven [Morrissey] was going to be our novelist, our Dostoevsky; in fact I lost a one-act play he wrote about eating toast in Hulme. But I got a phone call one day asking me to come over because he had something to tell me. I went to his mum's house and he took me into his bedroom with a poster of James Dean on the wall, and he told me that he was going to be a pop star. I had to stifle my laughter because I thought this was the last person in the world about to become a pop star. I had a conversation with Richard Boon, Buzzcocks' manager and a mutual friend, saying, 'Can you believe he'd ever be a pop star?' Four months later I went to either their first or second gig at the Manhattan club and I was utterly stunned. I remember walking out and Richard saying, 'Now do you believe?' Obviously I did, it was stunning.

JOHNNY MARR

Me and Morrissey both liked the idea of being on Rough Trade. I suspect on Morrissey's side it was primarily because the Fall, who he admired, had been on Rough Trade. I was going through a bit of a Monochrome Set* phase, as I do now and again, so Rough Trade sounded like a great idea to me. The anti-Factory thing was entirely me, because of my age. Even though I had respect for Factory, I totally understood that if you signed for them you were aesthetically identified with Factory. You became a Factory band and you might as well have started wearing short trousers and sandals straight away.

* Great lost band who released their early records on Rough Trade.

TONY WILSON

I felt that I couldn't sell the first James single or the first Stockholm Monsters single, and thought my company had lost something. I didn't know what it was we'd lost, but I wasn't going to saddle Steven with a shit record company. Now Rob Gretton, who was more significant within the company than me, was wandering around Manchester telling everyone that the Smiths were the new Beatles, but he was telling the Smiths that their demo was shit, and he wasn't going to sign them until they'd got a good demo . . . Pinnacle [later] went bust, and I probably lost about £150,000 in that. If the Smiths hadn't gone to Rough Trade that probably would have gone bust too, and the British independent movement would have ended right there, never lasted beyond the mid-eighties.

JOHNNY MARR

The reason that the flowers happened with the Smiths was not because of Oscar Wilde, it was because me, Joe Moss and Morrissey sat one night together and discussed [it]. We were about to play our first night at the Hacienda.* My and Joe's usual complaint about Factory and the Hacienda being a very cold environment resulted in Joe saying we needed to brighten the place up for the show. That's where the flowers came in. It wasn't either a hippie or an Oscar Wilde thing; it was purely to kill off that 1982 Factory aesthetic of austerity, of concrete and steel.

What else was being discussed with my general exuberant riffing was that it should be Morrissey and Marr on the songwriting credits. The 'and' should be in the middle, not just Morrissey slash Marr like the Americans say. And I said the first single should have a navy blue label. I wanted it to look like the Stones' Decca label – that was very important, because 'Not Fade Away' at that time to me was the first of whatever my hundred commandments of that week were. Billy Fury was also on Decca, so Morrissey didn't have a problem with that.

Even before I saw [Morrissey] with a microphone in his hand, I knew he was right. It was like he was prepared to do all these things. For a start I knew he was going to write a ton of great words. He regarded himself as a frontman, like I regarded myself as a guitar player. Normally frontmen were lads who looked pretty good and who were given loads of records to go and learn, but he was the only person I ever met who had been working at being a frontman since he was born! Like I had been working on being a guitar player, so I knew he was going to be great.

* 4 February 1983, the band's third ever gig, playing with 52nd Street.

The first time we got together with a drummer,* it was a bit frustrating because he wasn't really into it – he was a lovely guy, but it wasn't quite right. But the way Morrissey carried himself as a frontman even then, without being on a stage, in a crappy little rehearsal room in Beehive Mill, was perfect.

From the start he had words for a bunch of songs printed out on paper. I sat down with a guitar and played the riff and said 'What about this?' and he started singing over the top. Actually what he did was mime the singing over the top; he then encouraged me to put it down on a cassette recorder, and he took the cassette away and went away to find a way to shoehorn these words on top of the music. He would make up the melody lines and I would make up the guitar lines. He was humming it in his mind and he'd got the words written down. At first we couldn't work out if he would give me the printed words and I would put the music to that.

If I had any expectations about Morrissey's lyrics, I was expecting vaguely New York late-seventies punk rock or new wave lyrics because that was what I knew about him. That was my experience of the lyrics that he had written for the sort of faux-Slaughter and the Dogs, which were very good. It wasn't like a Tom Verlaine kind of thing, from what I remember it was more of a cross between Wayne County and Patti Smith, with a tongue-in-cheek New York hip street speak. But when he turned up it was way, way more northern and Mancunian. In 'The Hand that Rocks the Cradle' I remember the 'Climb up on my knee, sonny boy' line, not because of any controversy but because that said George Formby to me. That, coupled with the clothes that he was wearing at the time, which were cardigans, old man's suit trousers, brogues and quite a kind of defeated hairstyle, which was somewhere between where mine was and the Factory thing. He had a very bookish but contemporary look, whereas my style was a little more dynamic.

My thing was a dandified fifties look straight off the King's Road, which ended up being sold at my shop – it was straight from Robot or Johnson's. It was rock'n'roll but not rock'n'roll like the Rolling Stones. It was rock'n'roll a bit like the Stray Cats, or the younger brothers of the Clash; it was Theatre Of Hate entirely.

We did have a strong connection with the gay scene. The Manhattan was my night-time base and that was a gay club. There was only me and

* Bill Anstee, ex-Sister Ray drummer.

Andrew [Berry] and a couple of others in the place who weren't gay. The people who ran it could spot a straight guy a million miles away. At the time most of my friends were gay.

When we came out and when people think of the genesis of the band, doing a song like 'I Want a Boy for My Birthday', they put Morrissey's sexual ambiguity together and made five. But looking back on it, it was probably down to me that we were so linked to the gay scene. It has been said that I told people that our new band was a gay band and that might have been right for a week or two. I was into us being a new kind of rock group and certainly not like the bands at Factory at the time.

Johnny Marr saw the partnership as a classic songwriting team, but quickly realised that a band would be the perfect vehicle for the songs and set out to recruit a rhythm section.

JOHNNY MARR

The only place I knew where to get a demo made was Beehive Mill, so I went back there to do a demo with Si Wolstencroft on the drums, who had been drumming with Ian Brown and John Squire in a band called the Patrol, and Dale Hibbert, who sort of ran the studio, on bass. I blagged some studio time and we recorded 'The Hand that Rocks the Cradle' and 'Suffer Little Children'. I would play the demo in X Clothes in the middle of the Birthday Party and Psychedelic Furs and it would empty the place! I was going round saying, 'Listen to this!' and people wanted to slash their wrists! If you think we're miserable now, you should have heard us then!

We pleaded with Si to join. He looked great. He had been my mate and we really wanted him. Morrissey really wanted him in the band because as you can imagine, Si really looked the part. It was ridiculous that he wasn't in the Smiths.

On reflection though, Si's drum style wasn't right for the Smiths. It was too skippy. I guess, as it turned out, he wouldn't have been the right man for the job in hindsight. I realised that we needed someone who was a little more punky – he wasn't called funky Si for nothing.

I know Morrissey said quite humourfully that the two of us were bobbing about in our two lifeboats, but my lifeboat was jet-propelled with about 25 gay guys in it and with its own navigation system pointed to the word fun. We could not have been more different! What often gets left out is that we admired each other for our differences. My very active – hyperactive – lifestyle was great, but I wasn't looking at this person who was in self-imposed isolation in his bedroom thinking he was boring, but that he was fascinating and great. We did need each other, and we were of use to each other, but we really loved each other from the off. I knew what he loved about me and what I loved about him – which was that enigmatic aspect – and that was fine with me. I liked it but I didn't need to know everything about him. I didn't need to know his sources and his inspiration and I still don't.

He had very deliberate sources; I was more open and he was more closed. I admired that he could do that. I saw it as a strength. I would crack him up and he would crack me up. Really, to this day I feel very lucky to have had that opportunity, regardless of the success. It was just a nice thing to have in your life.

I was forever looking for band members and that's how I managed to find Mike Joyce. One of our mates knew of Mike, who he had seen in the shop a couple of times.

He came to the shop and struck up a friendship with me and said that he was a drummer. We needed a plan B if Si wouldn't join, so that was where Mike came into the picture.

I remember Mike being a Legends head . . . I used to go down there as well. Mike would go to Legends as well and he was still playing in that band Victim.* I could never work out what they were up to. They were from Northern Ireland. I could never work out why this Mancunian lad had 'Victim' on his drum kit. I don't think he was even playing when I approached him. When he was introduced in the shop as a potential drummer he expressed an interest. He was sat on the fence because of his commitments to this band.

Joe [Moss] was a massive part of it . . . Joe ran Crazy Face . . . and it was a prosperous, functional, wholesale business. I went in one Sunday and officially asked Joe to be the manager. There was just me and Morrissey there and Joe said, 'I don't really know what a manager does but I will help.' . . . He said, 'You need to get the rest of the group,' and I said we were just a songwriting duo and we would write songs for other people. God knows who I was thinking of – that idea was only going on in my mind, because I'm sure Morrissey wanted to be in a group and was pushing for other musicians.

Joe's building on Portland Street looked like our Brill Building. Very

---

* Victim were one of the many fine pop-punk bands signed to Terri Hooley's Belfast-based Good Vibrations records.

quickly Joe emptied the top floor for us, which meant laying off some machinists or moving them around, so he had already taken a hit financially in his business for me. He then bought a PA, which was another hit. It wasn't like he was a rich guy but he was a funky guy, very street. That all happened around the time we got Mike in the band, just before the Ritz gig.

Our first gig, at the Ritz on 4 October 1982 with Blue Rondo a la Turk, was put on by Andrew Berry. It was done for my benefit by Andrew. He needed to put a gig on for his mate and the only way to do that was to put on a fashion show, with us before it. We invited Blue Rondo a la Turk to be in it as well because they were in *The Face*.

At the Ritz we only had a few songs: 'The Hand that Rocks the Cradle', 'Suffer Little Children', 'Handsome Devil', and a fourth song – a cover of the Cookies' 'I Want a Boy for My Birthday'.

There was the famous story of Blue Rondo's roadie, a big bloke, coming up and saying that if we moved any of their equipment then we wouldn't get out of there alive. The problem with that was that their lead singer, Chris Sullivan, was a midget with a zoot suit on who had his mic set really low – so Morrissey, who had to use his mic, sang the whole set crouched down in sheer terror. Chris has since denied this; I'm sure he was quite nice, but the people with him were utterly obnoxious all day long.

We walked off to a smattering of applause from all 19 people there. Crucially for me, Joe Moss was stood at the back of the Ritz and he remembers being lit up like a firework – which is a shitty metaphor – by how I played guitar. That boosted my confidence no end.

After the Ritz I had arranged a gig at Manhattan. That was an important gig to me because we needed a full set and we needed to impress a lot of people. I was like OK, I'm going to have to go back and get my mate Andy [Rourke] in on bass.

The next thing that happened was that another mate of mine had some bullshit scouting job at EMI and he told them he was going to get a Manchester band. He was only employed there for a month, but he told EMI about us and got us a couple of hundred quid. So we went to Drone Studios in Chorlton and recorded the second demo and the three main songs we had at the time: 'Handsome Devil', 'What Difference Does It Make' and 'Miserable Lie'. Andy came down to help us out and that was his introduction to the band. You wouldn't bother using the word audition – I already knew he was right on the personal level, because he was my oldest friend along with Andrew Berry, and I knew he was right on a musical level because he is one of the best bass players to ever come out of this country. One of the best things about the Smiths records is the bass playing, which has dated really well.

Andy was the genuine bohemian in the group – his mother was an art teacher and I considered him quite middle class, which isn't meant as a putdown by any means. By that I mean I considered him quite cultured. What he brought in, which was crucial to the band's chemistry, was a way of handling me to everybody's benefit. I only realised years after the band split that the nature of our relationship was the tortoise and the hare – I was able to move super-forward and be very forceful [with] a sense of endeavour and was really super-driven, whilst he was very good at grounding me . . . We had this great chemistry. When that eroded over the five years of the band it would partly cause the demise of the Smiths.

At that point my life was amazing. I would go in and open the shop after sitting round with Joe for an hour and then a couple of mates would trickle in – not to buy anything, but to talk about the new Gun Club album or the impending Birthday Party show at the Hacienda or how crap Johnny Thunders was at the Hacienda the night before, and hang out and have a cup of coffee. I would make seven quid in one day if I was lucky! Then the other three Smiths would turn up and we would get in the service elevator and press the button and go up to our little world. It was on the top floor of this clothes factory in Manchester, but it was paradise to us. We started thrashing out the songs that me and Morrissey were writing. Me and him would get together on our own, recording on a Walkman between my knees, and I would put three songs down. In fact during that period I was giving him cassettes that I put together on my Teac three-track, which I've still got – it's an amazing thing.

I was getting loads of pressure because I was telling everyone how great we were going to be and everyone was going, 'Come on, then – get on with it!'

We did our first proper gig at the Manhattan* and all the [record label] heads like Tony Wilson turned up. Andrew Berry was DJing. It was our second gig but our first full set: we did 'Accept Yourself', 'You've Got Everything Now', but we didn't have 'Hand In Glove' then. We didn't get any real reviews for it, but we got mentioned in *City Fun* magazine by Liz Naylor and Cath Carroll, who were contemporaries of Morrissey. I regarded them as part of the older generation – the punk hangover, if you like. They were always very frosty towards me.

* 25 January 1983.

We did that Manhattan gig and were great. But while we were playing I knew people were looking at us thinking, 'This is weird music,' because it wasn't what you hear on the first Smiths album and it isn't what you hear on the bootlegs. The songs were physically in a lower key and Morrissey was singing in a lower register. That collection of songs that ended up on the Troy Tate album is a very odd group.*

ELLIOT RASHMAN

I knew Johnny Marr from the clothes shop so I went to see their second gig in a gay club in Manchester called Manhattan. I had booked the Monochrome Set at the Poly so I knew where they were coming from roughly, but I knew they were unique. It wasn't jingly-jangly, it was more West Coast, a northern psychedelic; there was also a bit of Freddie and the Dreamers in it, and the Hollies.

JOHNNY MARR

The big step was when we wrote 'Hand In Glove'. I had paid a visit to my mum and dad's one Sunday night and there was this crappy little guitar that my brother was kicking round with, which Andy had built for me at school. I was bored and started playing this riff on it that actually sounded like Chic. I phoned up Angie and I said, 'I've got to get round to Morrissey's and play him this song because I don't have a tape player.' So she borrowed her mum and dad's VW Beetle – she was only 17 at the time – and I jumped in the car with the guitar and went round to Morrissey's and kept playing the riff so I wouldn't forget it.

Luckily Morrissey was in again. It was the second time I had knocked on his door. He had a tape recorder so I just played it and he said 'OK'! When we were in that mode we were happy to let each other be in our [own] space. I was happy to get out of there because I was dying for a cig, and he was happy for me to get out of there because he knew I was dying for a cig! And he wanted to get on with writing the words.

A couple of days later we met. We got in the service elevator up to the third floor and we plugged in, and me and him just looked at each other and said, 'Shall we play the new song?' I said, 'Here are the chords.' Mike played along and Andy jumped in and our lives really changed at that moment . . .

We played it ten times on the run. We couldn't believe how good it was. Morrissey went into a different gear in terms of his singing and his metre and in terms of what he was projecting. The eleventh time I heard

---

* The initial sessions for the Smiths' debut album were recorded with Troy Tate of the Teardrop Explodes.

it I was able to piece together all the words, and what he was singing was so great and – crucially – so simple. It was simpler than the other songs we had done, which were very, very wordy. From then on our song-writing became more focused, we were absolutely enraptured with that.

Joe recognised how important it was and said, 'Alright, what do we do about recording?' He then paid two hundred quid for us to go into Strawberry Studios one foggy night. It was an absolute pig of a night in the winter of '82. There was a super Dickensian fog outside, which was perfect to record the first Smiths record, and it sounds like it! Out of the fog comes the fade-in and the night sounded like the record. We were ecstatic – except a few days later Morrissey insisted we rerecord the vocal, which was completely unheard of and unprecedented because we were all so skint. It was very insightful of him though, because the vocal wasn't quite right. We went in and redid his vocal, and within a matter of ten days we had the cassette. The redone vocal was more lyrical, it was less frantic and slightly more croony.

We had the cassette and an approach had to be made to Geoff Travis and Rough Trade. As was always the case when an approach had to be made to anybody, all three heads turned in my direction. I loved us (laughs) more than anything!

I made my way to Rough Trade and walked in the front door and said, 'Is Geoff in?' I was given a polite, 'Does he know what it's about? Does he know what it concerns?' I answered, 'No. I'm a kid with a great demo tape.' They said, 'I think we've heard that one before, perhaps you should write a letter and stick the demo in the post.'

I thought, what am I going to do? Then I noticed this van go round the back of the building and come back out really quickly. So I walked round the back where I noticed this loading bay. I went round the loading bay and stood looking at these records like I was in a library. I was immediately impressed because I had never been round so many records in my life and there was a lot of activity going on. I hung around very furtively. Luckily I could see Geoff Travis's office, which was pre-dominantly glass; I could see a lot of activity going on round this office, but because it was Friday I could see that he wanted to get off early, so I just hung out trying to look like I worked there and trying not to get kicked out. A couple of people asked me what I was doing there, so I said 'I'm waiting for Geoff' – like he was my best mate. Then, when he came out the building to get a cup of tea, I grabbed him by the arm and I said to him, 'Here's the tape of my band from Manchester, we're called the Smiths and you won't have heard anything like it. We are either going to put it out on our own label and you can distribute it, or you can sign us to Rough Trade if you want. But either way we are going to put it out and it's fantastic.' He kind of brushed me off, but then he took it and that was it.

GEOFF TRAVIS

It was a Friday afternoon and I was in the kitchen making a cup of tea. My office was the size of half a telephone box, so I was stretching my legs.

Whilst waiting for the kettle to boil, I was approached by two young men. One of them – who turned out to be Johnny – had the look of a young Keith Richards, which piqued my interest. He approached me and held out a copy of a tape that he said they had recorded. He said to me that it wasn't just any other tape and that I should listen to it.

I took it home and listened to it that weekend about thirty times.

On Monday I called Johnny and on Tuesday all four Smiths travelled down from Manchester to master 'Hand In Glove' at George Peckham's mastering facility. The Smiths had just mastered their first Rough Trade single.

JOHNNY MARR

When I got back to Joe's office on Monday morning at half ten, Joe told me that Geoff Travis had already rung at ten o'clock and said it was one of the best things he had heard for years and he wanted to put it out on Rough Trade. We were just delirious – right then I could see that navy-blue single label right in my mind's eye and Morrissey started putting the sleeve together straight away. This had all happened within six months of when we met. It seemed like a lifetime to me but it happened quickly.

One of the amazing things about signing to Rough Trade at that point was that you immediately had an agent, because All Trade booking was in-house. The bands on Rough Trade automatically got on to All Trade booking. Immediately we got phone calls at Joe's office saying, 'Do you want to come and play with the Red Guitars?' or other bands who were around at the time.

The phone was ringing all the time now to do other gigs. We then got offered a gig at the Rock Garden in Covent Garden,* which is a tin can, as you know. We played down there and it was horrible – you had to pay an extra twenty quid for monitors. But what was amazing was that when we got out of the van, which had no windows in the back – just a mattress on the floor, it was essentially a bong on four wheels (*laughs*) – there were

* 23 May 1983.

two kids, Josh* and Anna, standing there with flowers and a quiff and the female fifties equivalent. They had our look. Already. We bowled out of this van and these kids were holding flowers because they had heard us on the John Peel show.

I was so proud of us as we walked into the venue. I remember that was also the night I debuted my Rickenbacker. At that time I remember sunshine, new guitars and new clothes; balanced with this was this sensibility that has always been tuned to melancholia – which wasn't that difficult because me and Morrissey had that disposition in us. It was a strange thing: we were ecstatic about what was happening to us and we had the melancholy. Maybe it was an Irish thing, a weird schizophrenic disposition. As individuals, the two of us were harnessing that melancholy and putting it into our music.

ULU was our seventh gig and that was how we got the first Peel session. Scott Piering, who was our plugger, had invited Peel's producer John Walters down and he really liked us. Peel had already played the single a few times. Everyone knows the John Peel shows were like bulletins from the Smiths to our audience, and vice versa. I had never listened to the John Peel show before we were on it because I was out all the time. I was too busy! But I got well interested in it when he started playing my band!

The necessity to write songs for the sessions really brought the band along. I wrote 'This Charming Man' specifically for those sessions; this was despite some of the people that worked on them! I would say, 'Please let me put an acoustic on it,' and they would say, 'Must you? Are you any good on it? Are you fucking folk rock?' So I would bite my lip and carry on. It seemed like that culture suddenly had a visual focus and it was us! You had a new generation of students and teenagers listening to indie music and no new band to hang a hat on. The *NME*, John Peel, Rough Trade were waiting for a band to go to a new level as well; the *NME* was waiting to go to the next level themselves, somewhere very political, and they thought we were the band. We knew that we were that band and we basically became that band.

JON SAVAGE

When I got 'Hand In Glove' I thought it was a wonderful song. It was a time when guitars weren't big – you couldn't hear them in many groups. Just before there had been Orange Juice and a couple of other bands, but I really like clanging guitars in psychedelic music making a great noise, which the Buzzcocks had but the Clash didn't necessarily have. When I

* Josh would eventually front his own group called Loop.

got sent 'Hand In Glove' it took me some time to realise that it was Morrissey singing! I couldn't believe that he had actually done it because I thought he was going to be this tragic person. I was really pleased for him. I interviewed them at the time and I really liked Johnny, I thought he was great. I had never met him before I moved back to London.

JOHNNY MARR

Interestingly enough, when we got our first *Top of the Pops* there was still an issue around people I knew and at Rough Trade, which was, 'Are you going to do it?' I said, 'Fuck, yeah! This is what it's about. Get this shit to the suburbs, man!' We were like – it's easy to use the word ambitious instead of aspirational. We aspired to be great – the fame and the dough are a long way behind being great or being in the same pantheon as your heroes . . . If we were into it for dough and pure success we would not have been writing songs like 'Handsome Devil' or even 'Hand In Glove' . . .

When I got together with Morrissey, what he was doing was uncompromising and uncommercial and quite dark, and what I was doing as a musician was pretty dark as well . . . When your first songwriting session is 'Suffer Little Children', about the Moors Murders, you're not expecting big royalty cheques to come though the front door! I was in this for life and so was the singer I was going to work with. I love 'Suffer Little Children', and when your first single has a hot naked man on the front from a very specifically gay homoerotic image and you're coming out of the gay clubs, you're not thinking you're going to get in *Smash Hits*. I'm fine with that. I wanted to do what I thought was great.

We released the first album and everything blew up. We moved to London. I got a flat in Earl's Court and Morrissey got a flat in Chelsea. Despite this, I kept most of my clothes and belongings in my flat at Joe's, which Andrew was living in, and I still came back to write. It was Morrissey's decision to move to London and it was the right one. We had to work more closely with the record label because Morrissey wanted things to happen on a more daily basis. Joe had resigned as the band's manager by then, on 30 December 1983. That was the start of our managerless excursions and a period which has been well documented as a major part of the band's demise . . .

When we moved to London we spent all our time in cars. We were spending time in our flats listening to records and staying up late and also watching VHS cassettes, which had just become affordable. That was really important, as I was taping every bit of Dusty Springfield and the Rolling Stones I could get on these late-night shows. Nowadays you can't move for DVDs and YouTube, but then it was hard to see anything. I was able to buy a VHS player and bought *The Complete Beatles*. Me and Andy watched it over and over again and it gave us a template of where we were going to go next . . .

The band will tell you I was famously nocturnal. They would have to wait for me till four in the afternoon, which suited Morrissey as he was discussing artwork or interviews with Rough Trade. I was getting all my input during the night – the phone didn't ring, Rough Trade weren't on my case, because I was the band's de facto manager.

We had done the first album in Pluto in Manchester and there's a pattern there – when we had to do important stuff we retreated back up north.

We demoed the second album on a Portastudio and then we went back up north and stayed at the Piccadilly Hotel next to the Britannia. Pluto had closed down by then, and because we didn't like the sound in Strawberry, because it was very carpeted, and we considered anywhere in north Manchester past the Apollo too uncivilised (*laughs*), we ended up in Liverpool at Amazon. I remember Moz pushing for that because he liked a lot of the Liverpool music, like Cilla Black and all that kind of vibe, and since it was still very northern we went over there.

I remember we went to Amazon in this very seventies white limo – not a stretch limo, but it might as well have been, driving around this industrial estate in Liverpool where Amazon was.

ANDY ROURKE (Smiths bassist)
It was very much a basic stretch limo with an extra row of seats and a little footrest and an extra bit the length of this table attached to it, but it did stand out. What I remember about Amazon was that it was next door to a bacon barm place where I went to eat every day, but I wasn't meant to!

JOHNNY MARR
Andy was eating bacon butties whilst we were making *Meat Is Murder*! The band had got bigger and that album was number one.[*]

That night-time curve we were on was hedonistic but also really creative. It came out in the music and it definitely came out on *The Queen Is Dead*[†] because *VU* had just come out[‡] – this great unearthed Velvet

---

[*] *Meat Is Murder*, the Smiths' 1985 second album, was written during soundchecks on the 1985 UK tour. The album was a big leap forward from their debut.
[†] The band's third album, 1986's *The Queen Is Dead*, is the fans' and critics' favourite Smiths album and is felt by many to represent the band at the peak of their powers.
[‡] A 1985 release of Velvet Underground 'lost' tracks from the late sixties.

Underground album that never came out at the time. Andrew [Berry] was very important again, because he was an absolute Andy Warhol freak and he related to Andy Warhol because he had these Mancunian freaks all around in the salon in the Hacienda. He had based the idea for a salon on Warhol's Factory and encouraged lots of young girls to be around, and people were taking drugs and stuff.

In 1984/85 we came back to the UK to do a tour and to do a single and we could only breathe out when we got the third album together. There wasn't a tour in sight and we thought, let's move back to the north. I got a house and Andy got a flat and Mike got a house back up here in Manchester, which was sort of my call.

In Manchester it was hard for me to relate to what was going on by then because, as Noel Gallagher pointed out, what would I know – I was in the Smiths!

ANDY ROURKE

People's attitudes had changed towards us.

JOHNNY MARR

We weren't hanging round or going to gigs because we were playing gigs all the time.

ANDY ROURKE

We very rarely went out. We went to each other's houses, or usually Johnny's house!

JOHNNY MARR

We were knackered from touring and Manchester had changed because everyone looked like us. Manchester had become Mozchester. We were the biggest student band to that point. It wasn't like were we getting mobbed – we didn't go out. We were sitting round, staying up late, taking drugs and being in a band.

DAVE HASLAM

Very soon, something that I noticed happened with lot of Manchester groups happened with the Smiths. They start by being arty maverick weirdoes, when the only people at their gigs are what people would call weirdoes – people like myself, eccentric kind of people who think too much and are bothered about stuff that other people aren't bothered about. The band has success and suddenly the audience is very different. I would go and see the Smiths and it would be a convention for weirdoes who hate the world. And then the next thing you know there's loads of football fans there, throwing stuff around and singing 'Manchester la la la'.

JON SAVAGE

I saw them live late on at the Palladium in late '86. I didn't like the vibe round them, [it] didn't make me feel good.

MIKE JOYCE (Smiths drummer)

We had just come off a massive American tour where we were playing pretty big venues. I remember the late, great Bill Graham saying we would be playing stadiums the next time we were over. We were in massive high spirits, partying hard and giving the American crowd what they wanted. On MTV there was this thing about 'What is this phenomenon called the Smiths?' And we were playing massive venues without being at the top of the charts like Tears for Fears. Sire Records didn't know how to deal with us or how to market us, because twenty odd years ago America was very formulated, before Nirvana changed a lot of things.

Because of the American tour, we hit the road in the UK and I think we shocked a few people; people weren't expecting such a big sound. *Rank*, our live album, was recorded on that tour at the Kilburn National and it's a big sounding album – absolutely fantastic. It was great to have something committed to vinyl from when we were really rocking out. We were playing really big venues for us on that tour.

I think that tour was a culmination of all the gigs we had done in shitty little venues, struggling though a shitty little PA. That tour, everything was in place for us to come up with the goods. We had headlined before, but not on this scale, and it was down to us to come up with the goods. Which we did, because we had such a great album to cull the songs from.

I think Mozza really came out of himself on that tour, especially with the 'Two light ales please' sign.* Brilliant, absolutely brilliant!

The last gig was Brixton Academy in December; it was a charity gig for Artists Against Apartheid. It was a fantastic night. We had got to that point where we couldn't look after those people who had come to see us since the Rock Garden any more and there was a little bit of jealousy. I've felt that myself for a band as well, like they aren't yours any more, what are all those other people doing here? Don't be so bloody successful!

---

* Morrissey's handheld board was a pastiche of the Ramones' 'Gabba Gabba Hey' sign.

I'm sure we must have been exhausted at that point. If we weren't touring we would be in the studio, and if not that we were doing TV. It was non-stop, we didn't stop ever! I think it's hard for everyone, especially with somebody as un-rock'n'roll as Mozza, with his lifestyle of trying to look after himself and drinking a cup of tea backstage and trying to take it easy – that wasn't on the cards on tour. I learned over the years that to be a front person, it's a taxing thing, and not just physically – after all he wasn't exactly a bruiser. I don't know about now, but at the time he wasn't.

When you think about the mental gymnastics that he was having to perform on the stage and take that into consideration every night, you can see how difficult it was. Mozza always had that added pressure of having to be cool and having to sing; it's such a strange thing, a lot more taxing than playing the drums. He had the added pressure of being the frontman and I didn't really appreciate that in the early years. Later on, you realise that singing about how you feel about everything lays yourself open. There's a lot of internal angst being exposed. None of us were flippant about what we were doing. It was massively precious.

None of us thought that it was going to be the last tour. We recorded *Strangeways Here We Come** after that tour, which I thought was the best album we did – after *Strangeways*, what would have happened next? If we had carried on, I don't think the creativity would have dried up.

JOHNNY MARR

I was 23 when the band ended. I needed new air and I could see what was coming around the corner. There was this amazing new movement parallel to what we were doing and I was very aware of it. I remember that's what we talked about at the fateful meeting at the end of the band. I was saying, 'We've got to change, things have got to change – we can't just carry on and pretend we're in a black and white movie.' I was happy as a 23-year-old fan of music about what was coming along, coming out [of] my hometown – and it didn't have a name yet and it wasn't everyone in smiley T-shirts. I was getting tired of what indie had become.

---

* The Smiths' fourth and final album, 1987's *Strangeways* is the band's favourite album.

10

MID-EIGHTIES MANCHESTER: HYMN FROM A VILLAGE

Village Manchester, that is . . . that's what everyone called it then. It may have been a big city, but everyone knew everyone else and all the scenes overlapped. The Smiths and New Order had broken though and there was a lot of action going on in the city. From upcoming record labels to the squatted-out anarchy of Hulme and its own micro scene of bands, to several other bands starting on the very Mancunian long road to breaking through – years spent on the fringes of success, honing their sound to an original and wholly homegrown take on pop. The Happy Mondays and the Stone Roses were two of these bands, and another was James, whose gestation period is one of the oddest in the whole story.

JAMES

Keeping close to the no-rules post-punk ethic, James had been playing improvised sets with various vocalists until famously they saw Tim Booth dancing wildly at the Poly disco. Original band leader Paul Gilbertson asked Booth to be the band's dancer and it wasn't long before Booth was the band's frantic, charismatic vocalist. Early James were quite a different beast – there was a strangeness about them and a wilfully dark and dangerous kinetic energy, driven by Gavin Whelan's powerhouse drums.

MARTINE MCDONAGH (James manager)
The whole band was from Manchester apart from Tim. Tim was from Leeds and moved over to be at the university, but they were definitely part of Manchester.

TIM BOOTH (James vocalist)
It took me about two years to feel right in the band after the original singer. I felt like I had a lot to prove.

In August 1982 the band called themselves James, after bassist Jim Glennie's first name. Signing to Factory they released the Jimone EP, which was well received in the music press and got them a support spot on the Smiths tour in spring 1985.

MARTINE MCDONAGH

The first thing I did was the Smiths tour. I went on tour with them. It was exciting. We had this big old Bedford van to eat and sleep in and we stayed in dodgy bed and breakfasts. None of us had done that before and the band was getting lots of attention.

TIM BOOTH

We got on with the Smiths. I think Morrissey may have seen us as fellow travellers. He liked us and took us on tour. That's one of the best things about Manchester: we supported the Fall, the Smiths. And we've done the same, a lot of overlapping goes on. One of the big strengths of Manchester is that the bands have helped each other. The Smiths' attitude was great: instead of getting EMI to buy a band on to their tour, they took us instead.

When the band started we used to be into extremes; we'd write a lot of depressing songs. Eventually we thought, what's the use of playing this to people and depressing them? So whenever we came up with a depressing riff we would try and uplift it.

MARTINE MCDONAGH

I always felt they did have that commercial viability. They made music that lots of people could like. I also understood that it's not easy to convince labels. They were interested in the band because of the media interest, and the Smiths were promoting them, but when they realised the reality of what selling James records involved their interest ended because they didn't fit in.*

They weren't going to get daytime Radio 1 play at that time. The first band from Manchester to get that was the Stone Roses; not even the Smiths got that much radio play. In the place of that there was a strong network of independent programmes on local radio. And when we started to get into the charts without daytime Radio 1 play, people started to take notice of the indie bands who made great records. James were part of that – the scene that was unplayable on radio.

* Debut album *Stutter*, released in June 1986, was greeted with surprisingly average reviews and only got to number 68 in the charts. *Strip-Mine*, their second album, was released in September 1988 and did even worse. The band left Sire Records as a cult band, with a fierce following who appreciated the group's idiosyncratic and edgy music.

TIM BOOTH

Initially, living in Manchester, you couldn't help but sound like Joy Division. The whole city had a really depressing atmosphere and we tried to react against that. The attitude behind what we were doing was the same as behind Iggy, the Birthday Party, and people like that. James as a band really liked the Birthday Party. We used to travel down to London to see them – that was our roots. *Stutter* I would say had things in common with the Birthday Party.

Iggy Pop had the same unpredictability and violence. On stage he broke down barriers. We wanted interaction and spontaneity and we wanted to inspire people – it was great when the audience sat down during 'Sit Down'.

We would like the audience to present us with strange reactions, the weirder the better.

MARTINE MCDONAGH

I did the first shirts with the letters split up round the body. It came from someone in the crowd at a James gig in London who had made himself a T-shirt. I pulled him out of the crowd and asked if we could use that design and paid for it.

The reason we went into merchandise in such a big way was that we realised that was the only source of income we could have. It was a lot of effort setting that up – getting T-shirts in shops and finding designs that people would buy. This was in the time when people didn't buy indie band T-shirts. We did it to survive after being on Sire.

I remember when we moved into New Mount Street we used the same printer as the [Inspiral Carpets] did for T-shirts. We didn't really do it in cahoots with them. There was the Stone Roses T-shirt with the lemon on it at the same time – Gareth [Evans] made up absolutely shedloads of those and gave them away to people. They were a really good design and we knew we must do something for people to wear as a fashion item . . .

The curse of James? Well, we came out of our deal and put some stuff out on Rough Trade, and Rough Trade went under. We then focused on building the live and the merchandise side and then eventually we were selling two nights out at Brixton. Major labels said we should sign and we were getting lots of Radio 1 support. And then we released 'Sit Down', which was such a classic pop song, it didn't fall into any categories. It was a pop song and it got everyone interested in the band.

The album Gold Mother, *released in June 1990, saw the band swept up by the Madchester explosion; they had finally found their place. They released 'Sit Down', which hit number 2 in the UK charts and the album sold 300,000. James were finally a major act, although still with their own idiosyncratic approach.*

MARTINE MCDONAGH

There were some members of the band that meditated and [had a] very definite strict regime of vegetarianism and non-drinking and no drugs. They all had had their moments in the recent past.

I think they enjoyed living vicariously though. Everyone really liked the Happy Mondays – especially Shaun and Bez, who were great fun to be with when we toured with them. There were fights in hotel rooms, which was frightening, but we enjoyed being with them.

I personally worried about Shaun. I thought he was a fantastic bloke and it was scary to watch someone destroy themselves. He was the only bloke in his twenties who looked older than his dad.

Bez was always fantastic. I thought Bez could handle it better; he seemed to have a better constitution, and he could balance it out and combine the two lifestyles.

TIM BOOTH

Initially James were quite similar to the Happy Mondays – that's why we became what we became. We became quite austere because we lost a lot of friends – people who got quite heavily into that destructive world.

We saw what was happening so we swung around: we became quite austere for about three years; the last couple of years have been more relaxed. A number of things were happening, people were ending up in hospitals and prisons and we didn't want to go down that road. That's what songs like 'Johnny Yen' are about.

We related to the Happy Mondays when we first saw them; that's why we took them on tour. The Mondays were great and they probably influenced us, but they also used to be at a lot of our early gigs.

DEATH TO TRAD ROCK!

In the mid-eighties, Manchester had a distinct noise scene: bands often supported by John Peel, who played bass-led discordant anti-rock that broke all the rules. In the early eighties the author's band the Membranes were finally breaking out, with the successful single 'Spike Milligan's Tape Recorder' and a series of albums and world tours. The period also saw the breakthrough of other discordant groups such as A Witness and Big Flame, and of other bands who were based near Manchester like Bogshed, and to a certain extent the Inca Babies and a horde of Hulme bands like Dub Sex and Big Ed and his Rockin' Rattlesnakes.

VINCE HUNT (A Witness bassist)
I formed A Witness; our best known song was 'Lucky in London', which articulated how I felt about people who went down to London to 'make it'. Tony Wilson was a great inspiration, even from an early age. I remember we were all 14, 15 or 16 when punk first happened; there was Wilson on *So It Goes*, championing this music, these bands. Then after I came back from college in a band, he was saying, 'Don't go to London, do it here.' And Manchester – then, as now – seemed to have everything I needed to do it.

I went to see The Fall in about 1978 at Jackson's Lane Youth Club, the local comprehensive school where I lived in Hazel Grove, and it was one of those life-changing gigs. Mark E. Smith wearing a tank top, Martin Bramah playing the guitar left-handed, Una Baines plinky-plonking on a keyboard. They did 'Psycho Mafia', 'Bingo Master's Break Out', 'Industrial Estate', 'No Xmas for John Quays' – it was amazing.

What I liked about the Fall is what I still like about Manchester: you see a group of people hanging round the door, and they're probably the band. Then they get the bus home. It's such an accessible place and no one needs to play the star trip.

Hulme by the mid-eighties had gone feral, following the big brave new world of the late sixties clearance and demolitions. The families had mostly moved out and the students, squatters, junkies and freaks had moved in. The area had a whole new life, becoming the biggest squat area in Europe and by default a creative powerhouse that would affect the cityscape.

LIZ NAYLOR
I remember moving out of Hulme and Manchester; people were cashing their giros in Moss Side and getting robbed. It was good while it lasted – we were five minutes' walk from the Hacienda and everyone we knew lived in the Crescents and went in the White Horse and Grants – but it always felt edgy.

HARRY STAFFORD (Inca Babies guitarist/vocalist)
If you lived in Hulme in the early eighties, you were either a student, an artist, a doleite, a junkie, or indeed sometimes all four.

I was a student at Manchester Polytechnic reading, if you will, English Literature, majoring in the American Novel and Romantic Poetry. Hulme was for me the ultimate demi-paradise I had been looking for my entire life and didn't dare believe actually existed . . .

At this time the universities were alerted to the vast cheap housing only a stone's throw from campus, and in they poured like a Klondike gold rush to this cheap housing. All my friends moved to Hulme on the offer of such a good deal. And actually it made loads of sense. Hulme is basically a half-mile from the city centre, so it was walking distance; perfect. Also at this time the Hacienda had just opened, seven minutes' walk away. It was free to get in and staged arguably all the best gigs in town.

I moved into a friend's flat and that was that, and I reckon I probably squatted for the next six years. I don't believe I paid a single penny in rent because none of the flats I stayed in had my name on the tenancy and no one asked me to pay rent. I paid phone bills and electricity bills but the council never asked me for a single penny.

This oversight by the council meant that the occupants of these deck access flats felt that they perhaps could exploit the freedom of an unpaid-for dwelling . . . One resident removed all the walls and set up an art gallery; another created a gig venue for after-pub jams; some painted them black from floor to ceiling with the words 'burn baby burn' painted across the walls . . .

Because of the bohemian lifestyle that emerged, a lot of people set up bands. As many people were unemployed or dodging lectures, a lot of bands used the crescents to rehearse in. A Certain Ratio could be heard echoing across Charles Barry Crescent, Martin Moscrop's trumpet a shard of discomfort among the percussive shuffle. My band the Inca Babies began rehearsing in Charles Barry as well.

DAVE HASLAM

By the time I got to Hulme in 1982 the real Mancs had quite rightly fucked off. The council's policy was to move the families out, so it was kind of left to us. People are dismissive of it being full of students and arty types but the students and arty types re-energised it. I don't really remember paying any rent. Sixty per cent of the flats were unoccupied where I lived and ten per cent of the original inhabitants were left; the rest of the people were transients.

Pictures of Hulme in that era make it look like *Blade Runner* after the Blitz and that's how it felt. It did feel like a unique landscape really – all those tower blocks were falling apart and they stank. It was dangerous to walk around but you would hear great music from the windows: walk on further it would be a great dance record; walk a bit further and you would hear some kind of dub.

GREG KEEFE (Big Flame guitarist)

Before we formed Big Flame, me and Dil* theorised about the ultimate band for years. All the elements had to be totally sound and uncriticisable: politically it would have the rigour; it would never sell out; it was not money but pure art – non-commercial, popular; it would change the world.

As a band we loved practising. We built a practice room. I moved to Ermine Walk to get a room . . . I wandered around to find an empty flat. I found one with an extra bedroom in it [and] stapled carpets [to the] wall acoustically. Anyone who wanted to be in a band had loads of space in Hulme.

ALAN BROWN (Big Flame bassist/vocalist)

I moved to Hulme in 1981. I knew that there was a scene there with hopefully like-minded people, and so it turned out to be, although the nicey middle-classness was replaced by dropout middle-classness, which stood out starkly against the real people who actually had to live there through no choice. Hulme became home base on the cheap for the next five years or so, as it did for a lot of creatively minded hopefuls and wasters. So there was a fair pool of attitude to dip into – accentuated by the White Horse pub, PSV Club and the Hacienda of course.

I only got my nose broken once.

We had a statement of intent, a definite plan; it was very honourable, and there was no way we were going to deviate from this. It set out the lifespan and raison d'être of this band very clearly. And that was inspiring – here's the start and there's the end. [It was a] very logical way of ensuring we didn't end up being everything we hated about the music industry.

DAVE HASLAM

In the mid-eighties I had helped Big Flame with the Wilde Club. I was a fanzine editor; I had John Peel's phone number and they put up with me hanging around and playing records. I started DJing there. They said I need a DJ name and I turned up next day being advertised as DJ Miserable Dave!

NATHAN MCGOUGH

When the Boardwalk opened they were looking for people to run nights

* Big Flame drummer.

for them, and Dave Haslam said, 'Do you fancy co-promoting Saturday night in the Boardwalk?' We booked Sonic Youth, Mighty Lemon Drops, Primal Scream – we had everyone off that scene. One of the bands we booked was Laibach. I helped them all day long to set up – these antlers, the flag, they had a projector. I worked hard to make the show work. I could see this was going to be great. After the gig they asked if I wanted to be their manager, so I took them to Daniel Miller and got them signed to Mute, and left it there.

HARRY STAFFORD

One difference between bands today and bands in those days was that it was very important to look like a band. As members of the Inca Babies we were especially image-conscious. One of the most indelible images of my youth was the cover of the Ramones' first album. Four guys dressed in a punk uniform all the same, all dedicated to the cause, a true band of brothers. Me, Bill* and Mike especially wanted to have that for the Incas. At that time the look of choice was the demob suit with overcoat and George Orwell haircut, long on top but shaved close up to the ears. It was the look of northern miserablism, for a post-punk batch who had listened to just a little too much *Unknown Pleasures*.

We decided it had to be black glam. Big black hair, but a total mess. Black clothes, leather and drills but ripped like punks. Black pointed shoes but held together with gaffer tape. This was what we looked like and we were incredibly pleased with ourselves.

But, I hear you say, is this not the attire of goths?

No, no, no! This was the natural progression from the psychedelic garage trash bands of the sixties West Coast, like the Sonics and Link Wray, to eighties pre-grunge death rock. Admittedly we weren't alone in this. The Cramps, the Gun Club and the Birthday Party all led the way, but for our requirements we just wanted to fine tune it for our own urban 'raunchy death ray rock'. We were chuffed to see that C.P. Lee in one of his learned music texts had called us the Hulme Cramps.

Luckily these noisy bands had the best studio in the UK to record in: Cargo Studios in Rochdale.

JOHN BRIERLEY (producer, founder of Cargo Studios)

When I first opened Cargo, I sat around for about three months with hardly any bands coming in. I'd spent all I had on building the place and had nothing left for advertising. It was around then that the Gang of

---

* Bill Marten, the Inca Babies' bassist, sadly died in 2008.

Four came in from Leeds.* They were just looking for a studio and thought they'd give Cargo a try. They recorded their 1978 *Damaged Goods* EP for Fast Product. The recording had a very raw live sound which they liked. When the track came out it was immediately picked up by John Peel and from then on almost every indie band who heard it wanted to come in to Cargo. At around the same time Tony Wilson was starting Factory Records and he brought in Joy Division and Durutti Column to record the *Factory Sampler* EP.

Joy Division came in many times after that; their most famous recording from Cargo was 'Atmosphere'. Along with Joy Division came Factory producer Martin Hannett. Martin recorded many bands in Cargo: Joy Division, A Certain Ratio, Orchestral Manoeuvres in the Dark, Crispy Ambulance, Nico, Stockholm Monsters. Other well-known bands that came in were Echo and the Bunnymen, Teardrop Explodes, Dead or Alive, GBH, Discharge and of course the Membranes.

Most of the bands that came in were after the 'live' sound that Cargo had, and it was a good time for that kind of music; new wave, heavy metal and punk was rebelling against the 'disco' sound around at that time.

There were several factors that helped create that sound. From the outset I'd decided that I wanted a 'live' studio sound, so the recordings would sound almost as if they'd been on stage.

The Chameleons' melancholic rock should have filled stadiums but the band never quite reached this level, although they were one of the biggest Manchester bands of the eighties. Charismatic frontman Mark Burgess and guitarists Dave Fielding and Reg Smithies built up the dark dreamscapes of their imaginative yet anthemic songs.

JOHN LEVER (The Chameleons drummer)
Someone was saying the Chameleons were looking for a drummer. I phoned Dave Fielding and went to a pub. They had just got a publishing deal with Virgin and were sick of drummers turning up for the wrong reasons – fucking hippies turning up. I ran through the songs with Reg and Dave. Mark turned up, took a look at me and shook hands with me and said, 'You're in.' I said, 'I haven't even played yet!' He said, 'You're alright and seem like a nice lad,' and I was in. Basically they were sick of auditioning people.

It was a bit weird being in the Chameleons; I never felt I was good

* 28–29 June 1978.

One that got away: The Chameleons should have been massive, with their melancholic anthems. One of the biggest Manchester bands of the 1980s, they remain influential. (Photo: Ian Tilton www.iantilton.net)

enough. I lacked a bit of confidence. I wasn't sure of my ability. When it first sort of kicked off, they were a bit intense and I'm not an intense person. I became intense! We were playing London supporting stupid bands for showcases and then we got bigger and bigger. Especially in weird places like Spain – we were massive over there – and Greece and places like that. In Spain we would play to thousands of people.

Mark and Dave always had a love/hate relationship – all the time Dave's still got feelings for Mark deep down inside, but he's too intense with it all. It got more intense still when Tony Fletcher our manager died in 1987; it caused problems. He was like the dad who would slap their legs for being naughty – like the football manager. When he passed on it went tits up and the band fell apart. When we got back together after 14 years and we were friends again we were doing alright, doing great tours all over the world, but we started on each other again.

The Chameleons were always ignored by the Manchester scene. When the Liverpool and Manchester bands were playing a festival at G-Mex they asked all the bands like Echo and the Bunnymen and everyone and ignored us. Eventually Alan Wise, the promoter, rings us up and we said, 'Fuck you, you're only asking us because you couldn't sell all the tickets.' We were always ignored by the press, ignored by the radio stations, by the clubs, the other bands – the Hacienda being a prime example. I went there one night and said, 'I'm from the Chameleons.' They said they thought they'd heard of us and we could play the local band night on a Tuesday and get about 50 quid for playing. So we thought: let's just do it. And we did it and it sold out, completely sold out!

They knew we were out there in Middleton but everybody ignored us. We were ignored when we were doing important gigs, selling the Ritz out for two nights. We were doing things like that and still getting ignored. We were selling German and American tours out and still ignored by the press. The third album charted and that was with no hype at all.

Meanwhile, back in Manchester . . .

GRAHAM LAMBERT (Inspiral Carpets guitarist)
In the seventies I had missed punk by a few months. My sister got me into the Doors and when I started making music in the early eighties I saw the Prisoners on the tube and got into the whole Medway scene – the Daggermen, Milkshakes, and then into Spacemen 3.

I loved psychedelic bands and I also loved John Peel stuff like Bogshed, the Membranes – 'Muscles' was a great classic pop song – Three Johns and the Inca Babies. I was never into New Order and the Smiths – they were almost playing the game.

SCOTT CAREY (Paris Angels bassist)
I started getting heavily into West Coast stuff. I was into the Doors and Love and then the Detroit lot like the MC5, who I was introduced to by the Hyde lot who hung around with the Stone Roses. There was Simmy who eventually joined the Paris Angels as a lighting engineer, he was good mates with John Squire and his missus and worked at Cosgrove Hall, Phil Smith who now works with Oasis as their DJ and roadie, Chris 'the piss' Griffin who's now known as a major tour manager. The legendary Steve Adge, who worked with the Roses, was around as well, and his brother Mark Adge, who joined the Paris Angels eventually. They were older than me but took me under their wing. Those early Stone Roses shows were pretty violent shows. I was introduced to amphetamines and then LSD, which really introduced me to the psychedelic stuff. I was still at school where they pushed the idea that LSD was around in the sixties and that was it, but then I found out that you could still get it. I was like, 'Whoa!'

CLINT BOON
The Gallery was a great venue. I went to see REM there way back in the early eighties. It was their first British tour. I think the next night they played the Duchess in Leeds. At the Gallery gig the power went off and they carried on playing without the PA, doing Shadows songs. After the show they climbed off the stage and up on to the balcony around it to get off the stage. It was a classic gig. Really magical.

DERMO
I was into Buzzcocks, the Chameleons – some people saw them as 'goth' but I never did. Beautiful lyrics set to magnetic trance guitars and deep drums. Joy Division/New Order, James – 'If Things Were Perfect', so different. The Smiths, the Stockholm Monsters – *Alma Mater* is one of my favourite LPs. I would later see singer Tony France at quite a few Northside gigs.

SCOTT CAREY
I met Wags* because I had a bowl cut and this little American tie and

* Paul Wagstaff, later of Black Grape and the reformed Happy Mondays.

jacket and check shirt like Will Sergeant* – I was 17! At that age you took your image from someone else. But I got to know him and he was an intelligent lad. He turned me on to the 13th Floor Elevators and eventually LSD, so if it weren't for him I wouldn't be in the mess I'm in now! (*laughs*)

STELLA

I used to go to Rafters and see Bauhaus, Psychedelic Furs – brilliant gigs. When I first went out, like everyone from north Manchester I didn't get past Piccadilly. I went to Brewster's, till quickly I realised when I got my head stoved in by a few girls that that wasn't such a good idea. I discovered Exit and Devilles in 1981. The second week the Hacienda opened I had one of those honorary membership tickets. I couldn't get a proper one because I wasn't 18. I got it from the Stockholm Monsters. I knew them well because they had a big connection with Moston. They used to rehearse at Moston youth club, so that was an early introduction to Factory and to what all that about. Stockholm Monsters were sort of like an Oasis without the fighting brothers.

TIM BURGESS

'Blue Monday' came out when I was 17. It was the last year of school. When I was 15 I really got into Tony Wilson on *Granada Reports*, and *The Tube* was really big around that time, in 1983/84. I remember *The Tube* at the Hacienda round about this time.

My mum worked in a paper shop in Northwich and Alan Erasmus and Tony Wilson used to come in there and buy the papers. Alan Erasmus had a farm round there I think – my mum got friendly with them. She told them I was really into Factory and he had a Fac 51 badge on him. My mum recognised it from the record sleeve, so he gave my mum the badge and every time he came by he would drop off a Durutti Column record or New Order's 'Confusion' white label – or a signed copy of their *Low-Life* for my 16th birthday, which was really rare because New Order didn't sign records at the time.

NOEL GALLAGHER

I was into Yargo and the Waltones at this point. 'The Word' music page had started in the *Evening News*, with Terry Christian and Penny Anderson writing about bands. Then they started listing the gigs. At this point I was playing the guitar and going to Johnny Roadhouse.† There was

---

* Echo and the Bunnymen's brilliantly distinctive psychedelic guitarist.
† Mancunian music shop institution on Oxford Road.

obviously a thing happening, and then I discovered the Hacienda and what that meant and how it went back to punk. And I was thinking, wow, it's a fucking great city to be right in the middle of. I would spend my time in Johnny Roadhouse looking at guitars. I was really obsessed with music.

TIM BURGESS

The Smiths, I really didn't get into them to be honest. I did buy 'Hand In Glove', but in hindsight that was because of the hype really – it wasn't self-discovered. Everything else I bought on Factory because it was on Factory, and I found it myself on Market Street in Manchester Arndale. I think my mates were into the Smiths. I did miss out on them but I was always aware of them.

At that time the Fall became my favourite band for quite a long time. The first record I bought was 'Kicker Conspiracy', which was a bit bizarre for a first record to get into a group with; the next was 'The Man Whose Head Expanded'. It was the Rough Trade time, when they were putting out *Slates*.* *Grotesque* became my favourite records of all time. They were untouchable then. It was the Peel session of 'Container Drivers' – brilliant. I went to see the Fall about 100 times up and down the country in places like Preston and Northampton. After work I would drive there and drive back.

NOEL GALLAGHER

At that point in about '86/'87 there started to be a Manchester scene and the International started to put gigs on. That's when I started to go out, but not into town to discos and all that shit. I would start going to the Internationals to see a band. By that time I was hooked and I would go and see live music. I would go on my own because none of my mates went.

In the late eighties the noise scene was fizzling out and Hulme became a key player in the acid-house explosion. Again, the squats and the space were key, and several all-night parties and scenes would come and go, the Kitchen being the main scene. New arrivals in Hulme like Finley Quaye were making sense of all this musical variety . . .

FINLEY QUAYE

Hulme was like living on the Battlestar Galactica – like living on a huge spaceship with two great big arms that faced the Spinners pub.

---

* Arguably the Fall's finest moment, a mini-album of waspish bass-led songs released on ten-inch vinyl only.

I used to go to the Epping Walk blues and do stuff there freestyle. Manchester is a multicultural city and you would get exposed to a lot of different cultures; everyone walks around in Manchester with an eclectic attitude. I would be listening to ragga or Dub Sex.

Across the city there was a whole melting pot of mid-eighties action.

DAVE HASLAM

I was evangelistic about music. The whole idea of fanzines was to talk about stuff I was interested in. I was getting demo tapes from bands for the fanzine and friends at the *NME* would like them, so I thought I'll put them out. So Nathan [McGough] and I started Play Hard. We didn't have a business plan; we really shouldn't have done it. Basically we put some great records out: King of the Slums, MC Buzz B.

JOHNNY JAY

I did a record called 'Slaphead' with MC Buzz B about his teacher at school. We put a chorus on, sung by these two girls Pes and Pooch, and we took it to Dave Haslam. He said it was a great record and he gave us some money to go in the studio. We knew nothing about sampling, and we did the record. It was dreadful! Dave Haslam put it on a compilation and the next thing I know John Peel had played it. I'm saying, 'Who's John Peel!?' The next thing was that Radio 1 wanted us to do a session.

Nathan McGough, who was Dave's business partner at the time, knew Roddy McKenna at Jive Records. We went for a meeting and we were in there for ten minutes. Suddenly the door bursts open and this mad Scottish guy says, 'Who's done this tape?!' We get shuffled to the head of A&R and he's saying, 'I don't believe it, it's a rap record with hooks on.' I was thinking, 'What's he going on about – fish hooks?' It was all a bit of whirl; even Nathan was shocked.

MARTIN MITLER

The first record we did as Laugh* was a flexidisc for *Debris* fanzine and John Peel picked up on it. Morrissey went on John Peel and picked up on the record and said it was one of his favourite tunes.

We ended up on Jeff Barrett's Sub Aqua label, but the record never came out the way we wanted it.

The pre-dance underground was full of eclectic strands. Somehow a mini-scene of

---

* The first indie dance band, Laugh were marrying dance beats to indie guitars a good two years before everyone else.

youthful rappers and hip-hop heads were working with ex-prog-rocker Graham
Massey; this mix of musical styles was going to be very creative.

GRAHAM MASSEY

There's a funny period in the late eighties when everything had gone a
bit New Romantic. It was all a bit style magazine. Also going on was this
electronic thing that comes in quite heavily in the early eighties with
New Hormones and Eric Random. The 808 drum machine he got was a
very expensive piece of kit and everyone was in awe of it. Living a couple
of streets away from him was Jon Hurst. He had something to do with
Section 25. 'Gadget' we used to call him – he had a 303 and a few bits of
Roland kit. I presume he had something to do with Section 25's 'Looking
from a Hilltop' – he stuck this Roland gear in everywhere! He shared a
flat with Phil Kirby, who by this time was our drummer in Biting
Tongues because Eddie the other drummer had left to join Simply Red.

JONATHAN HURST

Jez and Pete from ACR used to have mushroom parties at my flat in
Heaton Moor, where I had an early synths, effects and tape studio. When
Tony Wilson got Donald Johnson to drum for ACR, a brilliant band was
formed and I was lucky enough to mix them live, along with the other
Factory acts on the Factory Extravaganza tours. Live production was the
order of the day, with lots of reverb etc. Later Section 25 offered me
studio space in their large Blackpool warehouse and we had plenty of
visiting Factory musicians.

GRAHAM MASSEY

There was this group on Old Lansdowne Road where Gadget lived called
the Mothmen. They were a sort of hot knife-wielding, psychedelic
freakout band, similar in a way to what we were doing – formless music
that was all about sound. There was a lot of reggae and dub influence . . .
[Gadget] used to do lot of work with Martin Hannett and had Martin
Hannett's ARP 2600 synth, which was a very posh bit of gear, on his
kitchen table. We used to sit round and worship it.

It was called Hit Squad but it wasn't really called that at all; the
individual names were Scratch Beat Masters, which was Tunes and
Gerald, and Spinmasters, which was Darren and Andy [Barker] and a
rapper called MC Shine. And the Shure 4 was another one.

It was a right mess really, but everyone would come and hang out in
the studio – 15 people all with an opinion, so it was bit of a nightmare.

I got to know Martin [Price] through working in the café across the road from Eastern Bloc. The Eastern Bloc lot were in for a brew all the time and I was constantly chatting to them. I was playing music in the café and they'd bring stuff over saying, 'Check this out.' I started doing a music course and Martin starts bringing rappers down there. He's trying to get grants off the government . . . The shop's a co-op pulling in grants from everywhere. They had this idea to bring kids in to do rapping for more grants, so we had all these meetings in Wimpy in Piccadilly with rappers turning up, talking about getting a record together. We got this record together in 1987 called 'Hit Squad MCR'.

We did it like a Coldcut record: stick a thousand records into a sampler and glue them all together. And it was a total disaster, too many cooks. Even the beats aren't looped properly, it doesn't even feel good. On the other side there's a track from MC Tunes and Gerald, because they had a group and they recorded a few things at the Kitchen in Hulme,* and another track from a bunch of rappers from Timperley. Also Darren and Andrew are involved – it's like Blazing Squad, like a huge team of rappers.

We put on gigs at the Boardwalk, a hip-hop night, and we'd have the Rap Assassins on. We would do gigs in places like Wrexham football social club or a pub in Bolton – odd random gigs with a dirty great team. I would be the sound man.

The scene in Manchester was a bit impenetrable for us. We were considered outsiders to it because it had grown from soulboy culture. The outer rim of Manchester had this soulboy culture going on in clubs. There's no name for it really. It was big in the mid-eighties – Jeffrey Daniels urban music programme, huge basslines, SOS Band . . . I was living in parallel to this in weird shared houses. I was in a bubble of weird Throbbing Gristle land – I'd got souly stuff and reggae from my girlfriend. I'd go to the Gallery . . . and the Reno club in Moss Side, which is like a basement thing. I would feel uncomfortable at the Reno, where they played Michael Jackson plus esoteric souly music with big basslines. A lot of electronic music came from that culture, the Mike Shaft era that had gone electronic in the mid-eighties. All the language of electronic music is already there.

By this time I was working at the Boardwalk doing sound, as I had started doing a sound course in 1987. By the time I was doing the course, Midi stuff was coming out. I was interested in the drum machines and I met

* The Kitchen was a studio as well as a club.

Danny Spencer, who would end up in Candyflip.* He showed me a lot of stuff and he was really into a lot of house music, but it was all that 'jack your body' stuff and I'm not really into all that. In 1987 we were starting to listen to Stu Allen's programme on Sundays, playing some of the early acid stuff which sounded weird, less mainstream, less cheesy. It really fitted more into the things we were listening to, like a lot of On U Sound System records. Also 23 Skidoo had moved into that area as well. We played gigs with them and were always stuck in the same paragraphs as them. We did a number of gigs with them and we saw them moving over to drum machines and hip-hop. I was now flirting with drum machines and hip-hop culture in a very leftfield, On U Sound kind of way.

Where Eastern Bloc record shop came in was that Martin Price was a character who bridged both sides. He had that soulboy element of knowing his onions, knowing everything that Spin Inn knew about. Spin Inn were their arch rivals, so when they were ordering records they had to know their shit so as to not tread on each other's toes. He knew this but he also knew all the anarcho On U Sound, the bands dabbling with sampling. There was this sort of thing of people messing with sampling; I guess KLF eventually fitted into that side of things. Another thing that glued all that stuff together was that Eastern Bloc had this huge section of Psychic TV albums. They were a band dabbling with very early acid house and they seemed to have a record out every week.

When we started 808 [State] it was as a sound system at the Boardwalk, with Gerald's homemade sound system joined to the Boardwalk sound system – it was quadraphonic, but it was really mismatched and out of phase (*laughs*). But we did a sound system with the acid thing. The house music was going off in Legends and there was Greg Wilson's thing, but we didn't feel part of that world. We did our thing. It was our version of that world.

* Candyflip would have a huge hit in the acid-house era with an indie-dance version of 'Strawberry Fields Forever'.

11

MADCHESTER: RAVE ON

In 1987/88 the last great sea change in British youth culture was gathering pace. This was especially so in Manchester, where the city's long tradition of club culture, dance music, drugs and electronic music combined with a band scene that was open to new ideas to make the city a frontrunner in the new youth culture.

Strange new sounds were being coaxed out of the Roland 303 by the likes of Chicago-based Phuture. Their groundbreaking 1987 release 'Acid Trax' utilised the squelchy sounds of the Roland TB-303 analogue bass synthesiser that had previously been considered a drawback of the machine. Phuture realised that these weird sounds were the synthesiser's strength, and created something far weirder, more tripped-out and hypnotic than anything previously produced in the house genre. Crucially, they created music that was far more potent and psychedelic than anything released in the dance genre before.

Within months a whole host of American innovators were making music coloured by its use of simple tone generators with tempo-controlled resonant filters, creating interesting sounds with the 303 by tweaking the resonance and frequency cut-off dials as they played.

There had been precursors to this new sound: you can hear echoes of it in seventies and eighties industrial bands like Suicide and Front 242 and the German post-punk scene – the stripped-down repetition and machine-driven grooves. But this was something else, a far more minimal, basic sound that conversely filled every corner of the room with its enveloping, pulsating beat. It was perfect for the Detroit and Chicago mid-eighties club scene and fitted like a glove in the post-Joy Division/New Order technocracy of late-eighties Manchester, where a city's love of electro and electronic and new sounds was amplified in big empty warehouse spaces, and by cutting-edge DJs such as Mike Pickering.

House was already established in the Manchester clubs. But the new twist, acid house, was something else altogether. Harder, more minimal and trancier-sounding, it kicked in with its perfect enhancer, ecstasy, which gave the experience an even more tranced-out, loved-up feel, echoing around the old warehouses at raves and in the Hacienda, where the big old building's industrial acoustics were perfect for underlining this new music's stark trippy minimalism. Acid house was the perfect soundtrack for the end of the post-industrial era – those battered, dingy warehouses suddenly went into full colour and sound systems boomed round Hulme and city-centre clubs.

This was a new psychedelic music that arrived when no one was looking. It brought with it a whole new culture, a whole new way of dressing and talking, a new drug culture. Before, acid-house drugs were for the bohemians; afterwards, they were everywhere, with whatever baggage that brought.

GRAEME PARK

The Hacienda was a club for hedonists run by hedonists – that's why it could never exist nowadays.

MIKE PICKERING

The reason the Hacienda had been known for being empty was because of Rob's idea, which was an amazing idea and came from the Danceteria* in New York, which was to keep it open every night as a meeting place. And everyone met and swapped ideas there. That's where village Manchester comes from.†

RICHARD BOON

It was dance that made the Hacienda. There would be 30 people to see the Pop Group and it was suddenly packed for the dance nights.

NOEL GALLAGHER

People were bringing those records back from Detroit to Manchester and Manchester always had this connection with New York. It's the same latitude. New Order always did legendary gigs in New York and you would always read about them. New Order changed their sound because of these clubs in New York. Cool people were always bringing stuff back from New York and the likes of Mike Pickering said, 'You got a fucking nightclub, you got to do something with it.' Every time I see Mike and introduce him to people I say, 'This is Mike Pickering – he invented acid house music!' And he goes, 'Did I?'

He's very humble – he will say, 'I was just playing records,' but it was way more than that. At this point Factory becomes central to it all and

---

* The club's layout was inspired by the New York clubs Danceteria, Fun House and Paradise Garage, which the Factory mob and New Order knew well from their adventures in America.
† The idea of 'village Manchester' was that despite it being a big city, everyone knew everyone else in the creative scene – no matter what they were involved in.

the Hacienda as well. The Hacienda was special. Nowadays everything is a business, but in those days that place was pissing away money. You always knew when they were up against it because New Order would play there for two nights when the tax bills came. To them it was art, not business sense. One of the brilliant things about Factory Records and the times of In the City* was that it was natural for Manchester to be the centre of the universe. I met people in the queue for the Hacienda from Essex and it was the most natural thing that could happen.

MIKE PICKERING

To be honest the Hacienda had been busy before 1988; the Saturday nights were always full and there were other nights that did really well. I had the Nude night on a Friday from about 1986 and there was always well over a thousand people at that.† The Saturday night was busy and was a more *Face*-orientated trendy crowd. It was just during the week that we had problems, because it was open every night.

One of the unique things about the Hacienda was its door policy. We let the casuals in, which was unheard of at the time. Because what I wanted was for my mates to get in. Everywhere else suits and ties were allowed in, even if you were a troublemaker. But if you wore a nice Armani top and some nice trainers, then you couldn't get in. And that was the sort of clothes we were all wearing. We made it free to people who were on the dole. It was brilliant − it was the first place to accept those kinds of people.

TIM LAWRENCE

These were the same kids who went to clubs like the Playpen, the Gallery, Berlin and Legend. Stu Allan, the DJ with the most influential house music slot on British radio back then, was a former Legend regular from the electro-funk days. A Guy Called Gerald, who recorded the quintessential British acid-house track 'Voodoo Ray', was, once again, a former Legend regular and someone who'd been on the scene since the jazz-funk era − 1987 certainly wasn't Day One for someone like Gerald, and although it's termed 'house', you can clearly hear the influence of electro, and indeed jazz-funk, in 'Voodoo Ray'. It's very much a hybrid track, hence its out-and-out uniqueness.

---

* Manchester-based music conference set up by Tony and Yvette Wilson that survives to this day.
† Mike Pickering is recognised as the pioneer house DJ in Manchester; along with Martin Prendergast and later Graeme Park, he hosted the visionary Nude night on Fridays that became the Hot night in 1988.

MIKE PICKERING

The Nude night was a big success. We were playing electro, and the music that would become house like Colonel Abrahams. There would also be northern soul, and Simon Topping used to have thirty minutes where he'd play Latin stuff he'd picked up in Lower East Side New York. If I liked it and the crowd liked it, then that was it really. So we had records that were really, really big at the Hacienda that have never been big anywhere else.

Within two or three weeks the club was right on its 1200 capacity. The fire brigade had put a low capacity on us, but it was still amazing. It was 50 per cent black, 50 per cent white. We had lots of little dance troupes from Hulme and Moss Side coming along.

TIM LAWRENCE

According to Pickering, Nude took off immediately. The numbers might be a little askew, but there's no doubt that the crowd, which had started to shift with Greg Wilson, became even more mixed.

GRAEME PARK

I met Mike Pickering at a photo session for new DJs in the north. I was playing these house records in 1986 and people weren't sure about them. But they sounded fantastic, really original, really DIY, like the early punk records . . .

Mike Pickering went on holiday for three weeks and I covered for him at the Hacienda and it went really well. I remember getting a train to Manchester and John Cooper Clarke got on. I thought he would be dressed like that only for the stage, but he walked round like that all the time. That seemed really cool and made Manchester feel even more exciting.

JON DASILVA (DJ)

I arrived at the Hacienda starting a new night for me to play with Mike Pickering and Laurent Garnier, who had to do national service.

Because it was my first experience of that kind of scale, I had no benchmark. The scene didn't really galvanise for me till later in the year.

DAVE HASLAM

I had been headhunted by the Hacienda in early '86. The Hacienda had been open for four years and it was losing money. They put on gigs and didn't make money. They kind of kept their world very insular. They then got this guy Paul Mason from Rock City in Nottingham and it was like they were saying, 'Let's roll the dice and get someone in who knows what they are doing.' One of the people was Paul Cons. They were given the brief. I think Tony Wilson went on holiday in the summer of 1986; I imagine he half-expected to come back and the club to be closed, but Mason and Cons had decided to put on club nights because the bands were losing money and Paul Mason had done a big *NME* student night at Rock City which had done well. He wanted to do that on Thursday night at the Hacienda and that's where I came in.

Mike Pickering and Martin Prendergast, or MP2 as they were known, were on a Friday night and me and Dean Johnson on a Saturday. They originally wanted me to do it on my own on the Saturday, but I literally didn't have enough records to do that. Dean Johnson was quite an intriguing individual, very into his street soul music, and he DJed around town. He was very purist about his music and he knew Kermit and the breakdancers and those kind of people, so he played jazz and soul. He would take a dim view of punters who asked for the wrong records! And occasionally get on the mic and say, 'This music's too good for you so you can all fuck off.' I quite liked that idea.

Everyone was saying it was fun for a while, but then people got fed up with the music being all over the place. That was when Jon Dasilva came in and started working with me.

JON DASILVA

I had been into On U and anything New York, weird stuff and Sugarhill Gang, Keith Leblanc, Velvets, etc. I would play squats, Labour clubs. When I moved to Manchester I set up an arts centre and played house music. Drifting to the Hacienda, I got subsumed by it and made my name.

PAUL RYDER

We would go to MP2, with Martin Prendergast and Mike Pickering, thinking, wow, these bass lines are excellent. I kept trying to rip them off but couldn't because they were all on keyboards. But the next Mondays album felt the influence of what Mike was playing.

MIKE PICKERING

There was this whole thing, the Baldricks.* This came from the Mondays and Phil Saxe – he got all the clothes together; Phil is where it all came from. Little Martin [Prendergast] who did the Friday with me was one of

---

* The Baldricks were a scally sub-cult named after Tony Robinson's character in *Blackadder*; they had the bowl-headed haircut and dressed in clothes too big for them. They were led by Martin Prendergast (Little Martin), who DJed alongside Pickering on the Nude nights.

them, a lot of the kids dressed like that at [Manchester] City games. I think a lot of that is down to Phil and the Mondays.

I found an old i-D magazine from Manchester and the next big thing I had put the working class are reclaiming the streets and the clubs and that's what we are going to do here at the Hacienda. We did think that. I wanted those people that looked like the Mondays and Ian Brown in the club.

My whole thing – and Rob's as well, and Tony's on a more intellectual level – was that we wanted these people in. We never had any trouble. People were grateful that they had a place to go . . . It was all set up: the music was there; the look was there.

JON DASILVA

DJ culture wasn't like now. There were no magazines and fan culture at the time. My approach to my set was open-minded. Krautrock – which was a buzz to hear loud on the Hacienda sound system – as well as reggae and dance. There would be some tension before we rolled out the four-to-the-floor kick drum a lot of people got into, and that was a great period, before it became gentrified and you had to be one thing or another.

The true Manchester had eclectic taste. I had been drawn into Manchester regionally because of Factory. The aura of Manchester is different, it's not London. It's got something about it that draws people in.

MIKE PICKERING

They put a mic in my DJ box and I said, 'Fuck off, I'm not into that!' A lot of DJs couldn't handle the Hacienda. I had DJs storming out!

I booked everything at the Hacienda. Rob was busy with New Order so I was booking the bands, the lighting guys, the VJs like Claude Bessey, all the DJs, as well as the bands. My band Quando Quango were big in New York and played at the Paradise Garage – Larry Levan had booked us.* The idea was to make the Hacienda and Manchester like New York. Our whole thing at the time was to stay in Manchester and make something out of it. In Liverpool, from the Beatles onwards, they had always been down the M6 before the ink dried on the contract. We wanted to make Manchester great so we didn't have to leave.

* Larry Levan was the DJ at New York City nightclub Paradise Garage.

JON SAVAGE

At that time I had just been to New York and discovered all those great breakbeat records in Downstairs Records; I was buying stuff like the Jimmy Castor Bunch.* Pre-acid house I was really into that, but I was also into early house because I had been to New York and heard a lot of it. In early '86 I went to New York and while I was there blagged some records. This guy gave me a 12-inch of 'Mystery of Love' by Fingers Inc, with 'Donnie' by the It on the other side. I fucking loved it and I took it back to London and played it. People said it was rubbish but it was brutal and psychedelic. It would be perfect for the Hacienda with its architecture and space and crazy sound system.

GREG WILSON

The original trendy crowd was no longer visible. Black kids and scallys dominated the floor.

Along with the likes of Stu Allan, Colin Curtis and Hewan Clarke (who were playing at the Gallery, the Playpen, Berlin and Legend), Graeme Park (the Garage in Nottingham) and Winston Hazel (Jive Turkey in Sheffield), Pickering pioneered the sound of house in the north of England. A 'young kid from Moss Side' handed him his first Chicago house record, 'No Way Back' by Adonis, and 'the club went crazy' when he played it. After that, Pickering started to develop as many fast-speed supply lines of American house as he could, with Kamins† one of his most important sources. Meanwhile Mike got test pressings of the early house music recordings via New York, often before they hit Manchester.

DAVE HASLAM

By the end of 1987 people had lost that raincoat-miserable world; that had been left behind. There was some resistance to it, people complaining at the DJ box, wanting to hear something more grey and downbeat. They were getting an upbeat experience and not liking it. I remember some guy saying, 'Stop playing this disco shit.' There was already a sense of something new, a new generation of people that weren't dressing in that dark raincoat way. By the end of '87 there was a good mix of students, street kids, black kids, gay kids, designer kids, hairdressers, all sorts at the Hacienda. I always thought that the crucial period was December 1987 to March '88. I remember having a conversation with Tony [Wilson] at the end of '87, talking to him about acid

* Great seventies novelty funk act.
† Mark Kamins, the DJ at Danceteria in New York.

house, and he immediately thought I was talking about drug culture. He was saying, 'Is this music that you take acid to?'

In his head he was thinking that this was the new drug music that I was interested in, so he invited me on to *The Other Side of Midnight* to talk about acid house. That was January '88.

JON DASILVA*
At first it was really rare to hear acid house. If you heard it coming out of [someone's] car you would cross the street and talk to them.

MIKE PICKERING
At the beginning there was quite a north-south divide. In Manchester people had been dancing to house music for a year before they were in London, where the rare groove scene was bigger. The initial northern house movement was basically Graeme Park at the Garage in Nottingham and me at the Hacienda.

It was quite telling [what happened] when I had done an exchange with a club called Fever at the Astoria. I came down in January 1988 and I distinctly remember playing Rhythm is Rhythm's 'Strings of Life' and getting booed. Six months later I went back and played virtually the same records and everyone was going crazy.

GRAEME PARK
Me and Mike would play the dance stuff and Dave Haslam would have the eclectic Temperance night.

JEFF COOPER (fan)
I felt like I lived in the Hacienda – Mike Pickering's groundbreaking Nude night for the full-on acid house experience and Dave Haslam's excellent Temperance night for the indie and the sixties and some dance music all mixed together.

MARTIN MOSCROP
Because we were on Factory we were honorary members of the Hacienda from the start, and because we were musicians we didn't have to get up in the morning. Every night there would be something on and we would be there. The Hacienda was good for us when we were little bit poorer.

---

* Following his youthful stints in punk-funk bands, Dasilva was typical of the eclectic crew of Hacienda DJs.

DAVE ROFE

The Gay Traitor bar downstairs in the Hacienda on a Friday, before it became the Fifth Man, was a total mixed bag. Upstairs it was house nation. Downstairs we would play anything – Yello, hip-hop, Kraftwerk – to a good mixed crowd.

MIKE PICKERING

We pissed a lot of people off at first. Local promoters weren't allowed to work with us and they weren't happy. The Hacienda had to be someone completely new who had never done it before to make it fresh.

IAN BROWN

The Hacienda was mega in the house days, wasn't it? Magical – everyone loved each other. My mate Stuart got a job as cellarman at the Hacienda so I would go down there. I lived in Hulme in '84, I used to walk in. I never joined but I would get signed in because my girlfriend was a member. I used to go to the Nude nights.

TIM LAWRENCE

The Hacienda soon had a slice of house that it could call its own: 'Carino' by T-Coy. Recorded by Pickering and [Simon] Topping, 'Carino' was probably the first UK house record to cause a stir, and its sonic blend reflected the Hacienda's fixation with the States.

MIKE PICKERING

It was a mix of Tito Puente and Adonis. We put 'Carino' together one morning in a little studio we borrowed in Didsbury. We recorded it on cassette and gave it to Stu Allan. He kept playing it and it went to number one on his chart. Then Coldcut Crew heard it and told Kiss, which was still a pirate station, about it. It was only then that it went national.

TIM LAWRENCE

Gerald Simpson, inspired by the electronic dance music he was buying from Spin Inn, the best-stocked supplier of US imports in the north, laid down 'Voodoo Ray' soon after.

A GUY CALLED GERALD

I had bought an 808 drum machine and a 303 bassline machine and was making electro and hip-hop in the style of Ice-T's 'Dog 'n the Wax'. I'd have reverb on the snare and this really heavy sound on the 303 bass. Then I heard these guys from Chicago using the same instrument, but they were tweaking it. I did a load of this stuff and gave it to Stu Allan and he was like, 'What the fuck! How did someone from around the corner do this?'

TIM LAWRENCE
Lost for a name when he played the material on Piccadilly, Allan introduced the producer as 'A Guy called Gerald', and a listener from Rham Records liked the music enough to put out the record: 'Voodoo Ray' by A Guy Called Gerald. Simpson took a white label of the track to Jon Dasilva, who was spinning at a new Wednesday-night slot at the Hacienda called Zumbar. Simpson returned to the venue a couple of weeks later.

A GUY CALLED GERALD
Either Jon Dasilva or Mike Pickering put the tune on and people were going fucking mental. I was like, "Shit!"

GREG WILSON
Graeme Park started DJing in Nottingham in 1984, when Rock City was at its peak and electro the dominant force. Colin Curtis said they had him on at Rock City a few times before he began to make a name for himself at the Garage.

GRAEME PARK
I became a DJ because Selectadisc record shop, where I worked, bought a nightclub called the Garage. They said if I didn't DJ for them I wasn't going to have a job in the record shop. When you are 22, 23 you do it. I found I was quite good at it. And unlike being in a band, you got all the money to yourself and you didn't have to pack all the gear up!

GREG WILSON
The manager at Rock City at the time was Paul Mason, who would move to the Hacienda in 1986. It was via the Mason connection that Graeme Park was brought to the club in 1988.

Graeme's other main club of the era was the Leadmill in Sheffield, which had been an all-dayer venue during the electro days. I DJed at an all-dayer there myself (possibly the first) in 1983. He'd appear alongside Jive Turkey's Winston Hazel at the Steamer nights in the Leadmill.

MIKE PICKERING
Friday night was free or a quid for people on the dole, and then we reversed the door policy so that the Perrys could come in. At that time it was 50 per cent black and white. We didn't need a smoke machine because everyone was smoking weed – every person in that club smoked weed. And then the Es came along . . .

Proving that the key player in all shifts of pop culture is a new drug, ecstasy changed everything, from people's clothes, music taste, hairstyle, language to the way they walked – suddenly everything was looser, baggier and weirder. Pop culture had shifted a gear and Manchester would never be the same again.

MIKE PICKERING

I always likened the E hitting the Hacienda to a Mexican wave. It started at the front door and moved down the club in a three-week period that changed the whole crowd.

IAN BROWN

All of a sudden it was really exciting. Everyone was dropping Es – that's what done it. My first E was amazing. We had been into tripping on acid in 1984/85 but that was nothing like when there were 2000 people tripping on Es!

I liked the house music before the Es because Howard Jones played us stuff; he had tapes off Mike Pickering. Cressa* had a couple of house tapes at the time. I thought it was ace – just a piano and a beat, dead simple. There wasn't much vocals attached to it. I remember going to the Chicago Jackmaster international tour in 1987 with Joe Smooth and Frankie Knuckles.† There was a big wooden chair nailed up to the wall by the sound desk and he was sat on that. I remember thinking then, this is something different. All the girls on one side and all the guys on the other side of the room were crossing the floor in patterns. He had all the blacks on one side and all the whites on the other and got them all to cross over in patterns. It was the Chicago thing, and he was disciplining everyone in the rules of the Chicago scene. It was really exciting and different. This was a year before the E came in . . . When that happened suddenly everyone was your best mate.

There were thousands of us, and more and more each week. I thought ecstasy was going to change the world – football violence stopped; violence stopped. It was a different atmosphere – you could bang into people and it was a laugh. Here were all the guys who had an edge to

---

* A mate of Ian Brown's from the scooter days, Cressa was also big mates with the Happy Mondays and was arguably the person who introduced the Roses to flares. Cressa would get on stage with the band and operate John Squire's effects pedals; his onstage dancing behind the amp was an integral part of the breakthrough Roses set-up.
† While studying at college in Manhattan, Knuckles became a DJ with Larry Levan, playing soul funk. In the mid-eighties, the term 'house' was applied to the music that he was playing at the Warehouse, defining the raw drum machine-driven new sounds he specialised in. Incidentally Frankie bought his first drum machine from a young Derrick May, who regularly made the trip from Detroit to see Frankie at the Warehouse.

them and they didn't have an edge to them any more! It made you feel sexy, it made you want to have sex, it was powerful, it was en masse – there were so many at it. You would go to a club and then back to someone else's house or the Kitchen in Hulme for an all-nighter.

MIKE PICKERING

Nude was the first big night for acid house at the Hacienda . . . when ecstasy hit, it swept through the club. Suddenly everyone was on ecstasy. I could just stop a record and put my hands in the air, and the place would erupt. The black kids disappeared and only a few stayed. Very quickly all the fashions changed and everyone started to wear baggy stuff. Leo Stanley got on to it at Identity;* I used to be quite friendly with him – great guy. He used to DJ at the Limit on Whitworth Street near the snooker club. He was coming out with T-shirts every week with slogans like 'Jesus had long hair'.

DAVE ROFE

The Hacienda was amazing at the time. I couldn't wait for the weekend, that kind of vibe. It was a social-cultural drugs thing, a new form of music . . .

There was lots of peripheral stuff; rave was everywhere. There was quite a few small clubs like Wiggly Worm doing stuff, adding wood to the fire. The Kitchen in Hulme was ace – a proper after-hours post-Hacienda meet-up when no one wanted to go home. It was all down the Kitchen – health and safety wouldn't allow it now.

NOEL GALLAGHER

I remember being in the Kitchen after the Hacienda one night and it was brilliant. I tell people now and they don't believe me, like it's some gritty northern drama but real. It was one of those the-sun-is-coming-up-in-the-morning jobs; I'd been stood next to this guy all night in the pitch black passing him a spliff, and the sun comes up and it's Mani! I was like, 'Wow! fucking hell!'

GREG WILSON

Once the drug ecstasy arrived on the scene and white ravers 'discovered' dance music in their droves, the years of groundwork laid by the black scene was, at best, obscured and, at worst, ignored.

Laurent Garnier, along with legendary Hacienda house DJ Mike Pickering, would observe that the original house crowd at the club were

---

* A clothes shop in Affleck's Palace.

mainly black kids – a vital clue when piecing together the true evolution of Manchester dance culture, and one that's still, more often than not, totally overlooked.

DAVE ROFE

Fonzo Bullah used to be the magical man on the stage. He would be doing the MVITA thing.* People like him, Cressa and Bez didn't do anything, but they made it all fun. Bands were less careerist then. If your mate was around then you would get him on stage with you.

JO SWEENEY (fan)

The Hacienda went from some place you never went to full of students into this amazing club. Suddenly it was packed, and packed full of mental ravers. You didn't even have to be on an E to get the vibe, the vibe just got you anyway! I've never been to a place like it, the atmosphere was mindblowing and the tunes were fantastic. All credit to Mike Pickering and Graeme Park, and Jon Dasilva as well – they had that place rocking. Totally rocking. For me the anthem was 'Voodoo Ray'.

KERMIT

'Voodoo Ray' by A Guy Called Gerald: I can still remember the first time I heard it. We were in the crescents in Hulme rehearsing with the Rap Assassins and Gerald had his studio in his flat down the corridor. He came round and said, 'Listen to this, listen to this!' and we said, 'Yeah, yeah, Gerald.' We went round and he played 'Voodoo Ray' and our jaws hit the floor. We went back and thought we'd better pull our fingers out now!

DAVE HASLAM

At the Hacienda we were on a journey and we didn't know where we were going. At no point were we controlling it or marketing it. We didn't have a focus group. I didn't have a single conversation with anyone about what to play. The Hacienda had gone from an empty club to Madchester central, swept up in the moment in an unselfconscious, organic, spontaneous celebration. That was my abiding memory of it. If we thought about it we would have probably fucked it up; if we played what they played at the Wag Club in London, we would have fucked it up. The great thing about the Hacienda was that you could act on instinct because no one was in control. I would turn up and Paul Cons had flown people in

* Fonzo was one of the real faces on the scene, with his flailing dreads and his 'MVITA' chant – MVITA standing for Manchester Vibes in the Area.

from New York, like a contortionist with vegetables. Paul would say that he had hired in naked human statues hung on meat hooks dripping paint and sweat off themselves.

ANDREW BARKER (808 State)

We set up, in my opinion, the first rave in Manchester on City Road. We went to the warehouse and changed the padlock; we went back a week later and no one had changed the padlock, so we knew it was empty. We cleaned the place up, got a generator and a sound system in and had a party that night. Someone phoned the police and said there was a party going on. There was a few cars outside and when the police came we said it was a private party – a works party. And off they went in their tag van.

GRAEME PARK

I remember one New Year's Eve, they had Christmas trees upside down in the Hacienda, said they were going to have a firework display. Me and Mike said, 'Are you sure about this?' and they said, 'Yeah!' This guy's hair caught fire but he kept on dancing, which sums up the spirit of the Hacienda for me.

MIKE PICKERING

I remember Nicky Holloway had taken over Saturday night as the Trip in London. People were in bandanas and had whistles and were going fucking mad. And it made my fucking year because I thought the cockneys were always miles behind us! At that time the place was really kicking off, but the Hacienda was a year ahead of London at least. In London they had been obsessed with the groove, which is what we were doing years ago!

MARTIN MITLER

I remember my first E in 1988. It was quite funny. We bought that at a pub nearby. We thought it was whiz. We snorted what we thought was the whiz. We thought it was horrible and we were going to have a word with the dealer. Twenty minutes later we got into the pub and it felt amazing.

PAUL TIBBERTS (fan)

I was about 19 and a Smiths fan and had never been a dance music fan, but I went down to the Hacienda in January 1988 to Mike Pickering's night and I took an E. And that was it. In place of Levi's and Doc Martens, we wore voluminous jeans, hooded tops and trainers; instead of beer it was E and spliffs. For two years I was out there: it was the Hacienda or

Konspiracy, then an all-nighter at the Kitchen in Hulme. The Hacienda was amazing, hot, sweaty and an incredible atmosphere – I've never felt anything like it. You would be best friends with people you just bumped into, you would be in love with girls you'd never seen before. The buzz of the Es was the best feeling I've had in my life and the people that went down to the club were the best.

BRIAN CANNON

Greg [Wilson] and I were in London in 1988 and it had gone off in Manchester when I went back. Manchester Hacienda from 1987 to 1989 was the Garden of Eden where it all came together. This was the crossroads of rock'n'roll and dance fused together. I was into the Roses and Mondays big time, and on the other hand I was pilled out my head in the Hacienda on a Friday night.

STEPHEN MORRIS

The only times I felt part of what was happening in Manchester was through the Hacienda when that was all going on. It was the summer of love and then you all felt part of something.

I didn't go to the Hacienda that often. On the odd occasion when they actually let me in I had a drink and they made me feel really welcome. A lot of it was because Gillian's sister would go along and would get in early by saying she was Gillian. We would turn up and say we were Steve and Gillian from New Order and they would say, 'Fuck off, you're already in!'

NOEL GALLAGHER

I fucking loved dance music from then. I got that Hacienda classics album which came out two years ago and I took it home and it brought a tear to my eye! It took me right back to that space and time. Every time I have a few people round I put it on and it's so evocative of that time.

TIM BURGESS

I would go to the Hacienda on Thursday, Friday, Saturday. Every night! And taking E and then hanging out in the daytime and getting interviewed by TV crews from London asking about the scene. Everything was a blur but it tied together – dancing at the Hacienda, smoking a spliff and listening to Hendrix in the early hours of the morning, then rehearsals with the Charlatans in the afternoon. It was a really good period, 1987 to 1993 – that was my life.

MARTIN MITLER

It wasn't just the E. It was the whole scene. At the time it felt like anything was possible. You would go to the Hacienda on the Wednesday and there was a bit of a community in Manchester at the time who'd lend each other gear and samplers. Things seemed easier at that time.

TIM BURGESS

I remember a few times walking back from Manchester to Northwich! Most of the time I was lucky and I got a train from Altrincham with a head full of E and spliffs, I suppose. It was amazing. What was so beautiful for me, I was probably wearing quite casual stuff and the Perry-boy thing was going on; older guys would have a flicker, Fila DJ tennis jackets and Kickers and stuff, like guys in Altrincham did anyway! A flicker bowl is not that high maintenance if you have the fringe cut straight across the front – really easy, just stays the same; my haircut was pretty legendary at the time, I think (*laughs*).

At the Hacienda I would see Bernard and Hooky and I got to be friends with a couple of guys who ran the bar, like Leroy, and we would go back to Salford and smoke draw. I used to go on Thursday night, [which was] Temperance night and Mike Pickering on Friday, and on Saturday if you wanted to see a band. I saw bands like the Birthday Party, Orange Juice and Einsturzende Neubauten at the Hacienda in the mid-'80s.

BEN KELLY

One of my favourite things was seeing people dancing on every space possible. It was this heaving mass. I was observing from the balcony a mist, steam rising above the heads of the merry band below. I was more than happy that my design had taken on a different life, more than I hoped would happen. You couldn't predict it.

For some people it really opened them up to possibilities; this sounds a bit like a notion of democracy through design – you can enable people to be free and exist within a democracy. Drugs had a big part in that with Es: music and fashion changed, recreational drugs changed, it was like a home . . .

GREG WILSON

Whilst the media was only just latching on to this new youth movement, the black crowd had already slipped out of the back door. Once their scene had been invaded by a seemingly neverending stream of E'd-up white ravers, many of whom would have told you that dance music was shit just a few months before, the black kids, who'd instigated the growth of house music at the Hacienda in the previous years, decided it was time to move on. So by the time the journalists got in on the act, the black presence was very much in the minority.

With the black crowd no longer the driving force, it was clear that the dynamic would change in the Hacienda, with house beginning to be played in isolation, whereas previously, as was the norm on the black scene, different styles and tempos were all played on the same night.

NOEL GALLAGHER

My first E was at the Hacienda. It was one of the yellow ones. I remember there was all the scaremongering at the time – that if you took one you'd drop dead immediately, that you have a great night and die in the morning. I remember thinking, 'Fucking hell, I'm not sure about that!' It was right at the time this thing started at the Hacienda –Temperance or Move night. I remember going; maybe I went on my own because the guys I grew up with weren't into music or drugs. They were into watching football, sitting in people's flats constantly, and I went to gigs on my own. I remember going to the Hacienda. I didn't know anybody there and ecstasy hadn't hit Levenshulme* yet, so I bought some speed – the good honest punk drug – and I remember standing there thinking: the music is utter shit. This is just monotonous, mechanical music,

I didn't know anybody, so I couldn't talk to anybody. Everyone was going mad and these people from Warrington had started talking. They said, 'Are you on one?' and I said, 'I don't know about that, I've read about that stuff!' They said, 'No, it's fucking great!' The next week I had my first one. The same music was on and it was like listening to music for the first time. That was the first night I went to the Kitchen in Hulme, because they went there as well.

I would never have dreamed of going anywhere near Moss Side and Hulme at three o'clock in the morning normally, and now it seemed like the most natural thing in the world to be walking round there! What could possibly go wrong or happen to us!

For two years it was like time stood still and everybody was having it. When the nineties kicked in, it was like people were bored of this – now let's go back to violence and intimidating people.

All that thing that you read about Manchester and acid house boils down to two years. It was utterly fucking inspiring. It was the centre of the universe. The Hacienda was amazing, the music was amazing, the people were amazing. New Year's Eve 1989–90 is when it all changed for me. As

---

* Area near where Noel grew up.

the clocks struck 12, someone got glassed and it changed immediately. It was never the same since. Then the all the bad drugs came into the city and all the guns – it was only fucking two years but it felt like a lifetime!

The 24-hour party could never last and the inevitable burnout came quickly. With the drugs came the gangsters, and the loved-up atmosphere turned sour as violence combined with the comedown from such an intense, euphoric experience. By the early nineties Manchester was basically knackered!

MIKE PICKERING

After E the Hacienda changed; it was obliterated overnight. In some ways the second summer of love was the greatest year in clubs. It kind of ruined the club though – despite it being a great house club we lost the other stuff. Before then we had William Burroughs reading poetry and bands like Pere Ubu and some amazing art installations – all that stopped in 1988. Two years into acid house I was saying, 'Shit! We fucked it up.' People said, 'You can't say that, you're a legend,' but for me in some ways it was better before! Imagine Simon Topping doing his 20-minute salsa break in the middle of the acid house era – he would get lynched! For two years, though, it was unbelievable; but it got sour.

TIM LAWRENCE

[Mike] Pickering, for one, was beginning to have his doubts about the direction of dance at the Hacienda.

MIKE PICKERING

I regretted the fact that once you'd come down off the E everything was pure house. I could tell even in 1989 that that wasn't a good thing and that what we were doing before was much more precious, because we were playing a wider range of music. By 1989 we were slaves to the beat. There were some amazing house records though, including Sueno Latino 'Sueno Latino', Rob Base & EZ Rock 'Get on the Dance Floor', Kid N' Play '2 Hype', 128th Street Crew 'I Need a Rhythm', Rhythm Is Rhythm 'Nude Photo' and Deee-Lite 'Wild Times'.

I felt I was drifting apart from Factory; these records we were playing were massive and I said we needed to have a dance label. Tony said, 'Dance music will never happen.' The funny thing with Tony was that he foresaw the DJ becoming a star but didn't want to put dance records out.

I had the T-Coy record and said, 'Let's put this out ourselves.' When Tony was alive, he openly admitted that he thought dance music would never sell, so I'm not slagging him off or anything. So, with my management at the time, we set up Deconstruction from a little office in Islington. I'd be getting white labels in a flat box on a Friday night and we had it signed by Monday afternoon. We were selling millions of records, and if Tony had let us do the dance label, [it] would have saved Factory.

Tony was supportive of us, sent me champagne when I went to number one. At the time they were putting out the Wendys and Northside and I was signing Black Box and T-Coy. Factory could have had those.

I went to the new Factory offices and Phil was doing A&R. I've known him since I was a kid; our families were close. It was the first time I saw computer screens and designer furniture in the new office and they had more computer screens than records sold! Deconstruction had a number one single and a number one album and we were in an office about as big as this table. Why would you need a massive office? If Factory had signed dance it would have been brilliant. We had a culture that was born in this city, it's what it was famous for, and we would have had a label releasing it.

I was getting white labels of stuff all the time and Black Box's 'Ride On Time' was sent to me on Thursday morning from Italy. I was sat at home in Chorlton and I remember I thought, 'Fuck, this is brilliant!' That Friday I put it on at quarter to 12 and the whole place went crazy. There was a phone number on the label and by Monday afternoon we had signed them to Deconstruction.

GREG WILSON

The underground scene went mainstream during the rave era – that was the big bang. Now everyone was into dance music, whereas previously many people looked down on it, viewing it as inferior to 'proper bands' with drums, guitar and bass. Ecstasy opened so many people up to dance, but the black crowd didn't need opening up because this was already their music. However, people got so whipped up in the frenzy of the times that they started to believe that they'd unearthed something new.

It wasn't long before the music took second place to the drug experience, and, to my ears, began to suffer as a result, becoming whiter and more European in flavour. Previously the drugs had supplemented the music, but now it was the other way around and the essence of dance culture pre-rave was seriously diluted, with many DJs beginning to believe their own myth, thinking they were some sort of shamanic figure, there to be worshipped. For me, it was always about respect, not adulation, so I found it somewhat unsavoury to see a new breed of DJs who clearly regarded themselves as first, with the music a distant second.

With this in mind it's not difficult to understand how they must have felt when, all of a sudden, there was no longer any room on the dance floor at the Hacienda, with people filling every available inch, packed together like sardines. When you watch the old footage from the Hacienda, you can see that there's hardly any foot movement, the dancing is pretty much all with the arms, hands and hips. This is a world away from how people danced in the black clubs.

For the black kids, who'd been brought up with dance, this was certainly not what they were about. It must have seemed like their party had been well and truly gatecrashed and, given the nature of the scene that they'd come from, there was no way they were going to stick around in that environment – at least not in the numbers in which they'd previously turned out.

TOM HINGLEY (Inspiral Carpets vocalist)

I loved the Hacienda. I did think there would be films about it at the time, like there was about San Francisco. It was a coming-together of a lot of people; people were hacked off with the economic situation and wanted a good time. There were a lot of elements of the Hacienda that made it work. It was really eclectic and you would get people who went there who ended up being brickies or bankers. It started the regeneration of Manchester by saying that the city mattered culturally. Just to have been involved with a scene like that is quite amazing.

GREG WILSON

I personally experienced the Hacienda at the peak of the whole Madchester period, and it was an amazing time when you really did feel you were in the centre of the universe. I don't want to take anything away from the Hacienda but, at the same time, I don't believe it should be given what doesn't belong to it. What happened at the Hacienda didn't come about in some sort of vacuum, but was very much dependent on the foundations set in place by the black scene. The fact that it happened in Manchester wasn't by accident, but had to do with the cosmopolitan nature of the city, with blacks and students/indie kids mixing together to create a cultural melting pot that would result in white bands like the Happy Mondays and the Stone Roses embracing dance music, whilst black artists (albeit lesser-known) like the Rap Assassins and MC Buzz B, drew inspiration from indie and rock music.

This is what made Manchester so special; it's just that most of the commentators forgot to include the black side of the story . . .

PETER SAVILLE
The Hacienda created a hipness and a youth culture that still resonates, and [it's] one of the things that contributes to the popularity of the universities. Young people think Manchester is cool.

GREG WILSON
The majority of black kids moved away from the four-on-the-floor playlist of clubs like the Hacienda to forge their own new direction.

Hip-hop, which had always been played alongside the early house stuff on the black scene in the North and Midlands, began to be fused with it, creating the early hardcore tracks, which, in turn, would evolve into jungle, the lineage continuing with drum & bass, UK garage and broken beat. Previously, black artists in this country had pretty much copied what was going on in the US or Jamaica, but this was a British take on things, bringing together various elements of black music past and present to create new hybrids.

In Manchester, the black crowd who'd attended the Hacienda could be found at Konspiracy, but with Madchester on the verge of being renamed Gunchester by the music media – the lucrative trade in drugs bringing in the gangs – it was all about to implode. Konspiracy would be short-lived, closed down by the police, whilst the Hacienda would eventually close for a period itself, given the escalation of violence both outside and inside the club.

But that's another story.

12

'GONZOID FUNK, MOTOWN PUNK, BIG ARMS, DANCING BEARS AND POETIC GENIUS . . .': THE STRANGE ENIGMA WRAPPED IN RHYME AND NO REASON OF THE FREAKY DANCING POSSE OF THE HAPPY MONDAYS

Shaun Ryder, the poet laureate of Generation E who claimed his brilliant words were 'just what came of his mouth', fronted the band whose gonzoid funk apparently 'just happened'. The Happy Mondays' lolloping groove machine is one of the most natural and utterly original distillations of funk, Motown, punk rock and all points in between to stumble into the charts. The band's series of singles and albums captured the day-glo chemical daze of the period perfectly.

TONY WILSON

The two American producers of the Joy Division movie [*Control*] were at the Mondays show and they said, 'Tony, we don't understand, when Shaun came out, the audience were already excited, but they raised it to a whole other level.' Well, number one, Shaun is the singer of one of the five great Manchester groups: Joy Division/New Order, the Smiths, Happy Mondays, Stone Roses and Oasis. Second, everyone knows Shaun has taken more drugs than almost anyone else, and this is a drug town and people respect that.

When I went to the Peruvian jungle to take ayahuasca for a Channel 4 documentary, I couldn't wait to get back and show off to Shaun. I said to him, 'I've been taking this amazing stuff in the jungle, ayahuasca,' and he just goes, 'Fucking great, in't it?' I couldn't believe it. 'How could you know?' 'I've fucking taken it.' And I'm like, 'I went to the far corners of the fucking rainforest to take it, how could you have had it?' He goes, 'Oh, Bez brought some back from his holidays.' And he described this Peruvian jungle hallucinogen in more detail and more eloquently even than the 60-year-old shaman I'd been working with in Peru. He said that it did change you, and that Bez was a totally different person for six months after taking it until it wore off. I guess I was too.

The third thing, actually, is that in Manchester we know that acid house was as big a youth explosion as punk, and was as colourful and wonderful and exotic. Everyone is now slowly beginning to understand that Shaun Ryder is the Johnny Rotten of acid house, and that is a major cultural thing, and that is why people went nuts when he came on the stage.

NOEL GALLAGHER

The Factory thing didn't appeal to me at first. It was way later when the Mondays came. I remember buying a Mondays single, 'Freaky Dancing', and when I finally saw them I thought, 'Wow! They're just like us!'

People forget how weird the Happy Mondays really were; to see them being the guys they are to play that sort of music they were playing in the early days like 'Tart Tart' – that kind of street funk Beefheart stuff . . . When people said, 'What are the Happy Mondays like?' I used to say, 'They're like Happy Mondays music – they aren't really like anything!'

ELLIOT RASHMAN

The Mondays story is interesting. Their music is black and they couldn't play it and it ended up as something else. They were from a generation of school kids who fucked off at 14 – the first non-aspirational sinkhole estate generation. They weren't like Roger Daltrey, coming from his estate and wanting the fish farm; they just wanted the drugs and the money and the cars and they didn't care about anything else.

SHAUN RYDER (Happy Mondays vocalist)

The first albums that I got was the two Bowie albums that I robbed from Scan's Superstore in Little Hulton in 1973 – *Pin Ups* and *Hunky Dory*. But at the same time, I think I also had the Rod Stewart album, with 'Maggie May' on it and 'Mandolin Wind'. I grew up listening to Irish folk music, country and western music, the Beatles, the Stones, Sly and the Family Stone. Fuckin' you name it. And anything that was in the charts as well. But then, you know, having older close relatives like our Pat [Carroll] and everyone – I mean they was all into northern soul, and then our Pete was into Commander fuckin' Cody and Captain Beefheart. I mean, fuck me, how many kids are in the Carrolls! All of 'em was into music or putting on music or whatever and it's still the same today with the younger ones.

Our family was always into music. Our Al, our Bern's husband, was on the fuckin' music scene – the folk scene, jazz scene or whatever, that was the sixties, early-seventies thing.

So we were listening to fucking everything. And I mean everything, from fuckin' Tom Jones, it was a big mixture. Then of course when you get to be teenagers it's like you're only allowed to be into one type of music, you know, either ska, reggae, punk, whatever rocked. The thing about me and Bez was, when we met what we had in common was we wasn't afraid to say, 'Yeah, we like The Specials but we dig Tom Jones . . . and Showaddywaddy, and Buddy Holly.' That was what bonded us together as well as other things – it was our love for music. And not to be frightened to say what you really liked.

From about 15 we was in the boozers in town. Anywhere that would serve us really. I mean I was 15 and I was working – I was a post boy. We were in Spring Gardens, going in the John Bull, watching the strippers at dinnertime and watching Bernard Manning.

The sharp-dressed iconoclast with a magpie eye, Shaun Ryder was dressing ahead of his running mates. He was part of the very early eighties split from the original Perry boys into a far more off-the-wall look that took several unexpected twists and turns . . .

SHAUN RYDER
I always had my own look. I can remember getting slagged off for wearing like Levi suede jackets and things like that with fuckin' beige Farrah kecks, you know, which ended up a year or two later with everyone else getting on that.

That must have been 1980, I mean before that I was on the Perry boy scene. I was like that from like 1978 – I started putting my hair in a side parting and things like that. But, certainly by 1980 we was all around Phil Saxe's stall, you know. That's where we met a lot of the other lads, football heads and lads that I still know to this day, 30 years later.

24 HOUR PARTY PEOPLE

*In which a bunch of kids come together accidentally to soundtrack
a new lifestyle*

SHAUN RYDER

I think I was 18 when we got the band together.* Gaz Whelan and Paul Davis was still at school, and I was 18. So they would just be 14, 15.

We really wasn't like other bands, we didn't come from music; alright, my dad did the working men's clubs and he played a banjo and that, but he wasn't a musician. We didn't go to college. We didn't knock about with all that scene. All our lot was proper fuckin' pure scallys.

In fact we was a bit embarrassed because we – well, not embarrassed ... but we weren't involved in that college crowd and that uni crowd, you know what I mean. It was like fuckin' hell, we'll rob these fuckers.

They looked down their noses at us. Even Hooky will tell you this: when we first came along he fuckin' hated us, he thought we was proper scum.

GARY WHELAN (Happy Mondays drummer)

When I was at school, I met big Bev Lomax. Her sister was getting married to Shaun – they went to different schools. I grew up in Swinton. I'd seen the sisters a couple of times and they looked really cool – like Bowie girls. Shaun had a bleached side parting and a blue suit and looked really cool. I looked up to him; he was three years older then me.

They were getting a band together. I'd bought a drum kit for my bedroom whilst I was at school. Mark Day was in the fifth year, Bez was in the third year, he was exactly the same at school as he is now – he's always been liked. His dad was a copper and Paul Davis' dad was a chief inspector. Mark Day was a prefect and had a motorbike and was into rock stuff like Queen, Rush and Genesis – you know the type.

SHAUN RYDER

Bez was a Walkden kid. Little Hulton, I mean it's Salford – it's a big place. We were Little Hulton, Bez is a Walkden lad, so you know, just around the area. Both of us had pretty naughty names for being lunatics so it was inevitable that we'd end up palling around together. Basically, the drug scene was really me and him.

Gaz went to school with him, and Mark Day, Paul Davis and Bez all went to the same school, all pretty much the same age group.

* In 1981.

GARY WHELAN

My thing was football. I had trials for Salford boys, then in 1980 I got into a soccer school trials at Moss Side. I got a letter because I had been picked for the England Schoolboys squad for a mini World Cup in Switzerland. I was on the bench and played for ten minutes.

I was told not to play football with my mates in the street in case I got injured. They were right, I did my knee in doing that, and after that the band started.

PAUL RYDER

In 1982 we started the band. It was our kid saying to Mike Sweeney,* 'I'm in a band, let us support you,' and Sweeney saying, 'Yeah, OK, go on then.' I remember coming home from the Bull's Head in Worsley saying, 'We got to start a band and play a gig.' It was as simple as that. We never did the gig with the Salford Jets but we got our shit together. I already had a bass. My dad knew Mark Day from the Post Office and me and Shaun knew Gaz Whelan from living near our grandma's. Paul Davis was Gaz's mate, so he was in.

SHAUN RYDER

We started the band for a laugh. I mean, when I got sacked from the Post Office – at the end of the day I didn't want to be a postman. It was great being a post boy, but being a postman was like fuckin' six days a week, getting up early for fifty-odd pound a fuckin' week. You know, once you became [a postman], once you got over 18 years old, then that was it, the fun fuckin' ended, in that game.

GARY WHELAN

Mark Day said, 'Do you want to rehearse with this band?' and Bez was getting confused with this other band so I kept putting it off. Then Shaun said, 'Come and rehearse with us,' and took me to his gran's. He sent his gran to the back room and got the whisky out.

SHAUN RYDER

Whelan was a little scally footballer, he's another Swinton kid. He used to live near me gran's so I'd seen all of 'em really since they was all about six or seven years old, but I didn't start speaking to 'em until they was about 14. I mean, I was pretty much, you know, the main boy round our way. You know, the Perry boy.

---

* Frontman of the Salford Jets, specialists in punchy power pop who had a mini hit with 'Who You Looking At' in the post-punk era, and local DJ.

GARY WHELAN

Shaun [had] been listening to Joy Division and stuff, loads of Velvets, Johnny Cash, Sly Stone, Funkadelic, Beatles, loads of Stones, Public Image, Africa Bambaataa – stuff like that.

SHAUN RYDER

I did have a drum kit but I couldn't play drums or anything. When we all started jamming around I ended up being the singer. We all had a go at singing and trying to write songs and out of the lot of us I was the best singer, the best frontman, 'cos you know you've got to be a clown. You've got to have a bit of knobhead personality to be a frontman, you know, you've got to be a jester and fuckin' all that sort of thing. I was like the comedy genius out of us all, I liked to clown around and write songs. Basically all the songs that was written was just to entertain us, full of in-jokes, snide meanings, subliminal fuckin' messages, just to our pals and us. And I was the best at that.

PAUL RYDER

Shaun was the singer because he couldn't play anything, plus he's born into it, a natural. He's a Leo, a natural big-mouth frontman. He said, 'I'll do that, I can sing, I can write poems – no problem!' And that was it, so he was the singer. He's always been good with words.

He used to say to the rest of us, 'You lot write some words,' and the rest of us were like, 'Fuck off! No chance – we're not doing that. I'm not baring my soul to anyone!' A lot of people don't know that the early Mondays lyrics were really personal to him and to me. A lot of the songs I knew exactly what he was talking about, but they were all cryptic – personal stuff – and every time he said that, we said, 'That's your job, mate – you get on with it.' Words are always disguised; everything was in a disguise, lots of little in-jokes.

SHAUN RYDER

It's like I thought Dylan sort of got away with not being able to sing. I mean, I think he's a great singer, but people say Dylan couldn't sing and that suited me especially, 'cos being a singer was, you know, a bit of fuckin' noncey.

At first I didn't wanna sing, but I did try. I did sort of learn to sing like Ian Curtis, 'cos we used to do Joy Division covers – we didn't play none of them live, it was just for our own amusement when we was practising.

PAUL RYDER

Our kid used to be really melodic. The early Mondays stuff was proper singing. I don't know why he doesn't do that any more, although he still sounds good.

GARY WHELAN

We used to rehearse at my old primary school – All Saints Methodist church school. We did a demo at Shaun's gran's on a cassette recorder. We sent it to a few magazines in 1981, and somehow we got two really good reviews. I thought they would be really bad, but both said we were like the Talking Heads, which we weren't! Mind you, everyone else we knew said we were appalling because they couldn't get round Shaun's voice. We said, 'Listen to Bob Dylan and John Lydon.' What helped us with journalists eventually with Shaun was his lyrics. Journalists like words. We used to write songs – just jam tunes – and we got Shaun on the floor scribbling lyrics. It had me in stitches what he was saying sometimes.

We were always adamant that we should never consciously do anything similar to anything else. Nothing cheesy. It had to be slightly different. When I played the drums I would play for the songs and not to show off. Drums are a difficult instrument – rhythmic not melodic. Charlie Watts and Ringo Starr are great drummers because they play for the song.

The punk ethic plays a part in what we were doing as well. We watched *The Filth and the Fury* recently and it was really similar to us in way. We also loved ACR and they're still one of my favourites. I loved the Buzzcocks as well, the first record I bought was 'Ever Fallen In Love'. I was still 11 at the time and I didn't know where they came from till years later.

SHAUN RYDER

When we was getting it together with the Mondays, we was influenced by everything, but we were really picky. If we started to sound too much like something the song would get scrapped. I mean, I loved the Stone Roses, but it was like, wait a minute, these sound like a sixties band.

PAUL RYDER

When we started we were just learning to play. I already had the bass and I knew one blues riff, that was all. The first song we learned to play together was a Joy Division song because the bass line was on one string. They had amazing bass lines – how can you get such a great bass line on one string? At the first early rehearsal we were trying to play a cover of 'Shadowplay' which we nailed a few weeks later. We also did 'I Fought the Law', the Clash's version, which was getting a bit more complicated for us. After that it was: 'Can't do cover versions – better write our own stuff.' The philosophy was as soon as it started to sound like somebody we would have to change it. If it was too much like the Beatles, Talking Heads, Joy Division, then change it. That was the philosophy, so we sounded original and different. What we ended up with was a kind of punk Motown.

SHAUN RYDER

I didn't want to sound like anyone else. I mean, my sort of thing, what I started off doing was more like rapping than singing, even though it wasn't rapping if you know what I mean. I certainly didn't want to sing. Basically the first songs we learned to play was songs like 'Transmission' and things like that.

You know, we was original. And that was the music and the way that we dressed really. Every fuckin' band nowadays is dressed with fuckin' hoodies and things, and jeans and trainers, but then it was unheard of. We'd had people coming from London and saying to us, 'You know there's something there, but you've got no fuckin' image.' You know, there's us in jeans, trainers, side partings, fuckin' crew cuts, whatever, you know, and there was no other bands dressed like that. But then we'd get told that we didn't have an image!

When we rehearsed we didn't want loads of people just hanging out. You know it was like: fuck off everybody else, this is us. We were quite strict. I mean people thought we were just absolute fuckin' loonies. Any gig we got paid for, we never touched that money – it went to get things for the band. It went to get us rehearsal rooms, get equipment, you fuckin' name it. Everything. I mean, even all the fuckin' craziness for the drugs and all that lot, you know, any dough that was made from that went into the band as well.

PAUL RYDER

The first gig we played was at a community centre in Worsley. My dad knew the caretaker and we did a 20-minute gig. It was local to where Gaz Whelan, Mark Day and my gran lived. We played in front of 20 people. The next one was the Gallery upstairs. We used to go downstairs in the Gallery on Saturday nights when it was the funk club. Me, our kid and Paul Davis were the only white faces in there apart from a few white girls. We sat in the corner smoking weed and all the black geezers loved us. We got right into the funk stuff. We knew the Gallery and they had bands on upstairs, so we played there.

SHAUN RYDER

I think the first gig we played was some youth club in Swinton, then the GPO club in Blackpool in 1983. That was the Battle of the Bands competition, I think. The venue had that glittery backdrop on the stage – strips of gold! Me dad got the gig through his Post Office connection where you get a weekly newsletter. We came last but one, brilliant (*laughs*).

GARY WHELAN

The first gig we played was the GPO club. We played three songs. We got the gig because of the Post Office connection.

PAUL RYDER

The Gallery was an amazing club: no violence, everyone was smoking big fat spliffs and it wasn't a big deal, a brilliant night out, really safe. I knew they put bands on upstairs. One dinnertime while I was working at the post office, I had a cassette on me and knocked on the door of the Gallery. This guy Pete Prestor who put the bands on and managed it, he put the tape on and said, 'Yeah, come and play in two weeks' time.' The goal at the time for us was to get a gig at the Gallery and get our name in the advert in the *Evening News*, and that was it! We got the gig at the Gallery and the name Happy Mondays in the *Evening News* gig list. It was like, 'Yeah! We've made it here! Job's a good 'un!'

GARY WHELAN

We always thought we were on our own. The Smiths were around and we made a point of listening to them and they were amazing. We didn't want them to rub off on us, though. We mixed with the Jazz Defektors, bands you wouldn't expect. We used to go upstairs at Boardwalk when we ended up rehearsing there and met bands like Curiosity Killed the Cat* – that was one of the wildest nights out we had!

We went to see the Roses at the International.† Cressa was the only other person who wore flares – he knew all the student lot at the Hacienda as well. Cressa lived in Chorlton; Chorlton to us was like another world compared to Swinton and Salford.

PAUL RYDER

We got to know the Roses through Cressa. Cressa was hanging out with

---

* Pop band who had a brief flirtation with fame in the late 1980s.
† The International 1 and 2 were two venues operated by Stone Roses manager Gareth Evans and his business partner Matthew during the eighties. Both venues were just outside the city centre on the border of Levenshulme. They were the main live venues in the city, where just about every touring band played.

us. He used to go to the Gallery as well. We got to know the Roses quite well; they were the only band we got to know. We would see them at Corbieres.

After the Gallery it all becomes a blur of doing loads of whiz, smoking lots of dope and drinking loads of beer. The first gig was on beer – three pints and two joints, that would kill me these days (*laughs*). I've not smoked weed for about 25 years – it would make me really paranoid. That's when Phil Saxe came along. We were getting our kecks from Phil and he started paying for our rehearsals. There was a rehearsal place on Adelphi Street in Salford – a sex shop with cocks fighting in the back of it in a big old warehouse with six rehearsal rooms, and there was a secret door to where the cocks were fighting. Phil and my dad were paying for rehearsal space and we had packed our jobs in at the Post Office. It was, 'Fuck this, let's be in a band!' That was the punk attitude.

GARY WHELAN

We had got replies from this cassette we sent out from London Records. This guy came up to check us out. He was an A&R whizzkid in London. He came to the school where we rehearsed, which was in this lower middle class area with private houses – nothing bad. We said, 'It's fine round here, we rehearse every Tuesday and Thursday.' And then ten minutes later a brick came though the window and he made [his] excuses and left.

PHIL SAXE

I was in the Hacienda one night. The Hacienda was the last place you would expect to see Salford kids, [but] I saw some of these kids and I went up to them and said, 'What you doing here?' They gave me a tape and I gave it to Mike Pickering. We booked them for a gig and then we got them on Factory. They asked me to manage them and then they started to hang around the stall. They were particularly cool customers – they were wearing paisley shirts. People like Clint [Boon] were hanging round the gigs as well; he would be at those very early Mondays gigs, some of the Roses would come in.

I was excited that there was a load of kids who dressed differently and had their own fashion and music. It was the first time that Manchester lorded it over Liverpool – they had tight jeans and training shoes – and now it changed, that was the time when we established ourselves as major musical force of the north west.

Punk was a London thing taken on by Manchester, whereas northern soul and Madchester were Manchester things. You didn't have to look to anyone else.

PAUL RYDER

We might have gone over Tony's head but Mike Pickering got it bang, straight off.

GARY WHELAN

When we played the Hacienda, I remember there was a poet dressed as Paddington Bear. He opened his battered old case [and was] reading poetry. There was some other bizarre stuff, eastern European folk music – you know what the Hacienda was like. We were asked to play a couple of weeks after Phil got Mike Pickering down to see us rehearse and Mike liked us. We had been mithering Phil Saxe at his jeans stall and we talked him into being the manager. He said he would pay for our rehearsals if we were in there every day.

SHAUN RYDER

You know Phil's stall was important 'cos he got the clobber in; he was cheaper than other places and he'd got the gear.

Twenty-odd inch bottom kecks like and we was asking Phil to get 'em. He'd go to the suppliers and they'd say, 'You don't want to be buying these,' and Phil would say, 'Give us fucking 1000 pairs,' or something. They let him have 'em for 50p each and I think he'd sold the fuckin' lot of 'em by the end of Saturday, you know, at ten quid or whatever.

Well, I mean, our little crew, you know, I'm not claiming I was the first but [I was] certainly one of the fuckin' first ones.

PHIL SAXE

I was always interested in looking for new bands, I always kept an eye on music. I went to the Hacienda opening night with Bernard Manning. It wasn't my sort of place. I didn't like that Manchester cliquish jazz scene, I thought the music and people were awful.

Me and my brother had a stall and we sold clothes to cool scallys. One day three girls came in and chatted to us. They said, 'Do you ever get flares in the warehouse?' We said, 'What do you want them for?' and they said, 'We're on the dole, we can't afford tight jeans and we want to be different!' I picked them up that night from the warehouse in Manchester and I made a couple of quid on each pair, and all of a sudden loads of people wanted to buy them. We were the only people in Britain that would sell them. It was months before anyone caught on and we were doing tremendous business in them. We were doing 500 pairs of Dickies cords, Levi's flares – we were doing really well with them . . . Also semi flares. At that time the people wearing them were the people who would develop into the Manchester music scene.

PHIL THORNTON

The footy look had changed. The white kids got more into that scruff look. From tracky bottoms it went to flared jeans and cords. The lad who used to work in Hurleys had that Manc look off to a tee: cropped outgrowing suedehead length hair, a Quaker-type beard, plain crewneck jumper, little pin badge, 24-inch flared jeans and Adidas Suedes or Jeans. The forecourt at Old Trafford would be full of these lads in 24-, 26-inch flares, beige golfing jackets, check shirts hanging out of the jeans. Phil Saxe had cornered the market for flares – he had about six months to himself and then other traders got wise to it.

MIKE PICKERING

The Mondays started coming to the Hacienda in 1985/86. Phil Saxe, who had the stall on the underground market with his brother, said, 'I'm going to start a movement with these lads – they look like beatniks, like Shaggy from *Scooby Doo* with little goatees, baggy jumpers and flares.' He had given me a lift at the time and said, 'Look at this.' He pulled up into a garage which was chocker with trousers. They were all flares and he started going on about them: 'They're tight here, they got a cord there . . .' He knew all the terms because his dad was in the rag trade.

He said, 'I've got this band and they got some good tunes.' I went to meet them and it was Shaun, Paul Ryder, Gary Whelan and 'Knobhead', Paul Davis. It was great. Then they did a gig in a youth club in Salford. I thought they were raw and very good. Shaun had a great voice that funnily enough reminded me of Feargal Sharkey at the time – a lot higher than it is now. I said, 'I can sign what the fuck I want with Factory and I think this would be great.' I said to the band, 'You should come to the Hacienda.' [It was] whilst we were trying to reverse the door policy, because people just didn't know that we were doing this and most lads thought they couldn't get in. So I got them in and they were fixtures and fittings from that time.

This was a year or two before the Es. I remember getting a couple of gigs with New Order at Salford Uni, and I got them three gigs with the Colourfield* because I knew Terry Hall. I then said to Tony, 'I've got this band, the Happy Mondays.' Tony said, 'Darling, you want to sign them then you sign them.' Rob said, 'I want to see them' – that's why they played with New Order – and Rob said they were great.

Enter the dancing bear, a fixed band competition, and an unconventional local record label . . .

---

* Terry Hall's moody dark pop outfit, post the Specials and Fun Boy Three.

SHAUN RYDER

How Bez sees it, we was at the Haci giving it at that Battle of the Bands and I said to him, 'Come on, get up on stage.' We was all tripping our nuts off and I shoved a maraca in his hand. When we did that Battle of the Bands we hadn't really played any gigs really.

You know that was double, double early, that. So when we started tripping out to London, to Leeds, you know – middle of wherever, upstairs pubs, back in the eighties, Bez was with us then, we'd done no more than four gigs without him.

PAUL RYDER

I remember Bez's mate got up before Bez did and we thought that was alright – at least it took the attention off us. At the end of the gig he said, 'You want to meet my mate Bez? He's coming back from living in this cave in Africa.' Of course we already knew Bez, but we hadn't seen him for a bit. A week later Bez arrived and it was like something from that film *24 Hour Party People*. He looked like he'd been in a spaceship. He actually had been living in a cave and travelling around for a year and a half, and this thing arrived that looked like Bez.

Then we played the Hacienda gig and Shaun said to Bez, 'Get up there on stage, I'm not going up there without you,' and he did.

Bez was really important. I wouldn't do interviews. I wouldn't open my mouth to anybody, I would sit there and listen to our kid and Bez; they thrived on it and they were speaking for the whole band.

SHAUN RYDER

Bez was always at rehearsals and when we were making albums, if you saw him nodding and dancing and smiling, it was getting approvals and the thumbs up. And if it's working on him you know it'll work on other people. We wouldn't let anybody else hear the stuff until it passed the Bez test.

GARY WHELAN

Bez joined because Shaun was a bit shy onstage, he was a bit of a crutch to lean on and take the pressure off Shaun. Just before him we had other people getting on stage for the odd song. We tried to get rid of Bez for six months (*laughs*).

Shaun reckons that getting Bez wasn't predetermined but he knew what he was doing, it took the pressure off him. We were really into Funkadelic and they did the same thing.

SHAUN RYDER

I got Bez up there because he was my mate, we was both off our tits and I was like, 'Fuckin' hell, I'm a lead singer, I'm getting fuckin' stared at.' It was like: get someone up and fuck about a bit. Plus he looked good, you know what I mean.

It was always about looking good as well for us, you know, so, I mean, me and him were pals and, I mean, you know it is a fuckin' weird marriage, me and him, but at the end of the day, you know, we are mates.

So we played that Battle of the Bands at the Hacienda. If you look at that gig at the Hacienda where Tony announced that we'd won, you know, I mean alright, it was probably a fix, there was some punters watching it who didn't really know, it was probably a pile of shite. But you know, there was bands up there – one wanting to be Duran Duran, another wanting to be Haircut 100, do you know what I mean, one wanted to be Madness. Not one of 'em was fuckin' original.

I mean, if it wasn't through Tony I don't think we'd have got where we got. You know it's like somebody like Tony telling me that I'm good, you know, is like good for me. It made me think, well, OK, there must be something there.

PAUL RYDER

We reached the final at the Hacienda and something happened to Mark Day. His nose wouldn't stop bleeding and he had to go to the hospital, so we couldn't play in the final. But according to Tony we'd already won it anyway. I went down and watched the final thinking, that cunt's in hospital because his nose wouldn't stop bleeding (laughs). A few weeks before Tony had seen us and I remember playing on the stage and thinking, shit, there's Rob Gretton.

I think the first time we might have flipped over Tony's head two foot, but I think Mike Pickering got it straight away.

ELLIOT RASHMAN

The Mondays made Factory a pirate ship. Suddenly what you had were the inmates taking over the asylum, living out the rock'n'roll myth. And people were thinking, 'Ooh, they're robbing people, they are rock'n'roll!'

SHAUN RYDER

Actually we'd already known Tony. I mean, this is another thing, right, me and Bez used to get up in the middle of the night and go and take Tony fuckin' supplies. We knew him anyway.

Yeah, he liked us. I mean, he did like me and Bez.

GARY WHELAN

We didn't think about making it. Me and Shaun thought maybe put a record out and that was it. Factory was the coolest label. We were the opposite to anything on Factory. We were the Antichrist! We weren't students doing jazz-tinted indie rock. Mike Pickering signed us to Factory. Mike was great. We went in with Mike to record the first single in two 12-hour sessions in Bury's Square One Studios.

SHAUN RYDER

When we recorded ourselves in the Boardwalk you could hear all the other bands on the tape. When we'd press play and record and play it back, you'd have the fucking Jazz Defektors kicking up on our tape and it used to sound fuckin' great, you know, all this noise going on in the background. We thought we should start fuckin' mixing that sort of stuff in (*laughs*).

We were dead lucky 'cos across the way we had A Certain Ratio and Martin Moscrop. They basically taught us how to fuckin' turn things on, press go and record. You know, fuckin' mix and all sorts.

DELIGHTFUL

In which the Happy Mondays make their first single

PAUL RYDER

The first single was produced by Mike Pickering, who said, 'It's a great cover but my name is too big.' It was bigger than the Happy Mondays and the song title! 'Delightful' was recorded in a proper studio. We thought, 'Fucking hell, this is brilliant!' It blew us away.

SHAUN RYDER

'Delightful'? Oh God, it's fuckin' horrible, I never liked it. It was when I was trying to literally learn what I was doing, try to write stuff. It was all originally sort of, 'Fuck, fuck, fuck, fuck – sort this mother-fuckin' knobhead out' lyrics, you know, and then suddenly you've got to go on record and you've got to have proper lyrics! I've gotta write a fuckin' song here, that's got no swear words in it, that has to have sort of something in it like a song.

It was too fast, you know, and to be quite honest to Mike we was all still learning then – everyone was still learning their instruments.

I though we'd started making that record way too soon. I mean, alright, we'd been jamming and practising for fuckin' years but I still didn't want us to go and make 'Delightful', you know what I mean. It was like, no, we're not ready to go and put anything down on vinyl yet, but Tony, he gave us a chance. He saw something in us.

GARY WHELAN

'Delightful' got played on John Peel and I was happy with that. I was sat in a car in Moss Side and he said on air, 'That's quite unusual, I quite like that,' and then he played some white noise by someone else! He asked us down for a session and we did it in a day. We did tunes like 'Kuff Dam' with Dale Griffin, who used to be in Mott the Hoople – he was difficult to work with! But he did a good job. We then went out and toured with the Bodines and the Weather Prophets – they were great. That led us to our first gigs in London. We played with Loop and Pop Will Eat Itself one week and then went down and played with Laibach the week after – they borrowed my kit. They said, 'Aaah: a blonde drum kit!' I liked them musically.*

PAUL RYDER

We played London, at the Black Horse in Camden at the Room Upstairs club, which had stuffed birds in glass cages along the walls. We set up in front of an old fireplace and played. Once Jeff Barrett† who ran the club had seen us, things stepped up a gear. Jeff got it like Mike Pickering got it. We were dressing different from the winklepicker, skin-tight jean bands around at the time and sounding different as well. He jumped on us like Mike Pickering did.

SQUIRREL AND G-MAN TWENTY FOUR HOUR PARTY PEOPLE PLASTIC FACE CARNT SMILE (WHITE OUT)

The Mondays' debut album proved that their quest for originality had not been a waste of time. Nothing sounded like this, from the band's swing to Ryder's brilliant words. This was the soundtrack to the real Britain, a million miles away from the indie charts or the mainstream.

SHAUN RYDER

Going to do that album was our first proper time in the studio for a

---

* A really unlikely pairing: the Mondays supporting the Slovene industrial music outfit!
† Gig promoter who went on to become Creation press officer and head honcho of Heavenly Records

length of time, you know, and we didn't have a clue. We didn't know what to do, we didn't know what a studio was like, you know. I can remember like, getting a load of beer cans and the mics in the vocal booth and I'm hitting the beer cans with a drum stick going, 'Wow, this sounds fuckin' great – let's do a song with this on!'

John Cale produced it. Of course we knew who the Velvet Underground were, we'd listened to them for years getting stoned, but I didn't know who John Cale was till Tony said he was in the Velvet Underground.

GARY WHELAN

We were all big Velvets fans; Shaun was a Lou Reed fan. John Cale had a great out-of-tune haircut. John Cale played the Hacienda and Phil talked him into it in January. We were there for six weeks in Swiss Cottage. He didn't know what to make of us. We didn't really connect – the band would turn up at the studio at midday with loads of drinks – he would go home at six and we would stay in there all night and record it all.

John Cale was clever though: he could hear a key clash and he would be right. We would play for half an hour and a couple of minutes would be great.

SHAUN RYDER

John [Cale] was a really nice bloke. It was a time where I think he'd just got himself straight, he was absolutely straight, he was eating loads of tangerines. He was very quiet, you know, a nice man. We was dead respectful to him and he recorded us virtually live – plug in, play.

PAUL RYDER

We did the album in Kentish Town with John Cale. We was all buzzing 'cos we were working with John Cale from the Velvet Underground, who took heroin and smoked loads of drugs. But on the first day he turned up with a big bag full of mints and a big bag full of clementines and no drugs because he was clean. I thought he was going to turn up with a big holdall full of stash, man, but he was just carrying the clementines and mints. But after five minutes of being deflated by that we said, 'Let's get on with it.'

Most of the album was recorded live. He made us play the song and then [he would] say, 'Stop – play it faster,' and he speeded all the songs up – it was really quick to do. It only took ten days. Phil Saxe was a massive John Cale fan.

John Cale had played the festival of the tenth summer at G-Mex.* That was when Tony Wilson or Mike or Phil had made the connection and said, 'Fucking hell, John Cale – why don't you produce the Mondays?'

I'm proud of it. It made us tighter as a live band. We did the songs 20 or 30 times on the same day. At the time a lot of people would say, 'You don't know what's going on when you see them, they can't play.' I thought we were a tight band. I would collapse when I came off stage – all the drugs and the drink would hit you afterwards. That's something else other bands wouldn't do: they would wait till after the gig to start partying. Where we would start at the soundcheck, they would do drink and drugs after the gig – 'Oooh, let's celebrate!' We would do more and more drugs before the gigs started; after the gig it would really hit me (*laughs*)!

PHIL THORNTON

Musically though, there was still fuck-all happening. I went to this hip-hop all-dayer at the Hacienda and a few of the Sunday all-dayers at the Apollo that Johnny Jay used to put on and you'd get a few lads in there, but by now that scene had gone a bit stale. The whole KRS-1, Public Enemy thing was kicking in, so it was even moodier for white kids. Which is why I think the house thing really went massive in Manchester. It just felt a bit less aggressive and fun again. I didn't really go to gigs, I went to see people like Gil Scott Heron, the Pogues around this time but gigs bored me, they still do. Just play your best six or seven tunes and get off, no one's that interesting! The only band I really got into was the Mondays and that was purely due to how they looked.

You have to remember there were no bands who dressed like we did back then; it was wall-to-wall fucking Duran Duran nuggets or else Smiths types. When I first saw the Mondays on the cover of *Melody Maker* around '86, I thought, 'Hey, these look like the kind of lads at the match.' It was that iconic cover with Shaun and Bez, Shaun rocking that Manc stubbly beard and manky anorak look.

PAUL RYDER

We started to get a bit of a following with Perry boys dressing like us and getting into the music. Because you don't think of Perry boys getting into music, do you? It's kind of standard now but people weren't like that then. They weren't dressing like that because they'd seen us, they were like that anyway.

* In 1986 Factory Records put on ten events, from art installations to a big gig at G-Mex, to celebrate the tenth anniversary of punk and the Sex Pistols' gig at the Lesser Free Trade Hall.

PHIL THORNTON

I'd been waiting for a band for years who I could identify with and suddenly they were here, the lads who sat in Phil's shop in the fucking Arndale Centre. Even before I'd heard them, I knew I'd love them and that first LP *Squirrel and G-Man* is still my favourite Mondays LP. *Bummed* was great too – that LP just summed up Manchester '88, that whole acid house, Madchester vibe – but *Squirrel and G-Man* caught them when Factory hadn't got a fucking clue what to do with 'em, didn't know what they had. John Cale producing but not really understanding them, how could he really? This Welsh classical musician, mate of Warhol, how could he possibly understand something like 'Tart Tart'? When I brought home the 12-inch version of '24 Hour Party People' and played it to my younger brothers who I'd indoctrinated into hip-hop and stuff, they just looked at me and went, 'You can't fucking like that!'

You have to remember no one sounded like the Mondays, they were totally original. I suppose you could sort of hear things like Can, and to me it was obvious that Shaun was into his hip-hop and northern and stuff – probably like me [he] felt a bit corny trying to be all cool and London trendy about it, but he made something that was entirely natural and convincing. It was white funk – not that ACR or Talking Heads type of white funk but dirty, hooligan funk.

PAUL RYDER

We were still not that big after the first album because there's nothing else like it. I can't really compare it to the Velvet Underground or the Pistols or something from Motown. There isn't really much to compare it to.

'WHO'S IN CHARGE HERE?'

A maverick band needs a maverick manager. When the Mondays teamed up with Nathan McGough it was a perfect combination. Supersmart, hip, and faster and looser than the band, Nathan was perfect. One of the key players in the late eighties Manchester scene, post-Mondays he went on to carve out a successful managerial career for himself.

GARY WHELAN

Nathan was managing the Bodines. They had an indie number one with 'Therese'. It wasn't working out with Phil for us and Nathan was getting into Shaun's ear, mithering us for months. Me and Paul weren't sure but Shaun chipped away at us.

SHAUN RYDER

Phil had gone, and by '87, yeah, Nathan had, well, took over. Nathan was like one of us, but you know, let's say an intellect.

Phil Saxe wasn't really full-time. He had to manage his shops and things like that. With Nathan, you know, he was on it 24/7. A lot of things got done in a short space of time. I mean, some of them used to slag Nathan off but if you think about it, he's a young kid in his fuckin' early twenties, you know, and doing some fuckin' really top stuff.

PAUL RYDER

Phil Saxe still had a business and he couldn't look after us as much as we wanted. We needed someone full time to take us to the next level. He had a wife and kid. Hats off to Phil Saxe, he said, 'Go for it, you need someone who can give you more time.' Nathan was brilliant, did a great job, he was partying harder than the band (*laughs*), which could have been a problem. He did the job well enough. He's a good guy, Nathan.

BUMMED

The Mondays' second album was produced by Martin Hannett – a perfect meeting between the two most maverick sets of chemical minds in Manchester. Something interesting was bound to happen. The resulting album, with its Hannett spaciness, was perfect for the E-frazzled minds in the studio, who were just embarking on their ecstasy adventures. Arguably this was the first and best E album; a perfect example of the form.

SHAUN RYDER

We was all off our tits on E when we was making that, dancing everywhere. I mean, fuckin' lunatics dancing in and out of fuckin' cake shops, you know, stopping our cars at traffic lights and getting out and dancing. We thought it was fuckin' normal.

Martin [Hannett] was brilliant, I mean he was pound for pound as drugged up and fuckin' as mad as us, which was brilliant. You know, it might have worried the fuckin' life out of other people but we thought it was fuckin' great. He is a geezer, you know that. A major producer, a major talent, and he's as off his tits as we are.

We'd never seen anybody back then just get a gram of charlie out and do it in one line. I can actually remember one time when he was passed out for a fuckin' full day on the mixing desks and I used to take over.

We ended up in [Richard] Branson's country manor house, you know, which was brilliant for us, you know, it was fuckin' rock'n'roll.

On the album I'm blabbing on about people like Henny Penny, Cockey

Lockey. I mean, they're people really that we had names for, you know, fuckin' madheads who used to come round the flat. People in our little gang all knew who this fucker was and who's coming through the door, 'cos we was always getting the odd lot coming round and everything. Once things started having to go on vinyl it was like: can you get away with saying things, you know. We had to think about it for a while and disguise it.

GARY WHELAN

Martin Hannett was fantastic. He was brilliant. We picked him up in a car. He'd been clean for years. We got to Bridlington and we sat down and had a beer at two in the afternoon. It was market and all day opening. Martin said, 'I'll have a coca cola,' and stayed in there all night drinking.

The good thing was we did the drums first. Martin had loads of stories and I got on really well with him. We would sit and listen to loads of house tapes from the Hacienda on a ghettoblaster, sit on the floor with loads of E – there was bags of it – and then back to the pub and studio. It was madness, like being in the Hacienda 24 hours a day. In fact we would go from Bridlington to the Hacienda – we were never all in the studio at the same time. It was: do your part and get out. There was always someone going back to Manchester, so you could jump back for a couple of nights. It was really good fun to make. I don't remember doing any of the recording on that record. I remember being in a room with Martin playing Tony loads of playbacks and that's it.

PAUL RYDER

Martin Hannett was an alcoholic by then. I took him to score once in the whole session and that was towards the end – I think it was to come down from the ecstasy and the coke! I remember me and him were on acid in the studio and got locked in, and we were trying to find our way out. It was hilarious, man – that studio in Driffield had a street inside it with a telephone box and a cobbled road and we thought we were outside for the first hour. We were saying, 'Where's the pub? Down the street?'

I loved Martin from the off but I really couldn't suss him out at all, he was so out there. I looked at him like: 'Wow, what are you? Who are you!' That spaciness to the sound – that was Martin. That's where I met John Pennington. He was 17 years old [and on] work experience. Martin used to say John's the only person who would set the mics right in five minutes. Everyone else would be scratching their heads. Martin loved John Pennington because he could do his stuff perfectly.

GARY WHELAN

I had my first E before Driffield. I'd been given one by Shaun. I had it in my pocket a couple of weeks and couldn't make my mind up about it. I was cautious about tablets. Once I'd taken it I went to my mate's pub in Swinton. I jumped on the bus and took a drag of a cig which felt like mint – like a freshness. And I started noticing women everywhere. In the bar next to Yates' on the high street I walked up to loads of women and talked to them without having a drink. When I left there I had four phone numbers in my pocket and I had never chatted up a girl in my life!

With E, I was dancing and not bothered about drinking. There was a lot of Es around the band at the time. There was also always a pipe on the go in the back of the van which was full of smoke, there was always something going on. Everyone had their own private thing going on. Weed was my thing by then – not hard drugs. In a weird way the Mondays saved me from hard drugs.

When we gigged we had all our friends backstage, like 40 people, and word started spreading and it started to grow. Everyone would do what they wanted and it was like a travelling club night.

With E you're in that kind of vacuum. You're in spacious sound and that Martin Hannett sound is perfect for E. It fitted so well with it. That empty-room sound of Hannett was the E sound. We called him Alf the alien life form. We would really, really rip into him and he did it with us. He was part of the gang.

JOHN PENNINGTON (sound engineer)

The owners of Strawberry Studios had sent Martin to rehab to make it possible for him to work. After he came out we did a track together. Martin took to me and gave me more work, which was the Happy Mondays. I'm not sure how he got the job because him and Tony weren't talking.

Someone in the Mondays camp was feeding him lots of different kinds of drugs. In the studio there was a delivery of cocaine every day, and there was acid and lots of other things going on to fuel him up for the day. As assistant engineer I had to translate what was going on in Martin's head to everyone else so they could get on with it.

My girlfriend was down in the studio while we were working on 'Wrote for Luck'. We couldn't find Shaun, and Martin was getting irate trying to find him to do the vocal. Sarah walked downstairs to the recreation room and found Shaun in there dancing to a 12-inch remix of Hot Chocolate's 'You Sexy Thing', dancing round in circles in the pitch black singing along. Shaun went upstairs and we tried to get the vocals out of him. We had mics set up at either side of him in case he wandered off into the studio. We were recording four tracks of vocals at any one time.

It was a very chaotic session. When we recorded 'Hallelujah' later on Shaun was doing the vocals with 30 people on the headphones with him while putting it down, so he could get the vibe of his mates being in the studio with him. On vocal takes you can hear lots of people humming – 30 people humming at the same time. It sounds like a weird Buddhist mantra. Some made it on to the mixes at the end . . .

That was the beauty of it when the Mondays came along – convention was thrown out of the window. You had to get something out of it, whilst Bez and Shaun were in cahoots doing as much damage as they could.

SHAUN RYDER

When I'm writing lyrics, initially it's a fuckin' massive rush that comes right off the top of my head and that will do while you're jamming around. And then when you've got to put them down on record you've got to really make sense of 'em. That's when you do have to sort of like spend time on 'em, you know. But I always find the ones that, if I spend more than a couple of hours on something . . . it's shite.

When people tell me [the] words are good I get a bit embarrassed, I don't know – it's something that I do, you know, OK. Sometimes I find it easy and sometimes I find it hard. Initially though, the reason I did it is because I did find it easy.

Most of our kid's bass lines are like northern soul, Motown rip-offs, which I'm not slagging off – that was great, that's what made it, that sort of thing. I mean, you know, Gaz found it easy to play along on the drums.

Mark was a good guitar player but he really didn't know what he was doing. It was great at first, before his bird came along: he would actually listen to what we would say. We'd say, 'Mark will you do this, Mark will you do that,' you know, and it worked fantastic, but then he gets a bird and he was like, 'I'll do what I bloody want to do, I do what she tells me to do now.'

Well, that was it, you know what I mean. He had no problem with us telling him what to do because it was like, he was a great guitarist, he was the only one of us who could read music.

The arrival of ecstasy on the scene ran parallel with the rise of the Mondays, who were sitting in their famous corner of the Hacienda pilled up, recording Bummed in a similar state of mind and getting a big crew of people around them in a similar state. Their chemical condition basically came out of that corner of the

Hacienda and took over the whole city; within months everyone was in a similar mindset and suddenly the Happy Mondays made sense.

PAUL RYDER

Shaun and Bez had friends who were bringing the ecstasy from London and brought a shitload back. That was excellent, that little corner under the balcony. It was during *Bummed* we got bang into it. I remember some friends coming back from London and driving straight to Driffield with all the ecstasy and that's the start of it all. You only needed to take one and you're away. It started to affect the music. It came halfway through the recording. It must have done something to Martin's ears, I think it made the music more uplifting to play. We would play faster and faster. We did one new song in the studio, 'Do It Better'.

How weird is that it takes a drug before everyone else gets on what we were doing!

SHAUN RYDER

The Es sort of opened everyone into different types of music. If you was only into indie music then you ended up into all sorts of dance music; if you was into dance music you end up going to indie nights. That's what E did.

Before 1988 we was playing to a couple of hundred people, right. You know, playing to, like, 300, 500 people sort of thing. And then in '88 we did the G-Mex and played to 9000 people. We never did the Apollo-sized venues – you know, with two-and-a-half, three thousand people or whatever. We jumped, really, we missed the old sort of venues out and went on to pretty big venues.

Everywhere we went, our pals who knocked out the E went. Which, you know, made it even better for the audiences.

DAVE ROFE

When the Happy Mondays supported New Order at G-Mex, the Mondays were wild. Wuzza, Duzza, Buzza – all the crew was there! Everyone blagging it. The security had their hands full that day!

SHAUN RYDER

We were all proud of Manchester kicking off. I think a lot of it had to do with the whole drugs scene there, the whole party scene, and the bands rolled along with all that. I mean, we had great bands as well, from us to Take That. Take That are still northern, you know, working-class kids.

Madchester was great for us. You could go to bed at night and actually be fuckin' looking forward to waking up in the morning with something to do, something to live for. We were living nice, a bit of cash, you know, a car – it was great. And we were still all young, all in our early twenties.

PILLS 'N' THRILLS AND BELLYACHES

No longer the weird outsiders, the Happy Mondays went to record their third album as consummate pop performers. The band was now one of the biggest in the UK and the resulting album was as slick and poppy as they ever got, with Paul Oakenfold at the helm. The record was big enough to fill stadiums and became the band's signature bestselling work.

SHAUN RYDER

'Step On' had come out because when we was off to the States to make *Pills 'n' Thrills* it was Elektra's 50th birthday, you know, and we got told we had to re-record a song from their back catalogue and we didn't really wanna do it at the time. And when the tape arrived, I think the first track on it was that John Kongos one. And just out of the fact that we didn't want to spend any time listening to anything and wanted to get on with our own writing, we did the John Kongos one – laid a few bits on it, sticking things like 'twisting your melon man' and 'call the cops' on it, you know, and sent it off. And it came out and tided us over till the album came out.

GARY WHELAN

We knew we had to make a progression – be more radio-friendly. We had to do an album like the Roses had just released. Cressa had given us a cassette of their album and it was good. We thought, there are some great songs on there. We knew [Paul] Oakenfold – Shaun and Bez had met him. Oaky was trying to get us organised, but when we got in the studio on the first day Bez come bursting in and he had crashed his hire car. We were in the studio that *Pet Sounds* had been done in, in LA.

We spent a lot of time partying. There was a guy sat in the studio for ten days on the trot. He was English and he had glasses on and a fur trapper's hat. He talked like a scouser. One day he took his hat off and he was Ian Astbury* and we didn't know! We thought the Cult were from Bradford.

---

* Born in Birkenhead, charismatic Cult frontman Astbury was a huge fan of the Mondays, namechecking them in endless interviews.

GARY WHELAN

People weren't happy with their roles in the band. Some people wanted to do more interviews. Bez was good on TV – you don't get sense out of him, people would want to interview Shaun with him. I would help out sometimes. Mark Day was always completely on his own, I don't think he understood what was going on – he always had nicknames like Pig Farmer Bastard. Everyone had loads of nicknames, like Moosehead. I loved his guitar bits but he never got it. He was always the outsider – never part of the gang. PD [Paul Davis] was just the craziest person, the maddest. We always had arguments on stage. Shaun always wanted to cut a song out – go to song number seven and we did song number six. Shaun and PD didn't get on at the end.

YES PLEASE?

The party had to end. The Mondays, worn out by living fast and free, were always going to be a car crash – indeed, during the recording of the last album in Barbados Bez had proper bike crashes. Yes Please, *produced by the ex-Talking Heads rhythm section of Tina Weymouth and Jerry Harrison, should have been perfect. After all, here was the rhythm section that had inspired the band in the first place and had had international success on their own as pop-dance act Tom Tom Club. Somehow it didn't work – the resulting album, although not a mess, was the band below their peak.*

SHAUN RYDER

Factory needed an album out. I wanted to wait for Oakenfold and Osborne,* so did Bez, right. So did Gaz, but, you know, Gaz will go with whatever keeps the peace. Now Mark Day, PD and our kid, it was like: 'Fuck Oakenfold and Osborne, they should be here now!' That was their attitude.

So Tony Wilson and our Paul go to Jamaica. [When] they come back from Jamaica they've got Chris and Tina with 'em, these are gonna produce the album. Well, no disrespect to Chris and Tina, they're great people, they're great producers, but it wasn't right for our band. We went right back to a way that didn't work, which was like, you know, spending five days setting up and mic-ing up a drum. Ten fuckin' weeks wanking off on a bass, you know, tuning a guitar for a fortnight – just a really slow way of working. Where, you know, you should get a fuckin' rhythm track going, bu-bum, bang that on, add, put the vocal

* Primarily a dance music producer, during most of the 1990s Steve Osborne was part of Perfecto Records, a production and remix collaboration with Paul Oakenfold. He went on to produce New Order, the Doves, Suede and Sophie Ellis Bextor, among many others

on, do that, done, dusted. We'll spend days and days on this bass line, you know, weeks and weeks on that guitar thing there, mic up the drums for days on end, you know, make 'em feel important, tell them they're fantastic.

The music wasn't going the way I wanted it to and I'll say it again: the first Black Grape album should have been the last Mondays album. Or not the last Mondays album, but it certainly should have been the next release. A lot of those ideas for the Black Grape thing was, you know, originally how we would have gone with the Mondays, with Oakenfold. I couldn't handle the way that the music was going and I just got completely off me tits, you know. I mean they really unintentionally divided the band, Chris and Tina.

You know, I did the best to write the words on that, for the tracks I weren't really feeling. I mean, to me it was like sort of a fuckin' limp hard-on version of Talking Heads.

PAUL RYDER
Do you know what, I loved that album. I think it's brilliant – a bit too light maybe in the sound. I was working with heroes – I loved Talking Heads. Most of the music was written in Barbados. We went with three songs. We went crack stupid – what a drug, crack cocaine. It was me, our kid, Bez and Paul Davis, we were the crack monsters – everyone else was smoking weed in abundance. Despite all that I'll always defend that album.

STINKIN' THINKIN'
The end of the Mondays

A fractured band, drugs, an album not as good as their peak – the cards were on the table. Even at this point the band could have pulled through, but fingers were now set firmly on self-destruct.

SHAUN RYDER
Well, I mean, the basic thing was the press had a go at us, right, for the first time ever, and the band just couldn't take that. The rest of them turned and blamed me for the press, you know, not liking that record. And I said, 'Wait a minute – we've had a fuckin' good run with the press, if they can't have a fuckin' little dig at us and you can't take it.'

GARY WHELAN
You got to be thick-skinned when it's mates. You know them too well. The problem is, people do change, but best mates don't want you to change. Even in Barbados it was still fun, right through to the end. There

was stuff going on. Mark got sacked from before Barbados and Johnny Marr was going to come to Barbados. Nathan said, before the end, that every member of the band had been to see him and wanted everyone else in the band sacked! Me and Shaun always got on. We agreed on a lot of stuff.

SHAUN RYDER

I'd always been into drugs. I'd been kicking about with heroin before the fuckin' E and all sorts. Drugs in our band was always there. What it was, was egos and jealousy that fucked it up and it's as straight and simple as this. You know we always thought we was a band of team players, [but] people were saying the songs were shit. And I was like: wait a minute, we've been on *Top of the Pops*. We were actually selling records.

I was splitting things equally with every member of that fuckin' band. Because we was all supposed to be pals and Tony had advised that, right?

However, so that was it, they decided to split the fuckin' band. Their decision again. You know, it was funny because they had this little plan at our last gig in Japan, where the geezer who was working at security with us at that time was going to be the singer.

I mean, Bez was there, we fought tooth and nail not to split that band up. But it was like, guess what, we're gonna fuck you and Bez off, right, 'cos we're jealous that you two are getting all the attention.

PAUL RYDER

There is that famous last meeting in Manchester. I think Shaun turned up off his head and said, 'I've got to go for a Kentucky's,' and I knew exactly where he was going. We had this meeting with a big label waiting there to hear these four new songs, because Factory had gone and we had some great offers and they wanted to give us £7 million.

Shaun goes off and it just so happens that no dealer's got any smack in Manchester, so it took him three hours to score. So by the time he got back to the rehearsal room Clive Black, who we were meeting, had fucked off back to London saying that if we couldn't turn up for seven million quid then fuck it.

I think something like the day after, Shaun phoned up and apologised. Everyone freaked out. Gaz Whelan panicked and said, 'No one likes us any more, the Swells *NME* interview has finished us.' But I said, 'The album *Yes Please* is top twenty.' Gaz thinking it's a failure – his arse just went. The last gig in Japan we did with Big Audio Dynamite. Gaz, Mark and Paul Davis were plotting to leave the Mondays and get Everton, our security guard, on vocals. When that happened I thought we may as well call it a day. I was too paranoid to work with anyone else the first year; I was a recluse. I was exhausted. I was fucked.

We should have taken a year out. Shaun said, 'Take a year out, do something else and then we'll come back with the new album,' and they fannyed out on us! *(laughs)*. And I didn't phone Gaz and Mark and Paul Davis like I usually did after an argument; normally I was Mr Fixit. I went back to my mum and dad's house and went to bed for a year,

GARY WHELAN
I said I wanted a break. I'm 25, I thought I could play football again – live off my royalties and do some semi-pro football.

Theoretically finished after the collapse of the Mondays, Ryder re-emerged in 1993 with Black Grape and astonishingly released one of the best albums of his career. Taking the Mondays' lolloping groove, he tightened it up into shorter, more focused but even more surreal blasts of dark pop, with the addition of Kermit's perfect rap foil. He was rewarded with 1995's huge hit album It's Great When You're Straight . . . Yeah.

SHAUN RYDER
Basically I went straight into Black Grape. I even offered our Paul to fuckin' come join in and do it. He came round to my house in Didsbury and put me windows through in my fuckin' house, you know, after the first fuckin' session, we had a big argument and he fucked off.

PAUL RYDER
I was there for the initial Black Grape sessions. My parting gesture was a chest of drawers through our kid's window – that was me quitting Black Grape and going back to me mam's, because I got a smack habit again. But when they got on *Top of the Pops*, no one was more proud than me to see that happen. People had been saying he was a big fatty walking round Didsbury, he can't do anything; but he comes back stronger and that made me proud.

*Driven by the lyrical genius of Shaun Ryder and the band's loose-limbed, tough and utterly original street funk from the Salford mothership, the Happy Mondays are pictured here at the pre-gentrified Salford Quays in 1988
(Photo: Ian Tilton www.iantilton.net)*

13

'IT'S NOT WHERE YOU'RE FROM, IT'S WHERE YOU'RE AT . . .': THE LONG AND STRANGE ADVENTURES OF THE STONE ROSES

IAN BROWN

I got to know John [Squire] in about 1977. He was getting his head kicked in at school and I knew he lived up our street. I wasn't hanging out with him at the time but I jumped in and helped him out.

That night, because I felt a bit sorry for him because of the fight, I took some records round. I already had 'God Save the Queen', the day it came out. I also took the first Clash LP and the Adverts' 'One Chord Wonders'. He had Beatles' *Live at the Hollywood Bowl* and the Beach Boys' *Golden Greats*. I played my stuff and he got it straight away and he got really into the Clash.

PETE GARNER (Stone Roses bassist)

I met Ian and John at a place called the Bridge near where we all lived in Timperley/Bowden. I'd seen them around a couple of times. One night we started chatting. I remember Ian saying he had been to see the Stranglers, which I was impressed by as he must have been about 13. There was a bit of piss-taking going on! John was quiet; he didn't say much apart from that. He played the first Clash album every day; Ian was more into the Pistols and the Jam. John for some reason was never having the Jam.

IAN BROWN

We started a band called the Patrol in 1979.* I played bass because it was

---

* The Patrol's line-up was John Squire on guitar, Ian Brown on bass, Si Wolstencroft on drums and Andy Couzens on vocals. Pete Garner was the unofficial roadie because 'I couldn't play' and taped all the band's rehearsals.

Iconic shot of Ian Brown in full flare mode.
(Photo: Ian Tilton www.iantilton.net)

the easiest thing to play. I must have been a frustrated singer then because I used to write the words and do the backing vocals. I used to say the intros to the songs as well. Andy Couzens was the singer. We had met him at college. He was weighing into this kid, fighting him, and we were impressed with his bottle because the other kid was bigger than him. We thought, let's ask him to be the singer. He was wearing winklepicker shoes, a long black Crombie and had a spiky haircut, so we knew he was coming out of the same sort of thing that we were.

He was a rich kid to us who had his own van and lived in a big house. So we rehearsed at his house in the cellar. He had the amps and the drum kit, I think my mate Si Wolstencroft and John broke into a school and nicked the school PA. We suspended it down a manhole for two weeks to hide it then sprayed it bright green because the Clash had one that was bright pink.

PETE GARNER
Si was into Topper [Headon] from the Clash. He was aspiring to that sort of level.

Ian was a pretty rudimentary bass player. His playing was pretty basic – classic punk style. John's guitar was really Clash. Their songs were like three-chord versions of the Clash and called 'Jail of the Assassins', 'Up on the Roof' and '25 Rifles'.

IAN BROWN
I guess we were Clash copyists really. We played in youth clubs and we played the Portland bars in town – that was our big gig. One night we could have supported Adam and the Ants at the Mayflower in 1979,* but we couldn't find our van to get into town and no one had a motor and we couldn't find Andy that night.

More than any other Manchester band, the Stone Roses were involved in the punk and post-punk youth culture, looking for adventure and taking risks on the abrasive late seventies/early eighties frontline. They ran with the gangs, wore the clothes, fought the fights; they were a mish-mash of punk rock, skinhead and Two Tone street culture. As the Patrol fizzled out, they drifted off into running with the scooter gangs.

PETE GARNER
Ian sold his bass and bought a scooter. Him and John had got into scootering with Mani, who I think was around at the time. I was

* 26 January 1979, on the 'Young Parisians' tour.

disgusted when they turned mod! Ian got into soul and stuff and I got into the Stooges and the Dolls.

ANDY COUZENS (Stone Roses guitarist)

The last Patrol gig was at the college that we went to. The last song we played was a cover of 'Blockbuster' by the Sweet with both me and Ian singing. That was the real turning point – everyone's tastes started to change slightly after that. Ian got really into his scooters and going out with a scooter mob and hanging out in the Horse and Jockey in Chorlton. He was really into it – like everything he did, he sucked it dry.

John bought a Lambretta – he didn't ride it that much but spent a lot of time pulling it apart, painting it, getting everything copper plated. Ian's bike was this amazing chopped-down thing painted pink.

IAN BROWN

Punk was going by the end of '78. We still liked the Jam, 'Setting Sons' had just come out. I was into the Pistols but they had split up so I was now into the [Angelic] Upstarts – their 'Murder of Liddle Towers' was a big tune; Cockney Rejects – 'Flares And Slippers'; Sham 69's 'Ulster' – that was their first record – and then 'Borstal Breakout', 'Angels with Dirty Faces'. Great records. I was really into them and then I started getting into early mod bands. I was getting older now so I started going to the Russell Club and saw Secret Affair, Purple Hearts and the Chords on the same night, and a band called the Killermeters from Yorkshire. I saw the first ever Madness show when they supported Dexy's Midnight Runners – the local Longsight skins nutted Chas Smash off the stage when he was doing his mad dance.

We got right into scooters in 1978. We weren't mods. You weren't allowed to be a mod to be on the scooters. We didn't have mirrors on our scooters. We would take the leg shields off and have them all boned down. I had a pink one and I put 'Angels With Dirty Faces' on the side of it. I had a two-tone suit and I had a green parachute outfit.

That was when I first met Mani, when was I was on the scooters. I used to hang out with lads from Chorlton and we knew lads from all over the city – Levvy, Longsight, Ardwick, Clayton, Wythenshawe. We also used to hook up with this crew from Moston and Failsworth and we heard about this kid up in Moston who had a swastika on his head, this skinhead who was causing all this trouble – fighting kids. I don't think he was a proper skinhead because when we went up there he had a white school shirt and black school kecks on, he was just a fucking idiot. He was causing untold grief so the idea was that 15 of us were going to give it to him. So we went down from Chorlton to this council house in Moston.

Mani was there, he's got a thick flying jacket on, one of those US bomber ones. I remember the first time I set eyes on him and I thought he's not a fighter, he's a lover – he's just here for the cause, not here for the fighting.

In '81/'82 I went all over – Great Yarmouth, Brighton. Not that many kids from Manchester used to go on all the runs. A hundred of us would go to Scarborough but only a hardcore of 10 or 15 went south, but there would be 10,000 other scooters when you got there. We used to meet outside Horners in Ayres Road. We were the Chorlton crew – the Trojans. We had chrome helmets with a fox's tail hanging from the back of them.

John had been playing guitar a bit and kept a band going with Andy Couzens on guitar and Mani on bass and with Kaiser on vocals. Chris Goodwin was on drums who ended up in the High. They were called the Fireside Chaps, then the Waterfront. I had met Kaiser in the 1981 riots in Manchester when it kicked off. I went down to Moston in the riots and watched Kaiser and the rest of them chucking bricks at buses.

ANDY COUZENS

I had started playing with John again at this time. This was as the Waterfront by now. I think we sat and watched a Marlon Brando film one night and got the name from there. Initially we had been called the Fireside Chaps, which we thought was funny. But when it came to the point of doing the demos we thought, 'Fuck, we can't put that on a demo tape box,' so we changed the name. We never played a gig but we went on for about a year of rehearsals in '82–'83.

IAN BROWN

The Waterfront played me the demo that they'd done. They were sort of Orange Juicey and I wasn't into that side of it, but I thought, wow! It sounds dead tuneful – like a proper band. They were into Josef K and Glasgow Postcard sort of stuff, as well as Green on Red, early REM, Rain Parade – I never liked any of that. They said, 'Do you want to join up singing?' so I rehearsed a couple of times with them. The idea was for me to join up on vocals with Kaiser and have two vocalists. We never played a gig and it didn't really happen.

ANDY COUZENS

The Waterfront demo was recorded somewhere in the back end of Denton, somewhere up Mani's way – in a little studio that someone had set up. We already had done some demos with the Patrol in Rusholme a couple of years before, in a studio just off Great Western Street where Mick Hucknall did a lot of stuff with his punk band Frantic Elevators.

IAN BROWN

In 1981 I was 17 and staying in Withington at my girlfriend's but then I broke up with her and that's when I moved into William Kent Crescent in Hulme. I sold my scooter and moved there.

It was Michelle, my girlfriend's 21st – the mother of my two eldest – birthday party. Gluebag Glen brought Geno Washington and his band back to the party in Hulme. I had never heard of Geno Washington at the time; to me he was just this dead cool old black guy who kept telling me that I was a star.

He kept going on all night: 'Hey man, you're a star, you should be a singer, man, look at how the people like you.' I said, 'It's our party, these are my friends! That's why they like me!'

It was Geno Washington who had sowed the seed. I told John what had happened at the party and he said, 'Why don't we give it a go?'

Me and John were still sort of mates, even though we hadn't seen each other properly for a year because we were leading different lives. We said, 'Let's get this band thing going,' so we met up and we wrote this tune 'Nowhere Fast', a song about our attitude that you don't have to go to work – it's punk rock! No fucker is gonna tell us what to do. By then I'd had a few shit jobs and now I was on the dole and that was it. I was never working for no one again.

I rung Pete up to see if he was up for it. He hadn't been into the scooter scene, so I hadn't seen him for a couple of years. I said to Pete, 'Do you want to play bass in this band?' and he was up for it. At the time John didn't want Andy Couzens to be in the band – he said, 'He's different to us.' I remember John saying, 'We've got to do it right as it is, we can't have Andy in it,' but I said we got to have him in.

ANDY COUZENS

I always thought there was something about Pete. He's just a great bloke,

Pete, someone who is great to have around. Whether he could play or not was irrelevant. John came in the end. Getting John in was almost like a default – he was like, 'Oh fuck it, go on then.' John said he would only do it if Pete was in the band. It ended up getting the Patrol back together – the big reformation.

PETE GARNER
The first rehearsal was February/March 1984 and the first song we did was 'Nowhere Fast'. This is with Si [Wolstencroft] who was now our drummer.

ANDY COUZENS
I had got Chris Goodwin in on drums initially. He came down for one rehearsal and left his kit in the cellar. It was like he was just looking for somewhere to store it.

PETE GARNER
You've got to remember that the only bass line I knew was the Sweet's 'Blockbuster'. I couldn't play bass at all and I'd only played that once, at that Patrol gig. I think it was a case of 'Always get your mate in on bass.' At our first rehearsal everyone strapped on guitars and I was thinking, 'What the fuck do I do!'

In the next few months we rehearsed everywhere. We even did the Boardwalk once and never went back because the room was shit. Later on, we rehearsed at the Chorlton Lock Up.

IAN BROWN
We had the Clash's last album and we thought, look how crap they are – we can do it! We saw the death of the Clash and they were the number one band for us. The Smiths had come out of Manchester that year and were now big. I used to go to parties with Andy Rourke, and everyone knew Johnny Marr because he used to run round the pubs telling everyone he's going to be number one. And a year later he was!

JOHNNY MARR
When I was putting Freaky Party together I got really tempted to go and personally talk to Ian Brown and say, 'Listen – come and be in our band.' I knew Ian Brown through Pete [Garner], and also Si our drummer had gone to school with him. We'd met a couple of times. We had that kind of respectful rivalry. I knew John Squire better. We were checking each other out like you do – we would talk about records. There was an unsaid

understanding that Ian and John were a musical item – so that's what stopped me asking Ian.

IAN BROWN
Johnny Marr is a great bloke, proper, really into music. He was only 23 when the Smiths split and we were 25 when we did our first album. We might have looked 19 – I thought, if we don't do it this year we'll never do it.

PETE GARNER
I liked the Smiths as people. When I was a bit younger I had met this kid who was into punk because we both got the same bus home from work and that turned out to be Johnny Marr. I was impressed because he liked the Heartbreakers. I had just bought the *Live at Max's Kansas City** album and I went round to his house.

JOHNNY MARR
When I was working at Aladdin's Cave on the ground floor of the Arndale,† I used to get the bus with Pete in the mornings and each night. He became a really good mate. He could see the way I was dressing and all of that and was interested. I really liked this guy. I remember we were getting the 99 back to Wythenshawe one night and he was trying to come up with a name for his band that he had just started in. He knew I was a Stones freak. He got off a few stops after me, saying the name had got to be as good as the Rolling Stones. I got home and the phone goes five minutes later. It was Pete and he says, 'I've been talking about it – what about the Stone Roses?' I said, 'Naah! That's too obvious, Pete!'

ANDY COUZENS
Si had left to join the Smiths when they started up. So we started auditioning drummers. I put an advert up in A1 Music in town. The drummer from the Skeletal Family came down but that didn't work out. We rehearsed for ages with no drums at all, which is ridiculous when you think about it – you'd get a drum machine now.

PETE GARNER
We put more ads up for a drummer and waited. It was the poster we put

---

* Classic Velvet Underground live album recorded in 1970 and released a couple of years later.
† In those pre-Afflecks Palace days there was a real hive of alternative culture in the underground market below Afflecks, noted for 'Bowie bootleg tapes and Tukka boots' among other things.

in A1 that Reni [Alan Wren] saw. He's told me since that it looked like there was something about it. It was a simple poster with list of influences on it and said: 'The Stone Roses require a drummer.' Even though no one had ever heard of us at the time, we put the band's name on it!

ANDY COUZENS

The first time Reni rehearsed with us was in Decibel Studios. We booked it to rehearse with Reni specially. Me and Ian went to pick him up. We knocked on this door in Gorton and Reni came to the door. I seem to remember he looked mad! He had a big long coat on and big furry moon boots, a pair of them awful stretch denim jeans – his dress sense was fucking terrible! We were a bit shocked! We put all his kit in the car and went back to the rehearsal room.

Yeah! It was weird. We loaded his gear into the car and went to the rehearsal room. We took the gear up three flights of stairs and he started playing. He was mad as a hatter. He played like Keith Moon, amazing. All those little things that he can do like double hits, unbelievable stuff, so fluent and no effort – he could actually do all that. We wanted him in – he was that fucking good, but we weren't sure if he was going to have it! We weren't that good at all, we were still pretty rough. He told me a while later that the thing that really struck was how much we believed in ourselves – the sense of belief that he got from us all. His best friend, Simon Wright, had been in a Manchester rock band called Tora Tora before joining AC/DC. If he hadn't had joined us he would have ended up as a jobbing musician. There was a deathly silence and someone said, 'Are you up for it or what, Reni?'

He joined us that night.

IAN BROWN

'Tragic Roundabout' was the first tune we did with Reni and we realised that this was it.

With the best drummer of his generation in the band, the Roses were ready to go out and play.

IAN BROWN

I read in *Sounds* that Caroline Read – who managed this Welsh band Mercenary Skank – was putting on an anti-heroin benefit at the Moonlight Club in London. So I wrote to her saying, 'We're surrounded by heroin in Hulme – can we play?' On the top floor of Charles Barry Crescent in Hulme, where I was living, there was an opera singer next to me and a dentist, and all them heads were all junkies. I said I wanted to do something about that. They wrote back and asked us to play and that was our first gig. Pete Townshend headlined and he got Reni up to play 'Pictures of Lily' and 'Substitute' with him. He then tried to poach Reni for his solo album and Reni told him to fuck off. We were made up because it showed the belief Reni had in us.

ANDY COUZENS

Our first gig was at the Moonlight. At the soundcheck the song that we did was 'Open My Eyes' by Nazz.* The version we did was really tough, it was a great song live. We'd had that much whiz by this point that we went off on one! The soundcheck sounded really good. People were going, 'Fucking hell!', coming up and saying, 'Where are you coming from? You sound amazing!'

HOWARD JONES

I was looking for a band to manage. It became a bit of a thing – 'I'm going to find a good band.' I went and saw the Roses rehearse in Spirit in town. They were absolutely fucking diabolical. It was a racket but one of those kinds of rackets that was so exciting. They had songs there. I couldn't believe some of the actual lyrical content. I'm into lyrics. I love Dylan. And Ian Brown's lyrics! Does Ian Brown realise how evocative they are? His words work on so many different levels; does he understand how powerful these words are? I got to know Ian and got to realise how deep a thinker he really is. There isn't a thing he doesn't think about and I thought, this guy is a great songwriter. They looked great, like a gang. There was a tall one, a thin one, a hard one, a soft-looking one – John looked like if you said 'boo' he would jump. Reni looked so young, I didn't realise he was so young. I couldn't believe it.† I had to become their manager.

At the time they hated the Hacienda and the way Factory Records dominated the Manchester scene. They saw me as an insider until I gave them my spiel and I said, 'I'm nothing to do with Factory.' Steve Adge had warned me about their attitude to Factory. I said, 'I'm resigning from Factory and the Hacienda and starting a company. We're going to start a label – if you go with me now, you'll have product out within months.'

---

* Todd Rundgren's great sixties psychedelic outfit.
† The youthful-looking Reni was 20 at the time, the rest of the band were 22 or 23.

TONY WILSON

The Stone Roses I hated. I'd seen them in the early eighties when they were a goth band* and badly dressed. By the time they started spreading their names all over Manchester they were managed by my first wife, my ex-partner, Martin Hannett, my ex-protégé from the Hacienda, Tim, and the guy who used to run the Hacienda, Howard Jones. So everyone who was an ex in my life was involved with the Roses, so I completely ignored them.

HOWARD JONES

That November me, Martin Hannett and Tim Chambers started Thin Line Records. And the following January we went to the studio and recorded the first demo with 'Tragic Roundabout', 'Misery Dictionary', 'Mission Impossible' and 'Self Respect' with Tom Oliver.

IAN BROWN

I was travelling round Europe and I was sat at a table in Berlin with my girl. I heard this bloke saying he promoted gigs in Sweden and I said, 'I'm in the biggest band in Manchester, called the Stone Roses' – although we'd never played Manchester at the time. He was called Alf and I made sure I got on with him to get this thing sorted out.

It was all set up in and in April '85 we went to Sweden. Alf's mate gave us his apartment and for a month we played five shows in Sweden with this Swedish punk band called Toxic Toy in places like Norrkoping, Malmo and Stockholm. At some of the shows, only two people turned up!

PETE GARNER

We went to Sweden for a month – all we had were our giros. Our roadie spent his giro in the casino in half an hour. We told Howard Jones, who was now our manager, that we had no money left and we had to get money off him. The first gig was totally brilliant. Loads of people there and went down really well, but the next one there was hardly anyone there. We started playing a new song, 'I Wanna Be Adored', in Sweden.

IAN BROWN

By sheer fluke I had started to jump out in the crowd at early gigs until 1988 and because of that I got on the front of a Swedish daily paper because of this gig in Norrkoping – because we'd talked everyone up about being the biggest band in Manchester. They put us in the paper, and word got back to Manchester that we were taking off in Sweden and

---

* The Stone Roses were never a goth band.

Tony the Greek played us on his Sunday night radio show. He played the demo of 'Tragic Roundabout' that we had just recorded. Loads of people loved it and kept phoning up to find out who we were.

TONY MICHAELIDES (Manchester radio DJ, aka Tony the Greek)
Howard Jones . . . called me up at home one time, late '84, and left a message saying he wanted to speak to me about a band he was managing. Later in the week he called over to see me at the radio station, but without bringing any music, and asking me if I'd play his band. Well, I needed to hear it first, naturally. About an hour before the show started on the following Sunday, he got the bass player Pete Garner to drop a tape off at the radio station . . . I told him I'd listen to it in the week as it was getting near show time.

As I walked back down the corridor I glanced at the tape box and was intrigued by the titles: 'Misery Dictionary', 'So Young', 'I Wanna Be Adored' (or 'Adored', if I remember it was titled back then) 'Heart on the Staves', 'Tell Me', 'Mission Impossible', 'Nowhere Fast'.

Time was tight but as there was no real preparation for the show I got hold of Paula and Ro and said, 'Let's go have a quick listen.' We went into the news booth off the side of the on-air studio and cued up the tape. 'Misery Dictionary' was the track I played and we just all looked at each other and thought, fuck, this is really something. Considering it was the worst time to listen to anything, 15 minutes before I was on air . . . We stayed there and listened to 'Adored' and 'Heart of the Staves'. I ended up rushing into the studio during the news and cueing up my first record, still clutching the Roses demo.

'I'm playing this tonight,' I said to the girls and they didn't need convincing. We played 'Misery Dictionary' and the phones just lit up.

PETE GARNER
After the Moonlight gig in 1984 *Sounds* journalist Gary Johnson got really into the band and interviewed us. The *Sounds* piece compared us to the Buzzcocks. It was a funny interview because it doesn't really say a lot, but in the piece Ian said that 'we played London and we blew Mercenary Skank offstage', which didn't go down that well. In the picture Reni looks about 15. The headline of the piece was 'flower power' – the first of years of crap puns on the name!

ANDY COUZENS
We didn't want anything to do with Manchester at all. We were opposed to all the raincoat-wearing Manchester Factory bands scene. All that cliquey elitism.

PETE GARNER
We played Preston Clouds and there was a kick-off.

HOWARD JONES
On 29 March, we did that gig at Preston. It was the start of the Roses thing. Loads of people travelled from Manchester to the gig. I'd never seen that before. It was unbelievable.

The crowd was quite heavy. There were some skinheads. A couple of people had these NF badges on and I told them to take them off and that nearly caused a riot as well!

I said, 'What the fuck are those badges?' There's no way I was having people with NF badges on, quite apart from the fact that Reni and Cressa were there. What did they feel like! I'd already been through all this with Factory, being accused of being Nazis and racist when it couldn't have been further from the truth.

PETE GARNER
I was glad I wasn't in the audience! It was really lairy. Loads of Mancs had come down and were fighting with people from Preston. All I remember when we were playing was the tension in the air beforehand and it erupted into a Wild West saloon thing. It was pretty naughty!

We then recorded the Tony Michaelides radio session with 'I Wanna Be Adored', 'Heart Of the Staves' and 'Tell Me'. They repeated it quite a few times.

TONY MICHAELIDES
We were contacted by Dingwalls to put on a showcase of Manchester bands in London. They wanted five bands in all – well, only four really, because it was obvious to all the Stone Roses were going to headline. We narrowed the list down: the final bill included Laugh, Communal Drop, Fictitious Minds and the Glee Company.

KAREN ABLAZE (fan)
Dingwalls was pretty much empty: just us and a couple of other people – two Japanese girls in the audience, maybe they got lost! Then we were driven back and we stopped off at Watford gap for nasty service station food and a game of football on the car park. It was mad how no one knew them outside Manchester at that stage.

JO BARTLETT (fan)
Danny and myself first saw the Stone Roses with original bass player Pete

Garner. Ian and John had paint-splattered clothes and guitars. They blew our minds. There were about 20 people in the audience watching them. Ian said, 'Clap, clap, clap,' when we clapped! He freaked some guy out by swinging on the pipes overhanging the stage, landing in front of him and removing the guy's glasses and putting them on himself. He played a couple of songs still wearing the glasses before swinging back and replacing them on the confused dude's face. We loved them so much we went outside and waved at them as their van headed off. Ian waved from the window.

PETE GARNER

We were in *City Life*. Bob Dickinson called us 'deviant Merseybeat' and asked, 'Can you like a band that does the finer points of the debate without the psychedelic drugs and the social vision?'

BOB DICKINSON

I interviewed them in a house on Zetland Road, Chorlton, where one of them was living. I'd seen them and I thought they were really exciting to watch, especially Ian Brown because of the way he moved on stage. In those days, he was quite athletic, or balletic, at times, quite unlike the way he looks now. And Reni was just the best drummer I'd seen since Keith Moon – afterwards, when they got famous, I think they told him to hold back a lot. As an interview, they were like a lot of new bands – very nice boys, a bit suspicious of journalists typecasting them, which I hope I didn't do when that phrase 'deviant Merseybeat' came to mind.

PETE GARNER

Ro Newtown's review of the Clouds gig appeared in *Melody Maker* that April and she said that 'they so blatantly lack originality and melody'.

We then finally played Manchester on 10 May at the International 1, supporting It's Immaterial. Loads of people turned up at that one. We were on a roll by then, well on a high anyway, coming back from Sweden. We were rehearsing every day.

HOWARD JONES

I was fired up from leaving Factory and I needed to prove to Tony Wilson that I knew a good band when I saw one. It was weird; everything happened so fast. Within three gigs, they had a full page in *Sounds* and were doing a single and album with Martin Hannett.

IAN BROWN

Howard then had us in the studio working on an album with Martin Hannett.*

He was losing it a bit by then. I would say, 'Hang on, I've got to get a drink of water,' and he would lean over and say, 'Ian used to say that.' He shut the control room and locked it so we couldn't get in. All the faders were pushed up the desk in the shape of his belly and his engineer Chris Nagle said, 'Leave it – that's "the curve", that's the Hannett sound!' So we left it. The version of 'So Young' was so trebly that when we went to play it in the car and turned it up, Reni's nose went 'bang' like that! It was too loud and trebly and so extreme, more extreme than the Mary Chain.

Martin had lost it. He used to play 'Transmission' quarter-inch tapes. He would put them on and bask in it as if he was trying to remember how to do it. We would say we wanted it to sound like Slaughter and the Dogs' 'Cranked Up Really High', which he had done, that's why we wanted to work with him. He didn't know what we were on about. Maybe it was the mastering that made that record sound so good.

ANDY COUZENS

'This Is the One' we wrote in the studio with Hannett. We recorded everything we'd got and he said, 'I'm going to the pub whilst Pete learns his bass to this other tune.' He then said, 'Write another song whilst I'm out,' and we went in and jammed 'This Is the One' out.

The warehouse parties are where the Stone Roses got clever. The first of these, in a railway arch near Piccadilly station, was also the first of three legendary gigs that set a precedent for the band's future run of classic appearances, from Blackpool to Alexandra Palace to Spike Island.

IAN BROWN

That July in 1985 we did the first warehouse party and that was a real highlight.

ANDY COUZENS

We didn't want to play Manchester again – it was a proper fucking pain. We went to Steve Adge and said, 'Can you put us on in town?' So he went out and rented one of those railway arches behind Piccadilly station.

---

* These sessions were never released at the time, apart from debut single 'So Young'/'Tell Me', but were released as *Garage Flower* by Silvertone in 1996.

PETE GARNER

Steve had been to London [and he was] buzzing about a warehouse party he'd been to. So on 20 July he booked the first warehouse gig.* He booked it secretly and photocopied directions of how to get there. People bought tickets without knowing how to get to it. Steve sold all these tickets that said to ring Spirit and find out where the gig was. He'd rented the arch and had to keep it secret because if the owners had found out it was a gig they would have pulled it. 'The only dress restrictions is no blue uniforms' was handwritten on the flyers. People would come down to Spirit, where they were checked if they were alright and given instructions of how to get to the party.

IAN BROWN

Steve put the three warehouse shows on in town. He said, 'I've got the place in Fairfield Street – do you want to do this party? It's called "The Flower Show".' He'd rented the warehouse off British Rail and it was a great night. It got us big in Manchester quick.

In those days gangsters used to run the posters in Manchester. One night we went out posting the warehouse gig, covering them all up on the Friday night when everyone is coming out of the clubs, and the posters said 'Gig on tonight, Stone Roses onstage at four'. Later on I was in somewhere like Corbieres and this guy came up wearing spats and looking like Oddjob. He said, 'You know I should really be breaking your knees.' I said, 'What for?' and he said, 'You've been putting posters over my patches tonight, guys get their kneecaps broken for less!' I said, 'Oh, I didn't know!' But he let us off – he knew our intentions were good. At the time I didn't have a clue what he was on about!

At the gig we had all our mates lined up to DJ. At about three in the morning this big Rasta turns up and says, 'I'm the DJ!' and we said, 'Yeah, sweet!' He DJed reggae all night, which was great. The warehouse parties gave us an underground vibe. They were the first warehouse parties in Manchester. We had the place done out with car tyres hanging from the ceiling and the police were outside drinking beer because we gave them a crate of ale to keep them sweet. When they turned up, there must have been 2000 people in there and we were saying, 'What are you going to do?' This was before there were flats in the city centre. It's not like we were going to disturb anyone.

* The Stone Roses played as 'The Flower Show' on 20 July and 30 November 1985.

We got round the licensing laws because we gave everyone a penny as they went in and said we were paying for them to appear in a video shoot.

SCOTT CAREY

The Roses' first Warehouse gig – my mate had just left school in 1985 and he told me about this band, the Stone Roses, who had been on Tony the Greek's show. So I went to see this band at the warehouse party. They didn't come on until one o'clock and I didn't know how all these kids were staying up that late – I was a bit too young to know they were using amphetamines. I was stood there thinking, Jesus, what time is this band going on? I'm going home! They ran out of beer and there were all these nutters hanging about. There was this group of lads called the Dancing Tarantulas from Hulme – they were proto dog-on-a-string Megadog types. They came in to play all the psychedelic stuff. About this time I was getting into psychedelic music as well and I was discovering groups like Nazz, Love* and the Chocolate Watchband, all that kind of sixties stuff. The Stone Roses came on and the first song they played was a song by Nazz called 'Open My Eyes'. I thought, this is amazing!

IAN BROWN

Howard Jones was now gone. We'd done the ten songs with Hannett. We'd gone to record the demos in some downtime and not an album, and they were talking about releasing an album. With Hannett it didn't sound right. He was a lovely fellow but he was so far out of it then, he didn't know where he was. He was sat under the mixing desk crosslegged like Buddha. He went massive in size and would wear a big black kimono. He was a dead intelligent head who lost it because he was too intelligent.

'GOOD EVANS'

In which the Roses get a manager . . .

IAN BROWN

Genevieve's had closed and become the International 1 and that was our first ever gig back in town after Sweden. The whole crew turned out – all my mates, Pete had all his mates from Paperchase, Mani who because he was our mate had a crew from Moston as part of our entourage. And that

---

* Arthur Lee's late-sixties LA psych-rock outfit, who were precursors to the Doors and a huge influence on the Manchester scene

was where we met Gareth – a year and a half before he became our manager. I remember shaking his hand in the soundcheck. We made him our manager when we did the university in 1986.

GARETH EVANS

The Stone Roses did a gig at the International early on with Howard Jones promoting it – I think it was their first proper Manchester show. Howard Jones had put an Easter festival on at the International with the Stone Roses and I watched the whole gig. I thought the charisma of John Squire just standing still was great. It reminded me of the bass player from Booker T and the MGs, who had a circle drawn around him – in his contract he wasn't allowed to move out of this circle. John Squire just stood there and looked so cool. Ian Brown – I loved the voice because I was always pissed off with these people going to stage school and just learning to sing. Pop is about your own distinctive voice. The Roses that night I really noticed.

IAN BROWN

Our look then was paisley shirts, leather trousers, and in 1986 black and red and white striped shirts, Pete had black hair and John had a bandana, which is what we were wearing when we first met Gareth.

We wore the leather pants because they were rock'n'roll but we tried not to be a rock'n'roll band – not in that kind of corny way. I've read an interview with John saying he was a big fan of the Mary Chain, but I don't remember wearing leather pants because of the Mary Chain – the Beatles had worn them in Hamburg, Rotten had worn them in the Sex Pistols, and Sid Vicious and Steve Jones.*

GARETH EVANS

I was into finance with gold bullion in the seventies and early eighties. I then heard that the Ocean's 11 club was for sale. I bought it and made it the International 1. I brought in Roger Eagle to book the bands and DJ.

IAN BROWN

We saw an advert in *City Life* saying that the International 1 had a

* The Roses have since been accused (not only by Tony Wilson!) of being a 'goth' band. In fact their whole look was a dandified take on their earlier mod-ish style, with a dash of leather trousers thrown in. The goth scene was a post-punk subculture into black clothes and darker, moodier music; curiously used as a putdown, the term 'goth' was never used by anyone in that underrated scene.

management company and they were looking for bands. We said, 'Let's have a look at that.'

GARETH EVANS

The story is I put an advert in the paper looking for bands. I deny this. A girl called Helen was helping me – she said she wanted to manage bands working from the office and I said, 'As long as you help do stuff in the office, that's OK.' So she put the ad in *City Life*.

The Stone Roses saw the advert. They came in Andy Couzens' big American car and pushed their way into the office trying to be rock stars, but I wasn't impressed with that. Then we started talking to each other.

IAN BROWN

We go to the International 1 and go upstairs to the office and walk in and Gareth is standing in the office. He drops his kecks and he's got this pair of super-tight Burt Lancasters with an apple on them. And he says, 'These are the underwear that I'm marketing. I can market anything, me.'

GARETH EVANS

I started saying things about the past and what I had been involved in. Maybe I like talking. And the story is true – I did take my pants down and show them some knickers with pommes on. I had got over £250,000 from some loan guarantees. So I got some Mitsubishi machines to make the underwear – the samples were made by real professionals and we sold them to everybody round the country.

IAN BROWN

He says, 'I'm also into gold bullion.' He opens this drawer and it's full of gold and with a jeweller's glass in his eye he starts looking at all this gold. He looks at us and says to Matthew,* 'They're like the Rolling Stones, aren't they?'

GARETH EVANS

I think the Roses played something to me and I said, 'I don't want to know, my job is to get you known, full stop.'

IAN BROWN

We knew Gareth didn't know fuck all. He had this club, though, and

---

* Gareth Evans's business partner.

not only could we rehearse there, we could fucking batter the bar while we were doing it! We would drink Black Russians and all that whilst we were on the dole. It was a big deal practising on the big stage through a big PA. We rehearsed at the International 2 and went to see all the bands that would come through there. We had to finish rehearsing when the bands started to soundcheck, so we would see everyone who came through – apart from Duran Duran, who were the only band that wouldn't let us watch their soundcheck! We would finish at five and watch everyone that would come through the venue because he was our manager. We would be in there every night seeing every act from Adrian Sherwood to the Bundhu Boys. It was Roger Eagle that was booking it all.

PETE GARNER

After the meeting we were managed by Gareth and we started rehearsing at the International. Gareth then got us a gig at McGonigles.* When we walked in all these heavy metallers were doing that dance to 'Smoke on the Water' and we were like, 'Oh for fuck's sake.'

As we run up to the stage, people were going, 'Fuck off, you English bastards. Get back on the boat, you bastards!' We only played about three tunes and then we were breaking all the furniture up in the dressing room because we thought we might have to fight our way out of there.

Andy, being loaded, flew back to Manchester. We had to wait eight hours at the ferry port playing shove ha'penny against the wall, waiting for the ferry. People weren't happy.

GARETH EVANS

I booked them at this place in Dublin and I knew it was like a rockers' place. I knew I wanted the press and the gig didn't go well. Andy Couzens said, 'I've had enough of this,' and got on the plane and flew back.† They came back in the van with no money. I lost my rag with Andy Couzens and said, 'You don't do that.'

IAN BROWN

When we got back we had a meeting in a café in Piccadilly. Andy Couzens had brought his dad's lawyer, who said, 'What can you do for this band?' Gareth immediately backs off and says, 'Until I get a deal I can't do anything,' and the lawyer says, 'Well fuck off then!' and he adds, 'You're not talking to my band like that!' We're all just sat there.

---

* 5 June 1986.
† Andy had had to fly home to get back to work.

We wanted to kick Andy out the band at this time. Musically he was covering everything over with his barre chords. John was getting really dreamy on his guitar – a lot more tuneful. We knew that was the way to do it: not to make a racket, get a really nice melody. You can be subversive that way – instead of playing punk rock, you can play it melodic and get your message through with nice sixties-style tunes. That's how we were going to do it.

Gareth and Andy not seeing eye-to-eye did us a favour really.

Andy said, 'You're not talking to my guy like that.' He looked around looking for support and we just looked at the floor. So Andy said, 'Right, we're off.' We just stayed there.

GARETH EVANS

Bands always make artistic decisions. I don't make artistic decisions. With Andy, the band never asked him back; it was a band decision. They could have asked him but they didn't.[*]

After Andy Couzens had been ousted from the band, Gareth Evans continued to try to find a deal for the group.

GARETH EVANS

The Roses had been hawked by Howard Jones around everywhere. I had to get them a deal – there were a few independent labels he hadn't tried. I talked to a few people. I needed an independent label, a person who could distribute it, and I found this person at Revolver.

I was doing crazy things to get the band known. Noel Gallagher said I gave 5000 comps away for early Roses gigs. It was always rammed, although we did sell a lot of tickets as well. I gave the band their mystique. I saw John Squire and I said, 'Don't go out front and talk to your buddies after the gig, you go out the side door and disappear.' They were dead sick because they had to go back round to Reni's house whilst I was having a great time at the club. But it worked.

NOEL GALLAGHER

The first time I saw the Stone Roses was at the International 1. I didn't have any idea who they were; it was one of those nights put on by Gareth where he would come up to you in the street and give you a ticket. You only found out years later that he gave out tickets to people he thought should be Stone Roses fans – I wonder what jacket I was wearing that day!

[*] Andy Couzens re-emerged in 1989 in the High.

I remember walking through town on the day of the Lord Mayor's parade, I don't know what I was doing in town. Gareth came up to me and gave me tickets and said, 'Have you got any friends?' I said, 'I got loads of them in Levenshulme,' and he said, 'Bring them all.' But nobody wanted to come so I went on my own.

The Stone Roses were in what was called their goth period, with their longhaired bass player and Andy Couzens on guitar. They were never a goth band though – fucking good is what it was. At one of the gigs, it was virtually empty and Ian was doing this thing where he was singing in the middle of the dance floor – he would go out and front people out and I thought, that's mad as fuck.

IAN BROWN

I always had a skinhead in them days. Every record company said, 'You'll have to grow your hair. We can't sign you, because in America they're going to think you're gay because Bronski Beat have got boneheads.' Gareth used to beg us, 'Grow your hair, grow your hair.' I was like, 'Fuck off! I like it like this,' but I grew it eventually because I wanted to.

The lads had been begging with me to grow my hair. I had been shaving my head for years, so, as a sacrifice to the band, I grew my hair in about '88 and that's when we got signed. We had the same tunes as we always had but the longer my hair got, the bigger the band got (*laughs*).

GARETH EVANS

I was still trying to find a deal for the band. Another guy came down and said, 'We don't want this,' because they associated them with 'Tell Me' and 'So Young'.

I got this guy called Dave who used to come down to the Internationals and persuaded him to open this label called Black on Revolver Records just for us. Revolver was an independent label. We didn't like the guy who owned it, but we got the record out and it got in the indie charts.

IAN BROWN

'Sally Cinnamon' is released by FM Revolver and then gets played on Janice Long and got us in the indie charts.* We had that punk rock heart that affected all our decisions as well. All the way through the Roses, that was how we worked. We were offered three nights at Ally Pally years later

---

* The Roses' second single was a swerve in direction from the band's strident 'So Young' debut and set the template for the band's new breezy, intelligent, mesmerising, psychedelic guitar pop.

and we said, 'No, fuck off – that's what a dinosaur band would do!' Our idea was to go to town, blow it up and then get out – all our decisions were based on that.

Then Pete left. When we were tripping, we could hear he wasn't on it and we were like, 'Oh fuck, what are we going to do?' Pete saved us the job of telling him when he said he got the feeling that 'You're going to be massive but I've got to pull out – I'm not made for this.' That saved us the job of sacking our mate.

SCOTT CAREY

I was in the Boardwalk with Clint Boon checking out bands. We had a membership to go there all the time and network, which we would call 'knocking about'. There was no one at the gig apart from Ian and John, who were just sat there with their haircuts and their sideys and both wearing black turtleneck jumpers looking dead cool – so I went over and bummed a fag off Ian. I was saying, 'What you doing here?' They said, 'Pete's left,' and my jaw just hit the floor! I went, 'What you gonna do?' and they said, 'We're going to look around for bass players.' Clint jumped in and said, 'You can't have him, he's our bass player!' I was tongue-tied, I didn't know what to say – so I shut up. So they got in one of the Hyde lot to play bass – Rob the Bob – and had their pictures taken with him as their new bass player. Rob couldn't learn the bass because he wasn't a musician, so he called me up and he said, 'They know about you and they want you to go for an audition.' But I was 18 and they were six years older than me, and that's a massive gap – they were just too cool for school. I thought, I'll be alright with the Inspirals. So I bottled it basically.

CLINT BOON

The next day I saw Mani's brother Greg in Manchester and I said, 'I was with Ian and John last night and they need a bass player.' Mani was working at the Opera House doing lights and I said, 'Get your brother in there quick.' Mani already knew them so he got in there. I'm given credit for that although it probably would have happened anyway. They could have met up with Garth out of the Buzzcocks, depending who came into the Boardwalk next, and history would have been different (laughs).

IAN BROWN

So we decided not come back from town till we'd found a bass player. We got off the bus at the Palace Theatre. Mani comes walking down the road and says, 'How you doing?' We said, 'We're looking for a bass player,' and he said 'I'm your bass player! You know I'm the best bass player in the west!' It was just like destiny, fate.

He might have been looking for us, I never knew. We went for a drink in the bar next door and that was it. He was in. Everyone who came to see the Roses at that point in '86 said that Mani was the final piece of the jigsaw. He looked great and could really play well.

'Elephant Stone' was the first song we wrote with him. We needed a groove and he put the groove in because he was a groove payer. He would play reggae all day long. Mani was into smoking weed and reggae and playing the bass. He was great. We used to think he had a little monkey face! He looked like the actor Hywel Bennett.

Cressa started doing John's guitar effects and we thought, this is great. As he started doing John's effects he started moving and that looked great. At the same time, Bez was starting dancing with the Mondays. We used to go to watch the Mondays in London and they would come to watch us. There was a mutual respect.

The London press used to always try and get us and the Mondays to be rivals, but we used to buzz about them. The press had no idea how tight we really were. Every time the Mondays had a big tour we would go to the party and send them off. We would be at each other's gigs. The Mondays were in the dressing room for our first big Manchester gig – the Clause 28 gig at International 2 with James.* Sean and Bez would be in the dressing room saying, 'Go on the Roses,' and all that. Sean used to tell me where my mam was in the crowd, because she used to come to all the gigs early on.

TOM HINGLEY

The first time I saw the Roses play was at the International 2 at the James gig where Ian Brown smashed up the microphone. Ian was abusing various people in the audience. The only thing I knew about the Roses was that someone had graffiti'd their name over the library.† That was the night Noel [Gallagher] and Graham [Lambert] met. I remember all the Inspirals were there. Without the Stone Roses, we wouldn't have had a career. When their album came out it was truly a groundbreaking record – a genre-defining record that picked up a change in the decade.

---

* 30 May 1988.
† In about 1987 the Stone Roses' name was sprayed on walls from West Didsbury to the city centre.

GARETH EVANS

I got to know a guy who worked for Zomba and lived in London. He would come down the club. He was dead cool. I then signed a deal for the Roses with Zomba. Eventually it all went to court and it got them press and everything. I knew you couldn't sign people for life. Bands can thank me for breaking the record companies' hold on bands – all I get is stick but I was brave enough to do it.

IAN BROWN

At this time, the Mondays were a little bit ahead and in autumn 1988 *Bummed* came out. We had recorded ours but ours wasn't released at the time. The Mondays started getting press and all that, which was great.

We were now selling the International 2 out and they were selling shows out everywhere – getting bigger and bigger. We were playing to 1000 at the International. Then we got to Leeds and we would play to 60, and 40 of them came from Manchester!

We played in Cardiff to 12 people and four of them were the Manic Street Preachers. At the time the Roses were only a Manchester thing.

Everyone was getting into acid house, Es and flares in 1988. John and Cressa had worn flares before. In '86 Cress had these bottle-green cord hipsters that were original Levi's. He gave me them to me and said, 'You should be wearing these.' The Mondays used to say about Cressa, 'Where's your mate – the funky monkey in the flares?' John had stopped wearing flares then. You can see it in pics at the time: all the band are wearing parallels except for me – they got baggy parallels and I was wearing the bottle-green flares.

With Cressa being the guitar tech, John was getting really good on guitar. If he wants a bit of echo on the chorus or delay on something, then Cress would press the buttons – number 72 or number 73. But as he's pressing the buttons he's throwing a few shapes and people were getting into that. He was our mate and it's great to have your mate with you but then it became difficult for him because he was sort of the road crew and also elevated because he was dancing on the stage.

When we did *Top of the Pops* the other guys didn't want him on because of Bez. They said, 'We're going to look like the Mondays – like we've got a Bez.' I said, 'Hang on, you're taking him out on all these shows and he looks good – he's a part of it and you won't have him on *Top of the Pops*.' I always felt sorry for Cressa because we got elevated to be pop stars and he didn't.

UNDERNEATH THE PAVEMENT . . .

*In which the Roses' debut album comes out
and slowly but surely changes the world*

*The Stone Roses' eponymous debut album is now regarded as one of the classic
British rock records. It captured the moment with euphoric songs that pulled off the
trick of combining classic rock'n'roll moments with the brand-new vibe. It was
the guitar record that caught the feeling of E without going acid house; it was the
future and the past captured in a nonstop series of fantastic songs that kept
building and building into a masterpiece.*

IAN BROWN

We recorded the songs in the summer of 88 during acid house. We
made them all before we took Es. But it made sense with acid house: we
were guitars and sixties melodies, but maybe Reni had the beat that
was connected somehow with acid house – it's up and we were about
the up. We were about community and the up, the positivity – nothing
can stop us feeling, we can do what we want, we're innocent. That
feeling when you took an E was: we are innocent – I've not done owt.
We used to freak journalists out because we used to have acid house
playing in interviews. they'd say, 'What's that you're listening to?' They
weren't into it, but we genuinely were playing it in cars and in coaches
on the way to gigs.

*On 12 August 1989 the Stone Roses played in front of 4000 people at the Empress
Ballroom, Blackpool.*

IAN BROWN

It was the big day out in Blackpool. It was the first time that we realised,
fucking hell, we got something here. We used to buzz off the fact that we
didn't look like any other band 'cos we'd got flares and John made our
shirts. With our printed psychedelic shirts we looked different.
Blackpool was buzzing. We looked at the crowd outside and we were
saying, 'Hang on, they got flares on and shirts like us!' It was an amazing
gig, the vibe was unreal. The video that was filmed of it is flat, it doesn't
capture it at all. The crowd were all E'd up, we were all together then. It
didn't feel like we were the superstar band and they were our fans. It felt
like we were all doing it together. It felt like it was a party and we were
playing the music.

GARETH EVANS

Blackpool was a day out and Manchester loves going to Blackpool. I wanted them to play different places where bands didn't normally go – places like the Winter Gardens, Ally Pally. I opened them up. I knew the scene was going to raves. It was the DJs I put on with the bands that made the gigs feel like raves.

IAN BROWN

There was general talk amongst us that we didn't want to just do the circuit – we never played the Boardwalk where everyone else played. We'd played the warehouse parties when we started and we wanted to take that further. We didn't want to play rock'n'roll venues. We wanted to play our own thing to keep it exciting – to keep it in line with that underground party atmosphere that was going on at the time. We'd done warehouse parties in 1986 and this was 1989 – we wanted to do places where bands didn't play. That was our number one priority.

All these kids at the gig weren't all Manchester kids: a lot came from Liverpool or St Helens – they were mainly northern kids. A lot of them were at their first gig. Maybe we were the first band they got into – they might not be regular gig goers.

STELLA

Blackpool I remember very well, and it was alright for the drugs at the time as well. Like the windowpanes* – everyone was tripping. There was flared pants; Joe Bloggs† – everyone found this little label.

The gig was just bouncing, sweating, tripping. Most of the audience were in the backstage bit; it wasn't all this, you know, You can't come in, it's VIPs only. I would have said about a third of the audience were backstage. It was that kind of feeling, a tribal feeling. We're all here, you know. Everyone knew about Blackpool. Got their drugs, everyone knew how they were getting there, got their lifts, you know everyone was getting in. I didn't buy a ticket, I don't know how I got in but I got in. It was silly to ignore that kind of fever, you know what I mean?

DAVE HASLAM

I was DJing at Blackpool; they asked me and Dave Booth to DJ. I think I got 50 quid for Blackpool and a night in a B&B.

---

* A type of acid.
† The Mancunian streetwear label that dressed the baggy hordes.

That day Blackpool was like Manchester on a day out. I can remember they set the DJ up at the back of the stage behind Jon Squire's amp.

Because I had been doing my night at the Hacienda, I knew exactly what to play and I have to say in that sense I was the perfect man for the job. I remember thinking everything I had learned about DJing for six years seemed to work that night. I really wanted it to work. I just knew the occasion for the Roses was really important. I had an hour to play before the band came on and it was absolutely fucking rocked with stuff like 'Big Fun' by Inner City. I remember playing 'Sympathy for the Devil', which was six minutes long, before they came on. If they were late, they would then have time to come on. I felt [it was] the right record, as one of the most memorable Rolling Stones gigs was in Blackpool, when it was a massive riot – it's only now I know the importance of that record in terms of Altamont etc. It's a big pop culture record and it had those 'woo woos' in it, which had the whole crowd grooving to it – it also had that baggy groove to it as well. I remember putting the record on and thinking, 'Yes, I've done my job.' Then the band came on and started with 'I Wanna Be Adored', and I suddenly realised that, where they had positioned me, I couldn't get off the stage. I spent the whole gig crouched down, so all I could see was the backs of the band. But I could feel this huge wave of audience excitement. There was almost a physicality about it. It was almost like I had been blown back – like a hurricane coming from the audience to the band.

IAN BROWN

Blackpool was like a rave. Everyone was on E except for us and my mum and dad! It felt like the city was behind us – they wanted us to go and make it. They wanted us to go and become massive – they wanted us to make it that Manchester thing. It was like that for all the bands. They say that the crowd is like the twelfth member in football and that was what it was like for all the bands. They put us there and the Mondays there and that started everything off.

On 21 November 1989 the famous Manchester takeover of Top of the Pops *took place, in the days when the programme and hit records still really mattered.*

IAN BROWN

Top of the Pops was absolutely fantastic. We shared a dressing room with the Happy Mondays. I remember being sat in the makeup room and Shaun [Ryder] being sat next to me asking if he could have my make-up, saying, 'He's a good looking fucker – look at my big hooter! Give me his make-up' (*laughs*). When we did the warm-up Mani went on the kit and

Gary Whelan went on the bass – we were going to swap and change about the line-ups for the actual take. It was Tony Wilson who persuaded us not to do it because outside Manchester no one would know who we were.

On 18 November 1989 the Roses took London, selling out the 7000-capacity Alexandra Palace.

IAN BROWN
Ally Pally was punk rock again. The place had a lot of history, this was where Pink Floyd had played in the psychedelic days.

DAVE HASLAM
Again they set me up on the stage, but this time I was near where the equipment was being brought on. I remember every time someone walked on, the record jumped. That gig felt like they were taking over London – there was that sense of an invasion, of an army changing the world, like away fans at a big football match going down to Wembley. The funny thing about Alexandra Palace was that there were people who had written Manchester off and suddenly they were all there.

JO BARTLETT
18th November, Ally Pally: that was our first Es! What a way to start! [Steve] Adge, who had been their tour manager when they played the Adershot Buzz Club, sorted us out passes for the aftershow at Ally Pally, then we went to the aftershow party at the Holloway Road studios. I think all the band apart from Ian were there. Mick Jones from the Clash was there.

IAN BROWN
The vibe was similar to Blackpool. Till showtime the vibe was amazing. Kids had travelled from all over the country to go to the gig and it was massive. There were 8000 people there. It looked massive at the soundcheck before anyone had got there. We had a quadraphonic sound system to get this mega sound. It was amazing by this time – we felt like the Beatles. We were the band of the time, but the actual show wasn't that great because of the sound – there was a delay from the back of the hall to the stage so what we put out was coming back a couple of seconds later and I don't know if we were out of time and all that. We were so tight as a band because we were so rehearsed. I don't think we enjoyed the gig on a musical level. I remember coming out with John afterwards to get in the car to go to the hotel and we were pretty long-faced because

we didn't enjoy the night. But it felt like a big deal – we were from the north and there were 8000 people there in London, at this place where the psychedelic happenings had happened in the sixties, and the atmosphere was fantastic.

DAVE HASLAM
The Roses were great because they had good record collections: there was something there if you were into the Byrds and there was that breakbeat-type element to some of the songs. A big part of the attraction was that kind of self-confidence, which was very key and very important as well. It felt very real and very authentic.

On 27 May 1990 the Stone Roses attracted 30,000 chemically altered people to a chemically altered location near Widnes with the unlikely name of Spike Island.

IAN BROWN
Spike Island was when I came out with, 'It's not where you're from, it's where you're at,' onstage.

It was almost like if you weren't from Manchester, you weren't cool, but what we buzzed off back to the Pistols was that the best music was trying to hit the doctor's son or the normal kid – everyone. It wasn't elitist. You knew you had all your mates with you; you knew everyone in the city loved you and it was about hitting the people that weren't like you, from a different part of society. That was what it was all about. I remember saying to Tony Wilson when he did the Madchester thing, 'It's not right, this – it excludes everyone else outside the Manchester postcode. It's saying like we are cool and they are not.' About two years later, when I did a documentary with Tony, he said, 'You know you were right. We shouldn't have done that. The Mondays never wanted to do that Madchester thing and we made them do it.'

PHIL JONES (promoter)
We drove round the country looking for these weird places to put them on at, like a motorbike dirt track in Essex where we met these gypsy guys who lived there who asked for too much money. Gareth lived near Spike Island and he heard that they did this annual small-town festival there. He went to have a look at it, met the council and signed up immediately. We wanted it to be in the north; it was a homecoming. Initially we were looking at doing two or three big gigs. Matthew somehow researched all the places – the more obscure the better. The deal was we had to play somewhere where no one had played before, somewhere outside the music industry.

JON SAVAGE

I wrote about the Roses at the time in relation to Morrissey, saying, 'He's the past and these guys are the future – they are saying something different.' I saw the Stone Roses and I had got the album when it came out and when no one really liked it. I saw them at Dingwalls and they were really good – the best time I saw them. I was really into the album. I was obsessed with 'Full Fathom 5' – I played it nonstop. Suddenly the scene is psychedelic-dayglo. I thought, great! Let's skin up – let's get going.

IAN BROWN

Spike Island was about not being a part of the system. I went round before the gig taking everyone's VIP passes off them. I was saying 'No VIPs.' I remember people with tears in their eyes because I was taking their VIP passes off them.

JIMMY MUDRICKZI (Puressence vocalist)

Me and Tony from the band went to Spike Island for some dancing in a field. The gig was so important. Look how many bands formed that day. The rest of the band were down there separately and [we thought], if they can do it then so can we. My brother knew Kev was forming a band. He rang me up, heard I could sing, so I went down and we formed Puressence.

IAN BROWN

There's a famous photo of Bonehead at Spike Island with his Pollocked-up van, his Stone Roses van all painted up. They all had the gear on.

GARETH EVANS

Spike Island was a year of meetings and committees. There was a march through Widnes against the festival with only two people with banners, saying they wanted me to go back to London. They obviously didn't know that I lived down the road in Northwich. Some people had a meeting, saying, 'Look at these needles full of heroin being left there.' I said we hadn't even been yet! A boat club there put a bridge in the canal to stop bridges [being built] to the island. Even when the army put the three bridges across the canal, it cost £60,000.

IAN BROWN

When we sat down and agreed to that show, we wanted it to break even. We wanted it to be 13 quid a head to cover the stage and PA. A few weeks later we found that they had made this money and people had had their butties taken off them at the gate – that sullied it for us on the night. The PA wasn't the best PA in the world; we should have had a bigger rig.

DAVE HASLAM
Blackpool was a celebration of something and Spike Island felt a bit more like the tail-end. I don't know, I felt it was chaotic – one of those gigs where I didn't think the band performed. It was also hard on the band.

MONKEY BUSINESS

In which court cases, legal issues, management wranglings, drugs and growing up all conspire to derail the Stone Roses

The Roses' weird career was about to get weirder. The band now had the whole world in their hands, but, after a handful of shows, they disappeared over the horizon.

STELLA
They weren't thinking about the dollar. I wouldn't have ever said that the Stone Roses were motivated by the money.

IAN BROWN
Glasgow Green was another great idea, the gigs in the big tops. Years later, when Radiohead did the big top tour, the agent said they took the idea from Glasgow Green, which was the ultimate Roses gig.

Glasgow was the best gig we ever played. It was raining in the tent with all the sweat, fantastic; the best gig we ever did.*

It all went downhill from there, it was really frustrating. We did the 'One Love' single, which I think wasn't too hot – the chorus wasn't strong enough. The B-side, 'Something's Burning', was great. If only we had done the 'Fools Gold'/'Something's Burning' style album at that time. What stopped us was that our lawyer said, 'If you release this in America, they can hold you to perpetuity and they can sign you forever. We can't let that run, plus your royalty rate is so so small.' So we got into a dispute with Zomba . . . We were looking at maybe only going to be able to do gigs and sell our own bootlegs and not make another album – which for me would have been a cool thing for a big band to do, sort of like the Grateful Dead did.

---

* The gig on 9 June 1990 in a 7000 capacity big top tent was perhaps the best gig they ever played and the last one with Reni.

We caught people with their hands in the cookie jar after Spike Island and we had all these court cases. We were keen not to blow it and to stay hungry. We had paid ourselves 60 quid a week until 'Fools Gold' came out and then we paid ourselves 100 quid a week, so we were still not lording it. And we were saying to Gareth, 'You look after the money, we'll sort it out later.' In the meantime we were still writing music. Me and John went up the Lake District to write some songs.

It was a bit strange because it was like we had written this masterpiece with the first album and now we had to follow it up. Looking back we had some really good tunes at the time that would have worked. So we had to start again and we got five or six pretty good tunes. I've got them on cassettes: there's one called 'English Electric Lighting' and one called 'Mr Shy Talk'.

We won the case in March 1991, so I bought a house in Wales, then John moved to the Lake District. We didn't know it then but we had started moving apart.

I had our Frankie in April '92 and John had a daughter at the end of '91 and that was another thing – we suddenly had kids and responsibilities and it wasn't a gang any more.

GARETH EVANS

The next thing was I got a letter from John Kennedy saying 'The band have sacked you.' And then we were in court.

They sacked me six months too soon – six months later I wouldn't have been able to afford to go to court!

IAN BROWN

John started writing over breakbeats and not really wanting to get anyone else involved in it.

We went out of our way to be a band without a frontman, to be a four piece – we were like the Beatles, there were four of us. U2 and the Stones lasted because they think, that's the singer's job, let him get on with it.

John was getting really into Led Zeppelin, but they didn't have the crowd we got. I remember saying to the rest of the band, 'Led Zeppelin don't have the plumbers, bricklayers, criminals and lesbians like us – potentially we got everyone in the world.'

In January 1993 we went to Square One in Bury and rehearsed every night till about June '93. We thought, shit, the songs are sounding great

– let's stay here, leave the gear here and get [John] Leckie* in and record. But it didn't work out, so we decided to move to a big house in Marple. Reni didn't start getting up till tea time and it frustrated Leckie because Leckie is a right grafter.

Add to this the combination of the court case and not having a manager – that did us in. We deliberately wanted to go with the biggest we could find and that's why we wanted to go with Geffen. The day we signed with Geffen, Maurice Oberstein from CBS drew up in his white Rolls-Royce and said, 'Come on Concorde now. I've got these seats booked and we'll sign on the plane.' We were saying, 'Fucking hell, what are we going to do now?' But we decided to go with Geffen because it was the devil we knew. It was LA, the Hollywood devil – they've got all this dough, let's go with them.

In July 1993 finally we went to Rockfield to record. We'd sacked Gareth by now, so it was four chiefs and no Indians. We loved the fact that we had been on Geffen Records for two years and they hadn't heard a note. We had been on there for two years, we got two million quid tax paid and had a million quid between us!

They say it took us five years to record but it was 15 months in that studio. I remember signing the guestbook when we left: 'quarter of a million and you get your dinner thrown in'. And in September 1994 we had finally finished the album.

THE RESURRECTION

In which the Stone Roses stumble in the mid-nineties daylight and find a world totally changed from the one they had last operated in

The second Stone Roses album, The Second Coming, *was finally released on 5 December 1994.*

IAN BROWN
We believed in that album at the time once we got it in the bag. I wrote a lot of lyrics on that album that I never put in. I changed all [John's]

---

* One of the most important producers in the UK, John Leckie has an extraordinary track record. Assistant engineer on the Beatles' *Abbey Road* and George Harrison's *All Things Must Pass* sessions, he worked on Syd Barrett's last ever recordings in 1974, as well as with Pink Floyd, before producing important punk and post-punk releases in the late seventies such as the Skids and XTC. Since producing the Roses' classic debut, he has moved on to work with bands like Radiohead and Muse. It was Mani's idea to use Leckie on the Roses debut album, because of his psychedelic production of XTC side project, Dukes of Stratosphere.

negatives into positives – there were loads of negatives. He had this line: 'I got his dead shrimp baby,' about male impotency and I said, 'I'm not singing that.' He was saying, 'It's dead powerful singing about male impotency,' and I was saying, 'I don't feel like that!' I wasn't a negative person; I didn't want to make a dark album. John's idea was the first album was all sunshine and colours so the second album would be dark. I was thinking, I don't like dark music – I love reggae and Tamla Motown and uplifting hip-hop and punk rock. I don't feel dark as a person. I don't feel I have a dark side. I mean, I might do, but I don't want to find it!

'Love Spreads' came out and went straight in at number two in the charts. There was a sense of excitement. We had a big world tour planned – the agent got out a world map and said, 'Here's a pin. Where do you want to go?'

But then Reni was out of the band. Me and him had a row. We were sick of it. We couldn't wait any longer for him. He didn't turn up for the interview with the *Big Issue*, which was our first interview – and was for the homeless, which would be a positive thing from us, for six homeless people in Islington to get homes off the money we raised. The next day we had a video for 'Ten Storey Love Song' to make and he didn't turn up for that either. We said, 'We can't wait for this kid any longer.' Then there was a cover of the *NME* that only me, Mani and John appeared on. It was like the comeback cover and there's only three of us on the fucking cover because he didn't turn up.

We just got fed up with Reni not turning up. One day me and him had a bit of a barney and he said to me, 'Right, get yourself another drummer,' so I did. I heard that Robbie Maddox was a good drummer, so I phoned him up and that was it.

The next day Reni phoned me and said, 'I need to get down to rehearsal early so that me and Mani can rehearse and you and John can come down later.' I said, 'I've done what you told me to do last night.' He said, 'What do you mean?' and I said, 'You told me to get another drummer, so I have.' I said, 'What you going to do now then?' And he said, 'Sign on, I suppose.' I said, 'I'll make sure you get your quarter of money.'

It was sad, but we couldn't be waiting on the kid any more.

John was going mad but John hadn't spoken to Reni for ages. To be honest it annoyed me, because it was like I had forced Reni to leave the band.

The world tour for the album was mega-fantastic. It went so well that at the end we were playing Sheffield Arena and Wembley Arena. Wembley was our last gig, then John leaves as well. As we left Wembley Arena that night, I remember seeing him waving from the window of the bus. Looking back now he was going 'Goodbye.' It was March 1996 and he left three months later, when he phoned us. I hadn't spoken to him in between.

On tour there was a distance between us because it was all different drugs. We set out to destroy the dinosaurs in the punk days and we had become the dinosaurs ourselves.

The last ever Stone Roses gig took place at the Reading Festival on 28 August 1996.

IAN BROWN

I honestly thought after John left, great, this is a brand new start – we can call ourselves the Brand New Stone Roses. John's left, you know, and Aziz [Ibrahim] is a fucking brilliant player and he's come in. I met Aziz through Robbie [Maddox]; they had played on the Rebel MC together, so I thought, let's give Aziz a shot. I had met him before I heard him play and I thought he was fucking brilliant. He was a fan of the Roses – he knew all the tunes inside out – and I naively thought it wouldn't matter, we could just carry on.

We did a few festivals round Europe and then Reading Festival. Slash offered to play at Reading with us and we said, 'Tell him and his boa constrictor to fuck off!' At the time we thought he was an LA twat, but we were wrong – it would have been really fucking amazing.

The thing is, we were ridiculed for that gig, but I saw thousands of arms in the air at the gig. I've heard the tapes and I know I was singing in a different key to the band for most of the tunes, but at the time I didn't see this mass exodus of people crying and people's worlds caving in. I just saw 60,000 arms in the air when we walked off the stage. As I came off stage there's our man Cressa again. I remember I was buzzing and I thought it was going to be ace. I came down the ramp and Cressa said, 'You got to end it! It's just a debacle.' I didn't realise till the next day that I was singing out of tune.

It was punk rock to play the big show and blow it – not many do!

We got in a room, got a cassette and recorded loads of rubbish for 20 minutes and posted it, saying, 'Here's our new tune now John's left.' I wish I had kept a copy – it sounded like the Fall or something . . . I said prayers and sent this poor B-side demo and got us dropped on purpose, luckily.

UNFINISHED MONKEY BUSINESS

In which Ian Brown goes solo

IAN BROWN

I was ready to sign on really. I sold my old Portastudio for 400 quid. I thought, I've got to make this 400 quid last as long as possible. Then I got a cheque for £8000, which was my cut of the publishing due from *The Second Coming*. I had given up music, thinking, what's it all about? I moved back to my mum's; I thought, what's it all about? I've not got a pot to piss in. I've got no band and two of my best mates have gone.

I then moved to Lymm. Aziz came round to the house one day, knocked on the door and said, 'Let's do some tunes,' and I got interested again. Nigel and Robbie rented a house in Lymm so we could all be close and work close. We were going to call the band the Brown. They said, 'We'll back you up and we'll write a song with just us,' because we couldn't find Mani – Mani went well wayward at the time!

We wanted to include Mani because we wanted that bass. He then phoned me up and said, 'Primal Scream have asked me to do a tour, but I want your blessing for it.' I knew that they had asked him to join, and he wanted my blessing. I was like, 'Fucking get out and do it!' It still touches me to know that he rang.

The guys said, 'Why don't you go solo?' I said, 'I don't want to go solo,' and they said, 'That's the obvious thing to do!' It was like when I first started, when Geno Washington said, 'You're a singer,' and I said, 'I don't know what you're talking about.'

The first album *Unfinished Monkey Business* was meant to be like you're sat in my bedroom, sat on my bed listening to my songs. *The Second Coming* was so overblown that I wanted my album to be the opposite.

I was really made up when 'My Star'* went straight in at number five – that was a fucking big achievement. Then the album went in at number four and I was like on fucking cloud nine, because suddenly I was back in the music. And I signed for five albums.

The 'Monkey Business' bit came from this *Guardian* story, when they rang Rockfield. Him out of Dodgy was staying there and they asked him about us making the Roses' second album. He said that 'He only answers to the name King Monkey,' which was fucking brilliant (*laughs*). He said, 'He's so up his own arse that he only answers to the name King Monkey.'

---

* The psychedelic tumbling arpeggio of 'My Star' was an impressive debut single.

MATTHEW PRIEST

I was a massive Roses fan and it turns out that we were next to them at Rockfield Studios when we were at the start of the recording for what was to become our *Homegrown* album* – probably around Nov '93, so the Roses had been 'quiet' for a few years now. We were recording with Ian Broudie at the time, so we would be finishing around midnight, which is when they would be starting with Paul Schroeder, who we knew because he produced our first three singles (mainly because we liked the sound he got on their first album). After a few days, Schroeder popped by and invited us round to the Roses' studio . . . They hugged us like old friends, were very warm and invited us to skin up on an Aerosmith CD from a fucking huge bag of grass.

We finished our session with Ian and moved up to the Chapel Studios in rural Lincolnshire to finish our album with Hugh Jones. I'd done my bits so I was kicking around trying to entertain myself when the phone rang and it was a journalist from the *Guardian*, asking if I was in Dodgy and did I mind telling her anything about the time we were recording next to the Stone Roses.

Now, I was a bit miffed at the fact that she didn't want to know anything about Dodgy, so I decided to wind her up a bit, and because there had been no news at all from the Roses camp in several years, she was desperate for any info.

So I told her that Reni played all the guitars; that the album was named after the KC and the Sunshine Band tune; that they were doing a cover of 'Desperado' by the Eagles. Then, just to really take the piss, I told her that Ian would only answer to King Monkey. Don't know where it came from but probably because he looks a lot like a monkey (*laughs*). Ian may have actually said, 'Never trust a man with a beard,' but I can't be sure.

Then that was it. She thanked me and I specifically asked her not to mention my name. I told the boys and we had a giggle, then thought nothing of it until the piece came out in the *Guardian*.

IAN BROWN

As far as I thought, I had already made the ultimate record with the Roses, so it was great to be making some stuff on my own. I could never be in another band like that. There was no point in even trying. I didn't have any ambitions to do it again.[†]

---

* Featuring 'Staying Out for the Summer' etc.
[†] Brown has gone on to release a series of brilliant, idosyncratic, highly original solo albums and retained his iconic status.

14

INSPIRAL CARPETS

After the Roses and the Mondays, the Inspiral Carpets were the third band of the late-eighties Manchester boom. Their Farfisa-driven garage pop had long roots, back to the early eighties when various Oldham bands gradually appeared. They were the first of the three so-called baggy Manchester bands to break though to minor cult status, followed by attention from John Peel and national tours; they then got swept up in the whole Madchester explosion with a number two album, 1990's Life, *several hit singles and three further top 20 albums – 1991's* The Beast Inside, *1992's* Revenge of the Goldfish *and 1994's* Devil Hopping *– before splitting in 1995.*

CLINT BOON
Graham started the Inspiral Carpets in 1981. They were called the Furs because Graham was a big Psychedelic Furs fan. They went through various line-ups before eventually becoming the Inspiral Carpets. I think they had 13 bass players by the time I recorded them in my demo studio.

GRAHAM LAMBERT
I formed the Inspiral Carpets in 1981. We couldn't really play proper instruments at first and just messed around with acoustic guitars. Someone eventually brought an electric round and we added that to our jam sessions. The other members all fell by the wayside because they were more into clubbing on Fridays and Saturdays – being a Peel addict I found that going out clubbing wasn't for me, I was more into seeing bands. At this time I was into Psychedelic Furs and Bauhaus, Sid Presley Experience and listening to John Peel or watching *The Tube* on TV.

The Inspirals had stopped for a few months and then I hooked up with Stephen Holt, who I knew from playing football for Oldham Boys. He was into indie bands like I was, but the lighter bands like June Brides, the Mighty Lemon Drops and the Shop Assistants. We were mates and avid

John Peel listeners so I resurrected the band with Stephen in 1983. By then I had learned to play guitar properly, learning chords from Johnny Cash songbooks. Now I could write a song based round four chords!

CLINT BOON

I was the company director in a furniture business in Guide Mill on South Street in Ashton and I had lots of space in the Mill, so I put musical equipment in there and opened up a demo studio and a rehearsal space. Chris introduced me to Mani, who was in a band called the Exit, in late 1983 in the Miners Arms pub in Oldham. They were Perry boys. I did management for the Exit as well as another band called the Klingons.

We decided to form our own band in 1984 called the Mill* with Mani on bass, Chris on drums and me on the organ. We were three like-minded individuals and we jammed every Sunday down the Mill, where I had my own home-built studio. I couldn't play anything properly at the time and we were playing all this mad music. It was bonkers. A lot of it was avant-garde, a lot of shouting.

Mani is great. He's always up for anything! And he played decent bass and guitar whilst I played the organ. We were really into psychedelic music and occasionally did covers of Joy Division or the Bunnymen. We were also doing stuff like Suicide's 'Frankie Teardrop' and recording smashing bottles and metal percussion. We sounded like Einsturzende Neubauten, but a more psychedelic version. We never did gigs, we just recorded rehearsals from 1984 to 1985. I've still got the tapes somewhere.

Mani knew Ian Brown and Andy Couzens and he heard that they were getting a band together, so we had this idea to get this sort of supergroup going with all five of us in it.

So a week later Ian Brown and Andy Couzens arrived at the Mill in this big flash car. Andy had this quiff and this nice semi-acoustic guitar and was into playing this jangly guitar stuff. It was pretty different from the sort of music that we were into! It didn't quite gel and they quickly left.

Andy was a rockabilly guitarist and Ian was a conventional singer, whilst I was into driving trucks over microphones and Mani was recording smashing bottles into bins. It always makes me laugh when I think of that meeting.

IAN BROWN

I met Clint Boon though Mani, who was in a band called the Hungry Sox

* Or T'Mill.

as well as playing with Clint. I went up to their studio for a meeting. I didn't want to sing the stuff they were doing. I didn't like the kind of music they were doing. So I pretended I didn't like the mike I was using and said I'd never sung in my life before.

CLINT BOON

A few months later, in mid '85, I got a call from Chris Goodwin, who had started jamming with the Inspiral Carpets and who wanted to record a demo at my studio with the band.

I took the demo to Spain on a two-week holiday and I thought, this is what I so want to be in – a punk band with keyboards. I had already bought a Farfisa keyboard because I was collecting instruments to make music with. I thought, if I put my organ into the band, then it will sound like the Velvet Underground.

When I came back from holiday I said to Graham, 'The demo is brilliant,' and told him that my organ would sound good on that. I went to a rehearsal and plugged the organ in and played. Craig, the drummer, was 14 and had just joined. He's said to this day he didn't know what was going on! There was never a conversion like, 'Can I be in your band?' 'Do you want to jam with us?' It just happened.

GRAHAM LAMBERT

We had started rehearsing at Clint's place in Ashton and slowly Clint worked his way into the band! He had been playing synth and managing T'Challa Grid but really wanted to play his Farfisa. In the autumn of '86, after we recorded the demo at his studio, I told him to wheel his Farfisa into the practice room to rehearse with us. Clint brought his organ in and we hit it off. It was brilliant for me because the others didn't have my drive, whilst Clint had this mad urge to be successful. Clint looked like one of the Seeds and he had a positive outlook on life and was brilliant at keyboards and backing vocals.

We played with the Happy Mondays at the Boardwalk in January 1987 – oddly it was the only time we actually played with them. Sean and Bez took Craig under their wing because he was a 15-year-old scally. Craig was a bit of a jack the lad who would have a case of beer from the venue and a spliff, so the Mondays liked him.

CLINT BOON

At first we were very psychedelic. But we had the advantage that we were diverse as people – I was 26 and listening to the Seeds and 13th Floor Elevators, whilst we had a drummer who was 14 and into hip-hop. That gave us another flavour and made us different and more modern. It was that mixture of styles that made us. Also Stephen Holt was a great singer. Then the bass player left.

GRAHAM LAMBERT
We were still going through line-up changes. That was our tenth bass player!

SCOTT CAREY
One evening I met Clint Boon in the toilet of the Castle in Oldham and nine days later I was playing bass with the Inspiral Carpets supporting the Bodines in London. I had a week to learn the songs and only made one fuck-up at the gig.

GRAHAM LAMBERT
Scott came in after Mark Hughes left in May 1987. We did the *Debris* magazine flexi in March 1987 and got to know Nathan McGough, who was managing the Bodines. By now the Happy Mondays were on the move with their debut album out, things were changing in Manchester. We also got to know Spacemen 3.

SCOTT CAREY
The Inspirals had the psychedelic oil lamps going on and Clint had a Farfisa going through a distortion pedal. We also used to do a 15-minute version of 'What Goes On' by the Velvet Underground which we were best known for.

GRAHAM LAMBERT
We did the *Dung 4* tapes on Cow Records – and then we supported the Stone Roses at the International 1, which was Mani's first gig with the Roses.

SCOTT CAREY
After gigs, we always went back to Guide Bridge to unload the gear but Reni was having a party and I thought, bollocks to this, Reni is having a party! It's the Stone Roses and I was invited! So I went. Two days later, Ricky Turner was round my house and we were getting stoned watching *Apocalypse Now* for the thirtieth time – we were into the psychedelic scenes and not so much into the political side of it back then. There was a knock on the door and it was the Inspiral Carpets with my bass and amp. I said, 'Hello, how ya doing!' I was a bit stoned. They said, 'We got some news, if you want to party you're in the wrong band, basically you

should help with gear.' I said, 'Bollocks. I love the Roses and that party was a one-off.' But that was it, I was sacked. It was Clint and Graham's band and they made the decision. That really hurt at the time. It was a bit ruthless! So me and Ricky formed the Paris Angels instead.

CLINT BOON
So we needed another bass player! And brought in David Swift.

We were doing gigs in Manchester and the faces started turning up, like Paul the hat man, who had the hat stall in Afflecks Palace,* as well as Geoff the pirate and all these other faces of Manchester – they were loving it. Then Paula Greenwood picked up on the *Debris* flexidisc and released the *Planecrash* EP on her label, Playtime in 1988. The *Planecrash* EP was titled that because I had recurring dreams about plane crashes. That song was about seeing someone's married life going downhill and that deteriorating relationship was like a plane crash.

GRAHAM LAMBERT
We got the *Planecrash* EP to John Peel in July 1988 and he started his show with it. I was on holiday with Karen in Scotland when he played it. I tried to find a phone box in the pitch black and ring the band but couldn't get hold of them. From then on it changed – we had a session and he played every track several times. It felt like we were on our way. But David Swift and Stephen had a problem because of their jobs. It was the lowest point of my life when I got back from rehearsal and Stephen said, 'I don't like the way it's going, it's going too fast.' We had strived for six years to get to this point. We were going to London to play gigs after work – we would get there at the last minute, then play 20 minutes and then drive back. It was insane but it was starting to take off. John Peel was all over us.

CLINT BOON
Noel [Gallagher] and Craig were at a party somewhere and bumped into Tony Wilson. Tony asked Craig to get us on *The Other Side of Midnight†* but, within a week or so, Stephen and David had left. So we phoned Tony and he said, 'Do an instrumental anyway.' He was well up for it so we played 'Directing Traffic'. To me that was the real cavalier attitude of

---

* Packed with great independent stalls and shops, the iconic Afflecks Palace (now called Afflecks) is the creative hub of the Manchester scene. Not just a place to buy clothes and cool bric-a-brac, it's a melting pot and a meeting place. It was opened in 1982 in the old department store, Afflecks.
† *The Other Side of Midnight* was a late-eighties Granada weekly regional culture slot, fronted by Tony Wilson.

Manchester. The never-say-die thing. That sort of spirit was crucial to the whole scene. Martyn Walsh came in on bass and this was his first appearance with us. It was our first TV break.

GRAHAM LAMBERT

So me, Clint and Craig held the fort whilst we tried to get another singer or knock it on the head. History says that losing your singer is like signing your own death warrant, but we got Tom Hingley from Too Much Texas, who had supported us at the back end of '88. He was different from us because he was a southerner from Oxford, but he was a really good singer. We also auditioned another singer from Burnage called Noel.

CLINT BOON

Noel was a friend and a fan. He was one of the first people who said he wanted to audition. All I can remember was that he was this kid with the broken leg from Burnage. That scally that used to follow us around and hang out with us.

NOEL GALLAGHER

I used to go and see the Inspirals at the International. I remember going to a band night that was being broadcast on some radio station in Manchester. On the bill it was the Inspirals, the Waltones and Ed Barton, who sang a song about his dog just dying. That was when I first saw the Inspirals. They did a version of 'What Goes On' by the Velvet Underground – they were brilliant then, when it was minimalist they were great.

GRAHAM LAMBERT

It was May '88 when I met Noel at a Roses gig.

NOEL GALLAGHER

At this Stone Roses anti-Clause 28 gig, I see a guy on the balcony and he's got a little tape recorder with the red lights on. He's obviously bootlegging the gig so I go up to him. At this point the Stone Roses had just released 'Sally Cinnamon' and I wasn't aware of their early records, but I had bought 'Sally Cinnamon' at their gig earlier that year at the International 1. I went up to him and said, 'What you doing there?' I didn't know him from Adam, so I said, 'If I give you my address will you send me a copy?' He said yeah, so we got talking. He asked what other bands I was into. I said 'I like the Waltones, Happy Mondays, the Inspiral Carpets . . .' And he said, 'I'm in the Inspiral Carpets.' We kept in contact through this fucking Stone Roses tape.

At the next Inspirals gig I saw him and it turned out to be their last gig with their singer Stephen Holt. I think Graham then called me up and said, 'You know the tunes, do you want to try and be the singer?' I thought, wow, fucking hell. I could be the singer! So I went down to audition. I had never sung before. They thought I knew the tunes and obviously I must have looked the part because I was in trainee hooligan gear – beige Lacoste bomber jacket, jeans and trainers, like the Happy Mondays wore as well.

CLINT BOON

Noel had been tagging along, coming to gigs, and Craig said Noel wanted to sing. We thought, 'He can't sing, can he?' So we had the audition. He came down. He also had a cassette with loads of songs on it which he'd been working on in his own time – there were no eventual Oasis songs on there. Noel auditioned with us on the night of the Lockerbie disaster, on 21 December 1988. That night while Noel was auditioning for the Inspirals that plane flew over Ashton, which is on the flight path – which is one of those weird moments. At about ten o'clock I went out to the car and put John Peel on. At midnight he finished his show and said, 'Thanks for listening and maybe we should go and see what's left of Scotland.' Then I heard the news that the plane had gone down at Lockerbie, where it turns left to fly over the Atlantic.

NOEL GALLAGHER

I went down to their rehearsal room at the Mill and I remember having to take about twenty buses to get there. It was fucking miles away! I'd never been that far out of town in my fucking life and it was on a real dark winter's night. This was all before mobile phones – you had to take someone's word that they would be there.

Outside the Mill there was this bus stop. I get there and there's Graham. So we walk around to their little rehearsal room, and we go in and he introduces me to everybody. They were talking to me like I was a professional audition expert – they said, 'What do you want to do?' and I was like literally saying 'I haven't got a fucking clue! I only asked him for a copy of the Roses tape!' I was winging it. They assumed I was a musician but all I am is a glorified glue-sniffing pothead from Manchester! The first song we did was 'Gimme Shelter' from the Rolling Stones and I shouted my fucking head off, then I did a few of their tunes. I remember it was quite alright, but they didn't say yes immediately, which is always a bad sign, although I didn't know that at the time.

Afterwards Graham kept in touch and asked me to be his roadie. I learnt to roadie on the hoof. All Manchester roadies were always like that, it was just people's mates.

GRAHAM LAMBERT

We didn't make him the singer and, still to this day, I don't regret it. I've got a lot of time for Noel. He turned out to be a brilliant songwriter, but his voice didn't seem to cut through on our sound. A lot of our songs were like heavy football chant anthems, whereas Noel has got a good voice – a soft and tender voice – so I didn't feel like he was the right choice. If we had picked him, it would have been a very different career for us. I think in the end everyone benefited from the decision we made when we got Tom – he had a great voice.

CLINT BOON

Stephen had a really powerful voice and Noel sings like I sing, which is a pretty thin type of voice. I thought, if I wanted a singer like Noel I could move to the front and do it. We wanted someone who sounded like a crooner and we had already heard Tom Hingley sing with Too Much Texas. We had done a couple of gigs with Tom and we heard their Peel session. They did this song called 'Jay', an amazing, beautiful piece of music with an incredible voice on it. We phoned him up and said, 'We're looking for a singer.' He said, 'I'm coming but I'm going to tell Too Much Texas first.' I think he had left Too Much Texas before he came to the audition. He did it as a sign of respect to them. He didn't want to be unfaithful. When he joined, our only conditions were for him to get a fringe, because he had his hair greased back, and to stop dancing on the stage, because he used to run around a lot up and down the walls – he did it at the audition a lot. At the next rehearsal he had a fringe and was standing stock still. That's why, on *Top of the Pops* with 'This Is How It Feels', he's as stiff as a board. He stood there like that because we told him not to move.

TOM HINGLEY

Too Much Texas had moved to Manchester from Oxford and Bristol. We did a Peel session and supported New Order and we did a single. It was going OK for us but we were struggling – at the same time I used to collect glasses at the Hacienda to make ends meet. We did loads of gigs at the Boardwalk. We supported the House of Love, the Beloved, the Vaselines. We then did the single on Uglyman Records and played in London at Dingwalls with Seymour, who became Blur. There was a handbags-at-dawn disagreement with Seymour.*

At the same sort of time that we had released the Too Much Texas single,

---

* This incident was obliquely referenced in the Blur song 'Mace', the B-side of 'Popscene'.

I went into Piccadilly Records* and I found a copy of the Inspirals' first single. I wish I'd bought it, it's worth £250 now! I saw an address for Playtime Records on the back, walked into Playtime and gave Paula Greenwood, who ran the label, a demo of Too Much Texas which she liked. We got some gigs with the Inspirals. Then when Stephen Holt left the Inspirals their manager Anthony Boggiano rang me and I auditioned with them.

GRAHAM LAMBERT

We were auditioning singers and Tom was really up for it. He had been the driving force in Too Much Texas. The rest of them hadn't been so driven, so he was keen to make a break.

TOM HINGLEY

I wanted a career in music and this was a great chance. Sometimes in life you have to be aware of opportunities to get your music heard on a wider stage. I had been playing in bands for 13 years and this was my chance. Also the Inspirals were really, really good. If they hadn't found a good singer, the band wouldn't have survived. They had done the work, they were already in John Peel's Festive Fifty. What I could bring to the Inspirals was a good vocal range – and I could write lyrics and interpret lyrics and bring something arty to the band.

After three weeks we went to record the vocals for the next single, 'Joe', in early 1989 for Playtime. Graham and Clint sat in the studio and said, 'Hey, you got a lisp!' I said, 'Too late, I'm in the band!'

Noel had broken his leg working for British Gas and came and worked with us instead. It was an interesting time because it wasn't like a party – everyone was working very hard and was part of a small entourage. Noel was young, very bright and very funny, there was a lot about him. I'm a southerner from a different place – I used to give him a lift home after gigs and got to know him quite well.

CLINT BOON

When we weren't on the road, Noel worked in the office, where he was doing things like answering the phone and replying to fan mail, sending signed photos, sending T-shirts. We employed him for four-and-a-half years. When people say he was our roadie, he was more important than that. He worked for us every day at our office in New Mount Street.

---

* The main Manchester underground and independent record shop.

Debbie, my girlfriend at the time, and Noel were our employees. Noel was included in everything we did, from our rehearsals to all the meetings. He was invited to meetings with Daniel Miller who ran Mute, our record label, or our publishers.

NOEL GALLAGHER

I just winged being a roadie till I learned how to do it. I remember changing strings on his guitar and he said, 'You don't half put them on fucking weird.' I was like 'Aaargh! Hope it stays in tune, you bastard!' Me, Graham and Clint really got on at the time – having a craic. I was really into music, I was into Yargo at the time – they were fucking brilliant – that album was amazing.* I still got the cassette that I bought and I still play it round at ours now. I'd say, 'If you really like reggae music, listen to this.' Basil Clarke was a great singer. I saw them quite a lot and the Carpets were like, 'Wow, you like that kind of music!'

CLINT BOON

We started the whole cow ethos round what we were doing. We were doing the merchandise because we didn't have a record deal and we had expenses running the office in Sackville Street. We needed to have money from somewhere so we started a range of T-shirts. The first cow T-shirt was a T-shirt I made myself for the *Other Side of Midnight* appearance. The cow shirt became quite iconic. When I made the 'cool as fuck' version with the cow in shades smoking a spliff, that was when it went mad. Everyone wanted it then – it didn't even have Inspiral Carpets written on it!

At the time only metal bands had T-shirts – you wouldn't see New Order, Bodines or Close Lobsters T-shirts, it wasn't the done thing. We made a name for ourselves as a cottage industry. We were self-sufficient, selling frisbees, balloons, baseball caps. If you could get Inspiral Carpets on it then you could sell it.

We released and sold loads of a cassette, *Dung 4*, which had original versions of the songs with Stephen singing. With that and the T-shirt money we recorded the first album and when we signed the Cow label to Mute they paid for the mixing and release.

GRAHAM LAMBERT

The style of shirts we did worked with our audience. The days of having all the tour dates on the back were over. We went to another level. We did quality merchandising. You still see them today.

* Yargo's dub-drenched, highly original music, as heard on their two albums, 1987's *Bodybeat* and 1989's *Communicate*, stands the test of time.

CLINT BOON

For a period we were on Playtime and we were hot property. We'd done the Peel session by that point and we were saying to Paula that we wanted to stick with her despite other people wanting us. The new single, 'Joe', was all pressed up and it started taking a long time to come out; then Playtime's distributor, Red Rhino, collapsed and left a lot of little labels high and dry. Paula was looking for another distributor for the whole label. We were worried we might miss the boat. We said to Paula, 'We can't wait any longer, we're setting up our own label called Cow.' And we left.

The Cow thing came from when, back in the eighties, I was photographing these cows. When the band started doing gigs, I projected the cow pictures behind us as visuals to detract from the fact that we weren't good-looking and we were a static band. I would set the lights, bubbles and smoke machine up after soundcheck. I controlled all the light show myself from the stage.

TOM HINGLEY

We set up our own label because there was no way we wanted to sign to Factory. With me working at the Hacienda I realised that, despite the fact that they found some fantastic bands, as businessmen they were bonkers.

GRAHAM LAMBERT

At the end of '89 we were in the right place at the right time. People were saying the next single would be top 40. We were getting more commercial as we went along. For me Peel getting behind the band was a major box ticked because I was an avid Peel listener. Craig quickly reminded me that there was more to life than John Peel – there was the rest of the world as well.

We toured in February 1989 when we dropped everything we were doing and decided to go for it full time. In April 1989 we supported James on a UK tour – they seemed massive at the time, playing universities.

We did the mileage with loads of gigs. The next single, 'Joe', came out in May 1989 and then 'Find Out Why' came out in August 1989 – each single was much bigger than the one before. We played the Hacienda in September 1989 and then put out 'Move', which was a lot more commercial, in November '89 and it was our first top 50 hit. We were on a roll at this point – big tour, Steve Wright in the Afternoon playing us. And then the big turning point was February 1990. 'This Is How It Feels' came out and we went into the top 20 and did our first *Top of the Pops*.

TOM HINGLEY

From early in our career we didn't want to be seen as a Happy Mondays support band. There was an occasion when their agent Brian Turner rang us up. They were playing G-Mex in March 1990 and we heard rumours that we were meant to be supporting them. It would have been a great gig but it was important initially for us not to be supporting the Happy Mondays, because we didn't want to be nailed on to someone else's career. We told our manager Anthony to tell them 'We're playing G-Mex ourselves in six months.' Anthony told them and then we rang up Simon Moran* and told him to book G-Mex for us. He said we were crazy but, if we gave him twenty thousand quid towards the gig, he would promote it. He did, and the gig was a sell-out.

GRAHAM LAMBERT

We were right in the middle of the Manchester scene when it took off. The Roses and the Mondays and the Inspirals – we were there. We didn't say it ourselves but we were put on the pedestal.

CLINT BOON

When Manchester kicked off, we were recognised as being one of the three. We just missed getting on *Top of the Pops* first out of those bands. We had brought out 'Move' at the end of 1989 and that was number 41 in the charts – in those days you had to be in the top 40 to get on *Top of the Pops*. A few weeks later there was that famous *Top of the Pops* that the Roses and the Mondays were on. I'm not convinced if we had got there first to *Top of the Pops* it would have been seen as such an iconic moment, but it would have been cool!

Our debut album, 1990's *Life*, is the classic band debut – you've spent five years getting your shit together and it comes out very diverse musically. A lot of debut albums are written over a long period of time with lots of different sources coming in, like leaving school, meeting girls, growing up. The record was very psychedelic with a patchwork of influences. The following year we released *The Beast Inside*, which was quite different. We got Chris Nagle in to produce because we wanted a darker sound. It was a record made by a band that was travelling the world and getting experiences of the world outside Oldham – writing songs about protestors outside the White House or visiting Dachau. In many ways, it was a reaction to the poppiness of the first album.

* Now a top UK concert promoter and still Manchester-based, Simon Moran runs SJM.

Anthony stopped managing us and Noel continued with us till early '92. But his heart wasn't in it, the drugs were playing a part in it as well, to the point where we couldn't work with him (*laughs*). But right to the end we treated him right.

GRAHAM LAMBERT

He had been with us from '88. At the end of '92 we need to have a clearout of backroom staff. They were getting jaded and had lost respect for the band. We slagged each other off all the time, but when the roadies are having a dig at the band as well, then you know you need a change. We were going to tour America in '93 and we decided to change things then. Noel had had enough standing around watching me play guitar – he was hanging around with Mark Coyle and they were jamming after soundchecks. He needed the break, even if it took him a year to get going afterwards. He wanted to play guitar all the time and not count T-shirts in our office.

It wasn't pleasant sacking him but we're not the first band that had to do it. Afterwards he said he would never have a roadie as lazy as he was when he worked for us!

NOEL GALLAGHER

On the first Inspirals tour, their monitor engineer was Mark Coyle, who I had met on the first night of the tour, and we decided that we were going to share a room together. On the tour, before the band did the soundcheck, he would get on the drum kit and I would get on guitar and we would play. He actually came up with the intro for 'Live Forever' way back because he would play that beat. I would play Graham's guitar, I would play these chords and Coyley would say, 'What is that? They're fucking great chords. You should write a song round that!' That was where 'Live Forever' came from.

So in the soundchecks he would play the drums and I would play chords on guitar and he would say, 'You're pretty good, man.' I had no ambitions to be in a group at the time. I thought, I've arrived here – that's got to be it.

CLINT BOON

Noel had Oasis at this point. We went to the early Oasis gigs to give him our support. When we sacked him we gave him a big chunk of dosh, we said, 'We're off to America and you've got Oasis now.' He was gutted but it had to be done. It was in the Roadhouse. We were rehearsing upstairs with the Inspirals and he was downstairs with Oasis. After the rehearsal, all five of us went down there to see him. He was sat there on one of the amps. He was cool about it. He said, 'You're a bunch of cunts,' and laughed. We gave him a couple of grand like a redundancy, knowing that money would help with his band.

Even right at the end and even after Madchester had finished, we were still having proper hits. The last album did well and 'I Want You', which we did with Mark Smith, was a top 20 hit in 1994.

We decided to use Mark Smith on the single because we were sick of remixing our tracks. We had used good people like Justin Robertson and 808 State but this time round we decided to do collaborations instead.

Mark Smith had been an icon of mine for years. I got to know him, I put the call in. He said 'Gimme three grand and I'll do it.' It was hard work – he's the king of chaos – we did a video with him, several interviews and the only *Top of the Pops* appearance that he ever made. It was an amazing thing to be a part of. But you couldn't do it full time. He offered me a place in the Fall after the Inspirals split but I thought it was better to remain a fan and a friend.

After those last hits, if we'd held on six more months we could have done what Pulp did and got big with Britpop. At the beginning of '94 we had a couple of hit records, headlined the second stage at Glastonbury, but then Daniel Miller, the head of Mute, said that they had done all the developing that they could and dropped us. We were shocked. No one would sign us even though we were top 20. We would have survived, as Britpop was just a continuation of the Manchester bands.

GRAHAM LAMBERT

Mute at the end of the day was just a business. We were the first band they dropped. Daniel Miller did say after he let us go he thought that we would have no trouble getting a deal, but we didn't. For a time Nathan McGough was interested in signing us to East West Records and there was some interest from Nude, but when you get dropped by the label it's a kick in the teeth! Clint wanted go for a job on MTV, Martin wanted to do solo electronic stuff, so we decided to call it a day.

CLINT BOON

I don't regret what happened. After it all gave me a life outside the Inspirals. We had ability in the band but I can't play like Dave Greenfield.* You can satisfy a stadium of people with what we do. I'm quite proud of the level of songs we could write – I wrote 'Sackville', it

* The Stranglers' masterly keyboard player.

makes me tremble I could write that song! I wasn't a fully developed person, and I wrote a song about prostitution and the red-light area which was well written. All my songs were conversational – I very rarely wrote about me – apart from 'This Is How It Feels', which was about my infidelity. I had to disguise what I'd done in a fictitious song in a family setting where a woman had an affair in the song. I felt so bad about what had happened so I put it into the song.

We did several world tours. Japan, Europe, Argentina. We got far in countries that we didn't expect. We were big in Argentina – we played the River Plate stadium with Paul Simon. We did a lot, we achieved more than we set out to achieve. We started as a garage band to play tunes after our day jobs, like the Seeds or Jefferson Airplane, and we ended up doing a world tour.

15

BAGGY

In the wake of the Mondays' and the Roses' big breakthrough, Manchester became pop central. There was a whole style, look and language with its own drugs and soundtrack. The city enjoyed one of those white-heat moments in pop culture when the glare is on a single location – like San Francisco in the late sixties or London during punk.

Madchester, as it was now known, had a second wave of bands who copped the critical backlash but were making great music. Like punk's second wave, these bands were inspired by or part of the initial explosion and then set out on their own idiosyncratic routes. Manchester's second wave was as disparate as you would expect, from the scallydelic guitar shuffle of Northside to the dark electronic pop of Paris Angels, from the northern glam pop of Intastella to the World of Twist's super-smart pop. Then there were the Charlatans, who became one of the biggest bands on the scene, with their Hammond-driven shuffling, groovy pop and charismatic frontman Tim Burgess, a music freak who was to become one of the pin-ups of the era.

TIM BURGESS

I remember the Charlatans and Northside were the buzz bands in 1990, then there was Wags and his lot the Paris Angels. I remember an article called 'The Second Wave of Manchester', which was kind of peculiar as it was only about ten minutes after the first bands had come out. They interviewed me and I ended up talking about non-league football teams like Witton Albion, who were the local team. And there was a great picture of me standing on the terraces.

MC TUNES

As soon as the T-shirts come out, Madchester was all over. Everyone was on the bandwagon. I saw bands that could have done interesting stuff and I don't hear about them now.

The Charlatans prepare for success.
(Photo: Ian Tilton www.iantilton.net)

JON SAVAGE

I remember coming up to Manchester in 1989 and going down Oldham Road. It was summer and everyone was in day-glo. It was fantastic, a really great vibe, but I think you can only just about put together a 'Best of Baggy' CD. For me, a lot of the records don't really stand up.

CLINT BOON

I would walk along Oldham Street every Saturday afternoon. I would go into Identity and blag free T-shirts from Leo Stanley and then go to Eastern Bloc to visit Martin Price, who had been in 808 State, and then hang around in Afflecks Palace. When people mention Madchester, I always think of Oldham Street and just hanging out, doing autographs and meeting all the other guys out of bands. It was a great time that; Oldham Street was like Haight-Ashbury.

GINA SOBERS

By the time of Madchester – the era of Happy Mondays, Stone Roses and later Oasis – this period oversaw the rehabilitation of Martin Hannett as he produced the Mondays and the Roses. That gave them a direct link with punk Manchester. The whole scene and city had blossomed from those days. Students poured into Manchester on the back of the Smiths' success, spawning more café bars and clubs in their wake, making it more of a 24-hour city than it had been in the mid-seventies. The Hac[ienda] was thriving as never before, having been losing money hand over fist due to dire mismanagement.

THE ONLY ONE I KNOW

The Charlatans make their move . . .

They had been around before everything kicked off. The original Charlatans were on the edge of the mod scene, playing a tight post-garage pop that also harked to the Medway scene of the Prisoners. They played a handful of gigs with the emergent Stone Roses, and, with new frontman Tim Burgess on board, their sound was swept up by the Manchester explosion – even if most of the band were from the Midlands.

TIM BURGESS

The Happy Mondays' *Bummed* really blew me away. I was still in Electric Crayons at the time. I remember buying that. I really liked the sleeve of *Bummed* as well. It then started to kick off for the Inspirals – I remember Steve Harrison putting in a word for me to be their singer when their first singer left and everyone went for an audition for them. I was about to go but they had found someone else.* That was when I knew I was going to commit to something, not just play with the Electric Crayons in youth clubs. I wanted to make proper records.

I joined the Charlatans from the Electric Crayons just after we recorded a single, 'Hip Shake Junkie'. We did a cover of 'LA Woman' by the Doors and 'Lucifer Sam' by Pink Floyd. Steve Harrison, who managed the Charlatans and managed the local record shop, took me to see the Charlatans and they asked me to join. Coincidentally 'Lucifer Sam' was the audition song for them. At the time I had a kind of crew cut when I joined and it evolved into a fringe.

I joined and things moved pretty quick. The Charlatans had a bunch of stuff that they had written with Baz [Ketley], their old singer, and I couldn't sing them. It was different, and deep down I wanted to sing my own words – we came up with stuff pretty quickly, like 'Sproston Green' and 'Indian Rope', which came up one weekend. Martin† wanted to get it going quick, so, by the time we had eight songs, we did our first gig, which was in Walsall. We wanted to keep a bit of the Midland connection – I had no idea why! We played the Boardwalk in 1989 and then it really took off.‡

I think at first Martin couldn't understand why it wasn't a Midlands thing, but Manchester was great because I finally got back to where I was from. It had been a long journey for me – I moved to Northwich when I was seven and when I was 21 I was back. I was born in Salford and lived in Worsley and ended up in Northwich.

The Manchester scene didn't really feel like anything to be honest – we were in a band and we heard our record on the radio and it was mind-blowing, getting into magazines I never even knew about was great. I was quite opinionated and people liked that. I think we were offered loads of TV shows – Saturday morning TV shows – but we were trying to keep a lid on it like the Arctic Monkeys do now and we turned them down. We were trying to make sure that we didn't blow it, that we didn't get over-exposed.

The band's debut album, Some Friendly, *was a number one.*

* i.e. Tom Hingley.
† Bassist Martin Blunt.
‡ The Charlatans' Boardwalk gig was packed; the band seemed to arrive fully formed and were welcomed with open arms by the scene. Within months their debut single, 'Indian Rope', was a hit and Madchester had another big band on its hands.

TIM BURGESS

When we went to America, it was considered a toss-up between the Charlatans and Jesus Jones who was going to be the number one. It was either 'The Only One I Know' or 'Right Here Right Now' and both, believe it or not, sounded quite similar – it could have been the production. They won it and went to number one in America. Everyone was saying that they had stolen our glory. That was quite weird really, because in hindsight really we could have been the number one band in the world!

The Roses couldn't get it together, could they? What we had was a record shop owner as a manager, we had a geek running the band! I think we had the songs as well. We had four full-on tours of America. Within a year we'd gone from a demo tape to touring America – it seemed really easy! Mind you, I wasn't doing the work!

We were the biggest British band since Johnny Hates Jazz, according to the *Daily Mirror* (laughs).

The Charlatans went on to become one of the UK's biggest bands, with a run of classic nineties albums – Between 10th and 11th, Up to Our Hips, The Charlatans, Tellin' Stories, Us and Us Only *and* Wonderland *– and three equally good but less well-selling 21st century releases,* Up at the Lake, Simpatico *and* You Cross My Path.

808 STATE

Finally coming together from a disparate range of personalities of varying ages, 808 State was like no other band operating in Manchester at the time. The loose affiliation of members gradually began to coalesce around an inner core and the band became one of the key outfits in the acid house era; 808 State were very much a precursor to the mid-nineties electronic dance bands such as Chemical Brothers or the Prodigy.

ANDREW BARKER

It's hard to place 808 State; you go into record shops and they don't know where to place us. Dance music went a bit strange and everyone had to be in a box.

MICHELLE SAINTE (DJ)

808 State was instantly legendary. I met Massey in '91 and made him autograph my 808 records . . . despite all of the amazing people I've met in this industry over the years, that's the only time in all my life I've asked anyone for an autograph.

Someone in 808 once stated that the people on the dance floor are onstage, not the DJ! I adhere to that philosophy to this day.

Graham Massey is a genius. Everyone seems to know this aside from him . . . truly a humble guy. Maybe they're not quite a household word in the US, but every good American DJ and producer worships 808 State.

GRAHAM MASSEY

In 1987 we started messing with the Roland gear 'cos there's a 303 that belongs to Gerald, so we decide to do some acid music – we do acid jams and everyone hates it! [But] we got some good tapes out of it. Then it becomes trendy and we start getting calls off ACR to come and support them at the Free Trade Hall.

And we start getting on Steve Barker at Radio Lancashire.* He's going in Eastern Bloc and talking to Martin Price who sold him the idea; John Peel gets on to it and plays it.

What we're doing is transportable: it's neat and we can get around and we just turn up, plug in and play.

ANDREW BARKER

Eastern Bloc Records was the nerve centre. They were getting the imported records. You heard all the records in the shop. There was a basement there where they stored all the records. Martin Price said, 'Let's use the room as a practice room with keyboards and a drum machine.' The shop would shut and we would pile in there and mess around with Graeme and Martin and Gerald. I don't know what happened but something fused. When they were making acid house we were saying there were no tunes there. I think they liked what we were saying, which was 'You need to turn it into a song and not just a backing track.' We started going in the studio together and writing stuff. That's how 808 State came about.

GRAHAM MASSEY

The original 808 was me, Martin and Gerald. Gerald had most of the gear – I had some gear. I was the Adrian Sherwood kind of figure with as many effects boxes as possible. Gerald continued being Gerald. He was making records with Chapter and the Verse. We were making records with MC Tunes and various hip-hop people, and making our own records. We didn't put a career plan into place. It was, 'Hey, let's make a record.' It didn't seem to take off at first, it didn't provide an

---

* Still the best alternative music show on the radio, Steve Barker's *On the Wire* has somehow persisted in the increasingly corporate world of radio.

income until later when ZTT started a bidding war. Then it became a viable thing for a career – that was 1989. Before that there was a blurry period of doing people's parties in places like Ancoats. I would do tours where me and Gerald would jump on a National Express bus with shopping bags full of synthesisers and play a gig and get the coach back in the morning. None of it was particularity ravey – we didn't play raves till later on.

We would play lots of soul weekenders in places like Southport. Adamski would always be there, everywhere we went, and Guru Josh* and us. You would walk in the dressing room and say, 'Oh no! Not you again!'

None of it glued together till the drugs kicked in. When E went big, just before that there was a big period of 'What the hell is going on?'

ANDREW BARKER

Everybody threw ideas into 808 State. You might have heard something at the weekend and say to the other members, 'Let me play you something.' I might have picked up a sample somewhere and said, 'Let's try this.' It was a melting pot of people's ideas; sometimes it worked out and sometimes it didn't.

GRAHAM MASSEY

I couldn't say I designed the band. It was the product of Martin's head. He was the mastermind, but you couldn't design it! The idea of going out and performing was interesting – no one had a background in performing or wanted to. We always thought Martin would be the MC but he backed down from that role.

When we started we had a slot on Sunset Radio – it should have been the Eastern Bloc show as all the music was provided by them. But it was the 808s' Darren and Andrew who took to it like ducks to the water, they were natural and funny as hell. Martin tried on the first show and it didn't work, he wasn't natural at it. Martin saw that and let them run with it. I wasn't involved. It wasn't my thing at all. The radio show was incredibly popular – tapes of the radio went right round the world. It was very culturally important for Manchester.

The band was an odd mix – once you form a group it's no one else's business how the music gets made, so we closed ranks. We definitely saw ourselves as a team of producers when we started, me and Martin wanted to produce other bands – in 1989 we produced that Inspirals track on

---

* Dance scene prime-mover from Jersey, best known for his three-time hit single 'Infinity'.

Playtime. Martin had talked us into doing it. Hundreds of mad projects – he was full of energy and ideas and he didn't finish any of them off!

Martin lived in Bolton and didn't go out a lot in the Manchester scene – he wasn't at the Hacienda a lot. He had his own scene that wasn't based in Manchester. Darren and Andrew, being young, found it hard to get in the Hacienda. They would get knocked back, so they had their own scene as well in other clubs. I was the only one who went there.

Darren and Andrew would DJ at Konspiracy* but the Thunderdome in north Manchester was their natural home. It was dark. It was like the Hacienda but with the heating up and the lights off. Rumour has it that it was home-brew that came out of the pumps in the club. I remember going in there and everyone had bowl cuts and proper rave gear on. All kinds of people at the Hacienda almost had an *i-D* magazine view of rave gear but at the Thunderdome the clothes were from mum's sewing machine or Joe Bloggs, not from a boutique. It was a fierce place, the escapism was much more pressurised and Darren and Andy ruled the roost. Eric Barker was like the Lord Mayor – he was Andrew's brother, that's why he was always with us on the side of the stage doing weird fan dancing.

Eric also ran our merch and he put the whole team together. He went on to promote the One Tree Island club nights.

ANDREW BARKER
I used to play 'Pacific' as a tape as the last tune at Thunderdome. The reaction we got off it on the dance floor, we thought, let's put it out as vinyl. And that was a reaction to that reaction.

DERMO
The Thunderdome! I always preferred the Dome to the Hac myself. Don't get me wrong, I loved the Hac, but the Dome DJs (808 State and so on) would play more underground tunes and seemed to be 'ours', while the Hac began to turn into a circus letting any clown in. I loved the smoke machines in the Dome, when you couldn't see your hand in front of you, and the strobes. Konspiracy was like that too.

GRAHAM MASSEY
We must have seemed really odd, these two young kids just out of school – me all technical and with a band background and Martin twice the size of everyone else. Take a photo of that and present it!

* A club established in 1980, the twisting tunnels and small rooms that had once been Pips closed in the mid 1990s.

We struggled to fit into that world of *Top of the Pops*. We played G-Mex* which was a real challenge. It was alright in a warehouse with no lights, but in a 10,000 capacity venue you needed some big ambition with lasers and a ridiculous sound system. I remember panicking about it. What the hell are we going to do? There was no performance. It wasn't all about what was going on on the stage. We used to have arguments about whether it was about performing or not, but, for me, coming from a performance background I could never cut that off.

PARIS ANGELS AND NORTHSIDE

The underrated Paris Angels were one of Manchester's second wave of bands. They released some great examples of acid house crossed with indie shuffle and had an east Manchester melancholy to their sound. Their best-known song, 1990's 'Perfume', stands the test of time.

Northside were the real deal, a gang of kids from the north of Manchester with a fanatical home-grown following who packed out their gigs from the start. Fronted by the charismatic urchin Dermo, they signed to Factory and recorded some inventive psychedelic-tinged guitar pop.

SCOTT CAREY

There were various different bands – very much a parochial scene – bands like Laugh who became Intastella, who I followed round for a few months trying to get a support gig with for the very early Paris Angels, who we had now got together.

Ricky Turner and me had been in a band when I was 16 called Jesus Rode a Surfboard and we tried to support the Stone Roses. Ian [Brown] laughed at the name which he thought and that was as far as it got. In 1990 Ricky said, 'Fuck it, we'll start a band.' I thought, I don't want to be in a band with Ricky again, but I was – for five years. Me and Ricky were like brothers. We used to argue all the time and then have a really good laugh.

The Paris Angels started that day I got sacked from the Inspirals. I knew this guy Wags and told Ricky about him. He was into psychedelic stuff and he liked *Apocalypse Now*. We thought, that's perfect, let's get him. There was a mate of mine in the Boardwalk and the Birch called big Simon, six foot four and 18 stone, who was drumming in a pub rock band. He knew I was serious because I'd been doing gigs all over the country with the Inspirals, so we poached him. We started rehearsing in Hyde police station, where they took the Moors Murderers when they

* 24 March 1990.

arrested them – we rehearsed in the cell where they were both kept. We took speed and LSD and rehearsed there all night. The guy who ran it gave us the keys – the doors were really solid and you would lock yourself in. We would go in at two in the morning whizzing our tits off and learn Velvet Underground covers.

Ricky started going out with this girl Jane and he said, 'I want to get her in to play keyboards and sing.' We said OK, and then Wags's mate wants to join on guitar but that didn't last too long. Then Steve Adge's brother, Mark, who was another mate, joined and we started playing at the Boardwalk. It was a serious thing now, instead of pissing about. This was 1988 and things were changing. Now, with the start of acid house and all this crazy music that sounded great with these little pills for 20 quid, it was another world.

The bands would pick up on the difference. It was like Haight-Ashbury now, it was a different drug, a different vibe. We had taken speed and LSD and when E came down to 20 quid from 30 quid this was the first time I bought some, because we just couldn't afford it before. At first I thought, What a rip-off this is shit, this is really shit. I got some slight hallucinogenic effect with the lights. The next week though I had it again and it really hit me. Ricky and Wags jumped on that and then the band stopped listening to the Velvet Underground and started listening to house stuff. I was quite resistant to it at first but it was like a wildfire. In a matter of weeks you would see people with big jeans and daft haircuts running around everywhere. We decided we wanted electronics in the band, so we got our friend in with a Moog synthesiser. He was an old punk who had never taken ecstasy. That was when it started to change . . .

DERMO

At the time of releasing our debut, 'Shall We Take a Trip', and recording the *Chicken Rhythms* LP, I was completely torn between extreme happiness and sadness. Only 12 months before we recorded 'Trip', my best friend Robo committed suicide in front of me and some friends in a way I'll never forget. Then, I'd just got back from London after recording 'Trip' and was chatting about the recording to a girl I knew when in the corner of my eye I could see one of my other brothers coming towards me, I knew what he was going to say. Steven was dead too. He'd jumped off [some] flats just like Robo. The dedication to Steven and Robo on the back of 'Trip' is the only time I made this public.

I was listening to punk rock, reggae because some of my mates went to Jamaica and brought LPs back – they were made out of melted plant pots, so I was told. I loved the idea of that at the time, not knowing it was probably due to necessity and not novelty. Yellowman was my favourite.

I loved his cheek, awareness and yet kiddish songs, like nursery rhymes, and then I saw a picture of him, an albino Rasta! This was something I'd never seen before and he fascinated me . . . Eek a Mouse had a top name and one of the most unusual, unique voices I've ever heard. There was Josey Wales and Augustus Pablo, people like that. And then acid house, the most original form of music I'd ever heard. I loved all the mad keyboard sounds and heavy drum beats.

SCOTT CAREY

We got on a compilation after playing the Boardwalk a few times. This guy who worked at Factory started this label called Sheer Joy. He got World of Twist and us and made this compilation called *Home*. He wanted to sign us and World of Twist but they had other ideas. But we went with this guy and he became our manager.

All the rock'n'roll pitfalls you read about happened to us, because we were more interested in partying than being in a band! It wasn't until we recorded our first single that we fully exploited the electronics. We recorded 'Perfume' in Suite 16 in Rochdale, which was Hooky's studio. We were using Cubase and all these keyboards, which was great in one way but was bad in another, because we had to start using a click track and that made us sound a bit like New Order.

'Perfume' was the indie chart's number one. I then had three years of brilliant, intense times with crazy memories of being on tour with seven people. We were young and it was full-on rock'n'roll. I liked the Zodiac Mindwarp ethos of touring and we did that in an indie working-class way – we partied a lot, to the detriment of the band. We couldn't survive as a seven-piece on Sheer Joy and we signed to Virgin, who wanted to make money out of anything that wore flares – although Ricky never called them flares, he said they were parallels! So we did what most bands do when signed to a major, we completely fucked it up. But we couldn't have survived on an indie label.

On our last tour we did 13 dates, partying every night. The last tour date was the Manchester date, which was fucking brilliant. We wanted to do it again but our contract came to an end.

DREAM SOME PARADISE . . .

Intastella

Intastella grew out of Laugh, with the addition of Stella on vocals. The fiercely creative Stella (she recently wrote and starred in a play about Nico) gave the band a charismatic glam edge. Intastella took Manc glam pop into another direction, before they were cruelly foiled by the industry and the foibles of fashion.

MARTIN MITLER

At the end of Laugh we turned down Noel Gallagher! Graham Lambert said, 'Try out our roadie, he's really good, he can play all our songs.' But we thought, the Inspirals' tunes aren't that good and not that hard to play – Noel missed out there. Craig Gannon was in the band and left us to join the Smiths . . . he didn't want to go; we had to persuade him to go.

STELLA

Intastella was a genuine northern line-up for a rock'n'roll band, something a bit different, and not obviously to make money. I think the ethos for all of us was, We don't wanna go on *Top of the Pops*, you're dead when you go on *Top of the Pops*. It's the complete opposite now, you have to start on the telly, then get your body together, you know what I mean? But the Factory stuff, I fell for all that, I liked all that. And I think where I made a mistake was I took that on with me in a band that was so obviously pop. Psychedelic pop, but pop with a blonde singer. But I think I still had that ethos – the Killing Joke ethos, and the credible artists I like.

Laugh were a good band but Martin was a bit wimpy, weren't he! I liked it, 'cos I like different kinds of frontmen. I'm not your normal kind of frontman woman – I was madly in love with Ian Dury as a very small kid.

MARTIN MITLER

We ballsed it up with Intastella, we went on the road before we were ready. There was a bit of over-confidence – *we can do anything*. We got a deal really easily because we did the first demos at Strawberry and Caroline* ran Strawberry. We got free time at Strawberry for an all-night session. We wrote five songs that way and we got a deal on the strength of that. We had a few offers and felt like things were happening for us . . . that and the class A's.

The Manchester backlash was about to happen and when we got pretty good the bandwagon rolled on without us (*laughs*).

* Caroline Ellary – the best A&R person in Manchester – worked at Strawberry at the time. She went on to manage Intastella and World of Twist, before years later signing Coldplay to their publishing deal.

STELLA

Intastella was too clever, because we wanted to fit too much in. It's a band and therefore everybody's opinion was worthwhile, but that can make for a cluttered kind of outlook, and that sometimes makes cluttered music as well.

Our records were six or seven minutes long. We discovered some brilliant noises that nobody else was using. I mean, I like Killing Joke and what have you, but I can't sing like that. And I don't want to sing like that 'cos I would sound like bloody Lene Lovich.

With me being a female, joining a band that had already been going for a while was hard. I had that other battle; I was battling my own band as well as everybody out there, you know.

I noticed a difference in how I was treated. I got on with all the producers I worked with. The producers . . . I don't know, I could relate to them, maybe I was more adaptable. I didn't play the total popularity game but I enjoyed working with these different producers. But the band tended to clash with them and get a bit shirty: 'My guitar's not out of tune.' I didn't fight with them as much. I enjoyed taking it to that next level with the producer. I think maybe 'cos the band was Laugh for so long they were a little bit more insular, more scared of it.

The original demos were the closest we got to being like [World of Twist], because Tony Ogden [World of Twist singer] did them and we had the same influences. It was useful to lump us together at first, but it didn't do us any good at all and it didn't do me any good as a songwriter, it being sort of the second band.

It was crap production on the first LP. We were looking to go and redo ours with Chris Nagle, but initially we were offered Craig Leon and I said yeah. He had a great track record. He had done Blondie, bubblegum, the Ramones, everything – on paper, perfect – but it didn't work.

LET'S TWIST AGAIN!

Intastella's friends the World of Twist, with their northern soul stomp and Nuggets psychedelia, were the great lost band from Manchester. They were formed in 1985 by Tony Ogden and Jamie Fry, brother of ABC's Martin, with Gordon King on guitar. Frontman Ogden was charismatic and had a brilliant mind. The group's stage shows were theatrical, but dashed with a northern working men's club reality and coloured in with a post-E trippiness. Their twisted pop combined northern soul, Hawkwind, sixties girl pop, psychedelia, the MC5 and the Stooges into something else.

Although their single 'The Storm' stalled at 42 in the charts and their brilliant updating of the Rolling Stones' 'She's a Rainbow' (incidentally one of Martin Hannett's last ever productions before his death in 1991) also just missed the top 40, World of Twist's début album, Quality Street *(1991), sold strongly. With expectations still high, the band started work on a follow-up album but it all ground to a halt when Ogden decided he didn't want to be the singer any more. Although auditions were held for a new singer, the band imploded and the second album was never released.*

Tony Ogden was fantastic on stage – he should have been a huge star – but it never happened. The music business doesn't understand bands like this; by 1992 they were dropped by their label and fell apart soon afterwards. Tony sadly died in 2006.

MARTIN MITLER

World of Twist were a brilliant band and good mates. I didn't think we were like them – Stella brought a glitzy element to Intastella, a shininess. We were about dance grooves and tripping out, whilst World of Twist – who had been going around a lot longer than us – had well structured songs . . .

JOHN PENNINGTON

The World of Twist were very misunderstood. They should have had more time and less pressure. Tony [Ogden] would be alive today if they had had time to do the album. He was on the edge as it was. He was a genius. I think it was communication with Tony – he could never get his point across succinctly. When we did the drum sound for the album version of 'She's a Storm', Tony said he wanted the drum to sound like a massive drummer hitting a really small drum kit. Now I understand it – he wanted a northern soul drum sound, powerful but small; the original northern soul drums were never big, the drums were far away with just one mic – but he could never really pin it down.

STELLA

Before they even had the signing party for World of Twist, Tony had lost it; he was spitting at the taxi driver and he was so angry. I thought, this is never, ever, gonna work, and I think the people at the record company knew it was never gonna work. They just thought they'd better do it, they thought it was trendy.

World of Twist got further than us, I think, because – and I wouldn't like to say this but, I don't know – they're more for lads, they're more of an anal, lads' Joe Meek type of thing. I know where those references come from. They kind of had a connection with London more than us and

Sheffield with Jamie Fry and all that, so they were almost more London-based than Manchester-based.

I finally saw the World of Twist's revolving heads show in London.* There was some Hooray Henry behind me saying, 'Ooh, they're hilarious aren't they, they're so funny!' but I was so pissed off how World of Twist had become this thing. Maybe people would have seen the irony in it, but Tony wouldn't have done. Tony wouldn't have wanted to be laughed at.

After they got dropped, they could have signed to Creation. World of Twist wanted the bigger money and Creation wouldn't give it them, and that was it for them.

Tony's vision was bubblegum. It wasn't like it wasn't completely honest music. He wanted to make pop music, but he wanted to be Brian Wilson. He wanted to be judged as a songwriter like Brian Wilson. He wanted to have the hang-ups of Wilson, he wanted to lock himself away and write the songs. Then the band would come and play, and he eventually said, 'I can't sing any more.'† And with the use of the drugs, he actually became that. But I do think he actually talked himself into that character when it didn't go according to plan and they didn't get the top 40, I remember he was very upset with what Bernard [Sumner] said about him on the telly – saying, 'We are weird.'‡

He shouldn't have said that. They should have backed that to the hilt, 'cos it was from Manchester. It was getting difficult for World of Twist.

It was all fragile. And when it's all about sales, as it was then, and your record company's looking at your sales and they've not gone top.

---

* World of Twist had an extensive live show with moving heads and other props.
† After the first album, Tony wanted the band to continue with a different singer.
‡ Barney from New Order commented when reviewing a World Of Twist single on TV that it was 'weird'.

16

HANGOVER

After the party comes the hangover. In the early nineties, the Mondays were staggering, the Roses slumbering, the Inspiral Carpets were having hits but were marginalised, the Hacienda was having bouts of trouble, the gangsters had moved in and the scene suddenly seemed sour.

MIKE PICKERING

In 1990, things were going wrong in Manchester and this came to a head in 1991. Manchester got lawless and the police didn't seem to want to do anything about it. When the Hacienda shut down for the first time, it was all over for me.

The drugs were worth millions – just imagine how much was spent each weekend on drugs – and it was inevitable that the gangs would take over. There were guns everywhere.

At the Hacienda, we had just got a four o'clock licence for the Friday night, which on paper was a good idea but in reality possibly wasn't. One night the police came barging into the club over a tiny incident on the door and everyone had to leave, with police bashing their riot shields and their helicopter flying overhead – a complete over-reaction. Then at the Hacienda's 11th birthday party I got threatened. I thought, that's it, and walked out of the club at that point.

The Hacienda staggered through the nineties. After the tragic death in July 1989 of teenager Clare Leighton, the victim of an extreme reaction to ecstasy, the club's demise was inevitable. The relative innocence of the Second Summer of Love was now entangled with drugs, gangsters and guns. During 1990, with Clare Leighton's death obviously in mind, the police had, under Operation Clubwatch, moved in on the Hacienda. In May of that year they informed manager Paul Mason of their intention to oppose an upcoming licence renewal. In July the club, fighting back with the assistance of George Carman QC, was granted six months to sort out the problems.

The following January, the magistrates decided there had been a 'positive change in direction' and renewed the club's licence. The management themselves decided to reintroduce the original membership scheme to try to keep troublemakers out. Within just a few weeks, on 30 January, Tony Wilson announced that the club was closing voluntarily after door staff had been threatened with a gun. A few months later it returned.

The Hacienda took the time out to apply a new Ben Kelly colour scheme and install airport-style security measures. It reopened on 10 May, with the long-running Saturday night with Graeme Park and Tom Wainwright and the phenomenal success of Flesh giving the club a third chapter in its history. But the intermittent violence eventually shut the club in 1997.

ERIC LONGLEY (managing director, Factory)

I originally met Wilson at some business thrash in the late eighties; we had similar interests in music, politics, philosophy . . . Factory were looking for a managing director. The problem was one of fiscal discipline and organisation, because they were growing bigger. This meant implementing management systems. I met with Rob Gretton and Wilson and Chris Smith, the finance director. They interviewed me for the job – we sat on the boardroom floor as there were no chairs. Wilson and Gretton rolled up joints and smoked their way through the interview. The major topic of conversation was the Marxist dialectic, how it differed from Hegel, what problems it threw up and how it had been misused by the British left. Wilson had a lot of questions and I suspect was using my knowledge to further his own, Gretton just wanted to know about what music I liked and what football team I supported. Chris the finance director hardly said anything. From this, they offered me the job of managing director.

I arrived at Factory and it was clear from the beginning that financially they were in a pickle. I instituted monthly board meetings with monthly management accounts to try to get a grip on what was happening. In my first three weeks, the Hacienda kicked off big time. First the manager complained that he wasn't getting financial information from the finance director, so I pointed out to him that if his bank overdraft was going up every month, that was sufficient to show we had a problem. At that stage the Hacienda had just finished an Inland Revenue inquiry in which the club appeared to have kept two sets of books and mistakenly gave the wrong set to the Revenue to review! The second big issue was that the police were trying to close the Hacienda, and then we had a gun incident at the club where somebody pulled a gun – fortunately no one was hurt.

We had a meeting of New Order, the board of Factory (Alan Erasmus, me, Chris Smith, Wilson, Gretton) and Mason (manager of the Hacienda).

We resolved to go on strike and close the Hacienda as a protest. The police were horrified because they wanted to close the club and they didn't want a bunch of gun-wielding amateurs from the city being the cause of the closure, so the police then spent the next four weeks suggesting how the Hacienda might be kept open or reopened.

We closed the Hacienda and I had to go and sit with Mason and hand out redundancy notices to a whole bunch of people who didn't deserve them. No one else would do this chore so it fell to me. Wilson avoided it even though it was his idea to close the Hacienda – I don't think he had thought through the consequences of his suggestion.

There were or are many stories about why Factory went bust. The usual suspects are the Happy Mondays but in reality they had no more to do with it than New Order, Northside, Cath Carroll or any of the other artists. The truth is complex but broadly Factory was in financial trouble before I arrived in 1991, deep trouble. The New Order album was well behind schedule and they were not to be hurried along – Hooky was deep into Revenge, his own band, which proved singularly uncommercial; the Mondays had released through some associates a truly appalling live album (Factory just shrugged and took the view that if the artist were stupid enough to put out a substandard album, there was nothing Factory was going to do about it) before jetting off to the Caribbean to record an album they hadn't yet written (you could see disaster written on this one before they even got there); there were no other major acts and we needed a record to plug the gap.

I suggested *Substances* by the Mondays. They were up for this, it would be remixes of their songs for a remix dance album. The Mondays also liked the little poke at New Order's *Substance*. The Mondays had a core fan base of about 40,000 in the UK so the album would have helped plug the gap and fill the coffers till the real thing was ready.

Instead Factory signed the Adventure Babies for more money than we could afford, and much more than I thought they were worth, as it happens – the public agreed with me on that one. We also launched Cath Carroll with an expensive promotional campaign, spending nearly £250,000 on an album that sold less than 4000 copies as I recollect; we released Palatine, a back-catalogue album of material from Factory's history, which sold less than 3000 copies. And we turned down the Smiths, Oasis and goodness knows who else!

In the final period, Factory looked to see if it could associate itself with a major and the first one approached – against my very strong advice – was Elektra. That approach was scuppered by my curmudgeonly act at a meeting with Elektra – my main concern was that they only had to look at the books to hang us out to dry and then buy the whole thing for less than a bad song, which is exactly what Roger Ames did for Universal when they bought Factory after I left. The underlying problem at Factory was that too many people were looking for escape routes (to sell the company, for example) rather than for solutions (commercial recordings and releases). It wasn't the Mondays that did for Factory – it was corporate suicide egged on by a management policy that was not in the long term interest of the company and artists.

In a funny way Factory was the epicentre of creative genius and fiscal incompetence – it developed ambitions in its later days that were far in advance of its roots or its ability to source.

We once went to a meeting with Alan McGee of Creation and Daniel [Miller] of Mute where we discussed a joint venture in France as a prelude to closer working together for the mutual benefit of our joint acts. This was a wonderful opportunity to get some muscle behind indie acts, but without losing our independence or the artists having to surrender their creative instincts or integrity.

On the way out of the meeting, Wilson commented that there was no way we were going to join in a business with someone who had no dress sense like Alan McGee – so McGee's sartorial elegance became the stumbling block to supporting our artists. For all Wilson and Factory said about supporting artists, it was on our terms or not at all – contradictory maybe, but somehow what you would expect from Factory.

Despite the hangover there was still a lot of great music coming out of Manchester . . .

TOM ROWLANDS (Chemical Brothers)

There's been no real master plan to the Chemical Brothers.* We've just sort of drifted into this. We started DJing for fun and then we got asked to do remixes and then it just seemed obvious to make an album. We

* They came out of dance to become one of the key mid-nineties UK acts and managed to have a top 20 album in America while they were at it. Mashing together huge beats with great textures and an ear for melody that came from their indie roots, they've cut some classic hit singles.

started at the *Jockey Slut** parties in Manchester – that always was a great night. We always like DJing in Manchester, in some ways it's sort of a homecoming for us.

I guess our background has helped us make the music this way. We've always been into lots of different things, we're still into bands even now in 1994, we listen to hardcore records and stuff like the Manic Street Preachers is really cool.

We've worked on the Charlatans, Primal Scream, Lion Rock, Bomb the Bass, the Prodigy and Saint Etienne. We've turned down Fatima Mansions, Echobelly and Deee-lite. I guess that gives you some idea of what we are about.

We were called the Dust Brothers and we got into trouble from the real Dust Brothers[†] for that. We didn't know that we were going to get famous! We were just DJing in cellars and using the name because we liked it, you could say that we sampled their name (*laughs*).

BRIAN CANNON

I bumped into Richard Ashcroft at a party in Wigan when he was a 17-year-old student. There was no Verve at that point. I was a football hooligan fashion-Nazi but I took to him, he was pretty cool – and I really hated students at the time. The next time I saw him was at the Stone Roses at the Alexandra Palace. I didn't see him for a bit after that and what happened was that the Rap Assassins were happening.

The Hacienda vibe had gone and it was at that point that I met the Verve, who were blending one into another. When the Verve took off in 1992 I met Noel and the whole Oasis thing happened and I was designing the Verve and Oasis sleeves.

The Verve was my band. Oasis were on a different level again – nobody in the Verve entourage was over 25 – so I drove the tour bus. I was totally immersed in that band. I've seen them 114 times, which has got to be a world record for the Verve. I wasn't working, I was turning up to watch them play.

RICHARD ASHCROFT (The Verve)

It's great that other bands really like us but we want the man in the street to like what we're doing. We wanted to make music with the greats like Miles Davis, Can or Chic, all of them rolled into one, but we wanted everyone to get it.

* A Manchester-based dance magazine. Wittily written and with great enthusiasm, it managed to achieve national distribution for several years.
† American production team who had shaped the Beastie Boys' sound.

I'd rather paint boats on the beach than taint my dream of what this was all about when I was a kid. We'll never lose the excitement of playing live or writing a new song.

What we go through when we make a record is like nothing else that anyone else will. When we record we want to be at such a level that if we aren't 'on', then we get very depressed about it, take time out and stop.

BADLY DRAWN BOY

I was a music paper reader then. The early nineties was a really good time for the *NME* as a reliable source of music; not to say it isn't that now but I was the right age to believe in it. I still wasn't sure I had it in me to be a musician or have a career in music.

After grunge, a strange electric scene emerged with people like Beck and Jon Spencer Blues Explosion – the fact that they all worked together and collaborated with the Beastie Boys made it even better.

I saw Jon Spencer play and it was such an electrifying gig. It was a Eureka moment, like when I first got into Springsteen. Jon made me realise I could do my own music in my own way. After that gig, I set myself up with a four-track recorder from *Loot*, it was the same model that Springsteen used for his *Nebraska* album. Things happen in your life and you can't read too much into them, maybe it's meant to be.

MIKE PICKERING

I was doing M People and that was going really well – that was something else that should have been on Factory!

I used to sing everything into a tape recorder and I had this mate Paul who had been in a couple of bands. I went to meet him and we had a couple of sessions and it was great. I would sing the song to him and play some drums off a record and he said, 'Mate, you're on to something here, these are great songs.' I said, 'I'll cut you in' and we got in Heather Small as the singer. Everyone was saying 'She's too shy, she's looking at the floor at gigs,' but I thought she had a great voice. We said this should be a band and we did 11 million albums. If we'd had a dance label at Factory, M People would have been on it. Factory could have had Kylie Minogue, because she was signed to Deconstruction as well – who knows where it could have all ended up!

Alan Erasmus drifted in and out of the Hacienda, God bless him, he was in a parallel universe. He came up to the flat I was living in above the Arndale at the time and I remember going into Dry Bar one Sunday night when 'Ride on Time' was number one. We were sat on our own and wondering where everyone was. Alan was saying, 'These records where everyone goes mad at the club, who puts them out?' I said, 'I put them out on this other label called Deconstruction,' and he said, 'Why are we not putting them out? You work here!' It had all passed him by. He said, 'That's a bit silly isn't it!'

MARTIN HANNETT RIP

The genius who did more than anyone to shape the Manchester sound died in 1991 after years of abuse had worn him out.

JOHN PENNINGTON

Martin had a specific sound and he would take it down by nuts and bolts to get it. He did like to have control. If he didn't get the sound that he needed, he would stick mics everywhere to get it – nothing was lost. He always resolved any problems in the mix.

Many boxes would be delivered to Strawberry Studios and it would be expensive reverb units hired for a day and used for a snare drum to give a track a special sound. The snare sound on 'She's Lost Control' is a snare drum put through a Marshall time modulator through a synthesiser. I would listen to him, whilst most engineers would say he was a crackpot. Martin liked me because I was up for anything, I knew what I was doing. I could use sequencers, and samplers were one of my passions as well.

I was there for Martin whenever he needed to do something. With the Mondays album I was there 24/7 in case we needed to get something – there was no rest really. Martin was being fuelled by chemicals – for me it was lots of coffee and chocolate and trying to sleep when I could. I had worked with him years ago and then he was off the scene.

He disappeared for a while from Strawberry and came back clean-shaven and a few stone lighter. He looked like a new man, I didn't recognise him walking down the road in a tweed jacket. Then he worked with the Happy Mondays and it went downhill from there really.

He would set the session up for the band he was working with and then go to the Waterloo pub across the road from the studio. Then I would go and get him out of the pub to finish the session.

Andy Couzens bought him a house after Martin had worked with the High. He moved him in there, sat him down in front of the TV and said he would come round the next day. Martin wasn't well, we had just finished a session with the High at Great Linford Manor and he was on his last legs. He was coughing and spluttering most of the time and asleep against the mixing console. Andy and I put it together. We would wake Martin up between takes and he looked like crap – all sweating, not talking. Two weeks after that session, he died – the next morning after Andy had moved him into the house, he was in there in the chair where Andy had sat him. Martin died in the armchair.

17

'1 WAS THE LAST ONE TO MAKE IT FROM MY CROWD': OASIS

The whole punk rock, post-punk, indie and acid-house generation had passed through and made their mark, and by the early nineties the dust had settled. Surely no one else could make it now?

NOEL GALLAGHER
I'm in Munich in 1991 on tour with the Inspiral Carpets and I call home once a week. I say, 'I'm in Munich,' and my mam goes, 'Where's that, in Germany?' I ask what Liam's up to and my mam says, 'He's in a band.' I say, 'He's doing what!' She says, 'I think he's the singer in a band!' and I'm saying, 'What band?' But the most shocking thing was when she said he was with Paul McGuigan. I said, 'What, Guigs!' And she said, 'He's got some guitar or something.' I said, 'This is something I've got to fucking see!'

I didn't even know [Liam] was into music. I remember we used to share a bedroom – him and his mates would all be going out doing mad shit and I would be staying in smoking draw and playing guitar. He would be like, 'You fucking weirdo, you're sitting indoors all night smoking draw and playing guitar!' He had no records, nothing, so it was a complete 'What the fuck!'

So I get back to Manchester and they've got this gig down the Boardwalk.* I go down to see them and all the Inspiral Carpets come down with us to see Noel's brother's band. Liam gets on stage and it's like 'Wow! He's a fucking singer!'

I remember my first ever gig was seeing the Damned at the Apollo in 1980. The lights were on and it was like, 'Wow! These are fucking

---

* 18 August 1991, supporting Sweet Jesus.

Liam and Noel in classic Oasis stage poses, 1995
(Photo: Ian Tilton www.iantilton.net)

brilliant!' When you see your little brother – even though it's not the Apollo and it's the Boardwalk on a Tuesday with about 11 people there, it's still dark, there were still lights and there was still sound coming out of the speakers, and it's 'Fucking hell, that's my brother on stage.' I went to see them afterwards and said, 'That's really fucking good,' and they asked me to be their manager. I say, 'I'm not a manager, what could I fucking do? Get a proper manager.'

A few weeks passed. They used to rehearse every Sunday at the Red House – a real shit-hole at the time, where all the band's gear was in one lock-up and if somebody's amp got nicked, a band would just nick somebody else's because theirs had been nicked. They kept asking me to come up and have a jam with them because I had an electric guitar by this point, but I couldn't be fucking arsed. One Sunday I wasn't doing anything so they call me up and say, 'Come on, get your guitar, you fucker.'

So I bring it and my amp and I get to the rehearsal room, I set my gear up and I'm bashing away in there. I'm sat on my amp before anything starts. They start playing their tunes and I start playing along. They were all stood up apart from the drummer, and I was sat down. Bonehead says, 'Have you got a guitar strap?' and it suddenly dawned on me that I had never played guitar stood up! I had played in the soundchecks but sat on the drum riser. It really freaked me out getting the guitar strap and playing standing up – that's fucking madness! I don't know what Bonehead was thinking. I think our Liam had bigged me up properly – I was the roadie from the Inspiral Carpets, I had an 'in' as it were.

Anyway we started playing and I remember them having songs which they had played at the gig. I then started playing the songs that me and Coyley had been messing around with, and to hear them all join in without Liam singing was the moment I thought, this is going to be fucking brilliant – it's your own music and there's a bass going on and then the drums! I immediately took the Paul McCartney role, saying, 'Don't play it like that, play it like this. You play it like this and I'll play along.' They were sat there going, 'You got to join the band, we got to write some words, this is fucking brilliant!'

LIAM GALLAGHER

The first time music ever did anything for me was when I heard the Smiths. Then I saw the Stone Roses at the International 2 just before the album came out and I thought, yes! That's here today, in my face, I can go with that. Morrissey was a bit weird for me, but Ian Brown was more of a lad. Him and John Squire were just lads, straight off the street, making this incredible music, and it really appealed to me. Everything just felt right that night. I went home and dreamt of being in my own band.

NOEL GALLAGHER

I said in a tongue-in-cheek way years ago that I came into the band and said I was taking over, but it wasn't quite like that! When I first heard them play 'Columbia', which was an instrumental, it worked. I had so many other bits of chords that the songs were already there. So if anybody was going to write one song a week, I was going to write five a day and they were all going to be better than theirs, so it was like, I'm going to do this and you're going to do that. It was kinda like, this is a brilliant song! Let's do another one which is even better than the last one! And at that point people stopped saying, 'Well, I've got a tune.'

Then I go away and start to think of it seriously – being a songwriter and writing some songs for this band. I was still with the Inspirals and this was when I'm starting to think in terms that this could actually go somewhere . . . And then of course Mark Coyle was my best mate and he was a sound engineer – he knew what he was talking about. He's got a portable recording studio at his house and he brings it down and he's going on about getting a better drum kit. He tuned it up for us and it was like a little family, with him making it all six of us.

Five days a week, Monday to Friday, we would rehearse. If you weren't going to the football you would rehearse – no argument. Guigsy, Bonehead and Tony all had jobs, but me and Liam, to coin his phrase, were 'living it' even though we hadn't done anything yet! We used to go and meet the rest of them from work – I guess the drug being the music. We couldn't make it ourselves, we were relying on them to play it and we used to push them to rehearse all the time. When you're young, you've got no kids and all that and music is everything. If you're not playing music, you're talking about it, if you're not talking about it you're thinking about it, if you're not reading about it you're writing it.

We had done a gig within three or four weeks of that first rehearsal. They already had four songs, and I had 'Columbia' and maybe one more of mine. So that's six songs – that's half an hour. And we're a band, we are Oasis.

PHIL SMITH (Oasis tour DJ)

I knew Noel from the scene. You would always see the same people and the same bands and you would always be nodding to people because you kept bumping into the same old faces at the gigs. And all of a sudden he had joined his brother's band. I didn't know he could play the guitar! I was living with Coyley and he said, 'Noel has got some great tunes, come and roadie for us when we get a deal.' So I did when things started happening for them, and then I started DJing on the 'Be Here Now' tour.

NOEL GALLAGHER

The actual story of where we got the name from is from before all this. I had this poster of the Inspiral Carpets tour dates on my wall at home and there was a gig in Swindon at the Oasis centre. I always used to say to Liam, 'Don't fucking take that – not the Oasis centre – when you can use the underground market where they sell really cool trainers.' But he wouldn't have it – that sounds miles better – in my own head we're the Underground Market but in his we're from a leisure centre in Swindon (*laughs*). Before that they were called the Rain. That was the shittiest name for a band ever, plus there was already another band called Rain in Liverpool. I said, 'That's rubbish, that's shit.' So they came up with Oasis.

BRIAN CANNON

The first time I saw Oasis play was at the Hop and Grape.* They were supporting Dodgy – this was a pre-record release and Noel had been mithering me to watch his band so long. I nearly never went – I thought, they've got to be shite, everyone's in a band and they're always rubbish – but I went along and bumped into Johnny Marr. He was there with Marcus Russell[†] and the gig blew my head off. I couldn't believe what I was seeing. The first time I met the entire band was at Sheffield when they played with the BMX Bandits.[‡] I brought my art books along with me.

NOEL GALLAGHER

At first the *NME* and all them thought Manchester was done and over. Luckily for us there was no next big thing. If there had been six bands coming out of Dagenham, we would have been on our arse.

Before Alan McGee turned up, from '91 to '93 we weren't particularly going anywhere but we still loved it. Nowadays two years without interest and you're finished, but back then it was different. It wasn't a career choice. It was something that you did because that was where you came from, whereas now it's like, 'Let's start a band,' and bands can get signed before they think of a name – you can be on MySpace

* July 1993. The Hop and Grape is now the Academy 3.
† Johnny Marr's manager, who once put the Sex Pistols on at Middlesex Poly when he was a student in 1976 – what better CV than to eventually become the Oasis manager?
‡ Friends of Teenage Fanclub and fellow Creation act, with a nice line in eccentric indie pop. The gig was on 28 Oct 1993.

and YouTube, you can be superstars before you've even got it together.

We recorded our first album as demos that never came to light and we were allowed to be shit for a couple of years. That first demo is quite Happy Mondays really and Liam sounds like Ian Brown. I guess you just copy your heroes, then you stumble across your thing if you're lucky.

PHIL SMITH

At first when they were playing fourth on the bill gigs, all they would do is four tunes. They would do tunes like 'Live Forever', 'Cigarettes and Alcohol' and no one would be clapping. And those are classic tunes. It didn't seem to take off at first. The Roses had a big Manchester following from the start but Oasis didn't. But as soon as we went to Glasgow and got a deal, at that moment it started.

NOEL GALLAGHER

We didn't think we were fucking great then but I knew we had something. Even to be a Manchester band and be shit is better than to be a fucking band from Liverpool and be shit, because we are from Manchester!

We did In the City at the Venue.* Pete Shelley was in the crowd and he came up to me and said, 'I really like the song with the wah wah pedal.' I didn't know what to say, he's from the Buzzcocks, man! They started the whole thing – never mind the Clash, it was them or the Pistols for me.

The same night as that gig we did 'Cigarettes and Alcohol' in a session on Mark Radcliffe's radio show. He would never have us on because he thought we were shit but he was on holiday and Lard† was standing in for him with Peter Hook. This was the session where Peter Hook barred us from the Hacienda live on air because we started taking the piss out of his leather trousers.

Anyway, when we were doing 'Cigarettes and Alcohol', on the 'sunshine' bit I said to Liam, 'Sing it like Johnny Rotten' – and that's where 'shiiiiiine' came from. You could see a light bulb come on in his head – that's it! I thought, it's only a matter of time now.

I remember Alan McGee being interviewed by Tony Wilson on *The Other Side of Midnight*. There used to be a big cardboard cut-out of him in Eastern Bloc Records. He used to go out with Debbie Turner,‡ who we used to share the Boardwalk rehearsal room with. She was in this band

---

* Manchester Venue, 13 September 1992.
† i.e. Marc Riley.
‡ Well known Manchester scenester and face about town whose nineties band Sister Lovers were another of the great lost groups.

called the Sister Lovers. I used to see Alan at the Hacienda and I knew he was the Jesus and Mary Chain's manager. I knew Creation Records and Primal Scream and all that, but at the time what was going on was Manchester, which was the centre of the universe. I didn't know his history – he was just this guy from London.

Before Creation, we only ever went to one label and that was Factory. Somebody came down to see us at the Boardwalk. I remember being sat in the new Factory offices when we went in and played Phil Saxe the tape – it was real early stuff, 'Columbia' was on it. He said he was going to send someone down to see us because we were playing the next week and I'm not sure if anyone ever turned up. I think he even said we were 'too baggy'!

PHIL SAXE

I went to see Oasis's first gig at the Boardwalk with Noel playing with them. I knew Liam before that – I knew Noel because he was a roadie with bands. Liam had a belt with Elvis on the buckle and he would say, 'We're going to be bigger than Elvis!'

We were trying to do a new bands album on Factory and I wanted to put Pulp and Oasis it. We couldn't have signed them, to be fair; we wouldn't have had the money to promote them.

NOEL GALLAGHER

Debbie Turner was doing a gig supporting 18 Wheeler in Glasgow.* She asked us to come up and play, and we said, 'Yeah, alright.' We shared their room because their drummer, Al Smith, was a roadie for Mondays. Because I was the roadie for the Inspirals we knew them from hanging out through Mark Coyle. So we shared a room and split the rent. We ended up going to Glasgow to do the gig – no one had told the promoter and he said he didn't have the licence to put on four bands on. We ended blagging on for four songs as the doors opened. [Alan] McGee was there because he had either missed his train to go back to London or he had turned up to see Debbie, who was by now his ex-girlfriend. He was there as the doors opened and he saw us play. As I came off stage, he came up and said, 'I really like your band, what are you called?' I said, 'Oasis.' He asked if we'd got a record deal and I went, 'No.' He said, 'Do you want one?' and I said 'Who with?' He answered, 'I run Creation Records,' and I said, 'Oh right! It's Alan McGee!'

He wrote down his number and I said, 'I'll give you a ring.' He asked if we had a manager and I said, 'No, it's just us.' We had the demo with the

* 31 May 1993 at King Tut's Wah Wah Hut.

swirling Union Jack thing on the cover – we had one in the van, so I went out and got it. I gave it to him and he said 'I don't want to hear it in case it's shit!' I gave it him anyway.

The only person that I knew in Manchester with any business acumen was Anthony Boggiano, the Inspirals' manager. I phoned him up and said, 'I met Alan McGee last night and he offered us a record deal – is he liable to be taking the piss or is he liable to be serious? Or is it the just the usual bullshit?' He went, 'I'll find out for you.' I don't know who he called but he rang back and said, 'He's deadly serious. Do you need a manager?' (laughs) I said, 'I'll get back to you – that's not my call.'

So once we knew that he was deadly serious we called him up. Then the famous meeting takes place. We go down to London and we go to Creation's office in Hackney – me, Liam and Bonehead. I was doing the Andrew Loog Oldham thing and I said, 'You leave all the fucking talking to me!' We finally found this place in Hackney and we were pretty underwhelmed by it.* I don't know whether I was expecting something like Factory Records – I was expecting something at least similar in London and it was kind of like just a door. This was before mobiles, so we knocked on the door. There was this huge sweatshop with what looked like illegal immigrants on sewing machines behind the door. This guy comes out and says, 'What do you want?' We said, 'We're looking for Creation Records.' He said, 'It's upstairs.' So we knocked on the door and it was tiny – like someone's bedroom. We walked in and they seemed to know who we were straight away, and the first person I saw was Andy Bell, who was photocopying some of his band Ride's reviews! It was such a cottage industry that Andy was doing his own press kit. In the corner, just written in black, painted like the Jam's logo, someone had written on the woodchip wall 'northern ignorance'. At that point I thought, this is going to be fucking great.

Creation was the right label. Alan shit himself for about four months after the gig in case we didn't sign, because when we had this meeting he said, 'You got to go and get yourself a manager and a lawyer.' I said, 'I don't know anybody but I'll find someone.'

There was always this guy at the Hacienda who used to go on about his brother being in a band. He was one of those guys that you used to meet but you never knew his name. When I came back to Manchester I had an HMV bag and I'd just bought 'Dusk' by The The. He said, 'How's that band of yours getting on?' and I told him, 'I've been offered a deal by Creation.'

---

* Creation's office was right in the heart of Hackney, a good twenty-minute walk from Bethnal Green tube station.

He asked, 'What have you got in that bag?' and I said, 'It's the new album by The The.' He said, 'Our kid's really chuffed with it,' and I said, 'Who is your fucking brother?' He said, 'It's Johnny Marr.' I said 'Wow! Man, I love the Smiths!' So we went back to mine and I gave him one of the demos – it had my phone number on it – and within two days Johnny had given me a call.

He called me and said he really liked it and he wanted to meet up with us. I met him and he said, 'I really like your stuff – what guitars are you using?' He was still like a big fucking kid (laughs). I said, 'I buy all my guitars in a place in Doncaster called Music Ground,' and he had never heard of it. I was like, 'Where do you get your guitars from?' and he said London. Then I said I was looking for a manager and he said, 'I've got a great manager – Marcus Russell.' He passed the stuff on to Marcus and we had a meeting. I said, 'If Marcus is good enough for Johnny Marr, he's fucking good enough for me.'

JON SAVAGE

For me the Stone Roses – I thought they lost their nerve, they weren't up to it. I really liked Oasis. I knew about them very early from Johnny Marr and Johnny's younger brother, Ian. I went to see Oasis at Water Rats in London and I remember getting into a huge row with someone about Blur, who I hated because they didn't rock and, like a lot of London bands, they do music hall – I can't understand it, if you're a rock band, fucking rock!

I went to see Oasis and I looked at Liam and thought, yeah, OK, they're going to be big, he's very charismatic. I went with Ian Marr to the Academy gig in Manchester. There weren't that many people there, and I remember turning to Marcus saying, 'Oh, I get it, it's the brothers isn't it?' He said, 'No, they're a band,' and I said, 'Marcus, c'mon!'

NOEL GALLAGHER

As soon as Marcus got involved, I went to see Alan McGee. Of course Marcus, being a manager, was trying to get a better deal – Alan shit himself for ages 'cos he thought we were going to cook it up a bit, there were little bits in the press everywhere. Marcus was saying, 'It's not a very good deal,' and I was saying, 'I don't care about the money, it's not important to me, it's the people.' You just know when you meet the right people.

I had been reading the NME for ages and I had read about the Jesus and Mary Chain and Primal Scream and how they were allowed to do virtually what they wanted when they were on Creation and it was about really natural cool people. Alan used to do things like phone you up on a Wednesday and say, 'I've left two tickets for you at Piccadilly station, pick them up and you and your brother come down – we're having a party at the Creation office!' We got to know all the people that were working there and they loved us. They loved the tunes and we hadn't even done any gigs in London at this point. So they weren't basing it on anything, just personalities. I remember saying to Marcus, 'I'm not bothered about the deal, I'd rather be at a firm like this than someone coming in and giving us a grand at the last minute to go off to Real World Studios and make a hit record.'

Alan was really shitting it waiting for us to sign. He gave us two grand to go to Loco Studios in Wales* and we did demos of 'Live Forever', 'Up in the Sky' and 'Bring It On Down'. We sent him the demos and he said he could only listen to them once because, if he didn't sign us, it would have upset him too much.

Signing to Creation was basically meant to happen. Alan's whole thing was, This is what we can afford to give you to make an album. It was like he was saying, 'I'm giving you a car, now do what you want with it but don't fucking crash it.' He didn't say, 'You have to work with this producer, or do this,' which was cool because I thought, hang on a minute. I've been doing this for three years – you can't tell me what to do or how my band should sound like. The Creation people were like, 'What are you going to do?' and I thought, what a brilliant question. It's not like they were telling you what to do. It was a marriage made in heaven.

We come back from London and meet Marcus and we then do a gig at the Boardwalk – one of the regular local band fucking nights. This time it was noticeable that people who looked music business or looked like journalists were turning up. There was a little review in the NME by a girl and it's a great review saying Manchester is starting to re-flower or something like that. Then we did the gig at the Water Rats – this was our first gig in London† and it was absolutely fucking rammed before that. I'm not sure of the time lines but we went to Liverpool to record more demos. We recorded 'Supersonic' by accident when we went to record 'Bring It On Down'.‡ Alan originally wanted 'Bring It On Down' for the first single and the idea comes that we should write a song. So I said, 'You lot go and take loads of drugs and watch the telly, and I'll go in the back room and try and write a song and be back in a bit.'

* September 1993.
† 24 January 1994. Oasis had spent two years touring the UK without playing London.
‡ Recorded at Pink Museum in Liverpool in 1994.

Then I could go round the back and write 'Supersonic' in a minute – whereas today I would be thinking of 15 reasons why it would be shit. It came out of nowhere and we recorded it that fucking night – we did a rough mix of it and we sent to Alan. I thought it was the best thing I'd ever fucking heard. Alan was adamant about 'Bring It On Down' being the first single because it reminded him of the Pistols and he loved that line, 'You're the outcast – you're the underclass.' But I was adamant that 'Supersonic' should be the first single because of the nonsense Happy Mondays lyrics and the fact that it wasn't a three-minute heads-down thrashy song but something different. He went, 'You know what – I think you're wrong, but it's your call.' I was only 24 at the time and for him to let us do that was great. As it turned out, it wouldn't have mattered what came out first.

The gig at Water Rats was mobbed and the review had that shot of Liam which became famous. When we first started, Liam used to stand like Ian Brown because that was what he'd seen. I think in that shot he looked a bit like John Lydon and someone said he was like a cross between Lennon and Lydon. I think that changed the perception he had of himself at that point.

Liam just kind of developed, as he calls it, his 'stillism' (laughs). I remember a couple of years later some American asked him, 'What's your stage persona, man?' and he says, 'Stillism.' This guy was writing it down dead seriously and we were cracking up.

It's like at the first gig, if he'd started behaving like Brett Anderson, we would have stopped the song and said, 'What you doing! What on earth are you doing!' Bez had done his gonzo dancing and Ian had done pretty much the same – you could act like them but the only progression on that was stillism! If he had moved, it would have been 'Whoa, whoa, whoa, stand still!'

LIKE AN AVALANCHE

With the 'Columbia' white label all over the indie shows on the radio, the buzz was massive. The gigs were packed and, without warning, Oasis had arrived.

NOEL GALLAGHER

People thought Blur or Suede would be it, but without anyone's permission in London, the masses decided what it was going to be. It's like the house lights went down, the stage was set and everyone was waiting for someone to walk on. The press were wanting Blur or Suede, but out comes 'Supersonic' and it was us.

It was that perfect moment for me that only lasts for two or three years – when you're the same age as your audience, you wear the clothes and financially you're in the same thing, you've not gone off to be pop stars yet. It's you and them and everyone else and it's magic. Of course, being a music fan I knew that this was going to be enormous. When I would say these things to Alan McGee, like we were going to be the biggest band in the world, everybody on drugs in the dressing room was going, 'Yeah!' I used to think I was the only person who believed it properly! It was unshakeable with me. I knew the songs that were going to be on the album and I knew the songs that were going to be on the next album because I already had them.

LIAM GALLAGHER

I can't say what I wanted from Oasis, 'cos it's too mad. I wanted to go to the top. To be the next Beatles, bigger than The Beatles. I didn't want to be the next Mondays, 'cos that's (holds finger and thumb slightly apart) that big. I wanted to be the biggest of our time. I wanted to be remembered as a top band who left a mark and did it our way.

Britpop, a word which your author shamefacedly admits to coining way back in 1988 when reviewing a La's gig in Liverpool, is often considered a separate musical movement, but in many ways it was Madchester part two. Oasis were part of that scene and bands like Blur, it could be argued, were initially London's answer to the Mancunian wave. Britpop saw the rest of the country play catch-up with an assimilation of the Manchester bands and culture. Loaded magazine exploded onto the scene in 1994 and lad culture became a way of life. The Manchester scene, boiled down to its bare bones of trainers, casual clothes, drugs and booze, became a live-for-the-weekend lifestyle.

Oasis unintentionally soundtracked this and became the pin-up boys of a boozy, belching generation. And what a soundtrack! The singles were coming thick and fast and were massive hits, each one bagged with its own distinctive artwork designed by Brian Cannon.

BRIAN CANNON

The cover of 'Live Forever' was the house that John Lennon grew up in, in Liverpool. We couldn't think of anything up till the last minute when we went round to Michael Spencer Jones's* house. He had that picture and I used a red film over it. The snow you can see is actually sunlight over it affected by the red filter.

---

* The photographer responsible for many of the shots used on Oasis artwork.

NOEL GALLAGHER

Britain was changing. The Conservative era was ending and something was happening in politics and fashion. Great Britain had gone from nihilism – optimism was coming back and it was all geared towards England. It was like year zero, big bang or whatever you want to call it. A lot of people were at the right age for fucking heroes. People didn't understand the Lycra shirts and the women's blouses worn by some of the bands, and a lot of people found Blur too clever. People wanted people like themselves in bands.

You got to make it look easy – that inspires people. Damon Albarn may be up there as one of the great British songwriters but, as I used to say to his guitarist, it's not about who's got the cleverest chords, it's about connecting with people. I don't know how I do it. I look out there at 125,000 people at a gig and not in an arrogant sense. I might think it's because I'm a brilliant songwriter but it's not because of that, it's because there was a bald guy in the band, because there are lots of bald people here thinking, if he can do it I can do it. A lot of it was because of Liam.

Also Paul McGuigan wasn't cut out to be a rock star but there he is on that stage. You can't put your finger on it because, if you could bottle it, some major label would sell it and it would be worthless. It's commonly known as magic. If it's there thank your lucky stars, and if it's not there hang onto its coat tails.

The ferry incident was before the record deal.* We were never worried because Creation was so laid back, we never felt we were letting anyone down. They sent us off to do our thing – but our thing happens to be getting into trouble, fighting and arguing, or the roadies shoplifting at service stations. When I phoned McGee and said everyone had been nicked, and I fucking managed to get away with it. It wasn't like he was saying, 'You'll never work again,' it was (*Scottish accent*) 'Fucking brilliant, that is total genius.' By the time you get back to England and read the story, they've cooked it up a little bit. Alan would also say they would normally have to make stories like that up, but with us every day he would go to work and there would be more stories – it was a dream come true.

---

* The first of many famous 'incidents' occurred in 1994 when Liam Gallagher was banged up after a drunken altercation on the ferry on the way to a very early Oasis show in Holland. This was the first of the endless boozing, brawling rock'n'roll tales from the band to grace the tabloids, amplified when the Gallaghers became the most famous faces in the UK.

The formative years of any band are naturally where it grows and grows and you're the same as your audience. Ultimately what separates you from your audience is the distance from them at the gigs. In a physical sense, you're fucking miles away, and then you start taking the big drugs and wearing the fur coats and several pairs of sunglasses. Those years are great as well – those years are fucking insanity, they're the rock star living – but the bit before is the magic bit, where you never knew what was going to happen but you knew it was going to be great.

Oasis' debut album, Definitely Maybe, *is the defining moment of the nineties. By default it was the moment that indie music ended and became a marketing term instead of an attitude. It was the sound of the UK and, more than any other record from the era, caught the mood of the country at that time. Noel Gallagher, the nice kid who worked for the Inspiral Carpets, had written the best guitar pop songs of his generation, stuffed full of hooks that went so much further than the simplistic view of the band as some sort of Beatles take-off. Add to this Liam's effortless swaggering charisma and fantastic rasping, sneering vocal and you have one of the great British albums.*

IAN BROWN

I met Oasis when they were doing one of the versions of *Definitely Maybe*.* I thought they were good lads. That was the first time I had met Noel, [though I knew] I'd seen him around in town because I recognised his face, and it was the first time I had seen Liam. I had heard a lot about Oasis off Steve Adge. He said that he'd seen them at the Boardwalk and that they were going to be massive and they loved us lot. Liam came down to our studio with a couple of his mates and Tony McCarroll, the drummer. When they were massive, I was buzzing for them. I remember when we were all watching *The Chart Show* on a Saturday morning in the studio and Oasis came on doing 'Shakermaker'. John said something like, 'The singer looks good but I am not sure.' I was saying, 'I think they're great, they're from Manchester and they've got bowl haircuts and it says on that little clip there that they love the Roses.' I thought it was really funny that we were supposed to be the masters, and the kids who loved us and grafted it had robbed us when we were asleep – that's music and that's great.

---

* Initially recorded in Monnow Valley Studios with Dave Batchelor, the result was too thin, so another attempt was made at Sawmills with Noel and Mark Coyle producing, and finally mixed to perfection by Owen Morris.

BRIAN CANNON

For *Definitely Maybe* we had Owen Morris in the background of the shot waving the master tapes of the album around, which when you're pissed out your mind is not the best idea! There was a mystique about that album cover. Whereas the first album was a kecks-down, full-on rock'n'roll sleeve, the artwork for the second album sums up the mystery of that record.

NOEL GALLAGHER

I was completely and utterly ready for it because I'd been with the Inspirals and I had travelled the world, maybe not in the same league but I knew what was going to happen. I'd read enough copies of music papers and watched enough documentaries about bands to know what was going to happen. I knew the record was good and it took a while to get it finished but I was like, Bring it on! I was a bit concerned for Liam at the time as he was only 19. I think it was lucky he had his brother in the band as he's a bit insecure at the best of times. He was a star though, he was a good-looking boy and all that shit – if he wore a binbag on his head it would have looked cool. I knew he was going to be some style icon.

BADLY DRAWN BOY

Oasis was a complete phenomenon. I hated them when they first emerged. I was in a nine-to-five job in Bolton and I heard 'Supersonic'. I thought it was rubbish, I thought I could write better songs than that. But that was completely unfounded, it's a brilliant song. By accident I ended up at the launch of *Definitely Maybe* at the Hacienda – my brother was more of a fan than me. I was in a competitive state of mind, thinking everyone else was rubbish and I was great, like you do before you've made it. I was reluctant to go because I didn't like them. I remember standing on the balcony and Evan Dando was standing next to me. Obviously I was a complete and utter no one at the time. I was directly in line with Liam's onstage eye line and he gave a power salute and looked me in the eye – or so I thought, it was probably Evan Dando! And I realised that Liam is probably the best frontman, in terms of someone who does nothing but has the charisma.

NOEL GALLAGHER

I was ready for it but for Guigsy it was the hardest. They just wanted to be in a band and play the local night at the Boardwalk. It's telling that they've never gone on to record a single crotchet of music since, they just wanted to get out on Tuesday night and play a guitar. I'm not putting them down, but they weren't playing with any conviction any more once they had become millionaires. Eventually they couldn't be arsed any more, which is fine. It hit Guigsy the hardest. He wasn't ready for it all.

ROCK'N'ROLL STAR!

The biggest band in the UK, Oasis left Manchester for London – perhaps the first band of any note for years to buck the stay-in-the-north trend. They had no choice – no one had got this big and things had become suffocating for the group.

NOEL GALLAGHER

We had to go where the action was. That's why we left Manchester. At the time in 1993, when I left, there wasn't much left here any more. The thing had gone. People were getting hit and mugged and where it used to be free and easy, nights out became like a military operation. If we hadn't had '88/'89 then '93 wouldn't have seemed so bad, but the dream had gone tits up and Alan McGee was drawing us towards London. So we went down there and found everyone loved us!

We got to London and whatever Manchester had lost, London had gained somehow. I moved to Camden and it was like being in the centre of town. The thing that became known as Britpop was just starting to happen. We followed the action – our record label was there, our manager was there and I got sick of getting that train to London and being delayed all the time.

We took Manchester to the national press. If we had stayed up here we would have been stuck. The *Guardian* and all those people didn't really get us. They didn't like people enjoying themselves – they are joyless cunts. They've never experienced joy in their lives. I'd do interviews and say, 'Why are you such a miserable cunt? You been to university.' And I always say to them, 'Your dad voted for Margaret Thatcher and now you work for the *Guardian* – you can't handle it when you rebel against your mam and dad, where I come from we love our mams and dads.' And for me that's the fundamental difference between the middle-class southerners and the northerners – it's too vast.

Moving quickly, Oasis ran through several landmark singles and a second album, (What's the Story) Morning Glory, that has become one of the biggest selling UK albums of all time. The high pressure of all this non-stop creativity and touring was bound to take a toll on some of the band, who must have been shocked by the group's rapid ascendancy.

NOEL GALLAGHER

When we all started we were on the same level musically, I think, but then I was at the turbocharger. I was writing all these songs that were orchestral things and the rest of them thought, where am I going to fit in with all this orchestral shit? I don't blame them for that. I used to feel sorry for them, but Guigsy would either not say a word for two days or be very nervous about doing gigs. It was a bit of a relief for Guigsy himself when he decided to call it a day after the second album, not that I've ever spoken to him about it yet. I knew he was going to be alright sitting in the garden, watching cricket and smoking without having me and Liam arguing about who was the greatest Rolling Stone or summat.

The Gallagher brothers' arguments are the stuff of legend. I was at Rockfield Studios when they were recording (What's the Story) Morning Glory and witnessed the biggest bust-up of them all, when they ended up fighting in the studio's garden and the band stopped for a couple of weeks. Before the fight the evening had been jovial; they had played us rough mixes of the yet-to-be-finished album and it sounded fantastic. The simmering tension and the brotherly love/hate relationship between the pair of them sits right at the core of the band.

NOEL GALLAGHER

We had a proper barney over what was the greatest Christmas single of all time. He said 'Imagine' and I said it doesn't get any better than Slade's 'Merry Christmas Everybody' – I was saying once Madonna starts covering a song then that's the end of that.* It was kind of a relief for Guigsy when he left.

WHAT'S THE STORY?

Oasis in their pomp were unlike any British mainstream band for years. There was a brash confidence and tabloid charisma about them that endeared them to the masses.

NOEL GALLAGHER

When we started – and although we get tangled up with that Britpop thing – we were essentially a punk band who did it for ourselves. We got up there and did it. There was no fashion thing. It was loud and it was strong songs about drinking and shagging. It doesn't get any better than that!

* Madonna covered 'Imagine' in 2004.

I used to get embarrassed by going to America and the Beatles thing preceding us. Over there people were always saying, 'I thought you guys sounded like the Beatles,' and I said 'I've never said we sound like the Beatles.' We sounded more like Slade. I love Slade, they're a seriously underrated band – just because of 'Merry Christmas Everybody' and Dave Hill, people forget how good they were. The first album, *Ambrose Slade*, is great – play it loud and you'll see what I mean. I met Noddy a few times, he's a real gent and he loves Oasis. I don't hear his voice enough. He's a great singer. They were part of my childhood with T. Rex and David Bowie.

When I try and describe what we sound like I always say 'rock'n'roll pop music', just like '20th Century Boy' and 'Cum On Feel the Noize' are – loud and euphoric.

I wrote 'Rock'n'Roll Star' in my flat on Whitworth Street before going out one night, with its 'We're out and we're having it large' lyrics. You're only aware of it ten years after – when you see 14-year-old kids at your gigs, and you're thinking, you weren't even around when 'Don't Look Back in Anger' was written.

BRIAN CANNON

The sleeve for 'Don't Look Back in Anger' came from the *Abbey Road* sessions, when Ringo left the Beatles but rejoined a day later. When he went back to the studio they had covered his drum kit in flowers.

JON SAVAGE

I saw Oasis later on and I noticed something very strange about them. They would start a number and for the first 20 seconds kids were going wild. Then they would calm down. I thought they didn't keep the excitement of the intros to the songs. I really like the first two albums till 'Some Might Say', which I still love. It was a very optimistic moment, it was the moment the Tories got trashed at the council elections – a great moment.

BRIAN CANNON

'Some Might Say' had the lyrics illustrated in the sleeve – all the references were there. About that time me and Michael Spencer Jones had a big fallout.

The sleeve for 'Whatever' was set on moorland near Sheffield. We'd gone to Monument Valley in Arizona – we'd flown a ten-thousand-mile round trip to do the picture, but the band had split up in LA after the gig at the Whisky a Go Go when Ringo Starr was in the audience. Noel was very upset and hit Liam on the head with a tambourine, so we never did the shot. Me and Michael Spencer Jones thought we should do a Verve-style shot with the band on the moors and it ended up looking brilliant.

At the time the Verve were the psychedelic freak-out wing of the new lad consensus. They had early connections with Oasis from taking them out on tour in the early days. The Verve's first tour of America as part of Lollapalooza in 1994 was fraught with difficulties, as the band's wired lifestyle saw them burn out on the tour. Typical of most UK acts in the nineties, they were walking the walk a bit too vigorously!

RICHARD ASHCROFT

The great bands take their lifestyle on the road with them. That's not just drugs but their mates, everything. Their whole environment, the whole thing is a 24-hour existence. I mean, drugs may help as a catalyst but they're part of a bigger thing, the feeling has to be there to start with. Too many people rant on about drugs. I mean it's easy to be some lead singer living in a bubble in a nice flat recommending drugs, but there's the man in the street in his crap environment taking drugs to block everything out. They're the ones that should be talking about, the reality of that existence. It's no big deal any more, everyone in our generation is doing drugs.

I think we've been cheated by our music biographers. When I've been on tour, I've taken it pretty far and I can't believe that people did it all the time. Take it from me, that lifestyle hurts, bad.

We're not interested in being written off as just that. Yeah, sometimes if you're on the road for a long stretch, just playing those ballparks like on Lollapalooza, then you do just go mad – but for us it's the music, that's the main thing. When we're on tour we'll have a great time, suck the marrow out of it all and come home like corpses, recharge our batteries and go out again. If someone gets blind drunk and throws something out of the window then it's because they're blind drunk, it's not a conscious rock'n'roll thing.

Mind you, I remember when we trashed that hotel in America, the staff were cheering us. It was like it was the last major hotel to not be smashed by a British band, ha!

In 1994 Oasis themselves were about to experience the reality of touring the States.

NOEL GALLAGHER

The thing about America is that you get away with unprofessionalism in the UK, but you can't there. They could not fucking understand out there how we could blow out gigs, or if the band was too pissed to meet the guy at the record shop who would rack the records. Marcus was back in England and we never had an American manager, so we were left to our own devices. Musically we could have smashed it but they're so attuned out there for people like Chris Martin and Bono who give a lot to a crowd. Liam's into his 'stillism' and they find that offensive out there (laughs). They had never seen people do interviews like ours – we were saying basically 'All American music is shit and has been shit since 1977.' They said, 'What do you think of Pearl Jam?' and I was saying, 'They are dogshit.' They couldn't understand that.

Alan McGee always said we were too Mancunian for them and it was no surprise that no one from the city had ever done anything there because we weren't meant to travel.* In a sense we were expected to go and repeat the staggering success of the UK in America. I'm sure McGee and Marcus weren't thinking that, but someone at Sony was obviously thinking, if they do this in England, which is an eighth of the size of America, they should therefore be eight times bigger. I'd already been to America loads with the Inspirals. New York and LA are great but the rest of it is shit – the rest of it is a Wednesday afternoon in Bury. The label must have thought, they sing in English and they like rock'n'roll so it can't fucking fail. But we're not that kind of band – the Americans are into showmanship and stage shows and they can't believe that 'you guys just stand there'. It's like you don't have to come and see us, you can listen to the records.

In America we were on Epic Records at the time and it doesn't get any more corporate than that. Their two biggest acts were Whitney Houston and Celine Dion, and then there was us. If you go there and act like Mick Jagger there they get it, but they were so intimidated by the way we came across on stage that they didn't know what to do!

The peak of the Britpop madness was the battle between Oasis and Blur for the number one spot. This was the high watermark of Britpop, with Blur releasing the jaunty Kinks vaudeville of 'Country House' on the same day as Oasis's 'Roll With It'. Blur, with the marketing muscle of EMI, won the day but when the Oasis album came out they were dwarfed by the sheer size of the Manchester band's sales. It was a great pop moment; the bands' genuine enmity for each other perfectly captured all the fault lines in British pop culture: north v south, middle class v working class, college v council estate.

* Although never enormous in America, Oasis, contrary to the myth, were big there. Even their recent album, 2008's *Dig Your Soul*, was top five.

BRIAN CANNON

The 'Roll With It' sleeve? God knows what that's about! They're all sat there looking at television sets. Liam was looking at Alex Higgins, Bonehead is looking at Peter Sellers in 'Party' and Noel Gallagher has got himself on the telly – that was a remarkable frame.

NOEL GALLAGHER

The broadsheets give me stick for my lyrics but the thing is I could convince anybody I was the greatest lyricist in the world. When an album comes out and you have to do a biog to explain all the songs, that's where they get all their soundbites from, but I don't want to dissect every line, then you spoil it for the kids. I don't want to know who the '20th Century Boy' was, it's me!

That's another difference between the working classes and the middle classes – we find something to enjoy. I'm not trying to be challenged by anybody. I don't need Brian Eno walking round with a big placard in the studio with 'golf course' written on it, or 'you must listen to this record with this in mind'. That's bullshit, because pop music is not about that. Pop music is 'Ob-La-Di, Ob-La-Da' – who gives a fuck what that means? It's what it means to you. What really annoys those people is that they can't define it.

All the great bands that ever were didn't have to explain themselves. I don't remember Johnny Rotten having to sit down and explain what every single song was about. It's either obvious to you or you're not a fan. Does no one believe in magic any more?

I remember saying to someone before our album came out, 'What was the capacity of Spike Island – 32,000?' I said, 'I won't rest till I've done a gig that's 33,000,' and that was it. The Roses were it for me. Although I really loved the Smiths and Joy Division, the Roses made me believe it and I made millions of other people believe it.

KNEBWORTH

August 1996 was when it got as big as it could get. 'Dare say it's bigger than God,' joked Noel, referencing John Lennon's controversial 'Jesus' quote from the sixties. When Oasis were busy selling out their two Knebworth shows they were the best known faces in the UK, which had become a whole country flavoured by Manchester. Oasis, the last band of their generation to make it, were the final part of the jigsaw that started when Pete Shelley and Howard Devoto drove down to London twenty years before to try to find the Sex Pistols.

NOEL GALLAGHER

It was mad that one in six people in the UK applied for tickets for Knebworth. That's where the story really does end. In a way after that it was all about statistics like 'one in seven people with red hair wearing black shoes went to the concert . . .'

Before Knebworth, I was on the way to another arena gig in Birmingham. I was driven to the site and went for a drive through the grounds with the manager. I got out in this huge field and said, 'Where is the stage?' He answered, 'You see over there where there is a vast sea of nothingness?' (*laughs*) 'See the tree right down there? Well, you see the other tree behind it? Well, that's where the stage is gonna be.' I said, 'How are they going to hear us!' After he explained all the technical things I thought, this is going to be brilliant! This is not only going to be a great show, it's going to be our Spike Island times fifty. I remember that summer was the summer we spent on helicopters – the gigs were so big, like Loch Lomond, that we would fly in on helicopters everywhere.

I remember flying over the site in the helicopter and thinking, I've seen that scene so many times on documentaries like the Isle Of Wight or Woodstock – you know, that shot from the helicopter. And here we are – it's us from fucking Manchester! It was the gathering of the masses. I was quite proud of those gigs – there was one arrest over two days and people were saying it was going to be a bloodbath, And that arrest was for pissing up against a tree!

It was a conscious thing to have John Squire on stage with us, it was like saying, 'Look what you could have been!' (*laughs*) John doesn't say a lot at the best of times – I always say that the two biggest cultural events of the separate decades were Spike Island and Knebworth, and he was at both. I think it was a beautiful moment – everyone onstage was a Mancunian. It was our way of saying that, if it wasn't for the Stone Roses, we wouldn't have been there.

There was of course a negative side to Knebworth. The people at Q magazine said it was the zenith and we all realised that it was too big. Alan McGee always gets melancholic about it because he went to rehab afterwards. But for me it was a vindication . . . it was the most natural thing in the world for me to rock up at that gig, plug in and have it!

I don't know what I feel about it now, maybe I wish we could have played better! We opened up the entire set with an album track, not even a single – with 'Columbia'. Bands don't do that any more. Whether it's the way we guinea-pigged it, maybe it was too big – maybe we should have underplayed it all, but I think the statement should have been made. I always said we would never be elitist and if a million people wanted to come we would play to a million people.

It was like the big raves I went to, like Joy and Dream. All those people in the field and it was beautiful . . . It wasn't about us up on stage. It was about everybody. It was about the kind of thing I would never say from stage because it would be considered too Bono. It was the last time that we were the same age as the crowd and on the same kind of standing.

I was never afraid of success because I knew I could handle it, because ultimately I knew who I was. I knew I wasn't a made man. I knew Phil Spector wasn't responsible for me, or George Martin or Nigel Godrich or Steve Lillywhite, I'd done it. I picked up that guitar and learnt to play it on one fucking string to get into that field at Knebworth. I signed off for years before Knebworth to be the biggest thing there ever was. I was going to drink and fuck and snort my way through the whole lot, but it was never going to beat me.

When you get on the fairground ride that is rock'n'roll, you're getting on the rollercoaster that's the most exciting ride and you've just got to enjoy it.

We made a film of Knebworth. It's called *Operation Gold* – a documentary that's never been put out. There were 15 cameramen travelling with fans on the train from all over the country, they filmed the police meeting rooms and all that. It cost us a fortune to make – it will probably get released on some anniversary. The gig was recorded properly with cameramen in the crowd filming from the fans' point of view. We were going to release it as a live album but I said it was too soon. But I think people will want to look back on Knebworth and say, 'Yeah! That was quite mental what happened to all of us.'

I guess the proof is when you speak to people who were there, people didn't give a shit that they couldn't see anything, it was to be with all those other people. I always said the best way to experience Oasis gigs is with other Oasis fans and not on a set of headphones at home – the essence of Oasis is in the gathering.

We went on the plane to America straight after and I guess sub-consciously we must have felt we had done it – *Morning Glory* was number five in the American [album] charts and 'Wonderwall' was number five in the American singles charts. Liam and Bonehead had a petty argument about a leather jacket and we were all on fucking drugs. I was like, 'Calm down, you're arguing for nothing!' and we blew out four really big gigs right at the point where it could have gone one way or another. I look back on it now and think subconsciously we must have thought, fuck it, that was it. At that point it has happened now and I thought, I've got to go and spend some money now, go and live it.

We got back to England and I couldn't believe the amount of press that was at the airport. We only cancelled four fucking gigs! It was insane. We had to be driven from the airport to a secret hideaway. Then the drugs started to take over. We were all doing loads of fucking coke and we decided to go and make the next album, *Be Here Now*, instead of all going, 'See you in a year.' The only regret I have from Knebworth is not coming off that stage and just letting *Morning Glory* go away and settle and let people say, 'What happened there! That was fucking brilliant!' Then just reappear three or four years later. I couldn't do it and we made the album, which was really overblown.* One day I'm gonna edit the *Be Here Now* songs and make them shorter.

I remember at that point, doing the record, thinking that everything I'd done had turned to gold. Like when I ambled in and did a song with the Chemical Brothers and it sold 250,000 copies! It was a massive single. I'd be doing the demos for a new song and thinking they were a bit long and no one said, 'Can you get them down to six minutes?' They all went, 'Great! Carry on!'

That's when the quality control started to go out of the window. I was thinking these random thoughts and believing they must all be brilliant, because everything I'd done before was random and brilliant.

I'm so glad we did Knebworth, because I meet so many people down the years with Knebworth T-shirts on who say it was an important part of their life. The Kasabian lads, for instance – their mams and dads dropped them off at Knebworth. I remember at the time saying everyone should go away and form a band. You think it's going to happen next year but it only became apparent when the Arctic Monkeys, the Libertines, Razorlight and the Coral and that little mini-explosion of bands came out, and they all said they learned to play guitar to *Definitely Maybe* . . . All those kids were at Knebworth and it's really special when people say it meant so much to them.

---

* Years later *Be Here Now* really works; the overblown long songs with their overdubbed codas are huge piles of sound to get lost in. This was the point the media turned against Oasis, but all their subsequent releases have been far better than history paints them, leaving them in the curious position of being one of the most underrated bands in the UK, albeit one that still sells millions of records worldwide.

It's a bit like the Sex Pistols thing at the Free Trade Hall – with that gig comes the Hacienda, comes acid house, comes the Stone Roses – comes the facility for us all to be sat here now. It takes years. I can see the aftermath of Knebworth and it doesn't leave a sour taste – I'm glad we did one of those things, like the Isle of Wight or Woodstock or Altamont. That was your thing, it was great. I was watching a documentary when James Brown, the journalist, said that for once the biggest band in the world was the best band in the world.

ENCORE!

Of course Oasis at Knebworth is not the end point. There is no end point. But it was a point in time when the whole generation that had grown out of Manchester since the Sex Pistols played the Free Trade Hall went mainstream. Oasis were the biggest British band since the Beatles. After the mid-nineties saw the whole of the UK attempt to be Manchester, it would inevitably change.

Manchester, though, is not a city of ghosts. Unromantic as ever, it quickly moves on from the past. There is no museum in the city celebrating Karl Marx, who lived with Engels in the city while they researched Das Kapital, and changed the history of the world; there is no museum for Alan Turing, who invented the computer in the city; most people know nothing of the city's radical past or the suffragettes; it's all been obliterated and bulldozed away like most of the Victorian city.

The past means nothing in the world's first modern city.

The groups, though, all continued. Still provocative, still liking it and lumping it, a new generation of bands emerged, with Doves, Badly Drawn Boy, I Am Kloot, Elbow and the Ting Tings all making great twisted pop music and all somehow sounding northern. In 2008 Manchester is a sprawling musical city and the whole city centre looks like a giant Hacienda. The Factory vision regenerated a whole city – without it Manchester would be a very different place today. Village Manchester doesn't exist any more and neither does the Hacienda, but go out any night of the week and you'll find a city drenched in its musical culture . . .

BERNARD SUMNER

Most of the time we looked to the future, most of the time we tried to do something new. But you can only reinvent music so many times – in a way we did that with 'Blue Monday' and we got a new sound. To expect us to do that continually, well, you end up in a Kraftwerk situation where every album that came out was totally innovative, until it eventually killed the group. The expectations were too high.

BEN KELLY

Working with Urban Splash,* they made no bones about that if Peter [Saville] and I hadn't jointly done what we did back then, then Urban

---

* The coolest of the property developers, whose innovative buildings and ideas were highlights of the huge redevelopment of Manchester in the early 21st century property boom.

Splash would not exist today. There was a point where I had no reason to come to Manchester and for ten years I didn't come to Manchester. When I came back I thought I had come out at the wrong city – the whole station had changed. As I move through the city it's so different, it's incredible.

There's a book published by Greater Manchester Council about the regeneration. There's a timeline at the beginning of the book and it goes through all the important things that happened in Manchester, and the second entry is the opening date of the Hacienda. It was great that there was a bunch of wackos like Factory who were doing their own thing independently with their own money, with no support from anyone, who went where others feared to tread on Whitworth Street West and changed the city. And that's thanks to Rob Gretton and Tony Wilson.

ERIC LONGLEY

Tony always told the story about how he interviewed a Californian rock star on his TV show and asked them to play a Gram Parsons song. Unfortunately they wouldn't. That night at the Manchester Free Trade Hall the audience were taken to California, soft warm red lights, softening carpets on the floor, potted palms and warm Californian accents. The artist did a couple of songs and then introduced the next one by saying that this 'next song was written by a great friend of mine, Gram Parsons, and I want to play it tonight for your own very wonderful Mr Tony Wilson.' Tony, sitting in the first row, shone, as this was the song he had asked for earlier that day in the TV studio. Before the Californian artist could say any more, immediately after the words 'your own wonderful Mr Tony Wilson', a loud, coarse, obviously Manchester-accented voice bellowed out 'Wanker!', completely destroying the ambience of the evening.

Tony told this story against himself because, despite all his self-appointed graces, at the end of the day he identified with Manchester and its working class and he refused to see himself above or beyond those roots. There's no shadow of a doubt in my mind that every band that went through Factory and the whole Manchester scene owed much to Wilson – he was a genius at promotion. He was also intensely loyal to Manchester and it owes much to him. There are many who criticise Tony as a wanker and his friends would openly admit he was a wanker (at times, who isn't?), but he was our wanker – and what a fantastic wanker, when you look at what he achieved for Manchester. I don't dispute the other groups would have got together, but whether they would have had the same attention coming from Manchester without Tony is doubtful.

GLOSSARY OF NAMES

Ivor Abadi . . . club owner

Karen Ablaze . . . fan

Barry Adamson . . . Magazine bassist

Louise Alderman . . . musician, Property Of . . .

Richard Ashcroft . . . The Verve vocalist

Tony Ashworth . . . drummer, Tunnelvision

Ed Banger . . . Ed Banger and the Nosebleeds vocalist

Andrew Barker . . . 808 State

Jo Bartlett . . . fan

Andrew Berry . . . Hacienda DJ

Clint Boon . . . Inspiral Carpets keyboard player

Richard Boon . . . Manager of Buzzcocks, boss of New Hormones records

John Brierley . . . producer, set up Cargo Studios in Rochdale

Alan Brown . . . Big Flame bassist/vocalist

Ian Brown . . . Stone Roses vocalist

Tim Burgess . . . Charlatans vocalist

Brian Cannon . . . sleeve designer for Oasis and the Verve

Scott Carey . . . Paris Angels bassist

Larry Cassidy . . . Section 25 bassist/vocalist

Hewan Clarke . . . DJ

Norman Cook . . . drummer in countless bands

Jeff Cooper . . . fan

Andy Couzens . . . Stone Roses guitarist

Kevin Cummins . . . photographer

Jon Dasilva . . . DJ

Dermo . . . Northside vocalist

Howard Devoto . . . Buzzcocks/Magazine vocalist

Bob Dickinson . . . journalist

Steve Diggle . . . Buzzcocks guitarist/vocalist

Billy Duffy . . . The Cult guitarist

Roger Eagle . . . DJ and promoter

Gareth Evans . . . Stone Roses manager

Evo . . . dancer from Street Machine

Liam Gallagher . . . Oasis

Noel Gallagher . . . Oasis

Pete Garner . . . Stone Roses bassist

Damien Gough . . . Badly Drawn Boy

Steve Hanley . . . Fall bassist

Dave Haslam . . . journalist and author

Alan Hempsall . . . Crispy Ambulance vocalist

Kevin Hewick . . . singer-songwriter

Martine Hilton . . . musician, Property Of . . .

Tom Hingley . . . Inspiral Carpets vocalist

Peter Hook . . . New Order bassist

Mick Hucknall . . . Simply Red vocalist

Vince Hunt . . . A Witness bassist

Jonathan Hurst . . . sound engineer

Johnny Jay . . . DJ and producer

Denise Johnson . . . singer

Howard Jones . . . manager of the Hacienda and Stone Roses

Phil Jones . . . Manchester gig promoter

Mike Joyce . . . Smiths drummer

Greg Keefe . . . Big Flame guitarist

Ben Kelly . . . designer

Kermit . . . rapper with Ruthless Rap Assassins and Black Grape

Graham Lambert . . . Inspiral Carpets guitarist

Tim Lawrence . . . author

C.P. Lee . . . key scenester and main man from Albertos Y Lost Trios Paranoias

John Lever . . . Chameleons drummer

Linder . . . artist and key player on the Manchester punk scene, Ludus vocalist

Rob Lloyd . . . Prefects and Nightingales vocalist

John Lydon (Johnny Rotten) . . . Sex Pistols vocalist

Johnny Marr . . . Smiths guitarist

Terry Mason . . . Joy Division drummer

Graham Massey . . . 808 State

MC Tunes . . . rapper

Martine McDonagh . . . manager of James

Nathan McGough . . . manager of Happy Mondays

Tony Michaelides (Tony the Greek) . . . radio DJ

Mick Middles . . . journalist and author

Bruce Mitchell . . . dubbed 'Mr Manchester' by Tony Wilson, been there from the start, Durutti Column drummer

Martin Mitler . . . Intastella

Stephen Morris . . . Joy Division/New Order drummer

Morrissey . . . Smiths vocalist

Martin Moscrop . . . A Certain Ratio guitarist

Jimmy Mudrickzi . . . Puressence

Stephen Murphy . . . God's Gift

Pauline Murray . . . Penetration vocalist

Liz Naylor . . . journalist

Peter Noone . . . Herman's Hermits vocalist

Jason Orange . . . Take That

Genesis P. Orridge . . . Throbbing Gristle and Psychic TV frontman

Graeme Park . . . DJ

John Pennington . . . sound engineer

Mike Pickering . . . Hacienda DJ and promoter, key player in acid house in Manchester

Matthew Priest . . . Dodgy drummer

Finley Quaye . . . singer

Elliot Rashman . . . Simply Red manager

Benji Read . . . dancer and playwright

Lindsay Reade . . . key player in post-punk Manchester and Factory Records, Tony Wilson's first wife

Alan Robinson . . . promoter at the Electric Circus

Dave Rofe . . . DJ and manager of the Doves

Mick Rossi . . . Slaughter and the Dogs guitarist

Andy Rourke . . . Smiths bassist

Tom Rowlands . . . Chemical Brothers

Paul Ryder . . . Happy Mondays bassist

Sean Ryder . . . Happy Mondays vocalist

Michelle Sainte . . . DJ

Jon Savage . . . journalist and author

Peter Saville . . . Factory Records designer

Phil Saxe . . . Factory Records and manager of Happy Mondays

Sefton . . . breakdancer for Broken Glass

Pete Shelley . . . Buzzcocks guitarist/vocalist

Adrian Sherwood . . . producer

Gerald Simpson . . . A Guy Called Gerald

Chris Sievey . . . Freshies frontman

Melanie Smith . . . fan

Phil Smith . . . Stone Roses road crew and Oasis tour DJ

Gina Sobers . . . punk scene face and member of the Liggers

Harry Stafford . . . Inca Babies guitarist/vocalist

Mark Standley . . . V2 guitarist

Stella . . . Intastella vocalist

Bernard Sumner . . . Joy Division/New Order guitarist

Phil Sutcliffe . . . journalist

Jo Sweeney . . . fan

Phil Thornton . . . author

Paul Tibberts . . . fan

Geoff Travis . . . Rough Trade Records boss

Gary Whelan . . . Happy Mondays drummer

Greg Wilson . . . electro innovator, DJ, journalist and producer

Tony Wilson . . . Tony Wilson

Richard Witts . . . The Passage frontman and cultural force

INDEX